T0342357

The Ukrainian Economy

Achievements, Problems, Challenges

The Ukrainian Economy

Achievements, Problems, Challenges

I. S. Koropeckyj, Editor

Distributed by Harvard University Press
for the
Harvard Ukrainian Research Institute

Publication of this volume was made possible by a generous donation by Ivan Pappas and Olha Guley Pappas.

ISBN 0-916458-51-2 (cl.)
ISBN 0-916458-57-1 (pb.)
Library of Congress Catalog Number 92-54348
Printed in the United States of America

Cover design: *Designworks, Inc.*
Typesetting: *Chiron, Inc.*

The Harvard Ukrainian Research Institute was established in 1973 as an integral part of Harvard University. It supports research associates and visiting scholars who are engaged in projects concerned with all aspects of Ukrainian studies. The Institute also works in close cooperation with the Committee on Ukrainian Studies, which supervises and coordinates the teaching of Ukrainian history, language, and literature at Harvard University.

This book is dedicated to the memory of two outstanding scholars, Vsevolod Holubnychy and Ivan Lysiak-Rudnytsky. Their lives' work was devoted to the cause of an independent Ukraine which, however, they did not live to see.

Contents

Preface

The papers constituting the present volume were originally presented at the Fourth Conference on Ukrainian Economics at the Harvard Ukrainian Research Institute, Cambridge, Massachusetts, in September 1990. The papers by Tetiana Pakhomova and Serhii Mischenko, and the four discussants were subsequently added in order to round out the volume. The conference was sponsored jointly by the Ukrainian Research Institute of Harvard University, the Michael and Daria Kowalsky Endowment Fund of the Canadian Institute of Ukrainian Studies, Edmonton, and the Department of Economics at Temple University, Philadelphia. I am grateful to these institutions for their generosity. The conference was the fourth quinquennial event within the project on Ukrainian Economics at the Harvard Ukrainian Research Institute. The previous three conferences took place at this forum in 1975, 1981, and 1985. Their proceedings, which I also edited, appeared under the following titles: *The Ukraine within the USSR: An Economic Balance Sheet* (New York, 1977), *Selected Contributions of Ukrainian Scholars to Economics* (Cambridge, MA, 1984), and *Ukrainian Economic History; Interpretive Essays* (Cambridge, MA and Edmonton, 1991). I would like to thank Stepan Chemych and Roman Procyk of the Ukrainian Studies Fund, for their generous assistance during this entire project, including the latest conference.

The Fourth Conference and the present volume are somewhat different from their predecessors, especially from the 1975 conference and its 1977 publication. The 1975 conference took place in times of RnormalS conditions in Ukraine's economy. This republic's economy, as well as the economy of the entire USSR, was muddling through the 1970s, as it had since the mid-1960s. No noticeable changes were expected to take place between the beginning of the 1975 project and the publication of its proceedings in 1977. In fact none did; neither was there any change during the immediate future after the publication. As a result, the analysis of the conditions at that time and some cautious predictions that were made for the future stood on relatively firm ground.

When the present project originated in 1986 and 1987, its objectives were similar—an analysis of the most recent conditions of the Ukrainian economy and some educated guesses as to possible developments during the next few years. However, the situation in the USSR was quite different than it had been in 1975. Mikhail Gorbachev was already at the helm of the Soviet Union, but nobody took his calls for perestroika, glasnost, and democracy very seriously. This situation changed quickly, so that when the conference papers were being prepared during the late 1980s, the transformation of the USSR was well under way and moving rapidly; specialists in the area were having trouble keeping up with the events in the Soviet Union in their research. Political and economic upheavals in the USSR continued during the period between the conference and the appearance of this volume, and culminated in the declaration of independence of Ukraine in August, 1991, which was convincingly upheld by a national referendum in December of the same year. Furthermore, conditions on the territory of the now former Soviet Union, including the newly independent Ukraine, are still far from being stabilized. No serious scholar would dare predict their final outcome. I therefore ask the readers of this volume not to expect to find an exhaustive analysis of the Ukrainian economy at the end of the 1980s and the beginning of the 1990s. It would be even riskier to attempt to make predictions about future developments in this new political reality. The papers included here are studies of the Ukrainian economy as it was on the eve of these epochal events. One can nevertheless occasionally find in these papers allusions to possible paths that the Ukrainian national economy or certain sectors of it might take in the future.

Attention should be drawn to three additional matters. First, practically all of the data included are based on official Soviet statistics. The scarcity and inadequacies of Soviet statistics have been discussed in Western literature innumerable times. The reader is advised to approach these data with the awareness of their limitations. Since conclusions are drawn on the basis of these inferior statistics, they should be treated with caution as well. No contributor, despite the most careful handling of these data, would insist on the absolute correctness of a certain numerical magnitude that he or she proposes. On the other hand, all of the contributors' results concur in that the Ukrainian economy's performance and conditions generally were below the union average during the 1970s and 1980s. This unanimity inspires our confidence in the general thrust of all the results and, at the same time, of separate findings in the volume. Second, to eliminate the data problem in future analyses of the Ukrainian economy, the quantity of statistics in Ukraine must increase and their quality must improve. I am sure that all the contributors join me in a call to Ukraine's statistical authorities: Please, publish more statistical information—most of it is available in your offices!—and standardize it according to Western methodology, as has been suggested by specialists of the United Nations. Third, and finally, Western economists are known to disagree with each other. The present authors also disagree with each other and with their editor on various issues, even important ones. Hopefully, the contributors from Ukraine and their colleagues there will follow vigorously this example of constructive debate in their future work.

There are many colleagues without whose help the Fourth Conference and the present volume would not have been possible. First and foremost, I am grateful to my friends, the authors of the papers in this volume, who devoted so much effort in preparing their informative and thoughtful papers, while having to define a moving target. Some of them are second- or even third-time participants in this project. I sincerely hope they will be rewarded for their contributions with the attention they so fully deserve. I would particularly like to thank my colleague Fyodor Kushnirsky from whose judicious advice I benefitted often in times of doubt, and on whose help I could always depend. I would also like to express my gratitude to Henadii Oudovenko, the Ukraine's ambassador to the United Nations, for his timely and interesting speech at the conference dinner. I am grateful to Adrian Hewryk for preparing the maps in this volume (and in the preceding volume as well). My thanks go also to Robert De Lossa for his thoughtful and thorough editing of the volume and, at the same time, vigorous efforts to publish it as soon as possible.

Finally the help of my daughter Sophia both in this and in previous projects as an editor, translator, researcher, and fellow economist is not only the proof of her interest in the subject matter but no less of filial devotion. The editor's usual expression of gratitude would in this instance not be adequate.

I. S. K.
January 1992

Note on Usage

Because of the changes in Eastern Europe and the former Soviet Union between the time that the papers contained in this volume were written and the present, technical difficulties arose in their presentation. Russian was the language of government of the former Soviet Union, but Ukrainian is now used in Ukrainian institutions where Russian was used before. In standardizing forms in these papers we have decided to give the relevant terms in the language chosen by the author or relevant to the source of citation. Not all those using this volume will be familiar with both Ukrainian and Russian. For this reason a table with Ukrainian-Russian equivalencies is provided below.

It is the policy of the Harvard Series in Ukrainian Studies to give placenames in the language of the nation in which they are presently located, except when standard English forms exist. Many of these placenames are familiar in this country only in Russian form. For this reason a table below gives the geo-political forms used in this volume, and other forms that might be more familiar to readers.

The papers have not been edited to take into account the changes after November 1990 except in one important area. Where usage dictated the name of an individual republic (e.g., Belorussia), the present English form chosen by that country is used (e.g., Belarus). This is an intentional anachronism and is meant to facilitate the correspondence between former Soviet republics and the present sovereign states of the Commonwealth of Independent States. In those cases where usage was clearly dependent on an understanding of the individual republic as a dependency of the USSR, then forms like Belorussian SSR or Kirghizian SSR were used.

As indicated in the editor's foreword, both the foreword and the introductory essay (Chapter 1) were written over a year after the other parts of this book. They therefore do reflect the changes in the former Soviet Union after November 1990.

Geographic Names

Alchevs'k (*for* Komunars'k)
Belarus (*for* Belorussia)
Cherkasy (*for* Cherkassy)
Chernihiv (*for* Chernigov)
Chernivtsi (*for* Chernovtsy)
Dniprodzerzhens'k (*see* Kamians'k)
Dnipropetrovs'k (*for* Dnepropetrovsk)
Donets'k (*for* Donetsk)
Ivano-Frankivs'k (*for* Ivano-Frankovsk)
Kamians'k (*for* Dniprodzerzhens'k)
Kharkiv (*for* Khar'kov)
Khmel'nyts'kyi (*for* Khmel'nitskii)
Kirovohrad (*for* Kirovograd)
Komunars'k (*see* Alchevs'k)
Kryvyi Rih (*for* Krivoi Rog)
Leningrad (when referring to the Soviet period only)
L'viv (*for* L'vov or Lwów)
Luhans'k (*for* Lugansk or Voroshilovgrad or Voroshilovhrad)
Lysychans'k (*for* Lysichans'k)
Moldova (*for* Moldavia)
Mykolaïv (*for* Nikolaev)
Ochakiv (*for* Ochakov)
Rivne (*for* Rovno)
Russian Federation (*for* Russia)
Saint Petersburg (when referring to the non-Soviet period)
Sevastopil' (*for* Sevastopol')
Sivers'kodonets'k (*for* Siverskodonetsk)
South (same as south region)
Southwest (same as southwest region)
Stebnyk (*for* Stebnik)
Ternopil' (*for* Ternopol')
Transcarpathia Oblast (*for* Zakarpats'k Oblast)
Vinnytsia (*for* Vinnitsa)
Volhynia Oblast (*for* Volyn' Oblast)
Voroshilovgrad, Voroshilovhrad (*see* Luhans'k)
Zakarpats'k Oblast (*see* Transcarpathia Oblast)
Zaporizhzhia (*for* Zaporozh'e)
Zhytomyr (*for* Zhitomir)

Political and Economic Terms and Expressions

Ukrainian	Russian
ekspertiza	ekspertiza
inzherneno-tekhnichni pratsivnyky	inzhenerno-tekhnicheskie rabotniki
Kolhosp	Kolkhoz
molodshy obsluhovuiuchyi personal	mladshii obsluzhivaiushchii personal
novobudovyi	novostroiki
okhorona/varta	okhrana
osnovni fondy	osnovnye fondy
proektni orhanizatsiï	proektnye organizatsii
robitnyky	rabochie
rozporoshennia zasobiv	raspylenie sredstv
sluzhbovtsi	sluzhashchie
vdoskonalennia	sovershenstvovanie
Radhosp	Sovkhoz
radnarhospy	sovnarkhozy
tekhniko-ekonomichni obgruntuvannia	tekhniko-ekonomicheskie obosnovaniia
pryskorennia	uskorenie
zastii	zastoi

It should be noted that the following words have become part of the English language, and therefore are given in their English form only: *chernozem, glasnost, guberniia (pl. guberniias), kolkhoz (pl. kolkhozes), kolkhoznik (pl. kolkhozniks), oblast (pl. oblasts), perestroika, sovkhoz (pl. sovkhozes).*

The yearly statistical compendiums *Narodne hospodarstvo Ukraïns'koï RSR* and its Russian-language version *Narodnoe khoziaistvo Ukrainskoi SSR* are referenced in the text as *Narhosp Ukraïny* and *Narkhoz Ukrainy*, respectively. *Narodnoe khoziaistvo SSSR* is referenced as *Narkhoz SSSR.* In the reference sections they are listed under their corporate authors: Derzhkomstat URSR (for *Narhosp Ukraïny*), Goskomstat USSR (for *Narkhoz Ukrainy*), and Goskomstat SSSR (for *Narkhoz SSSR*). This should facilitate location of these materials in library databases. Finally, the in-text references include the year of the statistical material, not the year of publication (for example, the text reference *"Narhosp Ukraïny 1989"* corresponds to the bibliographic entry "Derzhkomstat URSR. 1990. *Narodne hospodarstvo Ukraïns'koï RSR u 1989 r.* Kiev.").

List of Figures*

*Figures follow the "References" section of each chapter.

List of Contributors

Alan Abouchar
Department of Economics
University of Toronto
Toronto, Canada

Volodimir N. Bandera
Department of Economics
Temple University

Elizabeth M. Clayton
Department of Economics
University of Missouri

Ralph S. Clem
Department of International
    Relations
Florida International University

Leslie Dienes
Department of Geography
University of Kansas

Mariian Dolishnii
Institute of Economics,
    Academy of Sciences
Lviv, Ukraine

David A. Dyker
School of European Studies
University of Sussex
Falmer, England

Gertrude Schroeder Greenslade
Department of Economics
University of Virginia

Holland Hunter
Department of Economics
Haverford College

I. S. Koropeckyj
Department of Economics
Temple University

F. I. Kushnirsky
Department of Economics
Temple University

Ivan Lukinov
Institute of Economics,
    Academy of Sciences
Kiev, Ukraine

Blaine McCants
Central Intellegence Agency

Serhii Mischenko
ILTA Trade Finance S.A.
Kiev, Ukraine

Tetiana Pakhomova
Institute of Economics,
    Academy of Sciences
Kiev, Ukraine

Serhii Pyrozhkov
Institute of Economics,
    Academy of Sciences
Kiev, Ukraine

Stephen Rapawy
U.S. Department of Commerce

Andrii Revenko
Institute of Economics,
    Academy of Sciences
Kiev, Ukraine

Craig ZumBrunnen
Department of Geography
University of Washington

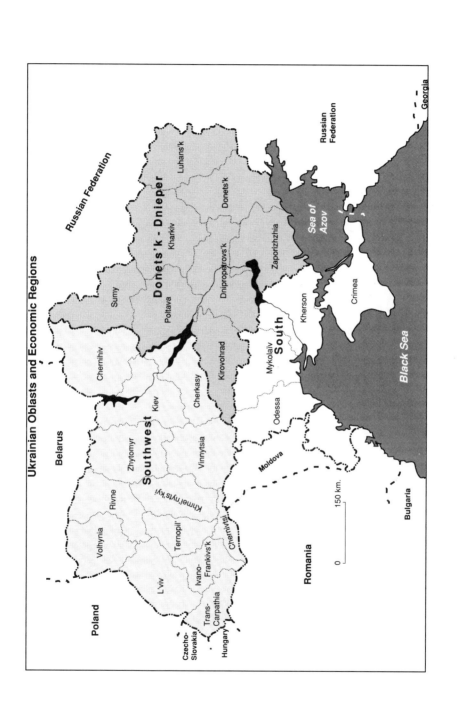

Ukrainian Oblasts and Economic Regions

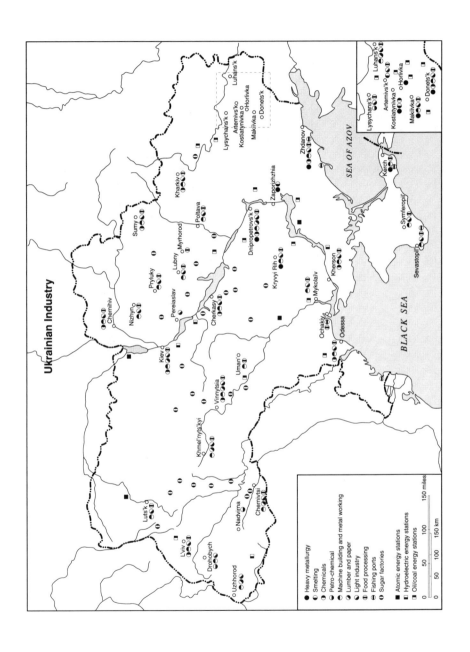

Ukrainian Industry

Lysychans'k o
Luhans'k
Artemiv's'ko
Kostiatynivka oHorlivka
Makiivka o Donets'k

Zhdanov

Zaporizhzhia

Dnipropetrovs'k o

Kryvyi Rih o

Kharkiv o

Poltava o

Sumy o

Myrhorod

Lubny

Pryluky

Nizhyn o

Chernihiv

Pereiaslav

Cherkasy

Mykolaiv

Kherson

Ochakiv

Odessa

Kiev

Uman' o

Vinnytsia

Khmel'nyts'kyi

Chernivtsi

Luts'k o

Nadvirna o

Lviv o

Drohobych

Uzhhorod

SEA OF AZOV

Kerch

Symferopil'

Sevastopil'

BLACK SEA

Lysychans'k o
Artemiv's'k o   o Horlivka
Kostiatynivka
Makiivka o
o Donets'k

● Heavy metallurgy
◑ Smelting
◐ Chemicals
◑ Petro-chemical
◑ Machine building and metal working
◑ Lumber and paper
◑ Light industry
◑ Food processing
◑ Fishing ports
◑ Sugar factories

■ Atomic energy stations
■ Hydroelectric energy stations
□ Oil/coal energy stations

0   50   100   150 miles
0   50   100   150 km

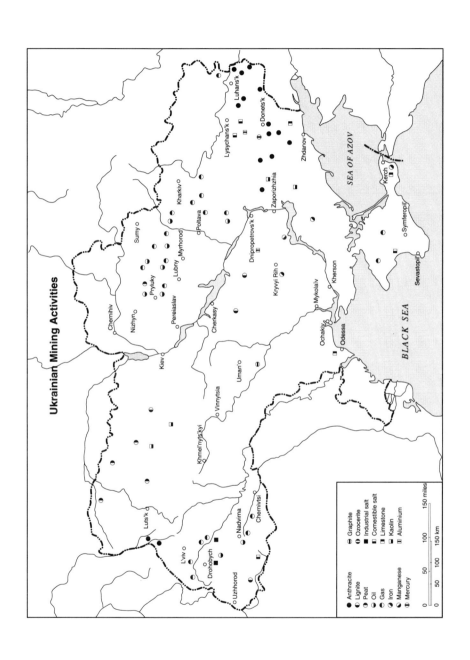

Ukrainian Mining Activities

SEA OF AZOV

BLACK SEA

Luhans'k
Lysychans'k
Donets'k
Zhdanov
Kerch
Symferopil'
Sevastopil'
Kharkiv
Zaporizhzhia
Sumy
Poltava
Myrhorod
Lubny
Dnipropetrovs'k
Kryvyi Rih
Pryluky
Pereiaslav
Cherkasy
Kherson
Mykolaiv
Chernihiv
Nizhyn
Kiev
Ochakiv
Odessa
Uman'
Vinnytsia
Khmel'nyts'kyi
Luts'k
Nadvirna
Chernivtsi
L'viv
Drohobych
Uzhhorod

Anthracite
Lignite
Peat
Oil
Gas
Iron
Manganese
Mercury

Graphite
Ozocerite
Industrial salt
Comestible salt
Limestone
Kaolin
Aluminium

0   50   100   150 km
0   50   100   150 miles

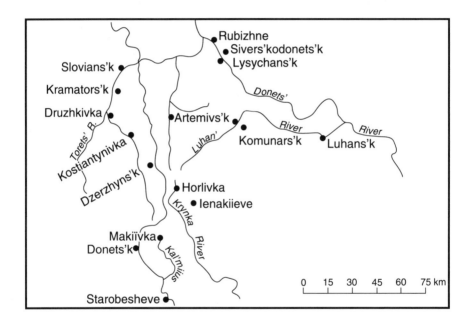

The Donbas Region

Selected Indicators of Recent Ukrainian Agricultural Development*

1. Share of Agriculture in Net Material Product (percent)

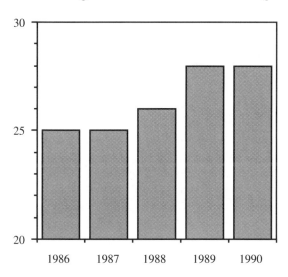

2. Distribution of Gross Agricultural Output by Major Sectors (1986–1990; percent)

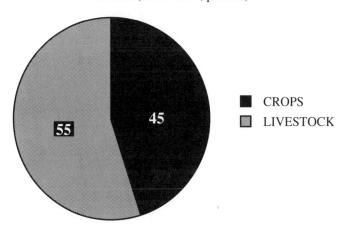

■ CROPS
□ LIVESTOCK

---

*Figures taken from: Narhosp Ukraïny 1990 (11, 329, 343, 345, 362).
N.b. These figures represent Soviet data, known for their inadequacies.

3. Average Annual Gross Output of Selected Agricultural Products (1986–1990; mill. tons)

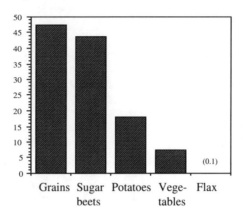

Grains Sugar Potatoes Vege- Flax
beets tables

4. Average Annual Gross Output of Major Grain Crops (1986–1990; mill. tons)

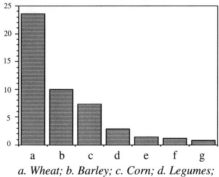

a. Wheat; b. Barley; c. Corn; d. Legumes;
e. Oats; f. Rye; g. Millet and Buckwheat

5. Average Annual Number of Livestock (1986–1990; millions)

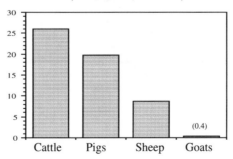

Cattle Pigs Sheep Goats

Part I: Framework

CHAPTER ONE
Introduction

I. S. Koropeckyj

The previous survey of the Ukrainian economy within the present research project covered the period from after World War II up to the early 1970s. Since then, dramatic changes have taken place not only in the economy of the now-former USSR, but in the state itself. The USSR as a political entity and its economy as an integrated complex have ceased to exist. Ukraine has become a politically independent state and the Ukrainian economy has become the national economy of this state.

An analysis of the Ukrainian economy during the years following the 1970s—the subject of the present volume—is facilitated by dividing this period into three parts: the early 1970s until 1985, 1985 to August 1991, and the short period since.

The first part, now referred to as the period of stagnation, marked the end of the system imposed on Soviet society by Stalin in the late 1920s. During the early stages of industrialization, this model registered some successes, but at tremendous material and, most of all, human cost. It failed, however, to deal effectively with some significant problems. Two of these problems deserve special mention: the inefficient utilization of resources and an inadequate mechanism for the introduction of technological innovations. Further growth in a moderately developed economy like that of the USSR, without available unemployed or underemployed resources, depends precisely on an appropriate institutional framework for the solving of these two problems.

The excessive centralization of decision making in the hands of the Moscow-based bureaucracy did not allow the economy automatically to correct itself to overcome these systemic obstacles. The Soviet leaders of this period, Leonid Brezhnev and his two successors, were unable and unwilling to radically reform the system. They merely tinkered with the system's planning and management mechanism, hoping that marginal changes would assure an acceptable level of functioning of the economy. These half-measures proved to be inadequate, and the performance of the economy deteriorated. The population's hopes for a higher standard of living were not realized and the Soviet Union's ambition to play the role of one of the two world superpowers could not be supported by the necessary economic strength.

The poor economic performance during this period was the main factor which compelled Mikhail Gorbachev, the leader from 1985 until the demise of the USSR, to change the entire political and economic system of the union. During the second half of the period under discussion, he attempted to introduce numerous varied political and economic reforms; however, they often were either ill-conceived, pragmatic responses to changing conditions, or a compromise among the contradictory positions of the decision makers, or the result of Gorbachev's indecisiveness, or, most likely, some combination of all the above factors. They proved to be unsuccessful and the situation in the Soviet Union became chaotic. While some of the components of the system (by now totally compromised) were dismantled, none of the reform proposals gained general approval and no new comprehensive and consistent structure of institutions was put in place. The consumer goods sector, especially the production and distribution of food, broke down throughout the country. With regard to political developments during this period, due to some democratization but, most of all, to the new openness of public life, the republics of the union intensified their demands for political sovereignty.

At the end of 1991, the Gorbachev period of Soviet history came to an end. The unsuccessful putsch of August 1991 accelerated the demise of the USSR. While a handful of the union republics had already declared their independence in 1990, the putsch galvanized similar declarations by the remaining republics. The third period, when fifteen independent states with their own national economies came into being in place of the USSR, is unfolding before our eyes (at the time of my rewriting of this introduction, January 1992.)

Ukraine gained its independence gradually and peacefully. The following steps in the process of independence should be noted. The declaration of economic and political sovereignty of Ukraine, accepted by its parliament on July 16, 1990, included all the political and economic prerogatives one would expect of an independent state, but it also implied loose membership in a reorganized USSR. In the referendum of March 1991, in response to a question formulated by republic authorities, 80 percent of Ukraine's population voted to stay within a new Soviet Union on the basis of the 1990 sovereignty declaration. At the same time, in response to a question posed by Moscow, 70 percent of the voters in Ukraine chose to remain in a renewed union. Immediately following the August 1991 coup d'etat (on August 24), the Ukrainian parliament declared Ukraine's total independence. This declaration was overwhelmingly approved by the population in the referendum of December 1, 1991, with nearly 91 percent voting for Ukrainian total independence.

On December 9, 1991, Ukraine, along with the Russian Federation and Belarus, announced the founding of the new Commonwealth of Independent States (CIS). At the same time, these states voided the Union Treaty of 1922 and proclaimed the dissolution of the USSR. The other republics, except the three Baltic republics and Georgia, joined the new grouping on December 21, 1991. The new agreement is vague. With regard to the institutions of the CIS, it mentions a council of heads of state, a council of heads of government, and foresees the functioning of the new agglomeration on the basis of cooperation among the member states through coordinating organs that have not yet been defined. The agreement states explicitly that this institutional framework is neither a state nor a super-state structure. The coordinating organs are supposed to deal with strategic defense, international relations, and many other spheres of social life. Economic cooperation is anticipated in a new "economic space," but the specifics of such a space are not spelled out. The selection of Minsk as the seat of the CIS is a transparent gesture to distinguish the CIS from the traditional centralized state associated with Moscow. A great deal of work on details will have to be done by the signatories of the CIS treaty in order to breathe life into the very general proposed structure of the new commonwealth.

Thus, a new political and institutional framework is emerging in Ukraine. On the basis of this framework, the Ukrainian economy is entering into a new stage in its development. Obviously, no analysis of this period can be undertaken as yet. The purpose of this volume, therefore, is to describe and and to analyze various aspects of Ukrainian economic development during the 1970s and into the late 1980s. Since the rest of the USSR was affected as much as the Ukrainian economy by Brezhnev's ideological-bureaucratic ossification and Gorbachev's pragmatic experimentation, the analysis of Ukraine's experience, in most cases, is conducted herein not in isolation, but in comparison with that of the other republics of the former Soviet Union.

Since four of the five sections of this book conclude with discussions which integrate the subject matter of each section's chapters and draw some conclusions, there is no need to do so once again here. It suffices to list the main topics covered in the book. In Part I, in addition to this introductory essay, recent economic developments, the need for economic reforms, and the desired characteristics and directions of these reforms from the vantage point of the late 1980s are discussed. Part II deals with the population as the labor base, various aspects of the labor force, and nonhuman resources. The latter include raw materials, especially energy and fuels, and capital stock. In Part III the growth of national income, and of industry and agriculture individually, are analyzed. For the first time, various macroeconomic indicators are discussed on the basis of newly available statistics. Part IV deals with the welfare of the Ukrainian population in terms of income and consumption, and also with regard to the economic development of Ukraine's regions. It also includes a discussion of Ukraine's catastrophic ecological conditions, probably one of the most pressing problems facing the country today. Finally, in Part V Ukraine's external trade and the problem of national income loss to the rest of the USSR are discussed.

The contributions contained in the present volume suggest the following overall conclusion. The performance of the Ukrainian economy in terms of the most important indicators has been mediocre compared to the other union republics during the period under discussion. During the last two decades the growth rate of the national income was the third lowest among the fifteen republics, it was the fifth lowest of industry, and it was the very lowest of agriculture. It has been estimated that Ukraine's performance in terms of technological progress in the entire economy was in ninth place (1981 to 1985), in industry it was below the union average, and in agriculture it was slightly above the average. With regard to national income and consumption per capita, Ukraine's place has been somewhere in the middle among the fifteen union republics. Welfare indicators on a per capita basis have not declined in comparison to other republics, primarily because Ukraine's population growth has been the lowest among the republics. Finally, ecological conditions and their as yet undetermined effect on the biological substance of the Ukrainian nation have acquired truly catastrophic proportions in some instances.

Ukraine was a part of a single, unified country. It shared the same political, legal, and institutional arrangements with each of the other republics in that country. Therefore, systemic factors of Soviet socialism—such as public ownership, central planning, and rigid centralization—depressed the economic growth and population welfare of Ukraine, just as they did in other union republics. There is no need to discuss specifically the influence of these factors on Ukraine's growth and welfare in this volume, because these issues have been extensively treated in recent Soviet and Western literature for the USSR as a whole, and the individual union republics as well. The overall systemic problem is treated here only insofar as it has had a differential effect on the republic.

There have been other determining factors specific to Ukraine, which have substantially contributed to the unsatisfactory performance of its economy. These have been extensively discussed in the volume's various chapters. The following factors deserve special mention: the exhaustion of the raw material base, low investment as compared to some other republics, superannuated capital stock and inadequate opportunities for the introduction of technological innovation (which result from low investment), an outdated economic structure, the unbalanced development of Ukrainian regions, administratively determined external trade, and the uncompensated transfer of a part of the Ukrainian national income to the Soviet central government and other regions of the USSR. In view of the rigid centralization of political and economic decision making in the former USSR, these factors must be understood as having been imposed on Ukraine by the central authorities in Moscow. Since the Moscow leadership's policies importantly affected the performance of the Ukrainian economy, the remainder of this essay will be devoted to a discussion of various interpretations of the relationship between Moscow and Ukraine, and to suggestions as to the possible future of this relationship.

Let us consider the views of the following three groups on this issue: Moscow-based (i.e., Russian, central) economists, the majority of the economists in Ukraine, and certain economists and political leaders in the West.

Because of the formally federal nature of the USSR and its multi-ethnic population, the economic relationship between union republics and the central government has always been a topic of considerable interest to Soviet economists. (At the outset, it is necessary to point out that in the discussion of these relations it is not always possible to completely isolate economic issues from political considerations.) The Moscow-based economists, taking the territorial integrity of the USSR for granted and concerned with the planning and management of the entire Soviet economy, paid relatively little attention to this issue during the pre-Gorbachev era. Subsequently, with the introduction of perestroika, they were largely preoccupied with the future model of the economy and with ways of attaining it.

When demands for independence by individual nations intensified, central authorities and the economists connected with them were compelled to confront directly the relations between Moscow and the republics. A reading of the voluminous literature on the subject leaves no doubt as to the following conclusion: Despite their differences on many issues, political leaders and economists representing almost the entire political spectrum in Russia—from reactionary nationalists to the most liberal reformers—have been determined to preserve the territorial integrity of the successor state to the USSR, including the unity of its economy. The late Andrei Sakharov and his widow, Yelena Bonner, are notable exceptions to this. The views on this subject by Russia's new leader, Boris Yeltsin, and his advisers have been ambiguous; on the one hand, he has stated on occasions that Ukraine has every right to be independent, while, on the other hand, he has argued that any community of nations (whatever its name) in place of the USSR cannot exist without Ukraine. At the same time, the need for such a community has been taken by him to be self-evident. Some of his closest advisers have been more straightforward than he in denying the right of political independence for Ukraine.

Integrating a number of national economies into one larger economy or, conversely, preventing a national economy from breaking up into a number of smaller economies is, of course, not a new idea. Over the years many economic rationales have been used to support such integration. In general, there are static and dynamic arguments. The former refer primarily to the redirection of trade among nations, which occurs as a result of integration or disintegration. For example, shifting importation of a product from a less efficient to a more efficient producer results in the lowering of the price of this product at home and thus contributes to the improvement of the welfare in a given nation without an increase in output. Furthermore, an integrated, larger economy can have the following dynamic advantages over an individual, smaller economy: specialization of resources, economies of scale, improvement in terms of trade with other nations, increased competition in resource utilization, and integration-induced increases in quantity and improvements in the quality of resources. Eventually, these advantages would be reflected in a decrease in production costs or an increase in output.

However, a multinational state with an integrated economy can encounter its own difficulties. The responsibility of any state's economy is not only to serve as the material basis for the standard of living of the population, as American economists often think. In addition to goods and services, each state's economy must produce public goods (lighthouses, national defense, etc.) Since the production of public goods would not be profitable to private enterprises, these goods are produced or subsidized by the state. An ethnically homogeneous state also provides a special kind of public good—various cultural goods (museums, theaters, literature, etc.) A multinational state is expected to provide such public goods specific to each ethnic group—national-oriented public goods. If several ethnic groups reside within a state and, in addition, are rooted in substantially diverse traditions, the integrated economy of this state may have difficulty supplying national-oriented goods to the satisfaction of each group. It is likely that individual nationalities would feel that central authorities have not allocated adequate resources to their particular needs. An integrated economy with a relatively small number of ethnic groups—all with a similar tradition—would probably be able to fulfill this responsibility more easily. Otherwise, the difficulties with national-oriented public goods could become centrifugal and politically destabilizing to such a degree that the economic advantages of integration would be outweighed. One can assume that there is some optimal size for an economic union in each region of the world.

While in general ignoring the problem of national-oriented public goods, Soviet writers who favored the territorial integrity of the USSR principally emphasized the first two dynamic advantages— specialization of resources and economies of scale—rarely mentioning the other purely economic factors. According to them, the geographical division of labor and the specialization of resources in their huge country enabled the enterprises to take advantage of economies of scale and to produce at low costs. Links of supply and demand among various industries and individual plants located throughout the country were established. The links, it was (and still is) argued, formed over a long period of time and proved efficient. They, in turn, led to the certainty of input availability to producers and to the elimination of uncertainty in the demand for products. All this ultimately improved consumer welfare. Any severing of these relations would require enterprises to establish new relations with concomitant higher production costs, at least during the transition period. In any case, decline in the population's standard of living would be unavoidable.

An additional, frequently heard argument stresses the fact that some important natural resources are available in one region of the USSR only. For example, the Russian Federation is the only major supplier of oil and natural gas for the entire former Soviet Union. Moreover, it supplied these products to the other former republics of the Soviet Union at a low price compared to world market prices. Russia also exported these two products abroad and thus earned hard currency for the entire USSR. Thus, some writers have asked, if some republics break away from the union, where would they get their oil, where would they be able to find such a low price for it, and how would they get the necessary foreign currency to pay for it? So goes the argument for the integrity of the former USSR.

Ukraine's economists obviously are well aware of the serious economic problems which could arise if its secession from the USSR were to be accompanied by the disruption of the existing supply and demand ties between Ukrainian enterprises and their trade partners in other republics. The links between Ukraine and the Russian Federation, with whom the bulk of Ukrainian interrepublic trade is transacted, have been particularly important. The Ukrainian economists, however, contend that there is no reason to assume that such ties must be interrupted by an independent Ukraine. They could continue as before, but as foreign trade, not internal trade. Furthermore, these economists note that should an independent Ukraine decide to trade with other countries rather than the former republics, such a decision would be made only if it were beneficial to Ukraine. It would allow Ukraine to adjust the part of interrepublic trade that was administratively determined and not economically justified in the past. In general, an independent Ukraine would be free to integrate itself into the world economy and not limit itself to its former Soviet partners. Its foreign trade would be truly based on the doctrine of comparative advantage, thereby promoting specialization and large scale production to a greater degree than under the past integrated Soviet economic system.

With respect to the supply of such critical commodities as oil and natural gas, which Ukraine has imported from the Russian Federation, Ukrainian economists argue that these commodities could be obtained also from sources outside the Soviet Union, for example, from the Middle East, through the mechanism of foreign trade. They acknowledge that their republic has been paying an artificially low price for these fuels, as well as for some other raw materials. But at the same time Ukraine has been exporting some of its products such as coal, meat, and processed foods to other republics at subsidized rates. Furthermore, they point out that there are many countries in the world which lack their own oil supply, but nonetheless fare quite well. In any case, a drop in Ukraine's national income could possibly be expected during the transition period following its political separation from other republics. If Ukrainians are determined truly to secede, these economists warn that they must be ready to face the consequences of the secession.

Two arguments which may potentially make Ukrainians skeptical about entering into some kind of economic and political integration with the Russian Federation, should be mentioned. They are more of a historical character. First, Russia, having been a superpower in the past, could have been expected to be able to protect Ukraine from its enemies. However, the experience of the World War I and World War II shows that Russia failed to do this; in both wars Ukraine was occupied and looted by Germans. Since these wars were caused to some extent by the imperial policies of Saint Petersburg and Moscow, one can argue that Ukraine suffered unnecessarily and, moreover, relatively more than Russia from the wars' devastations. Second, some portion of the population of an overpopulated Ukraine might have settled in Asiatic Russia, with its huge expanse, instead of migrating to countries overseas. It is true that many Ukrainians (by official accounts about 7 million) reside now in other republics, having taken voluntary advantage of such an opportunity or having been forced to migrate to these places before and after the 1917 Revolution. However, at the same time, Russians settled in large numbers in the southern and southeastern parts of Ukraine—especially in the urban areas. Between 1926 and 1989, their number increased from less than 3 million to more than 11 million, or from 7 percent to about 22 percent of the total population. As a result, the total population of Ukraine has hardly changed.

With the above considerations in mind, we can now ask: Overall, will Ukraine gain or lose economically by political separation from the former USSR? Only empirically can this question be conclusively answered, and it appears that nobody has undertaken such a study as yet. On theoretical grounds, it has been argued that the secession of a nation from a union would hardly be to its benefit if its production structure were similar to that of other members of that union. Since the economic structures of Ukraine, the Russian Federation, and other more developed republics are by and large similar, this reasoning may argue against Ukraine's successful secession. Furthermore, different national currencies in the newly established state—and the sentiment for the introduction of its own currency is very strong in Ukraine—would almost certainly not allow trade between them to reach the volume enjoyed before the dissolution of the union, with its common currency.

While theoretical reasons for and against economic integration are no doubt important, the striving of Ukrainian leaders and economists for the independence of their country is motivated to a greater degree by pragmatic considerations. The Ukrainian economy has been a part of the imperial economy of the Russian Empire and subsequently of the USSR for over three hundred years. In the past, Ukraine's interests often diverged from those of the entire Russian Empire/USSR. Regardless of the political and economic system in the Russian Empire/USSR, Ukraine's interests had to be subordinated to the interests of the entire national economy, as perceived by the central leaders in Moscow or Saint Petersburg. As a result, most of the specific factors mentioned above retarded Ukrainian development. Independent-minded Ukrainians are convinced that a Kiev government that is sovereign or a member of a loose economic commonwealth on the territory of the former USSR can cope with these factor on its own more effectively than a centralized government in Moscow.

Being independent, Ukraine can conduct the appropriate macroeconomic policies formulated to deal with such pressing problems as the modernization of the presently outdated economic structure, the equalization of interregional development, and the protection of the environment, including a ban on the development of nuclear energy. A free hand in conducting foreign trade, based on the availability of natural and human resources and the country's geographical location, could facilitate the transfer of new technology from abroad and enhance economic productivity. A halt to the unrequited transfer of a part of the Ukrainian national income, which has occurred mainly to support the military and foreign policy of the former Soviet central government and the development of Asiatic regions of the former USSR, would provide the resources needed to increase investment at home, making it possible to further technological progress, and to improve population welfare. Finally, a Ukrainian-centered cultural elite presently dominates political life in Ukraine. For them, there is no doubt that the demand for Ukrainian national-oriented public goods can better be satisfied by an independent government in Kiev than by any government centered in Moscow or Minsk.

The unfortunate experience of the Ukrainian economy within the Russian Empire and its successor the USSR is incomparably more important for the Ukrainian population than any possible theoretical advantages associated with a future association with Moscow. This most recently was expressed vividly in the above-mentioned democratically conducted referendum, in which the Ukrainian population convincingly chose political and economic independence from Moscow.

A final consideration is the attitude of Western political leaders and economists toward Moscow-Ukraine relations, and, in particular, their attitude toward the quest of Ukraine and other former Soviet non-Russian nations for political and economic independence. Naturally, the West is vitally concerned with the question of what economic and political structures will emerge out of the former USSR. Western leaders are unanimous in their conviction that a free market economy and a western democratic political system in the region would serve as stabilizing factors there and in the world as a whole. Since Gorbachev came to power, the policy of most Western leaders and economists, especially those in the United States, has been to support him while at the same time not supporting the devolution of the USSR into a number of independent states, even if the process is democratically chosen and peaceful. (An exception has been the halting support for the independence drive of the Baltic republics, whose annexation was never officially recognized by the United States.) This position was based on the premise that a free market and democratization could only be achieved in a unified USSR led by Gorbachev. Furthermore, these leaders believed that only such a government would be able to exercise proper control over the nuclear arsenal.

The unsuccessful putsch of August 1991 accelerated the dramatic changes already under way in the relations among nationalities in the former USSR. As was mentioned earlier, it facilitated the formal declarations of independence by all the former union republics. The emergence of fifteen independent states and the creation of the CIS precipitated the demise of the USSR and the departure of Gorbachev from the political scene. Yeltsin became the leading personality in the region. The United States had to reconcile itself with the disappearance of the familiar set-up in Eastern Europe and extended or promised to extend diplomatic recognition to the new states.

The situation in the Eurasian region which was once the Soviet Union is, however, far from stabilized. Disregarding any problems which may arise among various republics, the tug-of-war between the centrifugal tendencies of non-Russian nations and traditional centralizing tendencies of Russian leaders has not yet been conclusively resolved and will certainly continue for a long time to come. Therefore, it might be in order to offer a comment on the West's attitude, particularly that in the United States, toward Russia's—whether under the tsar or the general secretary—relations with the nations subjugated by it. This comment is appropriate in view of the fact that US policy for dealing with the developments in the area has yet to be shaped.

It is not clear why the formulators of Western policy chose to ignore the existence of non-Russian nations within the Russian Empire prior to and during World War I, and actively supported the defenders of the old regime during the Civil War. They subsequently favored the maintenance of the territorial integrity of the former USSR until the present. On practical grounds, a huge country like the Russian Empire/USSR would have been a potential, if not actual, adversary of the United States under any political and economic system. A number of relatively small successor states, unable to support any nuclear or conventional military build up, could never present a credible threat to the interests of the United States. Also, Russia by itself—without the non-Russian republics, not to mention the non-Russian nationalities within its boundaries—would be approximately half as strong with regard to population and about 60 percent as strong with regard to economic potential as compared with the Russian Empire/USSR. Over the years the cumulative savings on defense expenditures for the Western allies could have been quite significant. The possible advantage of having a large trading partner actually amounted to having no partner at all after the 1917 Revolution. The question of the contribution of the Russian Empire/USSR to the world's stability does not require any comment.

The moral justification of such a policy also should be questioned. This consideration is important in a country which prides itself on conducting its affairs according to accepted moral and ethical standards. The morality of a policy denying freedom for entire nations with developed identities and long histories, thereby condemning them to the loss of their cultural identity and assimilation into a master nation, is contrary to the foundations on which the United States was built. A possible explanation for such a policy toward the formerly subjugated nations of the USSR was the fear of a nuclear confrontation. This threat arose only in the late 1940s, but such a policy was in place long before that. Thus, the acceptance of this policy by most American leaders and most of the scholarly establishment certainly remains a puzzle from both pragmatic and ideological points of view. Extensive research of this phenomenon is acutely needed.

In the past, suggestions by a small minority of specialists on the former USSR that independence for the non-Russian nations was desirable for the West both on practical and moral grounds was dismissed by an overwhelming majority of their colleagues and Washington officials. Such ideas were treated as almost subversive. Incidentally, the tolerant attitude toward imperialism in the Russian Empire/USSR of mainstream specialists contrasts sharply with their hostility toward imperialism in other parts of the world. Nevertheless, as a result of recent events, they hopefully will rethink their positions and retool their skills in order to work with government officials to formulate policies appropriate to the new era. Unfortunately, one can still detect a lingering dogmatic preference on the part of these two groups for some kind of immediate political and economic integration among the independent states of the former USSR.

To conclude, it might be of interest to speculate from today's vantage point about the possible structures which could emerge in place of the USSR and what kind of relations one can expect between the Russian Federation and Ukraine in the future under these conditions. Three such possibilities deserve our attention.

Let us first consider an extreme. It is unlikely that the clock can be turned back to the Stalinist past. Potential promoters of such a move, the Communist Party and the KGB have been permanently compromised and legally banned. On the other hand, a coup by the army—the only relatively disciplined entity still in place with units in all parts of the former Soviet Union—or by some of its commanders cannot be excluded. But a military regime, without an ideological base (because of the preemption of Russian nationalism by Russia's president Boris Yeltsin) and probable hostility from the population, could hardly be a durable alternative. But even if such a coup were to succeed, the return to a Soviet-type centralized economic system would be highly unlikely.

The second alternative, a centralized empire, and the third alternative, a loose consultative commonwealth, can both evolve on the basis of the recently organized Commonwealth of Independent States. Which of them has a greater possibility of prevailing? Would the outcome be stable?

The historical tradition of the Russian Empire/USSR suggests that the second alternative could prevail. Ukraine twice signed agreements with Russia (the Pereiaslav Treaty of 1654 and the USSR Treaty of 1922), which foresaw practically full independence for Ukraine in some loose association with Muscovy first and with other Soviet republics in the latter case. Despite these high-sounding agreements, Ukraine became a totally integrated part of the centralized empire in both cases. A discussion of the various reasons for the subversion of the treaties is outside the scope of this essay. In any case, as shown above with respect to the Soviet period, the economic consequences for Ukraine have been highly adverse. Without going into details, the treatment of the Ukrainian economy by the tsarist regime was no better than by its postrevolutionary counterpart. Nevertheless, if historical tendencies are inevitable and the CIS should eventually become such an integrated entity, the question arises whether it will be stable and conducive to peace in the region and the world. Some economic reasons seem to suggest otherwise.

First, a characteristic of the CIS, in contrast to the relatively well-established regional integration of the European Community, is the membership of a disproportionately large country, the Russian Federation. This country—which comprises a relatively large number of non-Russian ethnic groups and is potentially unstable itself—accounts for about 54 percent of the total population of the eleven CIS members and for over 60 percent of their total Net Material Product. Because of its sheer size alone, if unchecked by institutional constraints the Russian Federation is bound to dominate the new entity. The non-Russian members of the CIS are well aware of this fact and certainly want to safeguard against the accumulation of decision-making powers in Moscow. They may, for example succeed in including in the agreement the requirement of members' unanimity in all decisions. But such an arrangement would in practice paralyze the effectiveness of the CIS. Therefore, decision-making power of individual member nations would have to be distributed formally or informally in proportion to their population or economic potential. Consequently, the Russian Federation would again be dominant. (The recent behavior of President Yeltsin may serve as a forewarning; he unilaterally announced the introduction of various economic reforms on January 2, 1992 in the Russian Federation without previous consultation with, much less the agreement of, the other republics. Because of the Russian Federation's importance in other republics' economies, they have had to follow suit with similar reforms.)

Second, the diversity of the CIS members is another destabilizing factor. The territory of the proposed CIS is immense—it spans eleven time zones, as compared with the two zones of the European Community and the three zones of the continental United States. The regions vary sharply with respect to climate, natural resource endowments, and economic development. Furthermore, the CIS is home to about 100 nationalities, who are compactly settled on their historical territories and speak their own languages. This results in rather low interregional mobility of the labor force. The introduction of a market system in the CIS would not lead to a nationally integrated market with equalized factor and product prices differing only by the cost of transportation. Local scarcity relations would lead to the creation of several autonomous regional resource and product markets, often coinciding with a given union republic or autonomous republic (of the former Soviet Union), and organized according to ethnic criteria, with differing per capita incomes. The CIS leadership would face a dilemma. If it attempted to compensate for the interregional differences in income per capita through national income transfers, it would most likely encounter opposition from donor members. If it did not, the republics with low per capita incomes would be dissatisfied. In either case, the destabilizing unrest in some republics would have to be either tolerated (but the stability of the CIS would be threatened), or the nationalistic expression of discontent would have to be suppressed by curtailing civil rights.

Third, a uniform privitization policy for the entire CIS would be ineffective during the transition from socialism to a market economy in view of the diversity of the CIS. For example, the same policy cannot be applied to the transfer to private ownership of subsidized coal mining in Ukraine and of profitable, but remote, coal mining in Siberia. Concurrent with the transition to the free market economy, macroeconomic policy will gain in importance. It is difficult to expect that, for example, the same monetary policy will be appropriate for cotton growing Tajikistan and the electronic industry in St. Petersburg. The likely result will be the centralization of structural and macroeconomic policies in various CIS committees, dominated by the Russian Federation. The centralized policies would require that the economic interests of some member states be subordinated to the interests of the entire CIS, as was historically the case in the Russian Empire and the Soviet Union.

Fourth, assuming that the CIS succeeds in evolving into a democratic community of nations without a central government, the Russian Federation would certainly want to play the role of a superpower internationally. Individual CIS members, we assume, would be asked to contribute a share of the necessary resources in support of such an activity. With the demise of a supranational ideology, no voluntary cooperation can be expected on the part of the non-Russian nations. Moreover, the policies of the Russian Federation government would be associated in their eyes with traditional Russian imperialism. To obtain needed resources, the Russian Federation government would have to force appropriate budget laws and other economic regulations on the member nations, even against their will. A gradual abrogation of their political and economic autonomy would then become inevitable.

Fifth, as was mentioned earlier, the responsibility of the economy of a multinational state is to provide specific, or national-oriented public goods to each ethnic group. If the past dismal experience of the Russian Empire and the Soviet Union serves as any indication, then it is likely that a centralized economy of the CIS (in legal and institutional terms) would be unable and unwilling to pay equitable (from each republic's point of view) attention to such needs of each ethnic group. This applies primarily to the allocation of sufficient resources to specific cultural and social needs, as well as for the protection of each republic's environment. An integrated economy furthermore would require the use of a common language—in this case the Russian language—in government, business, and the media. (While the European Community utilizes nine languages in transacting its internal affairs, to be equitable the CIS would have to use about 100 languages. This hardly is possible.) The resulting decline in the use and development of languages other than Russian, as history has shown, would lead to dissatisfaction on the part of the non-Russian nationalities and would further weaken the community's stability.

To counteract these centrifugal tendencies, the Russian Federation government, through its domination of the CIS, would have to curtail various civil liberties in the non-Russian Federation republics. The suppression of the cultural and political aspirations of non-Russian nations would not be able to coexist with freedom in other areas of social life and would inevitably cause a slide toward a totalitarian government, supported by the military, in the Russian Federation itself. It is a truism that a free market cannot remain free in the absence of freedom in other aspects of life.

The third alternative, a Commonwealth of Independent States limited to consultative functions among its members, something on the order of the Commonwealth of the British Empire, appears to be the best solution to interrepublic relations at the present time. The only executive role allocated to the CIS would be the responsibility of overseeing the nuclear arsenal of the former USSR prior to its complete dismantling. Economic relations among the member states would then develop on the basis of interrepublic agreements. Skeptics may argue that the ensuing economic exigencies in these nations will drive them back toward some kind of economic and political integration. However, one can argue that individual independent nations would take advantage of this arrangement in order to consolidate their national and political structures. Having matured and gained in self-confidence, these states could begin negotiations toward the gradual creation of a common market, comparable to that of the European Community, on an equal footing.

Of course, various intermediate solutions between the second and third alternatives are possible. But in general, tendencies toward these two alternatives can be expected. The outcome will depend on the dynamics of Russia's historical imperialism, on the one hand, and on the assertiveness of and cooperation among the non-Russian republics, on the other. After all, economic supra-national agglomerations are as a rule politically motivated. Only time will tell which alternative will prevail.

CHAPTER TWO

Radical Reconstruction of the Ukrainian Economy: Reasons, Reforms, Outlook

Ivan Lukinov

The last decade has been characterized by complex and contradictory social changes and the reorganization of the political, socio-economic, and cultural life of nations, both internally and in international relations. Depending on the region or country the trends and intensity of these processes manifest themselves in starkly different ways—ranging from revolutionary explosions to slow evolutionary transformations. While Western countries are gradually and consistently moving towards integration, the Eastern European countries are moving away from unity, which proved economically irrational, towards autarky. One phenomenon, however, seems to prevail worldwide: the abatement of hostilities among nations based on ideological differences and military power. Perhaps this gives our civilization a chance to survive and to progress further.

Ukraine is a large European country. It has been a member of the United Nations from the day of the United Nations' inception. Today it finds itself in the epicenter of the Eastern European processes characterized by the renaissance of national self-awareness. Ukraine has chosen the path toward real democracy and profound social, political and economic change. As in other nations in this part of Europe, the problems of national sovereignty for the Ukrainian people are particularly important. Demands for political independence for Ukraine, the freedom to choose its political and economic systems, the opportunity to develop its culture and language, and the freedom to structure international relations based on mutual interest and equality, make hardly objectionable goals in principle. Due to its geographical location, Ukraine is being called upon to play an increasingly important role in the international arena, particularly in the common European home.

The emergence of new political and scientific ideas in our time, and their rapid dissemination and adoption thanks to modern communication techniques have accelerated the changes taking place. These changes affect the quantitative, qualitative, and structural transformations of the factors of production, as well as the entire social and economic fabric, political ideologies, and the spiritual potential of the nations of the world.

Social dynamics result from the combination and effects of progress and regression. These antipodes accompany and sometimes determine the meandering path of mankind through the centuries. The periods of rapid growth give way to periods of stagnation, followed anew by a next cycle of growth. In other words, society develops unevenly, experiencing both large and small deviations from a trend line. Social reforms are important to nations, political parties, and their leaders if they are structured using appropriate measures which prevent stagnation and crises and at the same time facilitate progress. It should be stressed that changes brought about by bloody and destructive upheavals are unacceptable in today's civilized societies. Not only do they bring suffering to the people, but they are also incompatible with progress.

The purpose of this paper is to analyze and evaluate the rather complicated and contradictory situation, of critical proportions, which has arisen in Ukraine. It will examine the causes and consequences of this state of affairs in view of worldwide trends. The crisis has affected not only individual components of the existing economic system, but the entire system, including production, distribution, monetary circulation, prices, finances and credit, market conditions and consumption, and the environment. A way out of the crisis can be found only in a thorough transformation of Ukrainian social and economic systems. Reforms should include the restructuring of property ownership and of macro- and microeconomic management and economic policies; the promotion of wide-ranging profit-motivated entrepreneurship and of conditions conducive to individual choice and responsibility, and the development of markets and their infrastructure. The decisive components in this chain of reforms which will lead the country out of crisis and enable it to enter a new phase of healthy economic development are stabilized currency and its convertibility, business competition (regardless of form of ownership) satisfying consumer demand, the elimination of product shortages, and the fight against inflation.

Economic Potential and Structural Changes

Among the union republics of the USSR, Ukraine, with the exception of the Russian Federation, has the most favorable conditions and resources for diversified economic development and for sustained international economic relations on a mutually beneficial basis. This republic boasts a well developed industrial, agro-industrial, and scientific-technical base. Its population is nearly 52 million. Its sovereignty extends over a territory of 603.7 thousand square kilometers containing rich mineral resources, water basins and air rights, flora and fauna, and vast productive, social, and cultural resources accumulated over time. Although Ukraine in 1989 accounts for only 2.7 percent of Soviet territory, 18.0 percent of population, and 15.8 percent of the productive capital, it produces 17.6 percent of the industrial output and 22.6 percent of the agricultural output of the USSR.[1] Ukraine's share in the total output of the USSR in 1989 is, for example, in the case of iron ore 45.5 percent; pig iron 40.8 percent; steel, rolled steel, and steel pipes approximately 35 percent; various machinery approximately 25 percent; TV sets 35.9 percent; granulated sugar about 52.6 percent; and vegetable oil 33.2 percent.

The growth of consumer industries has lagged and, as a result, production cannot keep up with consumer demand. A relatively low standard of living is the consequence; an imbalanced production structure is to blame for this. Economic development has been lopsided with an emphasis on the steady growth of extractive industries and the manufacture of the means of production and armaments. Heavy industry's share in Ukraine's total industrial output amounted to 71.2 percent, while of consumer goods only 28.8 percent in 1989. For comparison, the corresponding proportion was 42:58 in 1928, 62:38 in 1960, and 71:29 in 1970. This trend has certainly contributed to the chronic consumer goods shortages. The relatively faster growth of

---

[1] If not otherwise stated, the statistical data are from various issues of *Narkhoz SSSR* and *Narkhoz Ukrainy.*

heavy industry branches was accomplished primarily by transferring investment resources from agriculture, forestry, and consumer goods industries.

Total collectivization, achieved by destroying prosperous private farms and exiling their owners ("kulaks"), led to the fatal weakening of agriculture. The state since then has purchased agricultural products from sovkhozes and kolkhozes at symbolic prices which barely covers one-third of the production costs. Labor and accumulated agricultural savings in agriculture have been utilized with the help of non-economic means in the development of heavy industry and urbanization. The country indeed has benefitted from the development of heavy industries and urbanization. But this development did not lead to the efficient utilization of resources, increased sales, national income growth, and the accumulation of investment and consumer funds.

Defense-related industries have had priority in the Soviet— including the Ukrainian—economy, absorbing the lion's share of all resources. For example, they absorbed nearly two-thirds of scientific-technical resources. Defense-related industries have contributed almost nothing to the civilian production sector, consumer market, and the improvement of the standard of living of the population. At the same time, the state has withheld sufficient investment funds and technological modernization from the most profitable economic branches, light and food industries and forestry, industries characterized by their rapid turnover, lower capital-output ratios, and resultant profitability, which is 1.5 to 3 times higher than the favored branches. The bulk of their profits and even depreciation funds have been absorbed by the state budget. The provision of consumer goods and services has not been considered a prestigious activity. Thus, paradoxically available investment funds have not been allocated to the sectors and branches in which they are most effective, as is the case in a normally functioning economy, but rather according to the central planners' preferences.

In the past the republic has had no sovereignty in the effective planning and management of its economy. It has been obligated to abide by the decisions already taken by union organs, such as Gosplan, ministries, and various agencies. It has not been able to fashion an economic structure appropriate to local conditions and peculiarities, one which would serve the interests of the Ukrainian people. As a result, the Ukrainian economy reflects the shortcomings of the standard structure of a Soviet-type economy; it is extremely rigid and unresponsive to changing consumer demand. The situation deteriorated significantly during the recent years of "inactive perestroika." Speculation, fraud, crime, and corruption have been rampant and the inflation rate has reached 7 percent.

Balancing a consumer goods market is impossible as long as the growth in effective demand is twice the increase in the supply of needed products. Furthermore, a balance will remain unattainable as long as the growth of investment and consumer product output remains at the same low level as in the past quarter century—this despite officially announced programs designed to accelerate the growth of the consumer goods sector relative to the growth rate of the producer goods sector. Even during the last years of perestroika almost three-quarters of investment in industry was allocated to the machine-building, fuel-energy, and metallurgical complexes, while only one-tenth was allocated to food and light industries.

Furthermore, storage and processing facilities for agricultural production in the USSR have proved to be very backward compared to the facilities available in developed countries. About one-third of agricultural products spoil as a result of late and low quality harvesting, transportation, storage, and processing into food products.

It is therefore necessary to modernize the production facilities in regions of raw material production in order to radically reduce these losses, to increase output, and to satisfy present market demand. The state trading network in almost all regions has been destroyed and consumer goods are now being channelled into a speculative shadow economy. The announcement of price increases for bread and some other foodstuffs by the union government caused speculative demand and panic among buyers. People buy everything that they can, whether they need it or not. They have become anxious about the planned transition to a market economy, which is erroneously associated with price increases and inflation. The difference between state retail prices and black market prices for consumer products has increased so much so that black market prices may be five to ten times higher than state prices at the end of 1990. Two to three years earlier, this ratio was between 1.5:1 and 2:1. Continued product shortages are in the interest of the people employed in the trade sector and black market operators because this market anomaly enables them to become wealthy at the cost of the consumers and the state.

The abstract two-sector model of economic development worked out by Karl Marx posited a faster rate of growth of the means of production branches relative to consumer goods branches. It was applicable, however, only to the initial stages of industrialization. The application of this model to the present level of economic development in the USSR has led to inertia, a lack of dynamism, and the failure to quickly adapt to changing consumer demand and existing market conditions in general. Increases in gross industrial output during the recent decades, which were effected solely for the sake of an increase—not in order to solve social problems and to satisfy consumer demand for high quality products and services— produced negative consequences, such as market shortages and the lack of a balance in the micro- and macroeconomic structures of the material, monetary, and value sides of production processes. Meanwhile, modern economics and production theory of large enterprises as well as rational societal structures have advanced beyond Marx's model. Two-sector models have evolved into mathematically highly accurate input-output analyses. The study of market conditions and the application of flexible economic policies, utilizing indirect regulating factors such as price, state budgets, money, and credit, have made the methods of the command system obsolete for achieving economic objectives.

At the present time it is of utmost importance to search for and implement scientifically grounded policies to overcome the complicated problems of the Ukrainian economy. A transition to an essentially new economic system would be the appropriate route for this purpose. This system should provide for the modernization of existing structures and the creation of new ones characterized by highly intensive and resource-saving technologies which would reduce waste or, ideally, eliminate it.

In order to carry out successful economic reforms and bring about the transition to a new economic system Ukraine must increase sales, define and rationalize horizontal and vertical relations, introduce reliable economic regulations, balance interbranch and interregional exchanges, and develop external economic relations. Obviously, it cannot build a sound market economy with all of its complexities simply with commands and pronouncements based on the existing distorted monetary, credit, and budget systems, the old price structure and mechanism, the devalued ruble, and in an environment of product and resource shortages, exacerbated by burgeoning consumer demand.

A radical reform of the entire economic mechanism, including prices, finances, credit, and taxation must be undertaken. Also, the factors which impede economic incentives should be eradicated and the concept of self interest in economic life should be promoted. Without these measures the existing crisis cannot be overcome.

It must be admitted that our economy was damaged not only by the factors discussed above but also by several serious blunders and mistakes in recent reforms. The poorly conceived anti-alcohol campaign, for example, not only destroyed budget receipts, but also promoted bootlegging and caused a shortage of sugar and confectioneries. The freedom for "co-operators" and private persons to engage in entrepreneurial activity without appropriate regulation opened up opportunities for speculation. This aggravated shortages of various commodities and services, and put pressure on the government to increase the emission of currency. To prevent financial and market catastrophe, the union leadership undertook various emergency measures. These measures, however, tended to suppress factors that stimulated the economy and resulted in a further decrease in the supply of consumer goods and services. The same, in essence naive, methods, have been used by republic authorities, causing further deterioration in economic conditions. All the while more money is being printed. Market shortages continue to worsen, and social discontent is growing.

One cannot ignore the fact that along with the aggravation of the political situation and confrontations between various groups, labor relations and labor discipline have worsened in industry, transport, and the trade and supply network. The established links among enterprises, industries, and regions also have loosened. This has contributed to the deterioration of the economic situation. State economic stabilization programs have not succeeded and the legislation intended to implement them has been stillborn.

Nor can one disregard the fact that during the past five years a number of catastrophes and incidents have occurred in the USSR which have caused considerable human and material losses. The Chernobyl tragedy—the explosion of the fourth block of the atomic electricity generating station—is, of course, the most well-known of them. The cleanup has already necessitated extensive financial and material resource expenditures and it will further necessitate such extensive expenditures in the future. The effect on the environment and on the health of the people exposed to the radiation still remains largely unknown. Other accidents include the earthquakes in Armenia and Central Asia, the explosions of pipelines, mine explosions, and transportation disasters. Consequently, the union and republic budgets have had to bear a heavy burden and deficits have increased. Several construction projects, including atomic generation stations and chemical and defense projects, are not being completed or remain idle because of pressure from public opinion. A large number of industrial, energy generation, and chemical complexes are located in Ukraine. The damage to its economy and environment has been especially acute. The amelioration of this dire situation has required substantial outlays of resources which may otherwise have been used to improve the standard of living of the population.

Changes in the Economic System

Ukraine's economy is characterized by disproportions in the system of current wholesale, purchasing, and state retail prices. This affects supply and demand and also the profitability of economic sectors and branches, artificially turning some of them into low-profit or losing ones. The equivalency of interbranch and interregional trade is distorted by this factor. Price distortions are particularly serious in the coal industry, substantial parts of the metallurgical and construction materials industries, and in agriculture. While the average recoupment rate for the entire industry (in 1988) is 15 percent, for the fuel-energy complex it is 8 percent, electro-energy 8 percent, and the chemical and petrochemical industries 11.4 percent (the most profitable branch in developed countries). At the same time light industry enjoys a 42.6 percent recoupment rate, timber, woodworking, and paper industry 29.4 percent, and food processing 17.1 percent.

The normal functioning of the economy requires more or less equal possibilities for individual sectors, branches, and enterprises. The same is true for enterprises, which are now leased or transferred to direct management or ownership by workers collectives, cooperatives, or private individuals. State budget subsidies are used to compensate branches or enterprises for the existing price distortions. But by doing this the state also levels off the results of both well-performing and poorly-performing working collectives. This levelling system has the effect of dampening economic stimuli. Those enterprises which function efficiently are required to transfer their so called profit surplus to the budget, while inefficient enterprises do not have any incentive to improve, because state subsidies protect them from being closed down. The deleterious impact of these policies led to the recent changes in the evaluation of enterprise performance. Economic entities are now being evaluated on the basis of final results and on their profitability. According to the recent laws, once taxes and insurance premiums are paid, the distribution of profits not absorbed by the state budget is decided by the working collective. Workers themselves allocate this money for such purposes as accumulation, incentives, and social and cultural activities. This is a crucial step for the working collectives on the path toward economic independence and responsibility. At the same time, workers are freeing themselves from the tutelage of the administrative bureaucracy. In addition, collectives can now decide to whom to sell their output, from whom to buy, and with whom to maintain complementary relations. Yet some economic functions, especially in the area of resource distribution, are performed the way they were under the old system.

The transition to a market system requires radical reforms in the areas of foreign exchange, finance, prices, banking and credit, taxes, insurance, structural changes, and investment. Thus, changes are required in the entire economic system. The market in this context not only includes the market for products, but also the market for money, various credit instruments, and the free interbranch flow of capital. The government should abstain from interference in these areas and should limit its activities primarily to policies promoting entrepreneurship and competition in various markets.

Longterm Development Trends

An analysis of Ukrainian economic development during the past quarter of a century shows a steady decline in the growth of the gross social product (GSP), national income, and fixed assets. Meanwhile, Ukraine has experienced increases in profits, investment, and the construction and installation of new fixed assets during the last ten years as compared with the preceding fifteen years (Figure 2-1).[2] The rising

---

[2] It is necessary to mention that the data shown in the accompanying table are based on official statistics, which are considered too high by Western scholars. This may be so, but no better data are available. Although official data need some revisions, they still reflect real tendencies. Further, the statistical authorities have been given the task of calculating corrected indicators in value terms for the USSR and

price level and costs of production have been largely responsible for this trend. The increase in investment and the value of new fixed assets was more a result of accelerated inflation than of a real increase. The same is true for the standard of living: income per capita increased in monetary terms, while it declined in real terms.

While the rate of economic growth in Ukraine amounted to almost 7 percent during the 1966–70 period, it subsequently declined, dipping as low as 2.5 to 3 percent during the years 1986 to 1989. The decline after 1970 probably occurred because the effects of the limited reforms of 1965 had been exhausted. The consequences of underlying stagnation and disproportional development became evident during this period. For example, the command methods of managing the economy became increasingly ineffective, and the slowdown in the modernization of productive potential and economic structures became more pronounced. For a while, the effects of these negative tendencies were dampened by rises in the price of oil on the international market, which earned more hard currency for the USSR than earlier. Some of the resulting benefits accrued to Ukraine as well.

Ukraine's internal economic and social situation, however, continued to deteriorate. Such industries as coal and iron-ore mining, and ferrous metallurgy suffered most; they experienced low profits or incurred losses. Their outdated facilities were not modernized because centralized investments were allocated for the development of atomic energy, construction of ineffective water projects, and the build up of military-industrial complexes. At the same time, the share of consumer industries as a proportion of the entire industry continued to decline (cf. *Vestnik statistiki* 1990, 36; *Radians'ka Ukraïna* 1990).[3] The shares of woodworking and construction materials industries also decreased. The above industries satisfy not only the basic needs of the population and of all industries, but they also have been the most important contributors to the state budget and thus provide the necessary funds for expanded reproduction.

---

individual republics. Initial steps have already been taken in this direction: in the table the gross social product and the national income estimates for 1985 and 1986 to 1989 reflect these new methodological approaches.

[3] The output share of light industries in total industry decreased from 13 to 11 percent and the share of processing branches in the agro-industrial complex from 23 to 17.5 percent between 1970 and 1988.

These harmful developments in Ukrainian industry occurred under the direction of the union ministries and agencies. One must remember that almost all Ukrainian industries were run by Moscow organs. Only 6 to 7 percent of its industrial potential was subordinated to the Ukrainian Council of Ministers in 1987. This number rose to 45 percent by 1989. All basic industries, nevertheless, continue to be run by Moscow (*Radians'ka Ukraïna* 1990). The republic's present sovereignty therefore does not include control over and ownership of most of its industry and a substantial part of its entire economy. In other words, the sovereignty remains fictitious. Members of the Ukrainian parliament object to this situation, justifiably demanding real economic sovereignty. Researchers from the Institute of Economics together with the Institute of Law of the Ukrainian Academy of Sciences took active part in preparation of laws designed to provide a legal basis for a market economy in a sovereign Ukraine. To this end the Ukrainian parliament accepted the declaration of "State Sovereignty of Ukraine" and the law on "The Economic Independence of the Ukrainian SSR" as well as laws on ownership, land, leases, entrepreneurship, enterprises, corporations, banks, the financial-credit system, the price structure, and external economic relations, among others.

In my view, however, the main task in this legislative activity has yet to be accomplished—namely, the working out of a new constitution of the Ukrainian SSR. Such a constitution should be framed without regard to the future changes in the political leadership, parliamentary composition, and political and economic systems. These changes should take place within the framework of the constitution and not the other way around, as has been the case to date: the constitution has been adjusted depending on who occupies positions of power and what the political climate is like. It should reflect the preferences of a nation living in a truly democratic society. It should guarantee human rights and thus function to stabilize the political and economic system.

It is obvious that it is impossible to create an effective market economy in Ukraine without a strategy and tactics for economic development different from those which have been in force until now. Ukraine, as an independent state, needs to simultaneously orchestrate the introduction of its own state administration, economic independence, economic responsibility (from the bottom up of all state and economic units), the restructuring of all economic sectors, and the development of social and market infrastructures that function more productively. A transition from an administrative distribution system, based on subjective considerations for the allocation of scarce resources, to a new system should take place. This new system should be characterized by creative entrepreneurship, vigorous economic activity, healthy economic initiative, and by competition among producers for consumers' money. At the same time, the state should limit its role in such a system to flexible regulating policies based on economic theory.

Interrepublic Division of Labor and Trade Relations

An analysis of Ukraine's economic sovereignty cannot be undertaken without consideration of the territorial division of labor within the USSR and the cooperation and inevitable integration of the union republics. The problem of the integration of independent states gains in importance as the number of independent nations increases. For thousands of years states, regardless of their race or nationality, have tended to maintain mutually beneficial economic relations among themselves. The opportunity to conduct mutually advantageous trade is even more important for the sovereign union republics. Such relations may include the construction of joint economic projects, united energy systems, the coordination of transportation and communications networks, as well as various other cooperative efforts. Various social groups and even state authorities sometimes put forth poorly conceived proposals for solving the present crisis. These proposals include rather abstract blueprints for the sovereignty of their republics. They ignore historically established international and interregional links and the present geographic division of labor.

It suffices to recall that on the territories of five union republics no oil or natural gas is available. Over 91 percent of the USSR's oil in 1989 was drilled in the Russian Federation. Nearly 77 percent of natural gas was extracted in this republic. Eight republics do not mine coal, eleven do not mine iron ore nor do they produce pig iron, and for all intents and purposes six republics do not smelt steel. Many other extractive and processing complexes and enterprises of light and food industries also are unevenly distributed. Special attention should be paid to the geographic concentration of the extraction of precious metals and diamonds which play an important role in economic life and foreign trade. The convertibility of currency without strong reserves of gold is impossible in times of shortages and in the face of poor quality of various products.

Zones of narrowly specialized agriculture also have been developed over time. For example, cotton is produced in the Central Asian republics and Azerbaijan only. Uzbekistan, Tajikistan, and Turkmenistan are the only producers of high-quality specialized cotton fibers, which are needed in all of the republics. Flax fibers are produced in the Russian Federation, Ukraine, Belarus, and Lithuania only. Georgia supplies almost 100 percent of the union's citrus fruits and 92 percent of its tea leaves, while the Russian Federation and Ukraine supply 92 percent of its sugar beets. The Russian Federation produces the bulk of timber, wood products, and paper in the Soviet Union. This concentration of production has been developed on the basis of objective factors and cannot be ignored. No closed autarkic economies can exist in developed countries. This reality proves that the economic disintegration of the USSR would not be advantageous for any republic. All of the republics, as independent states should develop on the basis of available resources and in view of established conditions—they should continue to be equal and stable trading partners, continuing to exchange the results of their labor equivalently and in a mutually beneficial manner, without being affected by price distortions. The unjustified transfers of national income from one republic to another should not be allowed.

The coordination of interrepublic economic relations is the objective responsibility of the center in any interrepublic cooperation scheme. But the role of the center should be different from the system of economic centralization which came into being in the USSR over the last seventy years. It no longer functions and has led to a cul-de-sac. For example, the percentage of the utilized national income redistributed through the state budget increased from 53.3 percent in 1970 to 73.5 percent (by expenditure) in 1989. The state budget is three times greater than the accumulation fund. The imbalances between production and consumption, the allocation of resources without compensatory remuneration, and the utilization of wealth without having contributed to its accumulation are only some of the most glaring consequences of overcentralization. An economic mechanism has been created which has thoroughly destroyed economic incentives and responsibility for the results of economic activity. This is exactly why the objective of self-administration and independence at each level of the economic hierarchy prevails in current economic theory and policy. However, economic independence and its stabilization cannot be accomplished by legal and political acts alone. The consistent and radical reconstruction of interrepublic relations, their optimization, and structural changes in the republic economies are necessary.

Reliable evaluation of vertical exchanges, between the republics and the center, and of horizontal exchanges, among republics, of the GSP, national income, and the net product of material production enterprises (NPMP) depends on the accurate estimation of these indicators. Price deficiencies, however, not only distort the equivalency of the exchange, but also make difficult the accounting of money and product flows. In addition, various products are produced and sold at a variety of ever changing contractual prices obscuring the real picture of these vertical and horizontal relations.

Receipts from foreign trade in general go to the central authorities. In the mid 1980s they accounted for approximately 10 percent of the national income of the USSR and between 8 and 12 percent of the national income of individual republics. Since data for the sale and purchase of each commodity for individual republics are not available, the reliability of the above percentages is not very high. Nevertheless the NPMP is increased by this percentage in the state statistics.

The volume and structure of imports and exports and their share of the GSP are undoubtedly important. Ukraine's annual turnover of imports and exports of 96.8 billion rubles in 1988 accounted for 36.8 percent (imports 19.0 and exports 17.8 percent) of its GSP (Ivanchenko 1990). The GSP's shares of imports and exports were respectively for Belarus 28.0 percent and 29.7 percent, Lithuania 31.3 percent and 26.3 percent, Latvia 31.5 percent and 26.4 percent, Azerbaijan 26.1 percent and 29.6 percent, and Moldova 31.7 percent and 30.1 percent (Granberg 1990, 95). Despite the fact that the Ukrainian economy now performs rather poorly, it nonetheless satisfies its domestic needs by 82 percent, while the RSFSR satisfies its needs by 86 percent, and the Baltic republics satisfy their needs by 71 to 73 percent.[4]

---

[4] For more on Ukraine's external economic relations, see Chapter 17 below.

The burden of defense funding for the USSR falls primarily on the Russian Federation, Ukraine, and Belarus. These expenditures accounted for 8.8 percent of the USSR gross national product in 1989 according to Soviet statistics (cf. Ryzhkov 1990, 33 and 35; Goskomstat 1990b, 5), and to 13.0 and 12.5 percent in 1980 and 1985 respectively, according to American estimations (U.S. Treasury 1989, 843). One can conclude from this that attaining economic independence for these three republics is rather difficult without the substantial conversion of military production to civilian use. Were such a conversion to be made, Ukraine could easily develop modern science-based production, especially in such branches as radio manufacturing, electronics, ship construction, and technological systems for light and food industries.

The future prospects for Ukraine's economy are diminished by the scarcity of its own fuel and energy resources. It should be noted that the extraction of oil dropped 61 percent, gas 49 percent, coal 13 percent, and fuel peat 49 percent between 1970 and 1989. The generation of electricity, however, increased 2.15 times during the same period, a fact which compensated to a certain degree for the decline in the output of other energy sources. Nevertheless, the expansion of energy-based products, the vigorous growth of the petrochemical industry, and growth in the number of motor vehicles have been responsible for a significant increase in the demand for oil and gas in Ukraine.

Energy conservation resulting from a reduction in energy intensive production processes and the introduction of energy saving technologies should result in a decrease in the demand for various energy sources. Because this trend depends on structural changes, it obviously takes a long time. In the meanwhile, Ukraine experiences constant shortages of fluid fuels and lubricants. The change in Ukraine's orientation from atomic energy to thermal energy generation will require additional imports of natural gas which, however, can only take place if new gas pipe lines, costing billions of rubles, are laid. The rise in the prices of petroleum, gas, and timber complicates the situation of the Ukrainian economy considerably. Most likely, the prices of Ukrainian exports also will have to rise as a result.

The success of Ukraine's economic independence depends on a thorough reconstruction of its foreign trade. The main deficiency in the present situation lies in the volume and structure of exports. As stated above, Ukrainian exports to foreign countries amounted to 6.9

billion rubles in 1988 (*Vestnik statistiki* 1990, 40). Metallurgical products, with 27.8 percent of the total, played the most important role in the export structure, followed by machinery products with 22.1 percent, coal with 10.1 percent, and chemicals and petrochemicals with 9.2 percent (*Vestnik statistiki* 1990, 40). The volume of machines exported, amounting to 2.4 billion foreign-exchange rubles, or 13 percent of the USSR's 17.8 billion rubles of exports, is especially low as compared with developed countries such as Japan, West Germany, the United States, and Canada (Goskomstat SSSR 1990a, 268). It is clear that its economic independence will remain meaningless if Ukraine fails to integrate itself into extended and intensive international economic relations, including trade in science-based production using modern technology. The solution to this problem requires, first of all, the reconstruction of the Ukrainian economy, particularly its industry.

The realization of Ukraine's economic independence also presupposes the right to decide who is entitled to utilize the output produced on its territory. Presently, some republics utilize more of the total union income than they produce. At the same time, part of the national income of the Russian Federation, Ukraine, and Belarus is transferred to other republics for investment or is used for the needs of the entire USSR. This discrepancy between production and consumption in some republics is understandably the cause of considerable social and national dissatisfaction.

For Ukraine, this outflow of a part of its national income is particularly sensitive. The loss of these funds creates a shortage of resources required for badly needed investment in Ukraine's basic industries, the light and food industries, and the agricultural sector. The shortage of capital investments is reflected in the decrease in the net accumulation of fixed productive funds. According to the estimates of the Kiev Institute of Economics, they amounted to 17.7 percent of the total funds in the USSR in 1970, 11.6 percent in 1980, and 10.1 percent in 1987. As a result, the national income per capita in Ukraine relative to the average for the USSR declined from 95 to 91 percent between 1970 and 1987.

Each of the union republics should be required to self-finance the investment and current expenditures needed to maintain a qualitatively modern economic structure capable of satisfying the social and cultural needs of its population. This is one of the basic conditions of economic independence. Furthermore, a republic's economic independence includes the ability to introduce radical reconstruction not only of its economic system, but also of the instruments of economic policy. As far as the instruments of economic policy are concerned, it is important to change the structure of budget receipts and expenditures, and to substantially increase the role of the budgets of lower administrative units with regard to saving, consumption, and participation in financing of high priority objectives of the national economy. Finally, the continual decline of the accumulation share in the national income must be arrested. Without such reforms, structural changes and the modernization of the existing productive potential cannot be achieved.

There are serious obstacles in the path of economic reform in Ukraine. In addition to the harmful heritage of the past and totalitarian approaches to economic life, mistakes made during the current reforms further complicate the social and economic situation. Ukrainians, as do other peoples in the USSR, expect the reforms to bring about improvements in their standard of living and cultural environment. Instead, while reforms are being announced and the parliament and government enact various pieces of legislation, inflation is rampant and market shortages are becoming more acute. The resulting decrease in the people's standard of living has evoked a negative reaction and a lack of trust in the decisions taken. The people have significantly reduced their initial expectations for a glorious future. Proposing new laws and projects is, of course, important. But it is imperative to determine the key issues for economic reform and to proceed systematically to deal with them in order to stabilize the national economy, to intensify economic development and structural changes, and to effect balances in the various markets.

Basic Approaches to the Solution of the Existing Crisis

Economic sovereignty coupled with political and cultural growth in Ukraine will lead to improved economic results, characterized by the interaction of economic activity, strengthened discipline, order and responsibility in the productive sphere, and the introduction of all types of businesses operating in well functioning markets. Important preconditions for economic progress are the freedom of democratic choice, independence in economic decision making, the importance of self-interest, and competition in the market place.

Economic development can be based on a system of small-, medium-, and large-sized enterprises and on various types of ownership, such as state ownership, corporations (including those jointly owned by foreign investors), cooperatives, and leased and other businesses. They all should be intensively involved in domestic and external economic relations. However, such enterprises cannot function efficiently without the stabilization of the value of money and the exchange rate, and the convertibility of the currency.

In view of the above and in connection with political sovereignty, it is necessary, first, to stabilize the value of money based on the competitiveness of products and services, price stability, and the convertibility of currency supported by sufficient reserves of gold and foreign exchange. Rigid control over the emission of money and its velocity, an active budgetary policy, and the elimination of budget deficits and inflation are absolutely necessary. Paradoxically, this can be accomplished not by dampening the factors stimulating economic growth (as the union government has done), but on the contrary, by promoting them by means of the activization of the role of prices, interest rates, and budgetary policies. A regulated market cannot function efficiently in an artificially frozen and deformed system of wages and prices. Sooner or later, preferably sooner, the government will be forced to undertake monetary and price reforms, without which no solution to the existing crisis is possible. The population will have to acquiesce to them.

Second, it is necessary to determine the strategic priorities for the economic development of Ukraine. Radical changes are required in the structure and forms of economic activity, including consumer goods and producer goods sectors of industry and agriculture. Equivalent relations between agriculture and industry and between urban and rural areas should be promoted. Structural and investment policy should be concentrated on supporting the growth of priority branches and economic systems capable, first of all, of eliminating the shortages of food and other consumer goods in domestic markets. This would contribute to the growth of gross and net national income and of the accumulation and consumption funds needed to solve the ever growing social problems. Consumer goods branches of industry, the agro-industrial complex, and the service sector can accomplish this task. Investment and other resources should be primarily allocated to them.

At the same time, it is necessary to reconstruct heavy industries by converting enterprises from defense to civilian use. But this is not enough. To eliminate consumer goods shortages, the diversification of investment and current expenditures in large enterprises and associations must take place. The purpose of this policy would be to create modern specialized production facilities for the output of quality industrial goods intended directly for the retail market and also of raw materials, industrial materials, and complementary goods needed for the production of consumer goods. According to some estimates, between one-third and one-half of fixed and circulating investment can be allocated for this purpose without any effect on the output of basic industries. These results can be achieved by accelerating capital circulation and increasing profitability, and thereby increasing accumulation in the entire economy. Thus, in effect, the entire industrial complex will benefit from this approach.

The conversion of defense producing enterprises to civilian use includes the transfer of workers after necessary retraining. The opening of additional work places within existing associations and enterprises will help solve an unemployment problem which may arise as a consequence of the transition of formerly stated-owned enterprises to leased and private ownership. It is estimated that in 1995 as the result of these changes product volume will rise by 1.4 times compared with the present level and the branch structure will look approximately as follows: heavy industry 40 percent, the agro-industrial complex 40 percent, and light industry 20 percent.

At the same time, Ukraine must restructure industrial branches of producer foods sector in favor of modern science-based products. Specifically, the following products should be emphasized in the Ukrainian industry of the future: radioelectronics, automatization and information equipment, computer and laser systems, new materials for space research, surface and water transport vehicles, new technologically advanced agricultural equipment, modern food processing and light industry equipment. These areas hold the most promise for joint ventures between Ukrainian and Western entrepreneurs.

Radical reform is also necessary in the extractive and processing industries, especially in the metallurgical and machinery branches. The technology and management of all low-profit and subsidized enterprises should be reorganized. If they continue to operate at a loss, these enterprises should be closed down. Particular attention should be paid to resource saving technologies in all industrial enterprises. This would lead to a partial solution of the present ecological crisis in Ukraine. Radical reforms as well as privitization and the transition to market conditions require a thorough restructuring and change in macroeconomic proportions accompanied by microeconomic improvements. The expansion of trade relations with other republics and other countries of the world should lead to the balancing of domestic markets. If trade were to reveal that domestic production is more expensive than imports, the respective enterprises would have to be closed down regardless of whether this enterprise is state or privately owned. In this way international economic relations will influence the structure of the domestic economy and would facilitate the effectiveness of investment.

The distribution of investment funds between producer goods and consumer goods facilities should change as a result of the new structural policy. At the present time this proportion is 71:29 percent. This should change, according to my calculations, to 60:40 percent at least. An especially high priority should be assigned to investment in the productive and social infrastructure of agriculture, rural construction, and technological equipment for agriculture. Without these improvements the solution of the food crisis in Ukraine is not possible.

Third, an important component of the economic reforms is the restructuring of ownership relations. These reforms cannot be undertaken administratively, by orders from the top. This especially complicated social process should proceed as a result of the conscious and democratic choice of the working people—of directors, specialists, working teams, workers, and farmers. They themselves should make choices and take necessary steps without pressure from political groups or parties. The present ownership system was determined by the reckless and poorly conceived policy of nationalization, by driving millions of peasants into the kolkhozes which subsequently were converted to state ownership. The same mistake, but in reverse, should not be repeated. Privitization and total rejection of state ownership imposed from above would lead once again to the destruction of the economy and thus to the brutalization of daily life. This is no way to improve the living standard of the people. On the contrary, this policy would lead to its deterioration for many years to come and would require additional resources simply to revert to the previous state of affairs.

Rapid economic growth cannot be achieved by completely rejecting the economic system which has evolved to date. It can occur by consistently transforming the old system into a new system characterized by highly intensive and effective resource utilization based on rational privitization, the use of property leases, specialization, cooperation, and technological innovations. According to legislation, workers should gain economic independence during the transition to new forms of enterprise management which would be based on their right to manage and to employ the means of production. Thus, state enterprises and associations would be managed by workers themselves. They will become fully responsible for the output they produce and for their relations with state and local budgets. The volume, structure, quality of produced goods, the satisfaction of market demand, timely deliveries, and the price level should be the sole determinants of the profitability of a given enterprise and of the income of each worker. Whoever works better should be better remunerated and should have better living conditions. This is the true socialist principle of the regulated market system.

The problem, however, lies not only in the transformation of the existing productive capacity, which is to a significant degree not only technologically obsolete but up to 40 percent worn out. No less important is the fact that Ukraine lacks various productive facilities. It is necessary to start new, especially small- and medium-sized science-based enterprises, especially for food processing and the production of other consumer goods. The number of such enterprises should approximately be doubled and they should be located in the rural areas that have the available supplies of raw materials. This policy will allow for the better utilization of the existing infrastructure and raw material reserves. The effective utilization of rural labor and material resources will make these enterprises profitable and, importantly, will counteract the negative consequences of the spontaneous flight of the rural population to the cities.

State agrarian policies aimed at the development of multifaceted farm enterprises should allow for privately owned large-sized farms as well as the freedom for peasants to choose how farms should be organized, without pressure for the rushed dissolution of kolkhozes and sovkhozes. In general, it would be a mistake to close down some types of current agricultural enterprises without first increasing their efficiency. Furthermore, market shortages of food products open great opportunities for peasants to choose which farms are the most profitable: privately owned or cooperative. Ukraine has an extremely limited amount of agricultural land per capita. There is only 0.81 hectares of agricultural land and 0.66 hectares of arable land per resident of the republic. Therefore the land must be utilized with a maximum degree of efficiency and must be continually improved. In considering land transfers regardless of the type of ownership, the state through the local soviets is responsible for monitoring land use and for assuring that the land and its high fertility is preserved not only for the present generation, but also for future ones. The choice of an owner should be made on the basis of the proposed owner's professional background and ability to farm with good results.

Agricultural land should be leased or sold to those farmers who can assure higher productivity than under the present circumstances. The ability of new owners to technologically improve the land under their control, and their ability to raise the necessary investment from banks cannot be ignored. In other words, agricultural reform— like the reforms in industry, the service sector, cultural life, and of the entire social system—requires balanced considerations, high professionalism, exact economic calculations, and a means to evaluate short term as well as long term results.

The scientific approach towards the realization of economic reforms, rather than rushed and ill-considered decisions and actions, is the only way to succeed relatively quickly and to steer the scientific-technological and economic revolution for the benefit of the Ukrainian people by raising the standard of living. A return to the level of the past, to some type of primitive economy and bazaar trade will not help to achieve this goal. The way to do it is by taking advantage of world progress (meaning new and higher levels of economic, organizational, and technological achievements,) fostering growth in entrepreneurship and market activity, and by strengthening and developing mutually beneficial relations with other countries. Ukraine could and should then become one of the most advanced and economically developed countries of the world.

References

Goskomstat SSSR. 1990a. *SSSR i zarubezhnye strany v 1988 g.* Moscow.

_____. 1990b. *SSSR v tsifrakh v 1989 godu. Kratkii statisticheskii sbornik.* Moscow.

Granberg, A. 1990. "Problemy mezhregional'nykh ekonomicheskikh otnoshenii." *Ekonomika i matematicheskie metody* 1:93–104.

Ivanchenko, I. 1990. "Kto kogo kormit," *Pravda Ukrainy* (15 April). *Radians'ka Ukraïna.* 27 May 1990.

Ryzhkov, N. I. 1989. *O programme predstoiashchei deiatel'nosti pravitel'stva SSSR.* Moscow.

U.S. Treasury Department, Bureau of Statistics. 1989. *Statistical Abstract of the United States, 1989.* Washington.

Vestnik statistiki. 1990. No. 3.

Figure 2-1. Selected Indicators for the Ukrainian Economy (1966–1989)
(percent)

	1966–70	*1971–75*	*1976–89*	*1981–85*	*1986–89*
Gross Social Product	6.7	5.6	3.4	3.3	2.6
National Income Produced	6.7	4.6	3.4	3.4	3.0
Fixed Productive Assets	6.9	8.0	6.4	5.3	3.5
Industrial Output	8.5	7.2	3.9	3.4	3.8
Agricultural Output	2.5	3.0	1.6	0.5	2.0
Construction and Installation of New Fixed Assets	8.0	5.7	1.9	2.7	4.1
Capital Investments	6.7	6.4	2.1	3.1	5.3
Profits	n.a.	8.9	1.0	5.3	11.5
Real Income per Capita	5.9	3.8	3.2	2.7	2.0*

Source: Various issues of *Narkhoz Ukrainy.*

* 1986–1988, unavailable since 1989.

Part II: Resources

CHAPTER THREE
Demographic Trends in Ukraine in the Late Twentieth Century

Ralph S. Clem

The demographic characteristics of a country or region are a product of the larger socioeconomic environment and also are agents of change in that environment. Economic development, for example, typically affects a population's fertility and mortality rates and natural increase, urbanization levels, and migration. These aspects of social change in turn influence further development, particularly through their impact—quantitatively and qualitatively—on the labor force. Following a period of very rapid population growth and the beginnings of urbanization and large-scale migration in the late nineteenth century, the population of Ukraine was dramatically transformed through massive and rapid economic growth. Tragically, it was decimated by the effects of war, famine, and political terror in the first half of the twentieth century (cf. Clem 1991). In the absence of catastrophic events of that magnitude, the last quarter of the current century—the focus of this paper—has witnessed a normal relationship between development and demographic change, as the population of Ukraine evolved further in the direction of the more-developed countries of Europe.

With this very general background in mind, we shall explain the main features of the recent, current, and near-term future of Ukraine's population, specifically population growth and its components (natural increase and migration), urbanization, age and sex structure, and ethnic composition. Finally, we will suggest some likely implications of these trends for the coming years.

Population Growth

With a population of 51 million (1989), Ukraine is the second most populous republic of the Soviet Union. In numbers of inhabitants, the Ukraine is about one-third the size of the Russian Federation, two and one-half times larger than the third most-populous republic (Uzbekistan), and almost 33 times larger than the least-populous republic (Estonia). In the periods between the three most recent censuses (1959–1970, 1970–1979, and 1979–1989), population growth in Ukraine was below the union-wide average, and as a consequence its share of the Soviet population dropped from 20 percent in 1959 to 18 percent in 1989 (Figure 3-1). Actually, the average annual growth rate of Ukraine's population has been dropping since 1959 (Figure 3-2); the average annual growth rate was lower in the 1979–1989 period than at any time in this century other than the catastrophic war era (1939–1959).

Within the republic, population growth rates have been relatively higher in the south region and lowest in the southwest region. As a result, the South's share of population has steadily increased, while the Donets'k-Dnieper and Southwest have lost ground. Nonetheless, Donets'k Oblast remains by far the most populous (Figure 3-3), followed by Kiev Oblast (in the southwest region), then Dnipropetrovs'k, Kharkiv, and Luhans'k oblasts (all in the Donets'k-Dnieper region), L'viv Oblast (Southwest), and Odessa Oblast (South).

Natural Increase

Since 1960, the rate of natural increase in Ukraine has decreased steadily to where it is now the lowest of any of the republics of the USSR (Figures 3-4 and 3-5). Preliminary figures for 1989 indicate another sharp drop for Ukraine, placing it even further below Latvia and Estonia (Goskomstat SSSR 1990, 45). As is clear in Figure 3-1, this is due to both a low birth rate and a relatively high death rate, although it should be noted that the latter is largely influenced by age distribution differences when compared to death rates in other republics or over time (Figure 3-5). Within Ukraine, there are major differences in natural increase (Figure 3-6), with the south region having generally higher rates, the Donets'k-Dnieper lower rates, and the Southwest intermediate rates. Figure 3-6 also shows that rural areas of the republic have very low rates of natural increase and, in many cases, actually are characterized by natural decrease. However, this is also primarily a result of age distribution. To find the principal causes of the decline, we must turn our attention to fertility and mortality.

Fertility

In recent years, the level of fertility in Ukraine has fallen to the point that it now ranks last among the 15 Soviet republics in most birthrate indexes (Figure 3-5). If present trends continue, the republic's population will not reproduce itself over the next generation. We will attempt to explain this phenomenon, bearing in mind that human fertility is one of the most complex aspects of society, since it is a function of demographic structure (age and sex composition), cultural patterns (marriage timing and duration), socioeconomic factors (education and work force participation levels among women), population trends (urbanization and migration), and the more intangible social-psychological influences that typically accompany modernization and social change.

In Ukraine, as in most other regions of the European USSR, low fertility is a fact of life in the twentieth century, during which the birth rate declined from relatively high levels to its current state. Data from the turn of the century indicate that fertility in Ukraine was among the highest in the Russian Empire, with six of the nine guberniias (which roughly correspond to the present-day Ukrainian SSR) having birth rates above the national average (Coale et al. 1979, 20–21). In succeeding decades, however, the influence of rapid and pervasive social change in Ukraine fostered an environment in which lower fertility eventually became the norm. The status of women changed through education and employment outside the home, the populace shifted from rural to urban areas, industrialization expanded, and traditional values associated with higher fertility eroded. (Coale et al. 1979, 205–206). The trauma of war, famine, and other events also had a negative influence on fertility levels, mainly by disrupting the age and sex structure of the population.

As a consequence of these and other forces, the crude birth rate in Ukraine fell from somewhere in the mid-40s per thousand at the turn of the century to about 27 in 1940, approximately 23 in 1950, and around 20 in 1960. After 1960, the decline continued to its level of between 14 and 15 per thousand (Figure 3-7), closely matching the nation-wide trend but dropping substantially below Central Asian republics such as Uzbekistan (Figure 3-4). Figures for 1989 show a further decline to 13.4 per thousand (Goskomstat SSSR 1990, 45). To understand why, it is necessary to breakdown the crude birth rate by age and sex by examining age-specific birth rates, the total fertility rate (total births to a cohort of 1,000 women), and the net reproduction rate (the number of surviving daughters per woman). These data (Figures 3-8 and 3-9) reveal two important facts: even though there has been a decrease in fertility since 1958, the most significant feature of current birth rate patterns is a pronounced urban/rural differential. This would appear to be at odds with the most recent crude birth-rate figures for Ukraine, which reflect a slightly higher urban fertility (Figure 3-6). The explanation is that the crude birth rate takes no account of age and sex differences; in the case of Ukraine, trends in sex and age composition are major determinants of fertility. For example, in 1959, 52 percent of women in the child-bearing ages (15 to 49) lived in rural areas, whereas by 1987 that figure had fallen to 28 percent. Likewise, changes in the age structure of the female population of Ukraine have resulted in proportionately fewer women in the child-bearing years. In 1959, 57 percent of women in cities of Ukraine were aged 15 to 49, while that figure dropped to 51 percent by 1987. In rural areas of the republic this change was even more precipitous, declining from 50 to 37 percent (Goskomstat SSSR 1988a, pp. 54–57). What we have witnessed is a relative shift of women from rural areas (higher fertility) to cities (lower fertility) accompanied by a decline in the proportion of women in the child-bearing ages.

The low fertility in urban areas in Ukraine is associated with factors that universally promote a reduced birthrate; especially significant are higher levels of education for urban women and employment in non-agricultural occupations. In terms of education, urban females in the republic are considerably better-educated than their rural counterparts, and female participation in the professional-technical work force is relatively high in Ukraine (Goskomstat SSSR 1988b, 119). It also may be the case that higher divorce rates and family instability in urban areas compound low fertility in cities. In 1988, Ukraine had the fourth-highest divorce rate in the USSR (3.6 per thousand population, Figure 3-5); preliminary figures for 1989 reveal a slight rise in the divorce rate to 3.7 per thousand (Goskomstat SSSR 1990, 48). A union-wide survey conducted in 1985 found that the remarriage rate in the republic following divorce was slightly below the union-wide average (Goskomstat SSSR 1989a, 206–207).[1] Although the data required to calculate a duration-specific divorce rate for 1988 are not available, the level of the crude divorce rate suggests that somewhere between 35 and 40 percent of marriages in Ukraine end in divorce. By comparison, the crude divorce rate in the United States (1986) was 4.8 per thousand population, and in Western European countries it generally ranged from 2.0 to 2.5 (United Nations 1989, 186–91). The tendency toward lower fertility in urban areas is exacerbated in larger cities, mainly because the conditions promoting it are more in evidence (Khorev and Kiseleva 1982, 47–81). Thus, while the divorce rate in Ukraine in 1979 was 3.6 per thousand, the rates in Kiev, Odessa, and Kharkiv were 5.4, 6.5, and 5.6 respectively (Khorev and Kiseleva 1982, 72). The incidence of particularly lower fertility in the largest cities becomes increasingly important in the Ukrainian SSR as the republic's urban centers continue to grow.

Given the long-term dynamics of socioeconomic change in Ukraine, the prospects are for continued low fertility and probably even a further decline. Although fertility in Ukraine is quite low in the context of the USSR, it nevertheless remains higher than most Western European countries or the United States.[2] Therefore, as the republic achieves still higher levels of development, incorporating more advanced education, further increases in urbanization, rising affluence, and growth of the non-agricultural sectors of the economy, the likelihood is that fertility will more closely approximate Western European levels.

Mortality

During the twentieth century, the crude death rate in Ukraine declined to very low levels, bottoming out around 7 per thousand in 1960 and then rising to its current level of between 11 and 12 (Figure 3-4). Currently, the crude death rate in the Ukrainian SSR is the third

[1] The figures are for remarriage after 5 and 10 years among divorced or widowed persons.

[2] For example, the total fertility rate in the United States (1985) was 1,842 and the net reproductive rate (1984) was 0.863, compared to Ukraine (2,026 and 0.957 in 1988). The respective rates for West Germany (1985) were 1,296 and 0.604, for Portugal (1985) 1,701 and 0.830, for Italy (1983) 1,551 and 0.741, and for Yugoslavia (1983) 2,098 and 0.964 (United Nations 1989, 1336–59).

highest in the Soviet Union. However measures that take into account age and sex differences in populations allow for a more refined analysis of mortality, and here Ukraine presents a more favorable profile than most republics. In terms of life expectancy at birth, the most sophisticated such measure, in 1988 Ukraine ranked sixth for males among the union republics (behind Georgia, Lithuania, Belarus, Estonia, and Tajikistan, in that order) and sixth for females (after Lithuania, Belarus, Georgia, Latvia, and Estonia; Goskomstat SSSR, 1989a, 494).[3] The gap between life expectancy for males and that for females in Ukraine (Figure 3-10) is typical of developed countries; for example, in the United States in 1985 life expectancy at birth for males was 71.2 years, while that for females was 78.2 years (United Nations 1989, 516). What is of note in Figure 3-10 is the substantial gap between urban men and rural men, a gap that is not reflected in the female population and that is growing.

The subject of mortality in the Soviet Union in the period after 1960 is rather contentious (cf. Dutton 1979, 267–91; Eberstadt 1981, 23–31; Feshbach 1982). It does seem clear from the available evidence that mortality, especially among males, began to increase in the mid-1960s, continued to increase or remain relatively higher through the 1970s, and then began to decline through the 1980s. Debate centers around the causes of the increase and subsequent decrease, with the following possible explanation: (1) the quality of life, and especially health care in the Soviet Union began to deteriorate in the 1960s, (2) long-term debilitating effects from the period of collectivization, famine, and World War II began to manifest themselves as peoples born during that time entered middle age; and (3) improvements in vital-statistics reporting resulted in an apparent increase in mortality.[4] The principal argument against the deteriorating-conditions hypothesis as a single explanation for a higher death rate is the decline in mortality that began in the early 1980s. With no evidence of improvements in health care since then, it is difficult to see how the relationship between the two trends can be sustained as a sole cause, although it is probably the case that over the long term,

---

[3] The figure for male life expectancy in Tajikistan is almost certainly spurious.

[4] Dutton (1979) believes that rising alcohol consumption is an especially important determinant of higher mortality. For a discussion of the effects of World War II, see Bednyi 1972, 181.

problems in the Soviet medical care delivery system, environmental degradation, and alcoholism have played a role in the increase in the death rate. Anderson and Silver (1989, 471–501), on the other hand, make a convincing case for a significant cohort effect on overall mortality trends in the USSR. Specifically, they demonstrate that males and females born during the Second World War and males who were young adolescents during the war (who were born during the 1930s) now experience higher mortality rates, probably as a result of the harsh conditions of those times.

Recently published figures for Ukraine reveal a pattern of higher age-specific death rates for the very cohorts identified by Anderson and Silver as prone to higher death rates (Goskomstat SSSR 1989a, 421). Additionally, the cohort of men who were of prime military age in the Second World War experienced higher mortality as they moved into the ages of 60 and over, again possibly from the delayed effects of wounds, disease, and the generally poor conditions incurred earlier (cf. Steshenko et al. 1977, 140). In the case of Ukraine, it would not seem likely that improved mortality reporting has had a major impact on the observed increase in the death rate, inasmuch as statistics from the republic are known to be of better quality than in most other areas of the USSR (due in part to the long tradition of Ukrainian demographic science).

The situation with regard to changes in the level of infant mortality in the USSR is even more controversial than that involving the general population (cf. Davis and Feshbach 1980; Jones and Grupp 1983, 213–46; Anderson and Silver 1986, 705–738). As is well known, the reported Soviet infant-mortality rate began to increase in 1972 after a virtually steady decline going back to the early 1950s. Probably in response to the attention given to this phenomenon in the West, publication of infant-mortality figures for the USSR were curtailed after 1975, and it is only recently that the complete series was released. The controversy focuses on whether the increase was real or whether it was the result of better reporting of infant deaths. Although at this point it is not possible to decide this issue definitively, evidence suggests that most, if not all, of the rise in infant mortality is attributable to more complete vital registration and changes in the definitions used to classify infant deaths (particularly the much greater emphasis placed on perinatal mortality in the early 1970s (Anderson and Silver 1986, 705–723)). It also has been suggested that in the early 1970s

Soviet physicians began more vigorous attempts to sustain the life of premature or other high-risk infants. In the event that these children died, they would be classified as infant deaths, whereas in the past they probably would have been recorded as stillbirths or miscarriages (Jones and Grupp 1983, 231–32). Nevertheless, there is legitimate cause for concern about the level of infant mortality in the USSR and the reasons behind it, particularly because the reported rates in the USSR are understated by about 20 to 25 percent due to deviations from international standards of classifying infant deaths. Such factors are excessive smoking and drinking by women, environmental pollution, poor nutrition due to an inadequate food supply, and the effects of multiple abortions all play a role in determining the health of newborns. The infant mortality situation in Soviet Central Asia is a genuine crisis, and contributes disproportionately to the overall USSR death rate.

Trends in infant mortality in Ukraine closely parallel those of the USSR in general, but at significantly lower levels (Figures 3-11 and 3-12). After declining through the 1960s and early 1970s, the infant-mortality rate in Ukraine rose after 1971 to peak in 1975, then declined again to still-lower levels. It should be noted that today, the infant-mortality rate in Ukraine has fallen to a level substantially below those of the early 1970s, while that of the USSR has not yet recovered all of its lost ground. Given that the under-registration of infant deaths in Ukraine was almost certainly not the problem, the increase after 1971 probably is due to changes in statistical classification procedures. There seems little likelihood that there actually was a temporary increase in infant mortality in Ukraine during that period, although—as is true for the USSR in general—there are grounds for concern about the continued high levels of infant death. A related matter is maternal mortality; here Ukraine ranked eleventh among the republics in 1988, although the absolute number of deaths (284) was not large (*Vestnik statistiki* 1990, 56).

Another aspect of mortality is the cause of death. Here again, the Soviet government recently released previously unavailable information that allows us to gain some insights into this aspect of the demographic situation. In 1988, the principal cause of death among males in the Ukrainian SSR was cardiovascular disease, followed by cancer, accidents, trauma and poisoning, and diseases of the respiratory system (Figure 3-13). The residual "other" category consists of infectious and parasitic diseases, diseases of the digestive system, and deaths from unspecified causes. Note that the "all ages" figure for cardiovascular and cancer deaths among males in Ukraine is slightly higher than the USSR level and considerably higher than that in Uzbekistan (provided for comparison). Because life expectancy is higher in Ukraine than in the USSR in general or Uzbekistan in particular, one would expect that degenerative diseases would play a more important role in mortality. On the other hand, the incidence of deaths from respiratory and other (probably parasitic and infectious) diseases in Uzbekistan is indicative of the relatively poorer health conditions in Central Asia; the pattern of death from these types of causes is typical of less-developed societies with lower life expectancies. A high rate of mortality from accidents among young males also is characteristic of developed countries, although this category may include a large number of alcohol-related deaths. Deaths among females in Ukraine are overwhelmingly from cardiovascular disease, followed by cancer, other, respiratory, and accidental causes (Figure 3-14). Female deaths by cause in Ukraine closely parallel the union-wide pattern.

Migration

For at least the past 300 years, the population of Ukraine has been shaped by the migration of millions of people to, from, and within the region. Migration to the forest steppe and steppe during the seventeenth and eighteenth centuries, migration to the southern steppe and then to the newly industrialized eastern Ukraine in the nineteenth century, and out-migration from the northern and western areas of Ukraine to Kazakhstan and the North Caucasus were among the most important migration streams during the Russian imperial period (Clem 1991, 233–45). In the first half of the twentieth century, the episodic calamities of war, civil war, and famine did much to alter migration patterns within the Soviet Union generally and Ukraine particularly. In addition, the scale of economic development in certain areas of the country and in the republic likewise had a major impact on the geographical redistribution of the population. Thus, the Donets'k-Dnieper region continued to be an area of substantial net in-migration, mainly to urban-industrial centers, while the south region attracted large numbers of rural in-migrants. The southwest region, on the other hand, was a major source of out-migrants, with millions moving to other regions of Ukraine, to the North Caucasus, or east to Kazakhstan and Siberia (Lorimer 1946, 45–49, 151–72; Lewis and Rowland 1979, 99–109). In the postwar era, the period between the 1959 and 1970 censuses witnessed net in-migration to the Donets'k-Dnieper and south regions of Ukraine, while the southwest region continued to experience net losses from migration (Clem 1980, 145–46).

During the two periods between the most recent censuses (1970–79 and 1979–89), both the Donets'k-Dnieper and south regions continue to be characterized by net in-migration, and the Southwest remains an area of net out-migration. In all of these cases, however, the volume of migration decreased between the two periods (Rowland 1990). Figures recently released by the State Statistical Committee (Goskomstat) provide the detail required to examine migration balances within Ukraine down to the oblast level (Figure 3-15). Here it can be seen that the regional pattern of in-migration from the Southwest remains evident through 1989, with the republic as a whole gaining a net of 44,300 persons through migration. Within the Southwest, Kiev Oblast and the city of Kiev are major points of in-migration, whereas in the south region, Odessa Oblast is—atypically—an area of out-migration and the Crimea an area of very heavy in-migration. It also is apparent that rural areas in the republic are overwhelmingly characterized by heavy out-migration, while most urban centers have positive migration balances. These data suggest that people are abandoning the countryside, as they have done for decades, seeking instead the higher standards of living associated with cities. In these uncertain times in the USSR, it is difficult to say where these trends might lead, but the long-term tendency would indicate that people will continue to leave rural areas, that the southwest region will remain as the leading source of out-migrants, and that the industrial centers of the Donets'k-Dnieper and the littoral of the Black Sea will be the destination for many.

Urbanization

The transformation of society from being predominantly rural to mostly urban, a process that typically accompanies modernization, is one of the most significant aspects of social change. Urbanization is important in its own right, but also is closely linked conceptually and empirically to other key features of modernization such as migration, lower fertility, the change from an agricultural to an industrial economy, rising levels of education, and even new forms of political culture. In the Soviet context, urbanization has played an even greater role in socioeconomic development, if for no other reason than the fact that the USSR probably has urbanized at a faster pace than any other country in history (Lewis and Rowland 1979, 158). Thus, since the beginning of this century, the level of urbanization (the percentage of the population residing in urban centers) in the Russian Empire/Soviet Union has increased from about 10 percent to its current level of around 66 percent. Although the level of urbanization today in the USSR is still not as high as those in most other developed countries, a shift of this magnitude within a relatively brief period is indeed a fundamental feature of life in a country whose experience of this century has often been dramatic.

Across the vast territory of the USSR and within Ukraine itself there have been major differences in the extent to which urbanization has taken place (Lewis and Rowland 1969, 776–96). As a rule, prior to 1959 Ukraine lagged behind the union-wide rate of urbanization, but within Ukraine, the Donets'k-Dnieper region, with its vast mining and industrial complexes, exceeded the national average in all intercensal intervals except the wartime-ravaged 1939–1959 period. Then, between 1959 and 1970, the Donets'k-Dnieper dropped below the national average and the South and Southwest exceeded it for the first time (Lewis and Rowland 1979, 212). As a consequence of these trends, by 1970 the level of urbanization in Ukraine (54.5 percent) was just below the unionwide figure (56.3 percent), but the Donets'k-Dnieper region (at 70.3 percent) was considerably above and the southwest region (at 38.4 percent) considerably below that mark (Figure 3-16). At the oblast level, the variation was even more striking, ranging from a high of 87.4 percent for Donets'k Oblast to a low of 23.3 percent in Ternopil' Oblast. Since 1970, the rate of urbanization in Ukraine exceeded the national figure, such that by 1989 the republic (at 66.9 percent) was slightly above the USSR level (65.9 percent). Within Ukraine, the relationship among the three regions remains unchanged in terms of rank, but the southwest has urbanized at a much faster rate than the other two regions, and therefore has taken in steadily larger shares of the republic's urban population (Figures 3-16 and 3-17).

Urbanization occurs primarily through rural-to-urban migration, which has been the case in Ukraine. Between 1970 and 1989, the rural population of the republic declined in absolute terms by more than 4 million (Figure 3-3), excluding gains from natural increase. In 1989 alone, the migration balance in rural areas of Ukraine was negative, −124,000 (Figure 3-15), with the bulk of those leaving the countryside coming from the southwest region. Prospects for a continuation of this trend are good; the coming decades almost certainly will witness a further decline in the rural population and a commensurate growth in rural areas.

Age and Sex Composition

The composition of a population by age and sex is both a determinant of and determined by other demographic trends. As was noted, the age and sex structure of a population has a marked influence on fertility and is itself shaped by fertility, mortality, and migration. Further, extraordinary demographic occurrences, such as a "baby boom" or catastrophic population losses, will echo through the population over the years as the affected cohorts age. It comes as no surprise, therefore, that the distribution of the population of Ukraine by age and sex has changed considerably due to the profound social and economic changes and severe demographic crises of the first half of the twentieth century, but now is stabilizing as the situation has normalized.

Most important, Ukraine's population has aged significantly over the last 30 years, as is reflected in Figure 3-18. In 1959, 26 percent of the republic's population was below 15 years of age, whereas the comparable figure for 1987 was 22 percent. On the other hand, the percentage of Ukraine's population over 65 has increased from 7 to 11 percent over the same period. Note that the trend in Ukraine approximates that of the national change but differs dramatically from that in Uzbekistan, where the proportion of the population in the younger ages has soared.

Also important is the movement through the population of the people born in and of military age during World War II. In 1959, there is a discernible deficit in the 10–14 and 15–19 age groups (who were born during the war) and again in 1987 in the 35–39 and 40–44 (the same group aged 28 years). Likewise, the cohort of males of prime military age during World War II is substantially underrepresented in 1959 (ages 35–39 and 40–44) and again in the 65–69 and over 70 age groups in 1987. As the male deficit cohorts have aged, the sex ratio in Ukraine has resumed a more normal pattern. As is evident in Figure 3-19, in 1959 there were major imbalances in the sex ratio in the age groups 35–39, 40–44, 50–54, and 55–59, groups in which men would have been subject to military service in World War II. By 1987, however, these deficits in the number of males had shifted to the 60 and over cohorts. Thus, in 1987 the typical pattern of male surplus in the younger ages, rough parity in young adulthood, and female surplus in the older ages prevails. Attention should also be given to the surplus of males in rural areas in 1987, which probably reflects a disproportionately high level of out-migration of young women. As the turn of the next century approaches—assuming that socioeconomic trends continue roughly as they have over the past 30 years—we can expect a further aging of Ukraine's population and the passing of most of the demographic effects of the Second World War.

Ethnic Composition

The dramatic ethnic plurality that characterizes the Soviet population and the ethno-territorial basis of the USSR combine to make demographic trends among the various nationalities of the USSR a matter of extreme political and social importance. Within the non-Russian republics, considerable attention focuses upon the proportion of the population made up of indigenous groups and especially by ethnic Russians. In Ukraine, ethno-demographic patterns in the first half of the twentieth century increased the Ukrainian and Russian share of the republic's population, in part because other groups were drastically reduced in number through the effects of war and international boundary changes (Clem *forthcoming*). The Russian population in Ukraine was heavily concentrated in cities and in the eastern oblasts; by 1959, Russians accounted for more than 30 percent of the urban population in the republic and for between one-sixth and more than one-third of the population of oblasts of the Donets'k-Dnieper region (Clem *forthcoming*).[5] Since 1970, the Russian presence in Ukraine has increased to 22 percent (1989), with the Ukrainian share dropping to 72.6 percent (Figure 3-20). This trend is partly due to continuing Russian in-migration to and Ukrainian out-migration from Ukraine. Between 1970 and 1989, the share of Ukrainians in the USSR who reside in Ukraine has fallen from 86.6 to 84.7 percent, reflecting a net distribution of Ukrainians to areas outside their republic (probably through migration).

[5] Figure 3-6. In the last regard, excepting Poltava and Sumy oblasts.

Data on urban in-migration between republics for 1988 show a positive balance for the Ukraine, but the nationality of those migrating is not given (Goskomstat SSSR 1989c, 51–58). Nevertheless, the pattern in the data points to the migration of Russians and Ukrainians into Ukraine from the Russian Federation and of Ukrainians to Ukraine from Central Asia and the Caucasus, perhaps in response to the unsettled conditions that have developed in those two regions. Other figures by nationality indicate that in 1988 there was a positive balance of about 180,000 Ukrainian migrants to urban places in Ukraine, suggesting the arrival of Ukrainians from the countryside and from outside the republic. It may be that the 1988 figures indicate a tendency for Ukrainians to return to their titular republic, reversing a decades-long trend to the contrary. The data only suggest this, however; a definitive analysis requires a longer time frame.

To the Year 2000

Projections of a population and its characteristics are inherently risky, as they involve several variables and considerable uncertainty as to the specific behavior of important factors. On the other hand, assuming that no major shocks occur, in the case of Ukraine we now have at least four decades of demographic experience to draw on to predict the near future.

Population growth in Ukraine probably will reach just over 53 million by the year 2000, with the average annual rate of growth falling to near 0.3 percent for the period from 1989 to 2000. Projections by the Foreign Demographic Analysis Division (FDAD) and its successor, the Center for International Research (CIR) of the Bureau of the Census (Figure 3-21) point to about this number (using the medium series of the FDAD projections). If anything, both of these projections may prove to be slightly high, as the fertility assumptions on which they are based are higher than those that we are currently obtaining.

Natural increase will continue to decline because fertility will drop due to further shifts in age distribution and higher levels of urbanization. Also, the mortality rate will improve for all ages but the crude death rate will continue to rise because of the further aging of the population.

Migration may be the most volatile component of population change in the coming years, especially if the political situation deteriorates to the point where ethnic turmoil generates large-scale movements. Here it is important to bear in mind that 6.7 million Ukrainians live outside the Ukrainian Republic; obviously, not all of them are candidates for migration, but the 1.2 million in Central Asia may be more prone than the rest to relocate to Ukraine. Within Ukraine, the Southwest region certainly will be a source of migrants over the next decade, the question being to which destinations.

Urbanization will proceed quickly, especially in the Southwest region, where rural depopulation is accelerating.

The age and sex composition of Ukraine will move further in the direction of an older population, and the sex ratio will be closer to normal as the World War II populations age.

The ethnic composition of Ukraine will change mainly as a result of trends in migration. If many Ukrainians move to the republic and non-Ukrainians are discouraged from doing so or even encouraged to leave, then the share of the population accounted for by ethnic Ukrainians may rise. A more likely scenario is for a continuation of the slow erosion in the Ukrainian proportion, but probably not much below 72 percent.

In conclusion, if political and economic conditions in Ukraine permit further development along the lines of Eastern Europe, then demographic trends will no doubt closely follow those what have already occurred in Eastern Europe. The prospects are for a continuation of the tendencies observed over the last 40 years as Ukraine has advanced toward modernization.

References

Anderson, Barbara, and Brian D. Silver. 1986. "Infant Mortality in the Soviet Union: Regional Differences and Measurement Issues." *Population and Development Review* 12 (4): 705–738.

_____. 1989. "Patterns of Cohort Mortality in the Soviet Population." *Population and Development Review* 15 (3): 471–501.

Baldwin, Godfrey S. 1979. "Population Projections by Age and Sex: For the Republics and Major Economic Regions of the U.S.S.R., 1970 to 2000." *International Population Reports* P-91 (26). Washington, DC.

Bednyi, M. S. 1972. *Demograf(cheskie protsessy i prognozy zdorovia naseleniia.* Moscow.

Clem, Ralph S. 1980. "Regional Patterns of Population Change in the Soviet Union, 1959–1979." *Geographical Review* 70 (2): 137–56.

_____. 1991. "Population Change in Ukraine in the Nineteenth Century," in *Ukrainian Economic History: Interpretive Essays*, ed. I. S. Koropeckyj, 233–45. Cambridge, Massachusetts.

_____. forthcoming. "Demographic Change among Russians and Ukrainians in the Soviet Union: Social, Economic, and Political Implications." *Russia and Ukraine in Their Historical Encounter*. Edmonton.

Coale, Ansley J., Barbara A. Anderson, and Erna Harm. 1979. *Human Fertility in Russia since the Nineteenth Century*. Princeton.

Davis, Christopher, and Murray Feshbach. 1980. "Rising Infant Mortality in the USSR in the 1970s." *International Population Reports* P-95 (74). Washington, DC.

Dutton, John, Jr. 1979. "Changes in Soviet Mortality Patterns, 1959–77." *Population and Development Review* 5 (2): 267–91.

Eberstadt, Nicholas. 1981. "The Health Crisis in the USSR." *New York Review of Books* 19 (February): 23–31.

Feshbach, Murray. 1982. "The Soviet Union: Population Trends and Dilemmas." *Population Bulletin* 37 (3).

Goskomstat SSSR. 1984. *Chislennost' i sostav nasleniia SSSR 1970 goda*. Moscow.

_____. 1988a. *Naselenie SSSR 1987*. Moscow.

_____. 1988b. *Trud v SSSR*. Moscow.

_____. 1989a. *Naselenie SSSR 1988*. Moscow.

_____. 1989b. "O predvaritel'nykh itogakh vsesoiuznoi perepisi naseleniia 1989 goda." *Pravda* (29 April): 2.

_____. 1989c. "Statisticheskii press—biulleten'." No. 4.

_____. 1990. *Chislennost', estestvennoe dvizhenie i migratsiia naseleniia v 1989 g*. Moscow.

Jones, Ellen, and Fred W. Grupp. 1983. "Infant Mortality Trends in the Soviet Union." *Population and Development Review* 9 (2): 213–46.

Khorev, B. S. and G. P. Kiseleva. 1982. *Urbanizatsiia i demograficheskie protsessy*. Moscow.

Kingkade, W. Ward. 1987. "Estimates and Projections of the Population of the USSR by Age and Sex for Union Republics, 1970 to 2025." *Research Note* (May). Soviet Branch, Center for International Research, U.S. Bureau of the Census.

Leasure, J. William and Robert A. Lewis. 1966. *Population Changes in Russia and the USSR. A Set of Comparable Territorial Units*. San Diego.

Lewis, Robert A., and Richard H. Rowland. 1969. "Urbanization in Russia and the USSR: 1897–1966." *Annals of the Association of American Geographers* 59 (2): 776–96.

_____. 1979. *Population Redistribution in the USSR*. New York.

_____. and Ralph S. Clem. 1976. *Nationality and Population Change in Russia and the USSR, 1897–1970*. New York.

Lorimer, Frank. 1946. *The Population of the Soviet Union: History and Prospects*. Geneva.

Rowland, Richard H. 1990. "Economic Region Net Migration Patterns in the USSR: 1979–89." Paper presented at the Annual Meeting of the Association of American Geographers, Toronto, Canada (April, 1990).

Steshenko, V. S., L. V. Chuiko, and A. F. Zagrobskaia. 1977. *Demograficheskoe razvitiie Ukrainskoi SSR (1959–1970 gg)*. Kiev.

United Nations, Department of International Economic and Social Affairs. 1989. *Demographic Yearbook 1987*. New York.

Vestnik Statistiki. 1990. No. 1.

Figure 3-1. Population of Ukraine
(1000s)

	1897	1926	1939	1959
Ukraine	29,164	38,026	41,318	41,869
Russia/Russian Federation	67,256	94,673	109,929	117,534
Russian Empire/USSR	125,043	167,656	193,077	208,827
Uk % USSR	23.3	22.7	21.4	20.0
Russ. Fed. % USSR	53.8	56.5	56.9	56.3

	1970	1979	1989
Ukraine	47,126	49,755	51,704
Russia/Russian Federation	130,079	137,551	147,386
Russian Empire/USSR	241,720	262,436	286,717
Uk % USSR	19.5	19.0	18.0
Russ. Fed. % USSR	53.8	52.4	51.4

Note: Figures are given for population within the current territory of Ukraine and USSR.

Sources: 1897, 1926, 1959, and 1970 figures are from Lewis, Rowland, and Clem (1976, 412); 1939 figures are from Leasure and Lewis (1966, 27); 1979 figures are from Goskomstat SSSR (1984, 7); 1989 figures are from Goskomstat SSSR (1989b).

Figure 3-2. Average Annual Growth
(percent)

	1897–1926	1926–1939	1939–1959	1959–1970	1970–1979	1979–1989
Ukraine	0.89	0.69	0.08	1.09	0.60	0.39
Donets'k-Dnieper	1.41	1.74	0.57	1.80	0.54	0.35
Southwest R.	0.67	0.08	-0.35	0.20	0.48	0.31
South R.	0.68	0.43	0.22	2.10	1.25	0.79
Russia/Russian Federation	1.14	1.28	0.34	0.92	0.62	0.69
Russian Empire/USSR	0.98	1.16	0.39	1.34	0.93	0.89

Note: Figures are given for population within the current territory of Ukraine and USSR.

Sources: See note to Figure 3-1.

Ralph S. Clem

Figure 3-3. Population of the Ukrainian SSR by Region and Oblast
(1000s)

Ukraine	1970 Total 47,126	1970 Urban 25,688	1970 Rural 21,438	1979 Total 49,755	1979 Urban 30,512	1979 Rural 19,243	1989 Total 51,704	1989 Urban 34,591	1989 Rural 17,113
Donets'k-Dnieper R.	*20,057*	*14,107*	*5,950*	*21,044*	*15,865*	*5,179*	*21,778*	*17,226*	*4,552*
Luhans'k O.	2,751	2,271	480	2,787	2,357	430	2,864	2,474	390
Dnipropetrovs'k O.	3,343	3,549	794	3,639	2,927	712	3,883	3,233	650
Donets'k O.	4,892	4,276	616	5,160	4,599	561	5,328	4,810	518
Zaporizhzhia O.	1,775	1,167	608	1,947	1,384	563	2,081	1,577	504
Kirovohrad O.	1,259	552	707	1,251	654	597	1,240	743	497
Poltava O.	1,706	679	1,027	1,741	875	866	1,753	991	762
Sumy O.	1,505	655	850	1,463	776	687	1,433	886	547
Kharkiv O.	2,826	1,958	868	3,056	2,293	763	3,196	2,512	684
Southwest Region	*20,689*	*7,940*	*12,749*	*21,578*	*10,165*	*11,413*	*22,257*	*12,272*	*9,985*
Vinnytsia O.	2,132	542	1,590	2,046	720	1,326	1,932	857	1,075
Volhynia O.	974	313	661	1,015	407	608	1,062	519	543
Zhytomyr O.	1,626	568	1,058	1,597	706	891	1,545	818	727
Transcarpathia O.	1,057	314	743	1,155	437	718	1,252	515	737
Ivano-Frankivs'k O.	1,249	384	865	1,332	485	847	1,424	598	826

	1970 Total	1970 Urban	1970 Rural	1979 Total	1979 Urban	1979 Rural	1989 Total	1989 Urban	1989 Rural
Kiev O.	3,464	2,287	1,177	4,068	3,015	1,053	4,542	3,644	898
L'viv O.	2,429	1,149	1,280	2,584	1,374	1,210	2,748	1,630	1,118
Rivne O.	1,048	288	760	1,121	408	713	1,170	530	640
Ternopil' O.	1,153	269	884	1,163	364	799	1,169	477	692
Khmel'nyts'kyi O.	1,615	431	1,184	1,558	560	993	1,527	723	804
Cherkasy O.	1,537	563	974	1,547	687	860	1,532	810	722
Chernihiv O.	1,560	540	1,020	1,502	665	837	1,416	756	660
Chernivtsi O.	845	292	553	890	337	553	938	395	543
South Region	*3,641*	*6,380*...							
Crimea O.	1,813	1,146	667	2,183	1,467	716	2,456	1,714	742
Mykolaïv O.	1,147	605	542	1,242	750	492	1,331	875	456
Odessa O.	2,389	1,335	1,054	2,544	1,588	956	2,642	1,745	897
Kherson O.	1,031	555	476	1,164	677	487	1,240	759	481

	1970 Total	1970 Urban	1970 Rural	1979 Total	1979 Urban	1979 Rural	1989 Total	1989 Urban	1989 Rural
South Region	*6,380*	*3,641*	*2,739*	*7,133*	*4,482*	*2,651*	*7,669*	*5,093*	*2,576*

Source: Goskomstat SSSR (1989a, 19–22).

Figure 3-4. Rates of Birth, Death, and Natural Increase
(per 1,000)

	Ukraine			USSR			Uzbekistan		
	Births	Deaths	Natural increase	Births	Deaths	Natural increase	Births	Deaths	Natural increase
1960	20.5	6.9	13.6	24.9	7.1	17.8	39.8	6.0	33.8
1961	19.5	7.0	12.5	23.8	7.2	16.6	38.2	6.0	32.2
1962	18.8	7.6	11.2	22.4	7.5	14.9	37.0	6.1	30.9
1963	17.9	7.3	10.6	21.1	7.2	13.9	35.8	5.7	30.1
1964	16.5	7.0	9.5	19.5	6.9	12.6	35.0	5.4	29.6
1965	15.3	7.6	7.7	18.4	7.3	11.1	34.7	5.9	28.8
1966	15.6	7.5	8.1	18.2	7.3	10.9	34.1	5.7	28.4
1967	15.1	8.0	7.1	17.3	7.6	9.7	33.0	5.9	27.1
1968	14.9	8.0	6.9	17.2	7.7	9.5	34.3	5.8	28.5
1969	14.7	8.6	6.1	17.0	8.1	8.9	32.8	6.0	26.8
1970	15.2	8.8	6.4	17.4	8.2	9.2	33.6	5.5	28.1
1971	15.4	8.9	6.5	17.8	8.2	9.6	34.4	5.4	29.0
1972	15.5	9.2	6.3	17.8	8.5	9.3	33.0	6.1	26.9
1973	14.9	9.3	5.6	17.6	8.7	8.9	33.5	6.3	27.2
1974	15.1	9.4	5.7	18.0	8.7	9.3	34.1	6.4	27.7
1975	15.1	10.0	5.1	18.1	9.3	8.8	34.2	7.2	27.0
1976	15.2	10.2	5.0	18.4	9.5	8.9	35.0	7.1	27.9

	Ukraine			USSR			Uzbekistan		
	Births	Deaths	Natural increase	Births	Deaths	Natural increase	Births	Deaths	Natural increase
1977	14.7	10.5	4.2	18.1	9.6	8.5	33.4	7.1	26.3
1978	14.7	10.7	4.0	18.2	9.7	8.5	33.9	6.9	27.0
1979	14.7	11.1	3.6	18.2	10.1	8.1	34.4	7.0	27.4
1980	14.8	11.4	3.4	18.3	10.3	8.0	33.8	7.4	26.4
1981	14.6	11.3	3.3	18.5	10.2	8.3	34.9	7.2	27.7
1982	14.8	11.3	3.5	18.9	10.1	8.8	35.0	7.4	27.6
1983	16.0	11.5	4.5	19.8	10.1	9.4	35.3	7.5	27.8
1984	15.6	12.0	3.6	19.6	10.8	8.8	36.2	7.4	28.8
1985	15.0	12.1	2.9	19.4	10.6	8.8	37.2	7.2	30.0
1986	15.5	11.1	4.4	20.0	9.8	10.2	37.8	7.0	30.8
1987	14.8	11.4	3.4	19.8	9.9	9.9	37.0	6.9	30.1
1988	14.5	11.7	2.8	18.8	10.1	8.7	35.1	6.8	28.3
1989	13.4	11.6	1.8	17.6	10.0	7.6	33.2	6.3	26.9

Sources: All figures except 1989 are from Goskomstat SSSR (1989a, 56–61). The 1989 figure is from Goskomstat SSSR (1990, 45).

Figure 3-5. 1988 Demographic Summary by Republic for the USSR

	Birth rate	Rank	Death rate	Rank	Natural increase	Rank	Net repro	Rank	Marriage rate	Rank	Divorce rate	Rank
Ukrainian SSR	14.5	15	11.7	3	2.8	15	0.957	15	8.9	12	3.6	4
RSFSR	16.0	10	10.7	4	5.3	11	1.005	12	9.5	4	3.9	2
Belorussian SSR	16.0	10	10.1	7	5.9	10	0.965	14	9.4	6	3.2	5
Estonian SSR	15.9	12	11.8	2	4.1	13	1.054	9	8.2	13	3.8	3
Latvian SSR	15.4	13	12.1	1	3.3	14	1.006	11	9.4	6	4.1	1
Lithuanian SSR	15.3	14	10.2	6	5.1	12	0.997	13	9.4	6	3.2	5
Moldavian SSR	20.9	8	9.7	8	11.2	8	1.234	7	9.4	6	2.9	7
Georgian SSR	17.3	9	9.0	9	8.3	9	1.058	8	7.2	15	1.3	13
Armenian SSR	21.6	7	10.3	5	11.3	7	1.023	10	7.7	14	1.2	15
Azerbaijan SSR	26.5	5	6.8	14	19.7	5	1.268	6	9.9	1	1.3	13
Kazakh SSR	24.6	6	7.7	11	16.9	6	1.437	5	9.8	2	2.8	8
Kirgiz SSR	31.2	4	7.4	12	23.8	4	1.841	4	9.5	4	1.9	9
Tadzhik SSR	40.0	1	7.0	13	33.0	1	2.388	1	9.3	11	1.5	11
Turkmen SSR	36.0	2	7.8	10	28.2	3	2.016	2	9.4	6	1.4	12
Uzbek SSR	35.1	3	6.8	14	28.3	2	1.943	3	9.8	2	1.6	10

	TFR	Rank	Young Mothers	Rank	Pre Births	Rank	Infant Mortality	Rank	M Life Expect	Rank	F Life Expect	Rank
Ukrainian SSR	2,026	14	53.1	3	46.8	9	14.2	11	66.4	6	74.8	6
RSFSR	2,130	11	49.6	4	52.2	5	18.9	10	64.8	10	74.4	7
Belorussian SSR	2,031	13	35.9	12	44.0	12	13.1	12	67.0	3	75.9	2
Estonian SSR	2,247	10	45.5	6	57.2	2	12.4	13	66.8	4	75.0	5

Latvian SSR	2,114	12	45.0	7	41.9	14	11.0	15	66.3	7	75.1	4
Lithuanian SSR	2,005	15	33.5	13	43.9	13	11.5	14	67.7	2	76.6	1
Moldavian SSR	2,635	7	47.5	5	54.8	4	23.0	8	64.3	12	71.3	13
Georgian SSR	2,261	9	63.2	1	49.5	8	21.9	9	68.0	1	75.8	3
Armenian SSR	2,512	8	61.5	2	58.9	1	25.3	7	61.6	15	62.4	15
Azerbaijan SSR	2,796	6	26.7	14	39.4	15	27.0	6	65.7	8	73.5	9
Kazakh SSR	3,126	5	43.0	8	52.1	6	29.2	5	64.8	10	74.1	8
Kirgiz SSR	4,000	4	38.6	10	51.3	7	36.6	4	64.2	13	71.8	11
Tadzhik SSR	5,348	1	38.4	11	56.4	3	48.9	2	66.8	4	72.1	10
Turkmen SSR	4,570	2	20.0	15	44.5	11	53.3	1	62.4	14	69.2	14
Uzbek SSR	4,283	3	42.2	9	44.7	10	43.3	3	65.6	9	71.4	12

Notes and Sources: Birth rate, death rate, and natural increase are expressed per 1,000 population. See: Goskomstat SSSR, (1989a, 56–72).

Net Reproduction Rate is a measure of the number of daughters that a group of females born at a certain time will bear during their lifetime assuming a fixed schedule of age-specific fertility rates and fixed mortality rates. In other words, it is a measure of the extent to which a group of newborn females will replace themselves given age-specific fertility and mortality rates, remembering that some females will die before attaining the age of reproduction, others will die during the reproductive span, and some will not give birth for other reasons. A rate of 1.000 means exact replacement; a rate below unity means that the population is not replacing itself. Figures are from Goskomstat SSSR (1989a, 114–16).

Marriage and divorce rates are expressed per 1,000 population. Figures are from Goskomstat SSSR (1989a, 117–23).

Total fertility rate is another measure of birthrate and is defined as the number of children that 1,000 women will bear in their lifetimes given current age-specific fertility rates. Figures are from Goskomstat SSSR (1989a, 328–43).

Young Mothers is a measure of age-specific fertility defined as the number of births per 1,000 women younger than 20. Figures are from Goskomstat SSSR (1989a, 328–43).

Premature births are expressed per 1,000 births and are defined as births occurring prior to the normal end of term and below certain body weight and size minimums. Figures are from Goskomstat SSSR (1989a, 411).

Infant mortality rate is defined as the number of deaths to children younger than one year of age per 1,000 births. Figures are from Goskomstat SSSR (1989a, 474–76).

Life expectancy is the expectation of life at birth. Figures are from Goskomstat SSSR (1989a, 494).

Figure 3-6. Rates of Birth, Death, and Natural Increase, Ukraine (1988, by Region and Oblast) (per 1000)

	Total Population			Urban Population			Rural Population		
	Births	Deaths	Nat Increase	Births	Deaths	Nat Increase	Births	Deaths	Nat Increase
Ukraine	**14.5**	**11.7**	**2.8**	**14.6**	**9.6**	**5.0**	**14.1**	**16.0**	**-1.9**
Donets'k-Dnieper R.	*13.6*	*12.1*	*1.5*	*13.8*	*10.6*	*3.2*	*12.9*	*18.0*	*-5.1*
Luhans'k O.	13.4	11.7	1.7	13.3	10.8	2.5	14.6	18.0	-3.4
Dnipropetrovs'k O.	14.2	11.4	2.8	14.1	10.2	3.9	14.7	18.0	-3.3
Donets'k O.	13.0	11.4	1.6	12.9	11.0	1.9	13.1	14.9	-1.8
Zaporizhzhia O.	14.3	11.3	3.0	14.3	9.6	4.7	14.4	17.0	-2.6
Kirovohrad O.	14.2	13.9	0.3	15.7	10.7	5.0	12.0	18.7	-6.7
Poltava O.	13.6	13.9	-0.3	14.4	9.9	4.5	12.6	19.3	-6.7
Sumy O.	13.1	14.0	-0.9	15.0	10.4	4.6	10.0	19.6	-9.6
Kharkiv O.	13.5	12.4	1.1	13.8	10.9	2.9	12.2	17.8	-5.6
Southwest R.	*15.2*	*11.5*	*3.7*	*15.9*	*8.2*	*7.7*	*14.2*	*15.7*	*-1.5*
Vinnytsia O.	13.6	13.8	-0.2	15.4	8.5	6.9	12.0	18.2	-6.2
Volhynia O.	17.3	11.3	6.0	18.4	7.6	10.8	16.1	15.1	1.0
Zhytomyr O.	14.4	12.5	1.9	16.2	9.0	7.2	12.4	16.4	-4.0
Transcarpathia O.	18.3	9.2	9.1	17.1	7.7	9.4	19.2	10.3	8.9
Ivano-Frankivs'k O.	16.8	10.4	6.4	16.6	7.3	9.3	17.0	12.8	4.2

	Total Population			Urban Population			Rural Population		
	Births	Deaths	Nat Increase	Births	Deaths	Nat Increase	Births	Deaths	Nat Increase
Kiev City	14.6	8.2	6.4	14.6	8.2	6.4	N/A	N/A	N/A
Kiev O. (without city)	15.4	12.4	3.0	16.5	8.3	8.2	14.2	17.4	-3.2
L'viv O.	15.6	10.4	5.2	15.1	7.7	7.4	16.4	14.5	1.9
Rivne O.	17.5	10.2	7.3	18.3	7.0	11.3	16.8	13.0	3.8
Ternopil' O.	15.4	12.6	2.8	17.6	7.6	10.0	13.8	16.2	-2.4
Khmel'nyts'kyi O.	14.1	13.1	1.0	17.1	7.7	9.4	11.4	18.0	-6.6
Cherkasy O.	13.5	13.7	-0.2	15.9	9.4	6.5	10.8	18.4	-7.6
Chernihiv O.	12.5	14.3	-1.8	14.9	9.6	5.3	9.7	19.8	-10.1
Chernivtsi O.	16.4	10.6	5.8	15.6	8.1	7.5	16.9	12.4	4.5
South R.	*14.8*	*9.6*	*5.2*	*14.4*	*9.9*	*4.5*	*15.8*	*13.3*	*2.5*
Crimea O.	14.8	9.6	5.2	14.5	9.5	5.0	15.4	10.0	5.4
Mykolaïv O.	15.5	11.5	4.0	15.4	9.9	5.5	15.6	14.7	0.9
Odessa O.	14.3	12.1	2.2	13.1	10.1	3.0	16.5	16.1	0.4
Kherson O.	15.6	10.8	4.8	15.7	10.2	5.5	15.5	11.9	3.6

Source: Goskomstat SSSR (1989a, 96–106).

Figure 3-7. Rates of Birth, Death, and Natural Increase, Ukraine
(1960–1989)

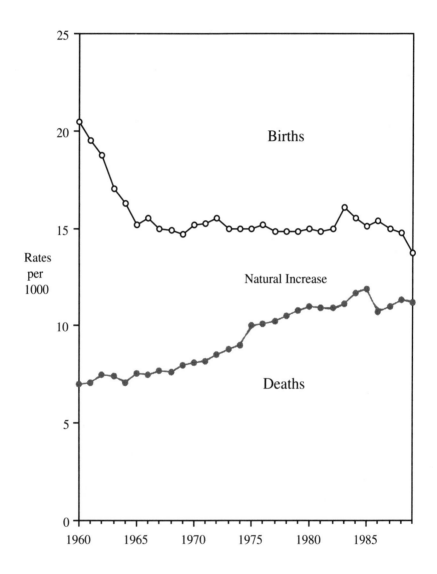

Figure 3-8. Age-Specific Birth Rates, Ukraine (1958–1988)

(Births to 1000 Women)

Ages	<20	20–24	25–29	30–34	35–39	40–44	45–49	15–49	TFR
Total									
1958–1959	28.1	150.9	137.4	85.1	44.6	11.5	1.6	70.7	2,286
1969–1970	33.1	160.1	110.1	68.3	29.2	7.2	0.7	55.2	2,059
1978–1979	45.9	163.3	104.2	54.1	19.3	5.3	0.3	57.3	1,957
1982–1983	49.2	170.2	109.0	54.6	20.3	3.7	0.3	61.1	2,024
1987	50.9	169.2	110.2	54.3	20.9	4.4	0.2	60.3	2,056
1988	53.1	168.5	106.2	52.5	19.5	4.1	0.2	59.5	2,026
Urban									
1958–1959	25.2	137.9	120.7	72.7	35.2	7.6	0.8	64.5	1,988
1969–1970	29.8	144.7	101.3	63.0	23.2	5.0	0.5	53.1	1,839
1978–1979	39.5	147.7	98.3	50.9	16.1	3.9	0.2	55.4	1,763
1982–1983	46.0	148.1	103.6	52.5	18.3	2.8	0.2	58.6	1,822
1987	46.0	159.8	99.2	50.7	18.7	3.5	0.1	56.4	1,894
1988	48.1	163.1	96.3	49.2	17.7	3.3	0.1	55.8	1,892
Rural									
1958–1959	30.5	165.4	153.5	97.9	52.8	15.1	2.2	76.5	2,582
1969–1970	39.0	192.9	123.1	76.5	36.4	9.9	1.0	58.4	2,439
1978–1979	60.4	202.6	119.8	61.7	25.0	7.8	0.5	61.1	2,444
1982–1983	55.1	235.7	123.7	60.6	25.1	5.3	0.5	66.9	2,592
1987	61.8	191.5	150.0	65.9	27.9	6.5	0.3	70.4	2,541
1988	64.4	180.7	142.5	64.0	25.5	6.2	0.3	69.7	2,436

Source: Goskomstat SSSR (1989a, 326–39).

Figure 3-9. Net Reproduction Rates, Ukraine (1969–1988)

		NRR	
	Total	Urban	Rural
1969–70	0.960	0.868	1.144
1975–76	0.955	0.864	1.161
1978–79	0.923	0.833	1.147
1980–81	0.910	0.818	1.163
1982–83	0.961	0.867	1.224
1986–87	0.991	0.910	1.229
1987	0.976	0.900	1.203
1988	0.957	0.895	1.148

Source: Goskomstat SSSR (1989a, 114).

Figure 3-10. Life Expectancy at Birth: USSR, Ukraine, Uzbekistan, Latvia
(years)

	1979–80		1987		1988	
	Men	Women	Men	Women	Men	Women
Total						
USSR	62.2	72.5	65.1	73.8	64.8	73.6
Ukraine	64.6	74.0	66.3	74.9	66.4	74.8
Uzbekistan	64.0	70.7	65.7	71.3	65.6	71.4
Latvia	63.6	73.9	66.3	74.9	66.3	75.1
Urban						
USSR	63.0	73.0	65.8	74.3	65.6	73.9
Ukraine	65.2	73.8	66.8	74.7	67.1	74.7
Uzbekistan	62.8	71.4	66.1	73.0	65.8	73.0
Latvia	64.8	74.4	67.5	75.4	67.3	75.6
Rural						
USSR	60.8	71.5	63.5	72.9	63.2	72.8
Ukraine	63.6	73.9	64.8	74.7	64.7	74.5
Uzbekistan	65.5	70.5	65.9	70.6	65.8	70.7
Latvia	61.0	72.6	63.6	73.8	63.8	74.0

Source: Goskomstat SSSR (1989a, 494–95).

Figure 3-11. Infant Mortality Rates: Ukraine and USSR (1970–1989)*

	Ukraine	*USSR*
1970	17.2	24.7
1971		22.9
1972		24.7
1973		26.4
1974		27.9
1975	19.7	30.6
1976		31.4
1977		30.5
1978		29.2
1979		27.4
1980	16.6	27.3
1981	16.2	26.9
1982	16.2	25.7
1983	15.8	25.3
1984	15.9	25.9
1985	15.7	26.0
1986	14.8	25.4
1987	14.5	25.4
1988	14.2	24.7
1989	12.9	22.6

* Deaths of children up to 1 year of age per 1,000 births in given year.

Source: Goskomstat SSSR (1989a, 473–74; 1990, 47).

Figure 3-12. Infant Morality Rate: USSR and Ukraine (1960–1988)

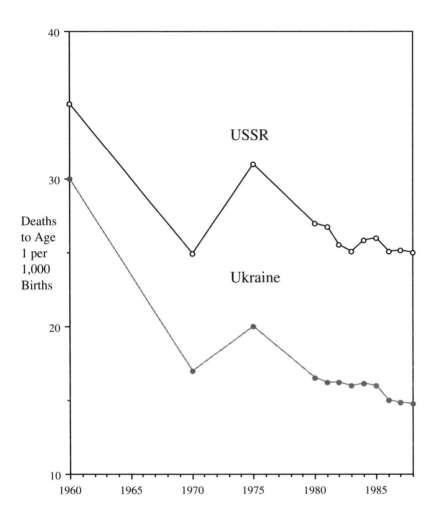

Ralph S. Clem

Figure 3-13. Causes of Death by Age, Males: USSR, Ukraine, Uzbekistan (1988)
(percent)

Males	Cardiovascular			Cancer			Respiratory		
	USSR	Ukraine	Uzbek.	USSR	Ukraine	Uzbek.	USSR	Ukraine	Uzbek.
<1	0.5	1.6	0.1	0.4	0.8	0.2	31.4	14.4	47.5
1–4	1.1	1.9	0.4	3.7	9.9	1.1	37.6	14.9	45.7
5–9	1.7	1.4	1.6	11.3	16.7	7.9	7.5	2.5	16.8
10–14	2.4	2.5	3.2	10.8	15.6	9.1	5.1	3.2	11.2
15–19	4.7	4.1	9.7	7.4	9.5	8.5	3.1	1.8	6.6
20–24	5.0	5.1	7.9	5.3	6.3	7.4	2.0	1.6	4.8
25–29	7.7	7.8	10.7	5.4	6.3	7.1	1.7	1.6	3.2
30–34	13.1	13.0	17.5	6.9	7.9	8.4	2.0	2.1	3.7
35–39	21.7	21.6	25.3	10.7	12.3	11.1	2.5	2.6	4.7
40–44	29.8	28.0	34.8	15.7	18.4	11.2	3.2	3.3	4.7
45–49	33.9	31.3	38.7	22.7	25.2	16.2	4.4	4.6	5.4
50–54	37.8	35.3	43.7	27.7	30.0	19.6	5.8	6.1	6.4
55–59	40.9	38.6	46.9	31.6	33.3	20.9	7.1	7.8	8.3
60–64	46.9	45.8	52.6	30.6	31.1	20.7	7.8	8.6	7.7
65–69	53.2	52.9	57.6	26.7	26.2	18.4	8.7	10.0	9.6
70–74	60.2	60.5	64.5	21.6	20.9	15.7	9.2	10.0	9.1
75–79	67.1	67.6	69.1	15.4	14.4	10.9	9.6	11.2	10.6
80–84	74.9	76.0	76.7	9.3	8.0	6.3	9.5	10.8	11.0
85+	80.6	82.7	82.1	4.3	3.3	3.4	8.4	8.5	8.7
All Ages	44.7	49.7	33.4	18.7	19.7	8.6	9.2	8.4	21.7

Males	Accidents			Other		
	USSR	Ukraine	Uzbek.	USSR	Ukraine	Uzbek.
<1	3.5	4.2	3.1	64.2	79.0	49.2
1–4	25.5	34.7	17.4	32.2	38.5	35.4
5–9	58.5	56.4	40.9	21.1	23.1	32.8
10–14	61.9	57.7	40.3	19.8	21.0	36.2
15–19	69.6	70.5	47.1	15.2	14.0	28.2
20–24	76.7	76.9	57.6	11.0	10.1	22.3
25–29	74.2	73.8	59.4	11.1	10.6	19.7
30–34	64.8	63.4	49.9	13.2	13.5	20.5
35–39	50.7	48.4	37.4	14.4	15.2	21.5
40–44	37.3	35.4	27.0	14.0	15.0	22.3
45–49	26.1	25.5	19.0	12.9	13.4	20.7
50–54	17.4	16.8	11.8	11.3	11.8	18.5
55–59	10.8	10.3	7.3	9.6	10.1	16.7
60–64	6.3	6.1	4.2	8.4	8.4	14.9
65–69	3.9	3.5	2.9	7.5	7.4	11.5
70–74	2.8	2.7	1.9	6.2	5.9	8.9
75–79	2.4	2.1	1.6	5.5	4.8	7.8
80–84	1.9	1.7	0.9	4.4	3.5	5.1
85+	2.7	2.2	1.7	3.9	3.4	4.1
All Ages	15.2	12.4	11.4	12.3	9.8	24.9

Notes: Percentage of deaths by cause of all deaths by age. The accidents category includes death from trauma and poisoning. Other category includes deaths from infectious and parasitic diseases, diseases of the digestive system, and unclassified deaths.

Source: Calculated from data in Goskomstat SSSR (1989a, 503–527).

Ralph S. Clem

Figure 3-14. Causes of Death by Age, Females: USSR, Ukraine, Uzbekistan (1988)
(percent)

Females	Cardiovascular			Cancer			Respiratory		
	USSR	Ukraine	Uzbek	USSR	Ukraine	Uzbek.	USSR	Ukraine	Uzbek.
<1	0.6	2.1	0.1	0.5	1.1	0.1	33.2	15.3	49.1
1–4	1.3	3.3	0.5	3.6	11.4	1.2	41.3	17.6	51.0
5–9	2.2	3.7	1.9	12.4	21.4	7.2	11.4	4.7	22.9
10–14	4.2	5.4	5.9	12.6	21.3	11.1	6.9	3.1	11.8
15–19	6.9	6.7	11.3	10.4	13.6	8.9	4.4	4.1	7.8
20–24	9.4	8.7	13.1	11.3	16.9	8.1	4.2	3.6	6.2
25–29	11.2	10.4	17.5	16.2	22.7	11.6	4.1	4.4	5.7
30–34	13.0	12.9	18.2	22.2	29.4	15.0	3.8	3.3	6.5
35–39	17.0	15.5	24.5	29.2	35.8	17.8	3.5	3.1	6.9
40–44	22.7	22.2	29.3	33.2	38.0	22.6	3.7	3.5	6.8
45–49	28.5	27.7	35.4	35.6	38.3	26.1	3.5	3.7	5.3
50–54	35.8	35.5	40.4	34.8	37.3	24.8	3.9	3.5	6.6
55–59	43.9	44.1	48.4	31.8	33.5	22.1	4.3	4.2	7.7
60–64	52.2	53.3	52.7	28.3	29.0	21.3	4.6	4.5	8.2
65–69	61.3	63.4	81.8	22.5	22.1	21.0	4.9	5.2	12.7
70–74	70.5	72.9	69.2	16.5	15.1	12.8	5.1	5.3	8.0
75–79	77.8	79.3	76.0	10.9	9.7	8.4	5.3	6.2	8.0
80–84	84.7	85.8	82.6	6.1	4.8	5.6	5.2	6.0	6.6
85+	89.0	89.9	86.6	2.7	1.8	2.4	5.1	5.5	7.0
All Ages	65.4	71.0	43.2	13.8	13.4	8.5	6.6	5.6	20.3

Females	Accidents			Others		
	USSR	UkSSR	UzSSR	USSR	UkSSR	UzSSR
<1	3.9	4.9	3.1	61.7	76.5	47.5
1–4	21.3	27.9	13.7	32.5	39.8	33.5
5–9	47.3	42.8	34.2	26.8	27.4	33.8
10–14	49.4	37.2	30.9	26.8	33.1	40.3
15–19	54.1	49.3	32.6	24.3	26.3	39.4
20–24	44.1	40.5	25.5	31.0	30.3	47.0
25–29	39.9	34.0	18.5	28.6	28.5	46.7
30–34	35.5	31.8	16.6	25.5	22.3	43.7
35–39	29.3	24.9	13.8	21.0	20.6	36.9
40–44	23.1	19.5	10.0	17.3	16.9	31.4
45–49	17.5	15.2	8.0	15.0	15.1	25.2
50–54	12.0	10.3	6.3	13.5	13.4	21.8
55–59	7.8	6.6	3.4	12.1	11.6	18.4
60–64	4.8	3.9	3.1	10.0	9.3	14.6
65–69	3.2	2.7	2.9	8.1	6.7	18.4
70–74	2.3	1.9	1.3	5.6	4.8	8.7
75–79	1.9	1.4	1.4	4.1	3.3	6.2
80–84	1.5	1.1	1.1	2.4	2.3	4.2
85+	1.1	0.8	0.8	2.1	1.9	3.2
All Ages	5.2	3.6	5.4	9.0	6.5	22.6

Source: See Figure 3-13.

Figure 3-15. Migration Balance, Ukraine (1989–1990)

Ukraine	Total 44,300	Urban 168,300	Rural −124,000	Rate 1000 0.9
Donets'k-Dnieper R.	*37,000*	*62,200*	*−25,200*	*1.7*
Luhans'k O.	2,500	2,900	−3,300	0.9
Dnipropetrovs'k O.	11,300	15,300	−4,000	2.9
Donets'k O.	6,100	10,300	−4,200	1.1
Zaporizhzhia O.	5,700	10,000	−4,300	2.7
Kirovohrad O.	2,200	5,400	−3,200	1.8
Poltava O.	6,200	3,200	3,000	3.5
Sumy O.	1,100	6,800	−5,700	0.8
Kharkiv O.	1,900	5,400	−3,500	0.6
Southwest Region	*−23,900*	*80,000*	*−103,900*	*−1.1*
Vinnytsia O.	−5,000	4,400	−9,400	−2.6
Volhynia O.	−3,400	5,100	−8,500	−3.2
Zhytomyr O.	−10,100	2,400	−12,500	−6.5
Transcarpathia O.	−3,700	3,300	−7,000	−2.9
Ivano-Frankivs'k O.	600	6,000	−5,400	0.4
Kiev O.	5,400	12,000	−6,600	2.8
Kiev City	9,200	9,200	N/A	3.5
L'viv O.	−6,000	7,900	−13,900	−2.1
Rivne O.	−3,900	5,500	−9,400	−3.3
Ternopil' O.	400	7,600	−7,200	0.3
Khmel'nyts'kyi O.	−4,800	5,900	−10,700	−3.1
Cherkasy O.	1,200	6,400	−5,200	0.8
Chernihiv O.	−400	4,600	−5,000	−0.3
Chernivtsi O.	−3,400	−300	−3,100	−3.6
South Region	*31,200*	*26,100*	*5,100*	*4.0*
Crimea O.	32,600	16,800	15,800	13.3
Mykolaïv O.	2,000	5,900	−3,900	1.5
Odessa O.	−7,900	−2,900	−5,000	−2.9
Kherson O.	4,500	6,300	−1,800	3.6

Source: Goskomstat SSSR (1990, 34–37).

Figure 3-16. Urban Population, Ukraine (by Region and Oblast, 1970–1989) (per 1000)

	1970 Urban	1970 % Urban	1970 % of UkUrb	1979 Urban	1979 % Urban	1979 % of UkUrb	1989 Urban	1989 % Urban	1989 % of UkUrb
Ukraine	**25,688**	**54.5**	**100.0**	**30,152**	**60.6**	**100.0**	**34,591**	**66.9**	**100.0**
Donets'k-Dnieper R.	*14,107*	*70.3*	*54.9*	*15,865*	*75.4*	*52.6*	*17,226*	*79.1*	*49.8*
Luhans'k O.	2,271	82.6	8.8	2,357	84.6	7.8	2,474	86.4	7.2
Dnipropetrovs'k O.	2,549	76.2	9.9	2,927	80.4	9.7	3,233	83.3	9.3
Donets'k O.	4,276	87.4	16.6	4,599	89.1	15.3	4,810	90.3	13.9
Zaporizhzhia O.	1,167	65.7	4.5	1,384	71.1	4.6	1,577	75.8	4.6
Kirovohrad O.	552	43.8	2.1	654	52.3	2.2	743	59.9	2.1
Poltava O.	679	39.8	2.6	875	50.3	2.9	991	56.5	2.9
Sumy O.	655	43.5	2.5	776	53.0	2.6	886	61.8	2.6
Kharkiv O.	1,958	69.3	7.6	2,293	75.0	7.6	2,512	78.6	7.3
Southwest R.	*7,940*	*38.4*	*30.9*	*10,165*	*47.1*	*33.7*	*12,272*	*55.1*	*35.5*
Vinnytsia O.	542	25.4	2.1	720	35.2	2.4	857	44.4	2.5
Volhynia O.	313	32.1	1.2	407	40.1	1.3	519	48.9	1.5
Zhytomyr O.	568	34.9	2.2	706	44.2	2.3	818	52.9	2.4
Transcarpathia O.	314	29.7	1.2	437	37.8	1.4	515	41.1	1.5
Ivano-Frankivs'k O.	384	30.7	1.5	485	36.4	1.6	598	42.0	1.7

(con't.)

	1970 Urban	1970 % Urban	1970 % of UkUrb	1979 Urban	1979 % Urban	1979 % of UkUrb	1989 Urban	1989 % Urban	1989 % of UkUrb
Ukraine	**25,688**	**54.5**	**100.0**	**30,152**	**60.6**	**100.0**	**34,591**	**66.9**	**100.0**
Kiev O.	2,287	66.0	8.9	3,015	74.1	10.0	3,644	80.2	10.5
L'viv O.	1,149	47.3	4.5	1,374	53.2	4.6	1,630	59.3	4.7
Rivne O.	288	27.5	1.1	408	36.4	1.4	530	45.3	1.5
Ternopil' O.	269	23.3	1.0	364	31.3	1.2	477	40.8	1.4
Khmel'nyts'kyi O.	431	26.7	1.7	560	35.9	1.9	723	47.3	2.1
Cherkasy O.	563	36.6	2.2	687	44.4	2.3	810	52.9	2.3
Chernihiv O.	540	34.6	2.1	665	44.3	2.2	756	53.4	2.2
Chernivtsi O.	292	34.6	1.1	337	37.9	1.1	395	42.1	1.1
South R.	*3,641*	*57.1*	*14.2*	*4,482*	*62.8*	*14.9*	*5,093*	*66.4*	*14.7*
Crimea O.	1,146	63.2	4.5	1,467	67.2	4.9	1,714	69.8	5.0
Mykolaïv O.	605	52.7	2.4	750	60.4	2.5	875	65.7	2.5
Odessa O.	1,335	55.9	5.2	1,588	62.4	5.3	1,745	66.0	5.0
Kherson O.	555	53.8	2.2	677	58.2	2.2	759	61.2	2.2

Source: Goskomstat SSSR (1989a, 19–22).

Figure 3-17. Average Annual Percentage-Point Change
in Level of Urbanization, Ukraine

	1970 %Urban	1979 %Urban	1989 %Urban	Average Annual %Pt Change 70–79	%Pt Change 79–89
Ukraine	**54.5**	**60.6**	**66.9**	**.67**	**.63**
Donets'k-Dnieper R.	*70.3*	*75.4*	*79.1*	*.57*	*.37*
Luhans'k O.	82.6	84.6	86.4	.22	.18
Dnipropetrovs'k O.	76.2	80.4	83.3	.47	.29
Donets'k O.	87.4	89.1	90.3	.19	.12
Zaporizhzhia O.	65.7	71.1	75.8	.60	.47
Kirovohrad O.	43.8	52.3	59.9	.94	.76
Poltava O.	39.8	50.3	56.5	1.17	.62
Sumy O.	43.5	53.0	61.8	1.06	.88
Kharkiv O.	69.3	75.0	78.6	.63	.36
Southwest R.	*38.4*	*47.1*	*55.1*	*.97*	*.80*
Vinnytsia O.	25.4	35.2	44.4	1.09	.92
Volhynia O.	32.1	40.1	48.9	.88	.88
Zhytomyr O.	34.9	44.2	52.9	1.03	.87
Transcarpathia O.	29.7	37.8	41.1	.90	.33
Ivano-Frankivs'k O.	30.7	36.4	42.0	.63	.56
Kiev O.	66.0	74.1	80.2	.90	.61
L'viv O.	47.3	53.2	59.3	.66	.61
Rivne O.	27.5	36.4	45.3	.99	.89
Ternopil' O.	23.3	31.3	40.8	.88	.95
Khmel'nyts'kyi O.	26.7	35.9	47.3	1.02	1.14
Cherkasy O.	36.6	44.4	52.9	.87	.85
Chernihiv O.	34.6	44.3	53.4	1.08	.91
Chernivtsi O.	34.6	37.9	42.1	.37	.42
South R.	*57.1*	*62.8*	*66.4*	*.63*	*.36*
Crimea O.	63.2	67.2	69.8	.44	.26
Mykolaïv O.	52.7	60.4	65.7	.86	.53
Odessa O.	55.9	62.4	66.0	.72	.36
Kherson O.	53.8	58.2	61.2	.49	.30

Source: Goskomstat SSSR (1990, 34–37).

Figure 3-18. Distribution of Population by Age: USSR, Ukraine, Uzbekistan
(percent)

Ages	USSR, 1959			Ukraine, 1959			Uzbek., 1959		
	Total	Men	Women	Total	Men	Women	Total	Men	Women
<5	12	13	10	10	11	8	17	18	16
5–9	11	12	9	9	11	8	13	14	12
10–14	7	8	7	7	8	6	8	8	7
15–19	8	9	7	8	9	8	8	9	7
20–24	10	11	9	10	11	9	9	9	9
25–29	9	9	8	8	9	7	8	8	8
30–34	9	9	9	9	9	9	8	8	8
35–39	6	5	6	6	5	7	5	4	5
40–44	5	4	6	5	4	6	4	3	4
45–49	6	5	7	7	6	7	4	4	4
50–54	5	4	6	6	5	6	4	4	4
55–59	4	3	5	5	4	5	4	3	5
60–64	3	2	4	4	3	4	4	3	4
65–69	2	2	3	3	2	3	2	2	3
70+	4	3	5	4	3	5	3	3	4

	USSR, 1987			Ukraine, 1987			Uzbek., 1987		
	Total	Men	Women	Total	Men	Women	Total	Men	Women
<5	9	10	9	8	8	7	16	17	16
5–9	8	9	8	7	8	7	13	13	13
10–14	8	9	7	7	8	7	12	12	11
15–19	7	8	7	7	8	6	10	11	10
20–24	8	8	7	8	8	7	10	10	10
25–29	9	10	8	7	8	7	9	9	9
30–34	8	8	7	7	8	7	7	6	7
35–39	7	7	7	5	7	5	5	5	5
40–44	4	4	4	8	5	8	3	3	3
45–49	7	7	7	6	8	6	4	4	4
50–54	5	5	5	7	6	7	3	3	3
55–59	6	6	6	6	6	7	3	3	3
60–64	5	3	5	3	4	4	2	2	2
65–69	3	2	3	3	2	4	1	1	2
70+	6	4	9	8	5	11	3	2	4

Source: Goskomstat SSSR (1988a, 48–61).

Figure 3-19. Sex Ratios by Age, Ukraine (1959 and 1987)

| | | 1959 | | | 1987 | |
Ages	Total	Urban	Rural	Total	Urban	Rural
<5	104.8	105.2	104.5	104.9	105.1	104.3
5–9	103.9	104.1	103.9	103.9	103.8	104.3
10–14	103.0	102.5	103.5	102.7	102.7	102.7
15–19	98.5	98.4	98.6	104.3	99.6	114.4
20–24	96.0	93.3	99.1	105.1	104.2	107.4
25–29	92.7	98.8	86.8	99.6	97.0	108.9
30–34	78.2	82.3	73.9	95.8	94.2	100.9
35–39	63.1	64.9	61.5	93.9	93.3	95.7
40–44	59.9	67.2	53.4	88.6	91.3	82.9
45–49	61.0	68.6	55.1	86.2	88.2	82.3
50–54	63.9	68.3	60.6	87.0	89.9	82.5
55–59	53.9	58.9	50.6	79.7	83.4	74.6
60–64	57.7	57.9	57.5	57.2	59.3	54.6
65–69	55.0	55.7	54.7	48.2	51.9	43.8
70+	49.0	46.1	50.7	38.2	40.3	36.1

Source: Goskomstat SSSR (1988a, 54–57).

Figure 3-20. Ethnic Composition of Ukraine
(1000s)

	1959	%	1970	%
Ukrainians	32,158	76.8	35,284	74.9
Russians	7,091	16.9	9,126	19.4
Jews	840	2.0	777	1.6
Poles	363	0.9	295	0.6
Belarusians	291	0.7	386	0.8
Moldovans	242	0.6	266	0.6
Others	884	2.1	993	2.1

	1979	%	1989	%
Ukrainians	36,489	73.6	37,370	72.6
Russians	10,472	21.1	11,340	22.0
Jews	634	1.3	633	1.2
Poles	258	0.5	258	0.5
Belarusians	406	0.8	440	0.9
Moldovans	294	0.6	324	0.6
Others	1,056	2.1	1,085	2.2

Figure 3-21. Population Projections for Ukraine
(1000s)

Year	CIR 1987	High Series	FDAD 1979 Medium Series	Low Series
1989	51,928	52,875	51,976	51,216
1990	52,061	53,102	52,118	51,281
1995	52,637	54,188	52,752	51,491
2000	53,207	55,232	53,248	51,474
2025	55,020			

Source: Kingkade (1987); Baldwin (1979).

CHAPTER FOUR
Labor Force and
Employment in Ukraine

Stephen Rapawy

This paper discusses the contribution labor makes to the Ukrainian economy. These labor inputs are measured by the size of the labor force or economically active population and are presented in terms of annual average employment, which relates the number of workers to the time they worked. Annual average employment is given for the state sector, collective farms, private subsidiary farming, cooperatives, and private employment. Share of industrial employment is presented by oblast. Labor force and employment trends are described and compared with those for the Soviet Union. Newly published data on the share of Ukrainians by branch of economy also are presented. Finally, such qualitative factors as education and level of mechanization are discussed.

Most labor force and employment data presented in the paper are either reported or estimated from official figures. Labor force participation and rates are estimated from the 1970 and 1979 censuses and projected to the year 2000. The 1989 census data were not available at publication. Employment figures generally are reported for the years prior to 1976 and mostly estimated for later years.

The Ukrainian Labor Force

The size of a republic's labor force is determined by the population census. In each of the postwar censuses (taken in 1959, 1970, 1979, and 1989), individuals were asked to declare their principal source of income. If the major share of an individual's income came from employment in the state sector, collective farms, or private subsidiary agriculture (private plots), then he or she was included in the labor force. This included individuals who are employed seasonally, those receiving training outside their workplace, and women on maternity leave. Pensioners working full-time at the time of the census were counted in the labor force, but pensioners working part-time were excluded, presumably because their pension was their principal source of income (Fedorova 1976, 211–27 and 1984, 172–82; Labutova 1984, 5–25; Goskomstat SSSR 1978, 54–55). Military personnel were included in the labor force and distributed among socioeconomic groups based on their occupation prior to induction. Indirect evidence indicates that prisoners were also included in population and labor force statistics.

Figure 4-1 presents labor force participation rates (the percent of the population working) by age and sex from 1970 to 2000. The rates were derived as a residual between the USSR rates and those for Central Asia. Thus, Ukraine is assumed to have the same participation rates as all of the non-Central Asian USSR. Outside Central Asia, the rates are fairly uniform and tend to be extremely high. The rates for Central Asia are weighted averages of the four Central Asian republics: Kyrgyzstan, Tajikistan, Turkmenistan, and Uzbekistan (Rapawy and Heleniak 1988, 15). The 1970 and 1979 rates for the USSR and Central Asia are based on the census data for 1959, 1970, and 1979 and projected to 2000. Projected rates were decreased slightly for the 16- to 19-year age group in anticipation of the longer period of schooling and were increased for the pension-age population to reflect a long-term trend. Rates for the remaining ages remain virtually unchanged. The 1979 rates, already among the highest in the world, are not expected to increase much, if at all, by the end of the century.

Figure 4-2 presents estimates and projections by age and sex of the population working in Ukraine. Between 1970 and 1990, the Ukrainian labor force increased at 0.6 percent annually. As a share of the Soviet total, it is expected to decrease from 20.4 percent in 1970 to 17.6 percent in 2000 (Rapawy and Kingkade 1988, 15). This relative decrease is due to greater population growth in the Central Asian and Transcaucasian republics. Despite the rise in female economic activity, the proportion of males in the economically active population is expected to increase, reflecting a population trend. After the mid-

1980s, males made up the majority of Ukraine's population.

Like the population, the labor force is aging. The pension-age group as a share of the total rises from 11.7 percent in 1970 to 14.9 percent in 2000. In 1987, the pension-age population made up 7.3 percent of the state-sector (government-owned enterprises and organizations) employment, both for Ukraine and the USSR (Goskomstat SSSR 1988c, 111). These figures exclude employment on collective farms and in private subsidiary agriculture, where the employees are believed to be considerably older. In the Baltic republics and in Georgia and Armenia, an even a larger share of the pension-age population continues to work.

In addition to age and sex, the level of education is another important measurement of the labor force. People with higher education (college level) comprise 9.6 percent of the Ukrainian labor force, compared with 10 percent for the USSR. In material production, 5.3 percent of the labor force has higher education in Ukraine, versus 5.2 percent in the Soviet Union. The share of the Ukrainian labor force with higher education in each of the branches of material production and the rank order of each of the branches are similar to those for the USSR. In the service sphere, 25.4 percent of the labor force has higher education, slightly lower than the Soviet figure of 25.9 percent. The branch rank order of social service branches is comparable to that for the Soviet Union. In the science and scientific services branch in Ukraine, the share of labor force with higher education amounts to 41.5 percent, the highest of any branch, followed by education with 37.8 percent. Both percentages are higher than those for the Soviet Union. The educational level of the Ukrainian labor force falls about in the middle when compared to other republics. Ukraine ranks substantially below Georgia and Armenia, the two republics with the most educated work force. In addition to the census data, educational attainment figures for the employed population are reported in statistical handbooks. But handbook statistics are usually limited to employees with higher and specialized secondary education. In 1970, 14.8 percent of the workers in the socialized sector had higher or specialized secondary education. By 1987, the proportion had increased to 27.1 percent, with 11.7 percent of them having higher education (Goskomstat SSSR 1988c, 118). Figures on the number of specialists published for benchmark years indicate an almost three-fold increase between 1960 and 1987. As Figure 4-3 indicates, the highest share of specialists is found in such branches as government administration, science and scientific services, education, and health. In relative terms, the greatest increase occurred in agriculture, where in 1960 there were 15 specialists per 1,000 employment. By 1987 the number increased to 137.

There is a strong relationship between urbanization, education, and, industrial employment. Statistically, the few heavily populated and urbanized oblasts affect the republic as a whole. At the end of 1985, two-thirds of the population, both in the USSR and Ukraine, lived in urban areas. The eight most populous Ukrainian oblasts have a share of urban population equal to or greater than that of the republic. These oblasts comprise 63.4 percent of the republic population.

Soviet statistics on nationalities are published selectively. Data are reported on nationality, language affiliation, and urban and rural residence from the censuses. Nationality data are published occasionally for Communist Party members, enrollment in higher-educational institutions, and for a few selected professions. Typically, figures are presented only for the titular nationalities (that is, the nationalities after which the republics are named) of the union republics and for the Soviet Union as a whole, but not by republic. Lack of detailed nationality data on the republic level precludes comparison of professions by nationality.

For the first time, the 1988 labor handbook reported the share of Ukrainians employed by branch of the economy (Figure 4-4).[1] Data are not reported for forestry, credit and insurance, and "other" branches. More important, collective farm employment, amounting to 3.7 million in 1987, or 15.3 percent of the socialized sector employment, is not reported by nationality. The nationality of collective farmers should be predominantly Ukrainian since Ukrainians are more rural than the total population of the republic. In 1970, the last year for which urban-rural nationality data are available, 54 percent of Ukrainians lived in rural areas, compared to 45 percent for the other nationalities of the republic (*Narkhoz Ukrainy* 1987, 227; Goskomstat SSSR 1972–1974, Vol. IV, 166–67; and Figure 4-4). Ukrainians comprised 73.6 percent of the republic population in 1979, but their share decreased to 72.3 percent in 1989 (Goskomstat SSSR 1989a,

---

[1] Data in Figure 4-4 refer to ethnic Ukrainians and not the total population living in Ukraine.

59). Arguably, the share of Ukrainians on collective farms should at least equal that of Ukrainians employed in state agriculture. Exclusion of collective farm employment most likely accounts for the smaller share of Ukrainians in the labor force compared to that in the population of the republic. Information is not available to explain the varying shares of Ukrainians in the remaining branches of the republic economy. Ukrainians made up 69 percent of the employment in the state sector in 1977 and 70 percent in 1987. As might be expected, the branch with the highest concentration is agriculture, followed by education. The larger concentration of Ukrainians in education probably is due to predominantly Ukrainian-language schools in rural areas.

For the Soviet Union as a whole, data occasionally are reported for selected professions by nationality. Figures on "scientific" workers by nationality are the most commonly published. Individuals are included in the scientific workers category based on educational attainment or on the nature of their work. This includes academicians, individuals who are candidates for or who already have doctoral degrees, and people with such academic or scholarly titles as professor, docent, senior or junior scientific worker, and scientific assistant, regardless of the work performed. At the same time, persons without higher education doing research in scientific establishments, higher-educational institutions, and industrial enterprises or comparable establishments are classified as scientific workers (Goskomstat SSSR 1988c, 287). The share of ethnic Ukrainians in the scientific workers category has been increasing and has reached 16.7 percent.

Annual Average Employment

Annual average employment is determined by the number of days worked during the year.[2] In the state sector, employment is divided into two broad categories: wage workers and salaried employees (*rabochie* and *sluzhashchie*). Wage workers are blue-collar workers usually engaged in physical work and are paid either on a piece rate or hourly basis. Usually, published statistics include apprentices in the figures for wage workers. Salaried employees fall into three categories paid on the basis of monthly salary rates. Engineering-technical

---

[2] The methodology used in determining annual average employment is described in Rapawy and Kingkade (1988) and Feshbach (1972).

personnel (*inzhenerno-tekhnicheskie rabotniki*) constitute the largest and most-important category among salaried employees. The group includes management and technical personnel, such as scientists, medical personnel, engineers, and technicians. The second group of salaried employees includes management and professional personnel in nontechnical categories, as well as clerical personnel. The third group is made up of minor service personnel (*mladshii obsluzhivaiushchii personal*) and includes custodial workers, messengers, chauffeurs, and security guards (*okhrana*).

Annual average employment has been published by branch of the national economy and by branch of industry for the Soviet Union through 1975. Employment data for the republics was published through 1975 by branch of the economy, but the coverage frequently was less complete than that for the Soviet Union. After 1975, the amount of employment data published dropped significantly, especially for the republics. Employment by branch of the national economy continued to be published for the Soviet Union, but statistics by branch of industry ceased to be reported. Published data for the republics after 1975 were dramatically curtailed. Republic employment by branch of economy and by branch of industry were no longer published. Republic employment for the state sector, state farms, and collective farms continued to be published (Gillula and Dunn 1983, 14), but collective farm employment excluded farms engaged in fishing.

This trend was reversed by the publication of a statistical handbook on labor in 1988—the first in 20 years (Goskomstat SSSR 1988c). The new handbook contains data on branch-of-industry employment for the USSR for mid- and end-of-decade years in greater detail than previously published. However, work-hour employment has not yet been released. Unfortunately, branch-of-economy figures by republic that were previously published for 16 branches now include only industry.

Now let us turn to labor inputs to the republic's economy, measured as average annual employment. Besides the normally reported employment in the socialized sector, estimates are made for employment in private subsidiary agriculture and for workers in cooperatives. However, because of the Soviet statistical procedure, not all labor inputs are recorded accurately. Part-time workers, employed either less than a full day or a full week, are recorded as having worked a full week ("Tipovaia" 1974, 6), thereby overstating actual employment. Judging by the Soviet literature, most part-time employees are women and pensioners. No data have been published by age and sex for part-time workers. As of June 1, 1987, 967,600 persons worked part-time in the state sector, representing only 0.8 percent of the sector's employment (Goskomstat SSSR 1988c, 141). However, the share of part-timers doubled during the last 10 years. Industry, health, and education are the principal employers of part-time workers. Figures for part-time employment by republic are not available.

A more serious distortion is created by excluding time worked on a second job from the annual average employment figures. On January 1, 1988, more than 5 million workers, representing 4.3 percent of the state-sector employment, had a second job (Goskomstat SSSR 1988c). Of that number, 2.5 million had a second job at the same establishment as their principal job. Information for this category of workers is not published. Figures for the remaining 2.498 million workers whose second job was at a different establishment have been published by branch of economy and by union republic. Dual-job holding at another establishment is more prevalent in the service sphere—4.5 percent of the total employment—compared to 2.1 percent in the material production branches.[3] Education includes the largest number of dual-job holders, 537,000, or some 6 percent of employment in the branch. In art, dual-job holders constitute 11.5 percent of employment, and in culture this figure is 11.2 percent (54,000 and 153,000, respectively). Health services are frequently mentioned in the secondary literature as having many dual-job holders, but the 247,00 dual-job holders in health comprise only 3.5 percent of the branch total. Possibly, holding two jobs is prevalent only among physicians. In 1988, there were 528,000 dual-job holders in industry and 347,000 in trade.

Data are not reported on the average number of hours worked on a second job per person, but the monthly wage earned is reported. A dual-job holder in the state sector earned 63 rubles of additional income per month as of January 1, 1988, which amounted to 31 percent of the average monthly wage earned in 1987 by a full-time worker. In construction, a dual-job holder earned 96 rubles a month, or 37.3 percent of that earned by a full-time worker, while in culture a

---

[3] The material production branches include industry, agriculture, construction, forestry, transportation, and communications.

holder of a second job earned 43 rubles, or 35.4 percent of the full-time branch employee. However, the share of wages paid cannot be assumed to equal the time worked.

Figures for dual-job holders are disaggregated by union republic but not by branch of economy, while wages for dual-job holders by republic are not published. In Ukraine, 311,000 individuals have a secondary job, which is 1.5 percent of the state-sector employment as compared to 2.1 percent for the USSR. Dual-job holding is most prevalent in the Baltic republics, with Estonia at 6 percent, the highest in the Soviet Union. Secondary jobs are least common in Central Asian republics and are the lowest in Uzbekistan and Tajikistan, where they represent 0.9 percent of the state-sector employment.

The Soviet Union's annual average employment, by branch of the economy, has been published annually since the mid-1950s. Data by republic have been published for some early benchmark years and by single year for the first half of the 1970s. After 1975, only total employment for the socialized sector of the republics was published regularly. Data by branch of the Ukrainian economy are estimated for the years after 1975 (Figure 4-5).[4] Recently, the Soviet press revealed that employment subordinated to the Ministry of Defense (MOD) was withheld from the published employment statistics since World War II. Calculations based on highly rounded data for the Soviet Union imply an annual average employment figure of 4.6 million in 1988 and 4.4 million in 1989. The sum of similar estimates for the 15 union republics is about 100,000 less than those two figures in 1988 and 600,000 less in 1989. The decrease is caused by an even-larger employment decline in the Russian Federation and Ukraine (Heleniak 1990d, 1–3). However, there are not any apparent reasons for the differences between the two sets of data. Evidently the MOD employees are not engaged in manufacturing but provide logistical and perhaps other types of support to the military. Information is not available on the level of MOD employment for earlier years, and reported data is not broken down by branch of the economy.

---

[4] Estimates, in part, are made by using RAS algorithm technique, where known elements of a matrix are used to fill in unknown elements. See Braithwaite and Heleniak (*forthcoming*) for a discussion of the method.

Comparing Soviet and Ukrainian employment excluding MOD shows comparable growth and a relatively stable distribution among branches of the economy over time. During the period from 1960 to 1989, state employment increased at an annual rate of 2.2 percent in Ukraine and 2.1 percent in the Soviet Union. In 1960, material-production branches accounted for 69.7 percent of the state employment in Ukraine and 69.8 percent in the Soviet Union, but by 1989 the share dropped to 63.4 percent and 63.8 percent, respectively. Employment growth in the state sector has been reversed during the last 2 years both in Ukraine and the Soviet Union. Between 1987 and 1989, employment decreased by 368,000 in the republic, resulting from a decline in industry, state agriculture, and transportation. The decrease has been offset, however, by a rise in employment in the newly established private sector.

Industry outpaced agriculture as the branch with the highest employment, both in Ukraine (1988) and the USSR (1978). The publication of information on employment by branch of industry by republic still has not been resumed. Figures presented in Figure 4-6 are estimated for post-1975 years. From 1960 to 1989, industry employment in Ukraine grew at 2.1 percent annually, compared to 1.7 percent in the Soviet Union.[5] As a result of this higher growth, Ukraine's share of national employment increased from 17.9 percent in 1960 to 19.9 percent of the Soviet Union's industrial employment in 1989. Industrial employment started declining in Ukraine and the Soviet Union after 1986. Between 1986 and 1989, Ukrainian employment decreased by 202,000, or 2.7 percent, while the Soviet figure fell 3.5 percent. Decreases occurred in most industrial branches of the republic, but employment increased slightly in construction materials and food industries, while the electric power figure remained unchanged.

Ukraine's level of industrialization is reflected by comparatively high employment in key branches of industry. Fuels employment decreased from 14.7 percent to 8.3 percent of the republic's total between 1960 and 1989. As a share of the USSR branch employment, however, it still amounted to 35.3 percent in 1989. Ukraine has large coal deposits and some natural gas. Coal mining is a labor-intensive activity compared to the extraction of other fuels, and accounts for the

---

[5] Comparison is made using the Soviet Union data presented in Heleniak (1990a).

republic's large share of industry employment. The steel industry has been a major industry in Ukraine since the turn of the century. Compared to the Ukrainian industry total, employment in ferrous metallurgy has been decreasing in recent years, but in 1989 it still made up 28.8 percent of the USSR's branch employment. Machine-building and metalworking (MBMW) is the largest branch of industry, both in Ukraine and the USSR. In the republic, this branch's share increased from 28.8 percent of Ukrainian total industry employment in 1960 to 44.0 percent in 1989 and made up 20.3 percent of the employment in MBMW for the USSR as a whole. Construction materials is a small branch, but Ukraine accounted for 21.4 percent of the Soviet Union's total in 1960 and 20.3 percent in 1989. The food industry is another relatively small branch of the economy in Ukraine, but it accounted for 20.8 percent of the Soviet Union's total industry employment in 1989.

A larger share of the population of Ukraine is engaged in industry than in the USSR as a whole. In 1985, 147.8 persons per 1,000 of the republic's population were employed in industry, compared to 136.7 persons for the Soviet Union.[6] As might be expected, industrial employment is concentrated in the heavily urbanized regions of eastern Ukraine. Of the seven oblasts with above-average industrial employment, the sole exception is the L'viv Oblast, located in the west, which also is urbanized and has a work force with above-average educational attainment. Although largely rural, Kiev Oblast includes the city of Kiev (the largest in the republic), which places the oblast among the leading Ukrainian regions in terms of urbanization and industrialization.

Ukraine's industry relies on the large deposits of coal and iron ore located in the southeastern portion of the republic. These deposits have been mined since the turn of the century and are substantially depleted. Nevertheless, in 1985 Ukraine still produced 36 percent of the Soviet Union's coal and steel, while employment in the two branches amounted to more than a third of the Soviet level. Coal is mined largely in Luhans'k and Donets'k oblasts. These two oblasts accounted for 85 percent of the Ukrainian fuel industry's employment

---

[6] Ratios on industrial employment by oblast were derived from unpublished employment figures by oblast and population reported in statistical handbooks and in Pistun (1984).

in 1985. Ferrous metallurgy is concentrated in the Dnipropetrovs'k and Donets'k oblasts, which accounted for 79 percent of the republic's employment. Employment in other branches of industry is distributed more evenly throughout the republic. MBMW is the largest branch of industry, amounting to one-fifth of the USSR's industrial employment and more than 43 percent of the republic's total employment. Approximately half of the MBMW employment is found in the eastern urbanized oblasts, and the rest is distributed among remaining oblasts. Construction materials, light industry, and food industry are the remaining large branches of the industrial economy. These branches are distributed more evenly throughout the republic, with the exception of the food industry, which is concentrated more in rural oblasts.

Employment figures are not published by nationality at the oblast level. However, population by oblast and nationality is reported for 1979, which permits us to make some inferences about the nationality levels in employment. Data are reported for a number of groups, but Ukrainians and Russians comprised 94.7 percent of the population—73.6 percent and 21.1 percent, respectively (Goskomstat SSSR 1984, 142). The 1979 census reported that 10.5 million Russians lived in Ukraine, of whom 8.6 million, or 82 percent, lived in the eight most-urbanized oblasts. This suggests that the educational attainment of Russians is above average and that they are more likely to be employed in nonagricultural work.

Besides measuring absolute growth of employment in industry, data are published on the effectiveness of labor utilization. Labor productivity is an overall indicator that measures the value of output in constant prices per blue- and white-collar worker. Data indicate that since 1980, the republic's productivity increases have been lower than those for the Soviet Union. Between 1980 and 1987, productivity in Ukraine increased 25 percent, compared to 27 percent for the USSR (*Narkhoz SSSR* 1987, 98; *Narkhoz Ukrainy* 1987, 55). This pattern is true for most branches with the exception of timber, woodworking, and pulp and paper, in which growth was 33 percent in Ukraine; and light industry, in which it was 19 percent. In the Soviet Union, the growth rate was 28 percent and 11 percent respectively in the two branches. The greatest difference occurred in the fuels industry, in which productivity in Ukraine increased 0.1 percent compared to 12 percent growth for the USSR.

The level of technology used in production largely determines the productivity of labor. Approximately one-third of the workers in the total economy are engaged in manual work as well as 34.9 percent of blue-collar workers in the industrial sector in 1985 (Goskomstat SSSR 1988c, 249). The Soviets define manual labor as those workers who basically work with their hands, but with the help of machines, simple hand tools, and other devices. Maintenance personnel work manually when repairing equipment but are not classified as manual workers. Despite its importance, manual labor has received little attention in Soviet literature. Statistics are sparse and usually are given as percentages when reported. The current reforms focus somewhat more attention on manual labor as an area where cost can be reduced and productivity increased. Despite the added attention, statistics continue to remain sparse. Data on the share of manual workers by branch of industry were published for the USSR in 1985, but only the share of the industry total is given by republic (Goskomstat SSSR 1988c, 253). For the USSR as a whole, the largest share of manual workers, 47.6 percent, is found in underground coal mining, followed by 46.1 percent in the food industry. On the other hand, oil extraction and electric power have the lowest shares, 14.4 percent and 16.3 percent, respectively. Ukraine, with 34.5 percent of manual workers, is close to the Soviet average of 34.9 percent.

Total labor input into the republic's economy, measured as an annual average employment, is presented in Figure 4-7. The data include employment in the state sector plus employment on collective farms, in private subsidiary agriculture, and in the cooperatives. Collective farm employment is the largest component outside the state sector. The number of people working on collective farms decreased 43.4 percent between 1950 and 1985, but collective farm employment was still 174 percent higher than that in the state agriculture.

Private subsidiary farming, in which farmers are allowed to cultivate small plots of land and raise livestock, dates back to collectivization. Private plots accounted for 2.7 percent of the total land cultivated in the USSR and 6.0 percent in Ukraine in 1987 (*Narkhoz SSSR* 1987, 186; *Narkhoz Ukrainy* 1987, 122). Despite the small holdings, subsidiary agriculture is highly productive compared with the socialized sector and provides one-quarter to one-third of a farm family's income. In Ukraine, for example, 24.9 percent of the milk that was produced in 1987 came from subsidiary agriculture (*Narkhoz Ukrainy* 1987, 134).

Private agriculture is labor-intensive and performed mostly on a part-time basis. The small parcels of land are used primarily to grow vegetables and are cultivated with simple hand tools, while livestock feed is obtained largely from the socialized sector. The amount of time expended in private agriculture is difficult to measure because most of the work is performed by individuals employed full time in the socialized sector or by housewives and pensioners. Budget surveys are the major source of information on the expenditure of labor in subsidiary farming. Labor coefficients used here are based on a 1958 survey of collective farm households. These data were used to calculate a set of labor coefficients for the number of work-days required to cultivate one sown hectare and to tend one cow, pig, sheep, or goat. Coefficients derived for the subsidiary agriculture of collective farmers are assumed to apply as well to non-collective farm households engaged in subsidiary agriculture. The coefficients are old but still applicable, since they measure labor input per unit of land cultivated or per head of livestock tended—not per unit of output. The coefficients thereby eliminate increased output due to better quality of seed or better livestock. Labor productivity as defined here can be increased only through mechanization, which has not taken place so far. The coefficients have the further advantage of being usable with land and livestock data published in the annual statistical handbooks.[7] Using national coefficients for a single republic introduces an unknown degree of error, however.

Private subsidiary agriculture has been stable during the postwar period. Approximately 2 million hectares of land are cultivated annually in Ukraine. In 1950, cultivated land amounted to 2.3 million hectares but included private non-collectivized farms, probably in western Ukraine. Livestock holdings also have been relatively stable. Cattle numbered 4.3 million head in 1960 and decreased to 3.6 million in 1987.[8] Hogs numbered about 4.5 million during that period, while sheep and goats decreased from 1.5 million to 1 million between 1960

[7] See Rapawy and Kingkade (1988) for a more detailed discussion on the estimation of labor inputs in private subsidiary agriculture.

[8] Data on cultivation of land and livestock holdings are published in annual statistical handbooks.

and 1987. Estimated employment was quite stable during this period since the holdings were multiplied by constant labor coefficients to derive employment. Private subsidiary agriculture employment was estimated at 2.6 million in 1960 and decreased to 2.3 million in 1989. Due to a substantial decrease in collective farm employment, however, the share of subsidiary agriculture employment in total agricultural employment increased from 26.2 percent in 1960 to 31.8 percent in 1989.

The current economic reforms generated two additional categories of workers: self-employed, or individual, workers and members of cooperatives. The antecedents of both groups are in Soviet economic history. Throughout the Soviet period, a small number of artisans without institutional affiliation continued to work independently. This group included such diverse occupations as writers, composers, artists, lawyers and physicians in private practice, artisans producing or repairing articles directly for the population, maids, nannies, and chauffeurs. Over the years, their employment decreased to the point of being statistically insignificant and was dropped from the statistical handbooks. Their continued existence, however, could be surmised from references made to them in census methodological material.

The 1987 law on individual labor, or the self-employed, dramatically increased the number of the self-employed. The figures for the group are presented as an annual average in the columns labeled "independent artisans" in Figure 4-7. Employment from 1950 to 1986 is estimated as a share of the USSR's figure in the same proportion as Ukrainian employment in the nonagricultural branches in the state sector. Employment data for the self-employed apparently have been published quarterly since 1987, but not all the data are available in the West. Most individuals are engaged in cottage crafts and personal services; half of them were not previously employed in the socialized sector (Goskomstat SSSR 1988c, 276).

Like the self-employed, cooperatives came into existence at the beginning of Soviet rule. After the nationalization of industry and agriculture, however, cooperatives ceased to be independent entities but were still reported separately. In 1960, all members of the producer cooperatives were transferred to the state sector. Of the 1.4 million members, 1.2 million were assigned to industry and the remainder distributed among construction; transport, trade, public dining, material-technical supply, and sales and procurement; housing, communal economy; and "other" (*Narkhoz SSSR* 1960, 632). Cooperatives were revived again in 1987 as part of the economic reforms. The new cooperatives could be formed by three or more individuals and do not resemble earlier cooperatives, which at least nominally were owned by a large number of members. Present organizations are privately owned businesses, but for ideological reasons were given a more acceptable name. As for the self-employed, employment in cooperatives has been reported as of a given date by quarters. The available number of observations has been averaged to obtain a figure more comparable to the annual average employment.

Employment in cooperatives presents some methodological problems when figures are incorporated with all the labor inputs into the economy. First, members working full time and part time are grouped together. Time worked by part-timers should be converted to work-year equivalents, making the time more compatible with annual average employment. Second, employment in cooperatives should be distributed by type of activity and assigned to an appropriate branch of the economy. Such distribution presents difficulties, however, since reported figures are identified by broad categories. Employment usually is reported for personal services, public dining, cottage crafts, processing secondary materials, and for other undifferentiated activities. However, employment has been reported in great detail for the last quarter of 1989, providing more statistics for major activities. At the end of 1989, employment in cooperatives totaled 779,400 in Ukraine and wages amounted to 2.5 billion rubles (Derzhkomstat URSR 1990, 122). Some 60.8 percent worked full time, while the remaining 39.2 percent were dual-job holders working part time. The largest share of cooperative employment, 30.8 percent, was in construction and related activities. Other or undifferentiated activities was the second-largest group, 23.3 percent, and includes production of construction materials, technical products, taxi service, and other unspecified activities. Dining establishments had an employment of only 5,600. Health services employment also was comparatively small, consisting of slightly more than 15,000 people, more than two-thirds of whom were also employed in state health services.

References

Braithwaite, Jeanine D. and Timothy E. Heleniak. *Forthcoming.* "Social Welfare in the USSR: The Income Recipient Distribution." *Staff Paper.* U.S. Bureau of the Census, Center for International Research. Washington, D.C.

Derzhkomstat URSR. 1990. *Ukrains'ka RSR u tsyfrakh u 1989 r. Korotkyi statystychnyi dovidnyk.* Kiev.

—————. Various years. *Narodne hospodarstvo Ukrains'koï RSR. Statystychnyi shchorichnyk.* Kiev.

Fedorova, N. V. 1976. "Sotsial'no-ekonomicheskii sostav naseleniia SSSR." In *Vsesoiuznaia perepis' naseleniia 1970 g. Sbornik statei*, 211–27. Edited by G. M. Maksimov. Moscow.

————— 1984. "Istochniki v sredstv sushchestvovaniia naseleniia SSSR." In *Vsesoiuznaia perepis' naseleniia 1979 goda. Sbornik statei.* Edited by A. A. Isupov and N. Z. Shvartser, 172–82. Moscow.

Feshbach, Murray. 1972. "Soviet Industrial Labor and Productivity Statistics." In *Soviet Economic Statistics*, 195–225. Edited by Vladimir G. Treml and John P. Hardt. Durham, North Carolina.

Gillula, James W. and Peggy Dunn. 1983. "Major Economic Indicators: A Survey with Selected Estimates." Report prepared for research project *Multiregional Modeling of the Soviet Economy.* Principal investigator: Fyodor Kushnirsky, Temple University. Sponsored by the National Council for Soviet and East European Research, (May).

Goskomstat SSSR. 1961. *Narodnoe khoziaistvo SSSR v 1960 godu. Statisticheskii ezhegodnik.* Moscow.

—————. 1972–1974. *Itogi Vsesoiuznoi perepisi naseleniia 1970 g.* 7 Vols. Moscow.

—————. 1978. *Vsesoiuznaia perepis' naseleniia—vsenarodnoe delo.* Moscow.

—————. 1984. *Chislennost' i sostav naseleniia SSSR: po dannym Vsesoiznoi perepisi naseleniia 1979 g. Statisticheskii sbornik.* Moscow.

—————. 1988a. "Press-vypusk" 367 (17 August).

_____. 1988b. "Press-vypusk" 410 (14 November).

_____. 1988c. *Trud v SSSR. Statisticheskii sbornik.* Moscow.

_____. 1989a. *Natsional'nii sostav naseleniia. Chast' II.* Moscow 59.

_____. 1989b. "Press-vypusk" 33 (3 February).

_____. 1989c. "Press-vypusk" 57 (20 February).

_____. 1989d. "Press-vypusk" 127 (April).

_____. 1989e. "Press-vypusk" 206 (16 May).

_____. 1989f. "Press-vypusk" 569 (5 December).

_____. 1989g. *Statisticheskie materialy ob ekonomicheskom i sotsial'nom razvitii soiuznykh i avtonomnykh respublik, avtonomnykh oblastei i okrugov Chast I.* Moscow.

_____. 1990. *SSSR v tsifrakh v 1989 g. Kratkii statisticheskii sbornik.* Moscow.

Goskomstat USSR. 1976. *Narodnoe khoziaistvo Ukrainskoi SSR v 1975 g. Statisticheskii sbornik.* Kiev.

_____. 1986. *Narodnoe khoziaistvo Ukrainskoi SSR v 1985 g. Statisticheskii sbornik.* Kiev.

_____. 1987a. *Narodnoe khoziaistvo Ukrainskoi SSR v 1986 g. Statisticheskii sbornik.* Kiev.

_____. 1987b. *Narodnoe khoziaistvo Ukrainskoi SSR. Iubileinii statisticheskii ezhegodnik za 70-letie velikogo oktiabria.* Kiev.

_____. 1988. *Narodnoe khoziaistvo Ukrainskoi SSR v 1987 g. Statisticheskii sbornik.* Kiev.

Grishchenko, Boris. 1990. "'Mass Unemployment' Facing Soviet Workers." TASS. Moscow. [Reported by Foreign Broadcast Information Service. *Daily Report: Soviet Union.* FBIS-SOV-90-171 (4 September): 61–62.]

Heleniak, Timothy E. 1990a. "Employment by Branch for the USSR and Republics: 1960 to 1989." U.S. Bureau of the Census, Center for International Research, *CIR Research Note* (April): Table 3c.

_____. 1990b. "Estimates and Projections of the Labor Force and Employment in the Soviet Union for 1988 and 1989." U.S. Bureau of the Census, Center for International Research, *CIR*

Research Note (March): Table 3.

_____. 1990c. "Industrial Employment by Branch for the USSR and Republics: 1960 to 1989." U.S. Bureau of the Census, Center for International Research, *CIR Research Note* (August): Table 4c.

_____. 1990d. "Ministry of Defense Employment by Republic." U.S. Bureau of the Census, Center for International Research, *CIR Research Note* (May): 1–3.

Kingkade, W. Ward. 1987. "Estimates and Projections of the Population of the USSR, by Age and Sex for Union Republics: 1970 to 2025." U.S. Bureau of the Census, Center for International Research, *CIR Research Note* (May): Table 1.

"Kooperatsii-dinamizm razvitiia." 1988. *Ekonomicheskaia gazeta* 34 (August): 12.

Labutova, T. S. 1984. "Zaniatiia naseleniia." In *Vsesoiuznaia perepis' naseleniia 1979 goda. Sbornik statei.* Edited by A.A. Isupov and N. Z. Shvartser, 5–25. Moscow.

Nikitin, P. 1990. "Formulas Based on 'Guess-Work'; Formulation of Employment Program Needs Public Monitoring." *Sovietskaia Rossiia*, 27 (March): 2. [Translated in Foreign Broadcast Information Service. *Daily Report: Soviet Union.* FBIS-SOV-90-023 (30 March): 52–54.]

Pistun, N. D. et al., eds. 1984. *Ekonomicheskaia geografiia* 36. Kiev.

Pravda Ukrainy. 1990. (2 February): 1.

Rapawy, Stephen. 1976. *Estimates and Projections of the Labor Force and Civilian Employment in the USSR: 1950 to 1960.* U.S. Department of Commerce, Bureau of Economic Analysis, Foreign Demographic Analysis Division, *Foreign Economic Reports* 10 (September): 36–43.

_____. 1979. "Regional Employment in the USSR: 1950 to 1975." In U.S. Congress, Joint Economic Committee. *Soviet Economy in a Time of Change* 1, 600–617. Washington.

_____ and Timothy E. Heleniak. 1988. "Labor Force and Employment in Soviet Central Asia, 1970 to 2000: A Compendium of Research Notes." U.S. Bureau of the Census, Center for International Research, *CIR Research Note* (January): 15.

_____ and W. Ward Kingkade. 1988. "Estimates and Projections of the Labor Force and Civilian Employment in the USSR: 1950 to 2000." U.S. Bureau of the Census, Center for International Research, *CIR Staff Paper* (September).

Romaniuk, V. 1990. "Zashchita ot infliatsii." *Izvestiia. Vechernii vypusk* (5 January): 8.

Shcherbakov, Vladimir. 1990. "Shcherbakov Warns of Increasing Unemployment." Hamburg. DPA in German. [Translated in Foreign Broadcast Information Service. *Daily Report: Soviet Union.* FBIS-SOV-90-023 (2 February): 111.]

"Tipovaia instruktsiia po statistike chislennosti i fonda zarabotnoi platy rabochikh i sluzhashchikh na predpriiatiiakh, v uchrezhdeniiakh i organizatsiiakh." 1974. *Biulleten' normativnykh aktov, ministerstv i vedomstv SSSR* 4 (April): 3–33.

Stephen Rapawy

Figure 4–1. Estimates and Projections of Labor Force Participation
Rates in Ukraine by Age and Sex (1970–2000)

Sex and age	1970	1979	1985	1990	1995	2000
Male						
16 to 19 years	53.1	49.0	48.6	48.5	48.4	48.3
20 to 29 years	90.0	89.9	89.9	89.9	89.9	89.9
30 to 39 years	97.8	97.7	97.7	97.7	97.7	97.7
40 to 49 years	96.4	96.2	96.2	96.2	96.2	96.3
50 to 54 years	90.3	90.1	90.1	90.1	90.1	90.1
55 to 59 years	79.8	79.6	79.6	79.6	79.6	79.6
60 years and over	49.6	47.3	48.5	49.5	50.5	51.5
Female						
16 to 19 years	47.9	44.0	43.6	43.6	43.4	43.3
20 to 29 years	87.1	89.3	89.4	89.5	89.6	89.7
30 to 39 years	93.0	97.0	97.0	97.0	97.0	97.1
40 to 49 years	91.1	94.9	94.9	94.9	95.0	95.0
50 to 54 years	77.7	84.2	84.2	84.2	84.2	84.2
55 to 59 years	44.7	43.9	44.2	44.5	44.8	45.0
60 years and over	25.4	24.4	24.8	25.0	25.3	25.6

Source: Rapawy and Heleniak (1988).

Figure 4–2. Estimates and Projections of the Labor Force in Ukraine
(1970–2000)

(In thousands, as of July 1 for each year)

Year	Total	Males	Females
1970	25,826	12,381	13,445
1979	28,460	13,843	14,617
1985	29,054	14,422	14,632
1990	29,278	14,658	14,620
1995	29,642	15,047	14,595
2000	30,221	15,452	14,769

Notes: These figures represent the labor force participation rates given in Figure 4–1 multiplied by the estimated population figures, by age and sex, from Kingkade (1987). These results are added up to obtain totals.

Figure 4–3. Number of Specialists with Higher and Specialized Secondary
Education in Ukraine, by Branch of the Economy (1960–1987)
(In 1000s)

Branch	1960	1970	1980	1985	Higher education	Specialized secondary education	Total
						1987	
Total	1,661.0	3,268.9	5,442.9	6,284.9	2,868.7	3,770.5	6,639.2
Industry	302.8	785	1,489.7	1,793.0	695.0	1,203.5	1,898.5
Agriculture	114.5	221.5	396.2	478.8	148.3	353.4	501.7
Transport	47.0	123.0	224.5	266.1	78.1	186.9	265.0
Communications	7.2	23.6	46.3	55.6	15.2	43.2	58.4
Construction	58.2	170.8	325.8	368.0	244.8	268.6	513.4
Trade, public dining, material-technical supply and procurement	57.4	194.0	416.6	503.9	110.8	411.1	521.9
Housing-communal economy and personal services	7.5	25.5	78.5	109.7	36.3	88.3	124.6
Health services	315.3	465.6	620.9	710.0	223.7	516.5	740.2
Education	458.6	670.3	837.2	924.0	709.3	286.2	995.5
Culture and art	34.6	64.7	127.3	158.2	62.8	106.8	169.6
Science and scientific services	117.8	187.0	337.0	359.1	289.1	91.3	380.4
Government administration	102.6	198.5	292.9	311.2	189.2	113.8	303.0

(cont'd.)

(In percent)

Branch	1960	1970	1980	1985	1987 Higher education	1987 Specialized secondary education	1987 Total
Total	9.7	15.1	22.4	25.5	11.7	15.4	27.1
Industry	7.5	13.0	20.4	23.8	9.2	26.0	25.2
Agriculture	1.5	13.3	6.9	8.9	4.0	9.4	13.4
Transport	4.4	8.2	12.0	13.7	4.1	9.7	13.8
Communications	6.4	9.8	16.1	19.2	5.3	15.1	20.4
Construction	5.4	10.3	16.8	18.8	12.4	13.6	25.9
Trade, public dining, material-technical supply and procurement	6.7	13.3	22.6	26.9	5.9	21.9	27.8
Housing-communal economy and personal services	2.4	4.7	9.6	12.6	4.1	10.0	14.1
Health services	45.8	45.9	47.6	55.4	17.3	39.9	57.1
Education	58.1	52.2	53.5	56.8	42.7	17.2	60.0
Culture and art	23.7	29.8	40.0	48.2	18.9	32.1	50.9
Science and scientific services	67.3	47.3	57.2	59.5	48.1	15.2	63.3
Government administration	47.5	60.3	68.9	70.2	41.1	24.9	66.3

Notes and Sources:

Absolute numbers: Goskomstat UkSSR. *Narkhoz Ukrainy* 1987.

Percentages: Derived by dividing reported figure in the above by the corresponding branches of employment in Figure 4–7.

Total and agriculture: Derived by dividing reported figures for specialists by the sum of state-sector and collective farm employment.

Health services, education, and culture and art: The 1986 employment figures from Braithwaite and Heleniak (*forthcoming*; Appendix Table III–3) are used to calculate 1987 percentages, but employment for education is reduced by 1,000.

Figure 4–4. State-Sector Employment in Ukraine, by Nationality
(1977 and 1987)

Branch and nationality	1977		1987	
	Thousands	Percent	Thousands	Percent
Total	19,134	100	20,718	100
Ukrainian	13,202	69	14,503	70
Industry	6,941	100	7,532	100
Ukrainian	4,512	65	5,122	68
Agriculture	1,399	100	1,413	100
Ukrainian	1,063	76	1,116	79
Transport and communications	2,048	100	2,211	100
Ukrainian	1,454	71	1,570	71
Construction	1,904	100	1,980	100
Ukrainian	1,295	68	1,366	69
Trade and public dining	1,777	100	1,879	100
Ukrainian	1,262	71	1,371	73
Housing-communal economy and personal services	743	100	886	100
Ukrainian	498	67	602	68
Health, physical culture, and social security	1,176	100	1,296	100
Ukrainian	811	69	881	68
Education	1,473	100	1,660	100
Ukrainian	1,090	74	1,228	74
Culture and art	298	100	333	100
Ukrainian	224	75	233	70
Science and scientific services	541	100	601	100
Ukrainian	319	59	355	59
Government administration	397	100	457	100
Ukrainian	294	74	334	73

Notes and Sources:
Total branch employment: Given in Figure 4–3.
Percent of Ukrainians by branch: Reported in Goskomstat SSSR (1988c).
Culture and art: Employment figures from Braithwaite and Heleniak (*forthcoming*; Appendix Table III–3). Employment for the two branches in 1987 is assumed to be the same as in 1986.

Figure 4-5. Annual Average Employment in the State Sector, by Branch of the Economy in Ukraine (1960–1989)
(1000s)

Line number Branch	1960	1970	1975	1980	1985	1986	1987	1988	1989
1 Adjusted total	(NA)	(NA)	(NA)	(NA)	(NA)	(NA)	(NA)	21,240	20,854
2 Reported total	10,659	16,200	18,356	20,042	20,679	20,747	20,718	20,523	20,350
3 Industry	4,056	6,036	6,602	7,308	7,534	7,554	7,532	7,421	7,352
4 Agriculture	965	1,213	1,362	1,568	1,619	1,589	1,560	1,499	1,405
5 Construction	1,087	1,658	1,854	1,844	1,839	1,862	1,908	1,995	2,001
6 Forestry	58	69	73	72	70	68	64	64	64
7 Transportation	1,062	1,502	1,702	1,822	1,863	1,836	1,756	1,647	1,652
8 Communications	113	241	275	283	284	282	270	262	263
9 Trade, public dining, material-technical supply and procurement	854	1,464	1,713	1,796	1,811	1,822	1,854	1,820	1,824
10 Housing-communal economy and personal services	315	540	701	806	866	889	907	891	894
11 Health services	689	1,014	1,144	1,219	1,315	1,334	1,374	1,425	1,425
12 Education and culture	881	1,431	1,625	1,806	1,857	1,898	1,954	2,030	2,030

(cont'd.)

Line number Branch	1960	1970	1975	1980	1985	1986	1987	1988	1989
13 Art	54	71	77	80	80	80	80	82	82
14 Science and scientific services	175	395	516	587	606	598	570	538	542
15 Credit and insurance organizations	46	68	92	115	118	116	117	119	120
16 Government administration	216	329	382	426	442	465	409	369	369
17 Other	88	169	238	311	373	352	357	361	328
18 Ministry of Defense	(NA)	(NA)	(NA)	(NA)	(NA)	(NA)	(NA)	717	504

NA Not available

Sources:

Lines 1 to 17: Heleniak 1990a.

Line 18: State-sector employment, which includes the Ministry of Defense (MOD) figure was estimated by multiplying the labor resource figure for 1988 (*Pravda Ukrainy* 1990) by a functional distribution of the labor resources (Goskomstat SSSR 1989g). The state sector, which exludes the MOD portion (Derzhkomstat URSR 1990), was subtracted from the estimated total.

Figure 4–6. Annual Average Employment, by Branch of Industry in Ukraine (1960–1989) (1000s)

	1960	1970	1975	1980	1985	1986	1987	1988	1989
Total	4,056	6,036	6,602	7,308	7,534	7,554	7,532	7,421	7,352
Branch									
Electric power	59	104	111	146	158	159	159	157	159
Fuels	598	572	520	579	620	618	606	602	613
Ferrous metallurgy	388	508	490	438	440	440	426	412	399
Chemical and petro-chemicals	108	271	311	288	297	297	293	289	292
Machine-building and metalworking	1,169	2,188	2,616	3,059	3,250	3,274	3,264	3,239	3,236
Timber, woodworking, pulp, and paper	261	307	313	371	374	374	374	366	356
Construction materials	338	428	458	467	458	460	456	454	471
Light industry	514	805	834	873	856	851	849	813	755
Food industry	451	625	654	644	652	611	610	606	622
Other branches	170	228	295	444	428	470	493	482	447

Source: For 1960–75, Rapawy (1979, 608–611); for 1980–89, Heleniak (1990c, Table 4C).

Figure 4–7. Annual Average Employment in the National Economy of Ukraine (1950–1987)
(1000s)

	Total (1)	Total (2)	Indus-try (3)	Nonagricultural sectors Other nonagriculture Total (4)	Services[1] (5)	Other[2] (6)	Inde-pendent artisans (7)	Co-oper-atives (8)	Agricultural sectors Total (9)	State (10)	Col-lective farms (11)	Private agri-culture (12)
Year												
1950	[3]13,674	6,439	2,509	3,823	2,319	1,504	107	(X)	7,235	611	6,624	(NA)
1960	19,819	9,723	4,056	5,638	3,230	2,408	29	(X)	10,096	965	6,487	2,644
1970	24,291	14,988	6,036	8,951	5,312	3,639	1	(X)	9,403	1,213	5,447	2,743
1975	25,835	16,995	6,602	10,392	6,250	4,142	1	(X)	8,840	1,362	4,975	2,503
1980	26,774	18,475	7,308	11,166	6,834	4,332	1	(X)	8,299	1,568	4,301	2,430
1985	27,049	19,061	7,534	11,526	7,097	4,429	1	(X)	7,988	1,619	3,958	2,411
1986	26,919	19,159	7,544	11,604	7,202	4,402	1	(X)	7,760	1,589	3,865	2,306
1987	26,799	19,181	7,532	11,626	7,267	4,359	20	3	7,618	1,560	3,748	2,310
1988	27,114	19,735	7,421	12,193	7,864	4,329	55	66	7,379	1,499	43,586	2,294
1989	27,370	19,816	7,352	12,097	7,789	4,308	38	329	7,168	1,405	43,485	2,278

	Socialized sector Total (13)	Workers and em-ployees (14)	Col-lective farms (15)	Private sector Total (16)	Inde-pendent artisans (17)	Co-oper-atives (18)	Private agri-culture (19)
Year							
1950	13,567	6,943	6,624	107	107	(X)	(NA)
1960	17,146	10,659	6,487	2,673	29	(X)	2,644

	Socialized sector			Private sector			
Year	Total	Workers and employees	Collective farms	Total	Independent artisans	Co-operatives	Private agriculture
	(13)	(14)	(15)	(16)	(17)	(18)	(19)
1970	21,647	16,200	5,447	2,744	1	(X)	2,743
1975	23,331	18,356	4,975	2,504	1	(X)	2,503
1980	24,343	20,042	4,301	2,431	1	(X)	2,430
1985	24,637	20,679	3,958	2,412	1	(X)	2,411
1986	24,612	20,747	3,865	2,307	1	(X)	2,306
1987	24,466	20,718	3,748	2,333	20	3	2,310
1988	24,826	21,240	3,586	2,415	55	66	2,294
1989	24,339	20,854	3,485	2,645	38	329	2,278

X Not applicable.   NA Not available.

[1] Includes trade, public dining, material-technical supply and sales, and procurement; housing-communal economy and personal services; health services; education and culture; art; science and scientific services; credit and insurance organizations; government administration; and Ministry of Defense.

[2] Includes construction, forestry, transport, communications, and other branches of material production.

[3] Excludes private subsidiary agriculture.

[4] Excludes students and collective farmers whose primary employment is in the state sector. In 1985, employment under this definition was 22,000 lower than the figure given in the table.

(See next page for *Notes and Sources*.)

Notes and Sources:
Column 1: Sum of columns 2 and 9.
Column 2: Sum of columns 3, 4, 7, and 8.
Columns 3, 5, 6, 10, and 14: Figure 4–5.
Column 4: Sum of columns 5 and 6.
Columns 7 and 17: 1950–86: Independent artisans for the USSR (Rapawy and King-kade 1988) multiplied by the ratio of employment of the state nonagricultural sectors in Ukraine to those for the USSR (sum of columns 3 and 4 to Table 4, column 3 in Rapawy and Kingkade 1988). 1987–89: Reported employment for different periods in 1988 (Goskomstat SSSR 1989b and 1989d) was averaged and multiplied by 0.5 (to eliminate double counting). Employment for 1987 and 1989 was estimated by an index of the USSR employment in Heleniak (1990b) (1988 = 100.0).
Columns 8 and 18: Data reported for various periods of time in "Kooperatsii" 1988; Goskomstat SSSR (1989b, 1988a, 1988b, 1989c, 1989e, and 1989f); and Derzhkom-stat URSR (1990). Zero employment was assumed for 1 January 1987. Data were distributed by year, averaged and multiplied by the USSR adjustment factors of 0.307, 0.532, and 0.644 for 1987 to 1989, respectively (Heleniak, 1990c) to eliminate double counting.
Column 9: Sum of columns 10–12.
Columns 11 and 15: 1950–75: Rapawy, 1979. 1980–87: *Narhosp Ukraïny* (1987). 1988–89: Derzhkomstat URSR (1990).
Columns 12 and 19: 1950–87: Labor inputs multiplied by corresponding land and livestock holdings. Methodology and labor inputs are given in Rapawy 1976. Land and livestock holdings are reported in the following sources: *Narhosp Ukraïny* (1970 and 1980); *Narkhoz Ukrainy* (1975, 1976, 1985, 1987); and Goskomstat USSR (1987b). 1988: Interpolated linearly. 1989: The 1987 figure reduced by the annual rate of decrease between 1985 and 1987.

CHAPTER FIVE
Energy, Minerals, and Economic Policy

Leslie Dienes

Well before the latest structural developments in the world economy, resource endowment was recognized as a dynamic, changing concept. As the determinants of final demand shift and as production technology and organization change, the relative advantage of countries and regions will change significantly. In the last few decades, the critical importance of infrastructure and information, management, labor skills, cultural-environmental amenities, and location have given new meaning to the understanding of resource endowment.

Historically, Ukraine has been the best endowed and, in an all-around sense, the most viable of all Soviet regions. Its mineral and fertile agricultural resources "were admirably suited to support a wide range of products of top priority for the national economy," beginning with imperial times and continuing into the era of the five-year plans (Dienes 1977, 157). Based on its pre-revolutionary foundation, a massive complex of interlocking heavy manufacturing was built up in Ukraine, specifically in its eastern parts, even as the republic continued its agricultural specialization and interregional "export" of food.[1] By the 1960s, the sheer bulk of the coal-metallurgy-heavy machinery complex of Ukraine exceeded anything found in Western Europe. In

[1] Even in 1985, the fuel and ferrous-metallurgical industries accounted for 20.2 percent of the value of all commercial-industrial production (*tovarnaia produktsiia*) in Ukraine as a whole. In the Donets'k-Dnieper Economic Region they accounted for 34.4 percent, a share matched only in West Siberia, where two-thirds of all Soviet oil and gas is produced. In earlier decades, fuels and ferrous metallurgy dominated the industrial structure of Ukraine even more strongly (Sagers 1990, Table 2).

the following 10 to 15 years, Brezhnev's aggressive ocean policy increased the significance of the Black Sea coast (which was not far from the centers of metallurgy), as a center of naval construction and as a heavily-used sea bridge linking the European USSR to the Soviet Far East.[2]

Under Khrushchev and in the first decade of Brezhnev, fertilizers, chemicals, petrochemicals, and synthetic materials also became priority industries. The presence of mineral chemicals in the Carpathian provinces and other areas and, more important, the rapid growth of an oil and gas pipeline network and the location of new refineries made additional resources available to Ukraine. From 1960 through 1975, this republic's share in the gross output of the Soviet chemical industry rose from less than 11 percent to more than 18 percent, dipping slightly below 18 percent again by the mid-1980s (Sagers and Shabad 1990, 42–43). Finally, the strengthening of economic ties with Eastern Europe during the Brezhnev years and increased participation in world trade prompted a great deal of new construction in Ukraine. Resource production and processing and power generation was expanded in the republic itself, at least partly for export, while its port facilities, terminals, and transshipment points were enlarged to handle the increased foreign trade (North 1983, 97–123).

In an earlier study I argued that roughly up to the Brezhnev era, the structure and functional specialization of Ukraine were economically rational from the vantage point of the whole Soviet system.[3] On the other hand, this specialization became increasingly disadvantageous from the Ukrainian standpoint. Yet, the two points of view could have remained compatible if (1) a determined effort was made to diversify

[2] As regional interdependence between the Far Eastern periphery and the European USSR increased through the Brezhnev era, a major decision apparently was made to establish a regular, extraterritorial sea line of communication linking the two by means of a 12,000 nautical mile route via the Black Sea, Suez Canal, Indian Ocean, and South China Sea. By 1984, the USSR was the world's largest user of the Suez Canal among nations in number of transits per year. The German intelligence service (BND) estimated at the end of the 1970s that four-fifths of the Soviet transcontinental freight; that is, that moving all the way to the Pacific coast, traveled via this southern sea route rather than by rail (Westwood 1985, 47). This estimate, however, is so high that it may refer only to military freight.

[3] Of course, not to maximize the GNP as such but the GNP of a predetermined economic structure, to use Koropeckyj's expression.

the republic's industrial structure, reducing its dependence on resource-intensive sectors, and (2) local energy resources were carefully husbanded and supplemented with in-shipments at costs no higher than the marginal cost of Donbas coal prevailing in the early 1970s (Dienes 1977, 155– 89).

Putting it another way, Ukraine should have capitalized on its resource endowment due to its relative infrastructural advantages, its labor force, and also its location in terms of the world economy. Except for the Baltic, no Soviet region enjoys a similar comparative advantage in all these factors. In addition, Ukraine has continued to excel in the potential for agricultural intensification. The fact that Ukraine could not make such an adjustment as an integral but subordinate part of the Soviet economy is a major theme of this conference. While system-related causes that affect the whole USSR, and indeed all centrally planned economies (CPRs), represent the dominant element in that failure, policy-related factors are also involved.

Diminishing Returns and Other Legacies

Mineral Depletion

Mining operations in the republic are threatened by rapidly worsening geological conditions. The famed Donbas has cumulatively produced about 8.4 billion tons of coal so far, more than any other basin in Europe and probably the world (Computed from Kortus 1964, 186–87; Shabad "News Notes," and Sagers "News Notes," various issues, April, 1991). Today, great depth and very thin beds, combined with insufficient maintenance, take a terrible toll on miners, even as the quality of the fuel declines due to increasing ash content.[4] The Donbas has long experienced more than 200 fatalities annually, but in 1989 the death toll was more than double that figure (SWB, 6 January

---

[4] More than half of all Donbas coal today is produced from below a depth of 600 meters. A third of the shafts exploit reserves between 800 and 1,000 meters, and the great majority of the 33 Soviet coal mines working below one kilometer are in Ukraine and adjoining Rostov Oblast (Marples 1988, 2; Sagers "News Notes," 1989, 331–32; "Bezopasnost' truda" 1989, 39). Fully 70 percent of the remaining reserves are found in beds of less than 0.9 meters. Half of the coal is already mined from seams of 0.9 to 1.2 meters thickness, and increasing quantities originate from beds of 50 to 60 centimeters (Zagumennov and Sokolova 1985, 58; Fedorishcheva and Alymov 1986, 140).

1989, 14; Marples 1990, 17). About 1,200 miners are maimed each year (*Sotsialisticheskaia industriia* 8 August 1989, 2). In addition to the physical conditions of the mines, an acute lack of medical equipment and drugs lurks behind these horrendous figures. The whole mining complex of Donets'k Oblast possesses but one resuscitator, for example (*Rabochaia tribuna* 1990, 1).

Geological conditions in the iron ore field of Krivyi Rih, which in 1970 still produced the cheapest ore in all the USSR (Dienes 1977, 164), have also worsened significantly. Conditions also have deteriorated in manganese mining. Ukraine accounts for almost three-quarters of Soviet production, but has been unable to satisfy the growing demand for manganese (Tereshchenko 1986, 14). At Krivyi Rih, a major shift from underground to surface mining has taken place in recent years. Much of that crude ore represents very low-quality quartzites, however, and extracting it inflicts immense environmental damage on fertile agricultural land.[5] During the 1981–1985 five-year plan alone, Ukrainian ferrous metallurgy had to devote one-fifth of all its investment simply to counteract diminishing returns in the mining of iron ore (Starosel'skii 1987, 47–48).

The three petroleum-rich regions of Ukraine (one geological "province" and two "oblasts") have long faded from national significance. Cumulatively they produced almost 1.5 trillion cubic meters of gas and a third as much oil in heat equivalent (Dikenshtein 1983, 60, 170, and 209; Sagers, "News Notes," various issues, April 1991). These are large volumes. Yet by 1989 the USSR was extracting 75 percent of that cumulative output in a single year. (*Pravda* 28 January 1990, 2). Future reserves in all these regions are scattered among many small prospects in depths of 3,500 to 6,000 meters.[6]

[5] Many open pits at Krivyi Rih are 260 to 280 meters deep. Mine heaps and tailing cover 14,000 hectares of agricultural land (Tereshchenko 1986, 14; Gavrilenko 1986, 2).

[6] In addition, the Dnieper-Donets'k graben, the largest of the three, is a province with extensive salt accumulations of various geological ages, which greatly complicates geophysical exploration for the deep-lying sub-salt deposits (Dikenshtein 1983, 260).

Air Pollution

Extractive and primary industries, particularly when spatially concentrated, take a heavy toll on the environment and human health. In
the historic citadels of heavy metallurgy, including Eastern Ukraine,
the situation is aggravated by technology that is even more obsolete
than the average for the country.[7] Since 1975, death from cancer in
Donets'k Oblast rose by one-quarter (*Molod' Ukraïny* 1989). In
Zaporizhzhia and Dnipropetrovs'k, two of the oldest Soviet steel mills
are completely enveloped by urban construction. Here the mortality
level for children is 25 to 45 percent higher in any given year than the
mean for the republic (*Sovetskaia kul'tura* 22 August 1986, 8; Sagers
"News Notes," May 1989, 399 and 404).

Geographic and Structural Imbalances

The delayed structural shift away from capital-intensive primary
industries, which are subject to locational inertia, has retarded the geographic spread of manufacturing in Ukraine (Dienes 1977, 157– 59).
Since the late 1960s, the geographic imbalance has improved greatly.
A large proportion of that development was not environmentally
benign, however, and consumer industries continue to be underrepresented. As late as 1989, almost four-fifths of all state capital
investment was directed to the electric power, coal, metallurgical,
chemical, and petrochemical industries (JPRS-UEA 30 October 1990,
66–67). In particular, the share of light industry in 1986 still
accounted for a mere 7 percent of the value of aggregate industrial
output, a lower proportion than in Siberia without the Far East (*Narkhoz Ukraïny* 1987, 62–63; Granberg 1986, 25). New data for 1988
shows that in light industry products, Ukraine experienced a 90 percent deficit in interrepublic exchanges, slightly greater than the Russian Federation. By contrast, Belarus and all non-Slavic republics in
the European USSR (including Transcaucasia) registered substantial

---

[7] Although Ukraine has made significant progress in recent years in modernizing
its steel industry, oxygen converters and electric furnaces still accounted for only 46
percent of the republic's steel production between 1988 and 1989, versus 48 percent
in the USSR as a whole and more than 77 percent in Kazakhstan (Sagers "News
Notes," May 1990, 392–94).

surpluses (*Vestnik statistiki* No. 3, 1990, 39–53).[8]

The improved geographic distribution of industry among regions and the city network simply spread the structural deformities over most of Ukraine. By 1987, the formerly Polish Volhynian and Carpathian oblasts received as much investment as the Donbas area, with such construction channeled into the northern tier of the republic as well. (*Narhosp Ukraïny* 1973, 350; *Narkhoz Ukrainy* 1987, 257; Ishchuk and Kiretskii 1988, 73–74). During the 1970s, more than half of the new building (*novostroiki*) in the entire western half of Ukraine and a still larger share in the coastal provinces occurred in settlements with a population of less than 50,000 (Ishchuk and Kiretskii 1988, 73–74). Yet, the bulk of that construction represented the extraction of mineral chemicals, synthetic materials, and intermediates and the expansion of nuclear capacity at a reckless pace.[9]

Energy Shortfalls—A Clear and Present Crisis

The burden of the resource-intensive sectors, with their worn out, wasteful plants, is perhaps most dramatically apparent in the severe energy shortage that has overtaken Ukraine. The republic's ferrous metallurgy, petroleum refining, chemical and building-material industries, which nationally accounted for almost 23 percent of final energy use and 20.5 percent of aggregate fuel consumption in 1980 (Sagers

---

[8] In Soviet domestic prices, Ukraine's negative balance in inter-republic and international exchanges with respect to products of light industries is almost 80 percent as great as its negative balance with respect to oil, gas, and petroleum-refinery products. The deficit is more than 2.2 times larger than Ukraine's surplus with respect to products of the food industries. These prices, of course, significantly undervalue fuels and raw materials and overvalue consumer soft goods, but the magnitude of these balances still is instructive.

[9] The Carpathian foothills, in particular, have become a major source of mineral chemicals, especially of native sulfur and potash, with production both from surface and underground operations. Kalush is one of the largest centers for caustic soda and chlorine and an important producer of vinyl and polyvinyl chloride. In addition, the populous western provinces of Ukraine and other border provinces of the USSR are an advantageous location for Western companies supplying their European firms and customers with petro-chemicals when the raw materials are easily transportable, since labor and capital costs in these areas are much lower than east of the Urals. However, a joint venture with Occidental Petroleum at Kalush ran into heavy local opposition on environmental grounds. In April 1990, Goskompriroda ordered a halt to the project (Peterson 1990, 9).

and Tretyakova 1988, 10–11), suffer even more from obsolescence than Ukrainian industry as a whole. The first two industries, in which 53 to 54 percent of the capital stock was already amortized at mid-decade, must have been especially extravagant consumers of energy (Figure 5-1). In Ukraine at that time, for example, energy consumption per ton of steel exceeded that in Japan by a full 60 percent ("Krupnye regiony" 1989, 60).

No other region or republic has seen its energy position change so rapidly for the worse than Ukraine. In less than two decades, from 1970 through 1988, that republic went from a small energy surplus to a 42 percent overall net fuel deficit in heat equivalent units (Baramyshkov and Nevelev 1990, 5; Goskomstat SSSR 1988b, 67). Equally important, the marginal cost of fuel supply in Ukraine is among the highest in the Soviet Union today. Ukraine no longer has any advantage in terms of energy, even compared to the St. Petersburg area, Belarus, and the Baltic states.[10] The difficulties and delays involved in tapping the vast gas deposits and in replacing oil reserves in the West Siberian arctic's biggest fields were instrumental in the overworking and premature peaking of hydrocarbon reserves in Ukraine and the nearby North Caucasus. A substantial portion of that gas also was piped out to Moscow, Belarus, and abroad (Dienes 1983, 392–97 and 401–404).

Today Ukraine is a net "importer" of each major fuel from other republics, although its minor in-shipments of coal are more than compensated for by net exports abroad. Its traditional dependence on other Soviet republics for crude oil and refined products has intensified in recent years: besides the Russian Federation, Belarus refineries also show up as major suppliers (Goskomstat SSSR 1988b, 145). Since 1980, however, gasoline and diesel fuel consumption in Ukraine declined, dropping by 13 to 14 percent in the first half of the decade.

---

[10] Currently, the increase in supplies of fuel (crude oil, natural gas, and cola) for the European USSR originates from West Siberia and Kazakhstan. West of the Urals, therefore, marginal costs vary only by distance and the transport charges from these suppliers. Costs also vary, to some extent, by differences in the mix of these fuels required by the industrial structure of the various areas and the technology at major consuming centers. Earlier, then Ukraine still played a role in incrementing supplies, the western provinces of Ukraine still could claim lower marginal costs for boiler fuels than the Baltic Republics or the Saint Petersburg-Novgorod area of the Russian Federation (Dienes and Shabad 1989, 245–49).

The level of consumption probably is even lower today, given mounting troubles in the Soviet oil industry (Cooper 1989, 3; Dienes 1989, 1–5; Sagers "New Notes," September 1989, 605 and April 1991, 251–65). In the summer of 1989, serious shortages of motor fuel and lubricants hampered farm work in some oblasts of the republic as well as elsewhere in the USSR (*Izvestiia* 20 June 1989; *Gudok* 19 September 1989, 1). Ukrainian authorities have now decided to limit the outshipment of a number of products, including motor fuels (Baramykov and Hebelev 1990, 10).

Most dramatically, however, Ukraine, which until 1978 both exported and provided natural gas to other regions, now must pipe in two cubic meters for every cubic meter it still produces from its own fading fields (Sagers et al. 1988, 890; Sagers "News Notes," April 1991, 290; Shabad 1979, 258). Ukraine also no longer is a net supplier of electric power to other Soviet republics, but remains so with Eastern Europe (*Vestnik statistiki* No. 3, 1990, 40). The republic, the southern Urals, and the Caucasus were apparently among the regions that were hit the hardest by power shortfalls during the winter of 1989–90 (TASS 6 September 1989; *Radio Moscow* 12 September 1989; Sagers, 1990 308–309). Reserve generating capacity in Ukraine has fallen to a mere 2 percent, well below the critical level for any power system (*Ekonomika i zhizn'* No. 20, May 1990, 5). The current shortages and the gloomy prospects of power supplies in Ukraine also have international implications. Hungary, in particular, cannot replace even a fraction of its considerable electricity imports (28 percent of its consumption) from Ukraine and is increasingly concerned about the reliability of that source in the future (HVG 9 December 1989, 70–71; 10 November 1990, 5–6).

Spatial Optimization and Regional Equity in Energy Allocation

In the Soviet economic structure, the out-shipment of Ukrainian gas, coal, and some other mineral resources was largely an example of spatial optimization in distribution. Assuming comparable labor productivity in Ukraine as in industrial centers elsewhere in the European USSR, such interregional exports also reflect a basically rational pattern of allocation for the larger economic system as well.[11] In

---

[11] In other words, economic gains from the spatial optimization of the fuel mix was

addition, the favorable location and geological conditions of Ukrainian mineral resources other than coal and oil have yielded large rent payments, resulting in very substantial income to the Soviet state. This was particularly true of natural gas output annually from 1963 to 1974 (Dienes 1977, 173–74; *Narkhoz Ukrainy*, various issues). The coal industry was subsidized through most of the post-Stalin period, generating economic rent for only a few years after each major price revision. Today, surplus value earned by the other minerals produced in Ukraine, with the possible exceptions of manganese and sulfur, also seems to have been eliminated. Large rent-like "surpluses" collected by Moscow on Ukrainian resources probably are limited to those derived from the republic's fertile and well-situated farmland.

Yet, while static economic criteria in the spatial allocation of fuel and other mineral flows may have been satisfied, the same cannot be said of equity criteria. On one hand, these resources have been withdrawn from Ukraine without any interest or severance payment. On the other hand, fuel and energy at least (though clearly not minerals) represent a critical component of final demand and not simply inter-industry inputs. The manner of allocation of different energy forms, therefore, significantly influences consumer welfare.

As in the rest of the USSR, so also in Ukraine, the municipal economy and the consumer, particularly in the countryside, have not been allowed to modernize their energy use as much as other sectors of society. By Soviet estimates, the inadequate modernization of energy consumption by households and by the municipal economy adversely affects the lives of 50 million people (Melent'ev and Makarov 1983, 52). It is notable, however, that in this respect Ukraine is worse off than the European part of the Russian Federation taken as a whole. In the municipal-residential sector in certain parts of the Russian Federation, such as the rural *raions* of the non-chernozem zone, the lack of quality fuels is even greater than in Ukraine. Consumers in Siberia and the Far East are still more deprived. However, it is more logical to compare Ukraine with European Russia, as a whole, because of Ukraine's size, population, and geographic location.

---

not overwhelmed by higher labor productivity in Ukraine than in the European part of the Russian Federation, Belarus, and the Baltic republics.

Per capita gas consumption in the residential-municipal sector of Ukraine has consistently remained below that in the European part of the Russian Federation and the Urals, even as Ukraine was providing a third of the USSR's cumulative output through the 1960s and one-fourth between 1970 and 1977 (*Narkhoz SSSR*, various issues; Shabad "News Notes," April issues). As the Ukrainian fields were drained and increments were shifted to the giant North Tiumen' deposits (and to some extent Central Asia), supplies became less accessible to the republic. The furnishing of gas to the Ukrainian residential-municipal economy slipped further behind in a relative sense. For 1970, the per capita gas consumption of this sector fell 16 percent below that of the European part of the Russian Federation. Between 1975 and 1980, Ukrainian gas consumption averaged 30 percent less, and in 1985 it was still 20 percent below that of the European part of the Russian Federation.[12]

The residential and municipal consumers of Ukraine have not fared any better in the allocation of electricity and centrally supplied heat. From 1970 through 1985, per capita usage of electricity in this sector remained a full third lower than in the Russian Federation. Even in the 1980s, Ukrainian households also received less than half as much centralized heat as Russian households. The fraction was much smaller during the previous decade. The difference is too large to be explained by the harsher winters of the Russian Federation. District heating and co-generation is clearly less developed in Ukraine,[13] and the population is assigned a much smaller proportion of centrally generated heat

[12] Gas consumption (by sectors) is available only for the whole of the Russian Federation. The overwhelming portion of that gas, however, is used in the European part of the Russian Federation and the Urals. The small amount consumed in Siberia and the Far East (mostly by industry) can be estimated from pipeline capacity (Goskomstat SSSR 1988b, 89–96).

[13] Of all "teploenergiia," or heat furnished by pipes to districts or apartment complexes in the USSR, Ukraine received 12.1 percent in 1985, while the Russian Federation received 71.6 percent. The former is far lower, the latter far higher than the respective shares of these republics in the Soviet population, despite the unquestionable neglect of the Trans-Ural regions of the Russian Federation, which also suffer from the harshest winters (Goskomstat SSSR 1988b, 89–94). In Ukraine in 1989, only 11 percent of all electricity was expected to be generated by cogenerating turbines (bleeding turbines that supply steam for space heating as well), only a fraction of the corresponding share prevailing in Minenergo of the USSR (Pronin 1989, 18).

than in the Russian Federation (Goskomstat SSSR 1988b, 91–94). The heating network and equipment is in a wretched state: 55 percent of it is not only amortized but is physically worn out (Pronin 1986, 35).[14]

The converse of this centralized neglect is that households in Ukraine burned more than half as much state-furnished solid fuels than households in the Russian Federation, although Ukraine's population was only one-third as great (Goskomstat SSSR 1988b, 91–94). In the countryside, of course, stoves are the universal means of heat supply, not only in Ukraine but everywhere in the USSR. Even in urban households in Ukraine, space- and water-heating stoves provide 35 percent of the heat they received (Pronin 1986, 35).

Investment Policy and Modernization

The voracious energy needs of the Soviet economy and the pivotal role of hydrocarbons in hard-currency earning has distorted the Soviet investment budget. The need for energy has preempted funds that could have gone into modernization and diversification, which are needed everywhere but especially in regions top-heavy with primary and resource-producing industries. Since the mid-1970s, an increasing percentage of total industrial investment has been shifted to the energy sector, particularly oil, gas, and nuclear power. To make matters worse, this period also coincided with the construction of the Baikal-Amur Mainline (BAM), the continued Far-Eastern military build-up, and, later, the Soviet invasion of Afghanistan.

The experience of Ukraine during this investment crunch, however, differed somewhat from that of the Russian Federation. Russia's claim on Soviet investment allocation as a whole rose substantially, from 50 percent in the ninth five-year plan (1971–1975), to more than 50 percent in the eleventh five-year plan (1981–1985), and to almost 53 percent in 1987 (Goskomstat SSSR 1988a, 65). By contrast, Ukraine's share of the allocation was dropping sharply, from close to 17 percent of the country's total in the first half of the 1970s, to below 14 percent between 1980 and 1982, and remaining under 15 percent for the rest

---

[14] The 200,000 km heat distribution system for the entire country is also in a parlous state, however. "Losses in heat pipelines average 13 percent, while norms call for losses of only 5 to 6 percent." The poor quality of insulation is the most important reason for such enormous losses (Sagers and Tretyakova 1987, 13–14).

of the decade. Throughout the 1970s, the fuel and electricity branches of Ukraine's economy persistently claimed almost as high a portion of the republic's aggregated investment as they did in the Russian Federation, while the portion was only moderately lower than that during the early 1980s.[15] (Goskomstat SSSR 1988a, 36–39 and 55; *Narkhoz SSSR* 1983, 365). The continued prominence of the Ukrainian energy sector thus was squeezed out of an investment total that declined drastically in relative terms. In reality, aggregate investment for Ukraine and all the other republics was not the result of prior regional allocations, but basically of mechanical summations of branch investments made by national ministries in Ukraine.

The modernization and retooling campaign, begun under Brezhnev and cresting with Gorbachev's machine-building crusade in the first two years of the twelfth five-year plan, did raise the growth of capital allocation channeled into the machine-building and metalworking (MBMW) sector of Ukraine compared to that of the Russian Federation. The proportion of industrial investment directed to the MBMW branches increased sharply in Ukraine (as it did in Belarus) and declined slightly in the Russian Federation. Yet the historic lag of Ukraine concerning MBMW investment has merely narrowed and is far from eliminated. Per capita, the MBMW sector of Ukraine still received only 73.5 percent as much of an outlay in 1987 as it received in the Russian Federation (Figure 5-2).[16]

[15] In the first half of the 1980s, slower growth of investment in the Ukrainian fuel industries was more than counterbalanced by the reckless nuclear program.

[16] This gap is even more poignant in light of recently released statistics by Goskomstat. The per capita value of interrepublic machinery trade in 1988 was far higher for Ukraine than for the Russian Federation. The per capita value on interrepublic export of machinery was 65 percent higher and the per capita value of such import was 79 percent higher in Ukraine than in the Russian Federation. Both Ukraine and the Russian Federation registered substantial trade surpluses in machinery and equipment with the rest of the Soviet Union, though the dominance of interregional export of machinery over import was substantially higher for the Russian Federation. (Belarus, however, overwhelms the other two Slavic republics both in per capita interrepublic machinery trade and the relative size of its machinery export surplus. *Vestnik statistiki* 1990, 39–41). Clearly, by now Ukraine has become a critical equipment and machinery supplier to the rest of the Soviet Union. This industry is so intertwined through input-output linkages with industries in other republics that its modernization appears essential not only for Ukraine but for other republics as well. The sharply rising prices for equipment during the past decade doubtless introduces some regional

New data by Goskomstat also reveals that in 1988 the Russian Federation was the beneficiary of almost four-fifths of all MBMW products imported by the Soviet Union from abroad, while Ukraine received barely more than 11 percent—one-seventh as much as the Russian Federation (*Vestnik statistiki* No. 3, 1990, 39–53). Obviously, not all MBMW imports represent capital goods, but the majority, perhaps even the bulk of them, do. The overwhelming dominance of the Russian Federation and the puny share of Ukraine in the import of foreign machinery and equipment temper somewhat the recent narrowing of the investment gap between the two Slavic republics in the MBMW sector.

Despite the declining share of overall capital allocation in Ukraine and the feeble contribution of imported machinery, the following must be noted. The investment squeeze resulting from the country's rising energy burden plus Brezhnev's other ventures pressed on some Russian regions equally hard. The crash development of the Tiumen' oil and gas complex and BAM alone swallowed up well over half of all investment growth in the Russian Federation from 1975 through 1988. During the 1980s, the Urals experienced *relative* reduction in capital allocation even more severe than Ukraine.[17] The Far East, as a whole, suffered a substantial absolute cut, despite BAM and the naval buildup (*Stroitel'naia gazeta* 5 April 1988, 1–2).

Restructuring, Regional Development, and Ukraine

Crucial cultural factors aside, relative position and accessibility have always been critical variables in regional development. Position and access, however, must be understood in terms of both geographic space and political-economic power, whether one takes a national or a global perspective. Political subordination to outside centers of decision making has been the fate of Ukraine. Given its manpower and locational advantages, its economic interests cannot be willfully

---

distortions into interrepublic comparisons. However, given the size and complex industrial structures of both Ukraine and the Russian Federation, such distortions between these two republics should not be very significant.

[17] See my calculations and sources in Dienes (1989, 255–56).

ignored without damage to the whole Soviet system.[18] In the short run, however, the maximization of benefits for an entire regional system rarely, if ever, coincides with the maximization of benefits in its specific constituent parts.

Gorbachev's perestroika has gone through drastic swings in immediate goals and investment priorities in response to unexpected economic and social developments during its five years. The immediate stress shifted from centrally targeted modernization and intensification of the capital stock to partial and confusing delegation of authority to the enterprise level, with more rational input combinations by firms to be aided by newly introduced users' fees on labor, capital, and natural resources. Between 1989 and 1990, the deepening social crisis first produced a recentralization, with allocation priorities on the social-consumer sphere, then new proposals based on bolder reforms. These years ushered in acrimonious debates and a set of decrees concerning republic and regional autonomy and the restructuring of the Soviet federation. Some of the objectives of the Gorbachev years so far remain wishful thinking, though with different urgency, even as they appear largely contradictory. All of them have regional implications, not the least with respect to resource use, investment, and structural change in Ukraine. In addition, the severe investment constraints imposed under the pressure of the huge budget deficit have unavoidable regional significance.

Intensification in the context of perestroika involves shifting new investment into retooling and expanding existing facilities rather than into new construction. That goal was already a propaganda theme of much of the Brezhnev era. In its original version, Gorbachev's twelfth five-year plan (1986–1990) specifically stressed that investment should focus on the high technology renovation of existing plant capacity in the European USSR, and that new projects elsewhere in the country be restricted essentially to the extraction of fuel and strategic metals.

---

[18] Yet this is precisely what happened in the first five-year plan, the collectivization campaign, the Famine of 1933, and a number of other situations. The huge losses sustained by Ukraine clearly damaged not only this republic but sapped the strength of the Soviet economy as a whole.

The policy of intensification and the clear stress on the region west of the Urals was expected to benefit Ukraine. The plan was to accelerate the structural shift in the Ukrainian economy from resource-intensive to higher value-added, technology-intensive manufacturing more in accord with the republic's comparative advantages in the new industrial era. According to one source, Ukraine and the European Russian Federation, the two core regions that have roughly equal weight and that balance one another, were to assume the role of two locomotives during perestroika (Sokolov 1989, 10–11). These "foci of territorial concentration of human activity...[serve as the] generators and diffusors of innovation" to the hinterlands. In the Siberian, Central Asian, and Caucasian hinterland, the development lag in the short term may increase when compared to the geographic cores of the economy (Bond 1987, 497– 503; Treyvish 1986, 623).[19]

Gorbachev's first major reform attempt to increase the decision making authority of the firm was expressed in the Enterprise Law of June 1987. The December 1989 reintroduction of detailed quantity planning for all consumer goods and infrastructural construction (while retaining the high proportion of state orders for capital goods and commodities), essentially squashed this budding autonomy. However, the bulk of investment responsibility, shifted onto the shoulders of the firms by the Enterprise Law, apparently is to remain there in most industries (Il'in 1989, 29–30). Therefore, primary, resource-intensive industries, which face sharply deteriorating geological conditions and escalating prices for equipment, should stop expanding in Ukraine and retrench. The new payment of user fees for natural resources, capital, and labor also favors the engineering and consumer branches against mineral and other primary industries in Ukraine. Given resource depletion and unfavorable geological conditions in Ukraine, the mineral and primary industries tend to be both labor- and material-intensive and, thus, are subject to high user fees on all counts.

---

[19] Interestingly, "the explanation for this progressive evolution, i.e., the mechanisms by which economic benefits are to be transferred from regions of high investment priority to outlying areas of lower potential, may seem strongly reminiscent of growth pole theory, now considered by some as ineffective." The theory also is strongly criticized by western radicals as "a tool for perpetuating regional inequality" (Bond 1987, 502–523).

Republic Self-Management

Republic self-management and accounting could have more substantial influence on regional economic structure if agreement could be reached on its controversial and contradictory features. The proposals in this case were galvanized by the issue of nationality and have had great emotional appeal to most Soviet citizens. The General Principles of the original Draft Program, published in March 1989, put forth a circumscribed autonomy for republics. Republics would gain jurisdiction over 36 percent of Soviet industrial production as a whole, as opposed to the mere 5 percent they controlled in that year. This share, however, would vary from 27 percent in the Russian Federation, to 42 percent in Ukraine, and as much as 75 percent in Moldova because of the differences in their industrial structure. The fuel-energy, metallurgical, and machine-building complexes, and most chemical branches, all of which are very important in Ukraine, still would be controlled by ministries in Moscow (*Economicheskaia gazeta* No. 12, March 1989, 10–11). Much greater authority concerning polluting firms supposedly would be given to republics. However, the republics' power over ecologically damaging plants that are under Moscow's control is not yet spelled out. (SWB-SU 1 April 1989, C3; FBIS-SOV Daily Reports 3 April 1989, 67).

Yet, pressures from republics to secure more radical autonomy from Moscow already have made the General Principles obsolete. Recently, more than half of the USSR republics, among them Ukraine, adopted resolutions to take control of most economic activity on their territories and to claim ownership of natural resources. In the case of Ukraine, all fuel-energy, metallurgical, machinery, chemical, and microbiological-medical industries are to be under the control of Kiev, according to no less an authority then the Deputy Director of the Ukrainian Gosplan (Baramykov and Nevelev 1990, 8–9. See also Mihalisko 1990, 17–19). Gorbachev's response, a new union treaty, would also go further in accommodating republic autonomy than the General Principles. Yet, Moscow still would execute a common policy on the fuel-energy, transport, and communication systems, on credit, finance, and monetary matters, on gold and diamond reserves and, of course, on defense and foreign affairs. The republics were promised the right to participate in these crucial, union-level issues but the central Soviet government has not explained how they will participate. In addition, while the proposed union treaty grants the republics full rights over their land and natural resources, it ominously states that the exercise of these rights cannot hinder Moscow in the realization of its own sovereignty (*Izvestiia* 24 November 1990, 1–2).

In and of itself, however, autonomy will not solve the economic problem of resource allocation and use, even in industries transferred to republic control. Centrally set prices still would give incorrect signals; innovation still would face the same disincentives as before. Particularly in Ukraine, a republic with the size and population of France, overall efficiency may not improve much, if at all. On the other hand, pressed by the upsurge of nationalism, the Ukrainian leadership must be more responsive to regional health and environmental concerns. Probably, it will push harder for higher value-added and consumer industries and will retain in the republic more of the food it produces.

Ironically, increased economic autonomy and power could also have highly irrational consequences. Shutting down unprofitable enterprises may become more difficult under republic control unless the plants are a clear danger to the public health. Coal miners everywhere resist pit closings. In the Donbas, the fight is on to preserve jobs in 21 collieries marked for liquidation, and a dozen such mines that were planned to be closed during the previous 15 years so far remain open (*Pravda* 8 July 1989, 2). The miners have become highly politicized, and the strike committees have turned into alternative power centers (*Rabochaia tribuna* 25 April 1990, 2). Marples (1990, 16–18; 11 August 1989, 10–12) has noted that the public hostility to nuclear power and the growing militancy of the miners in Ukraine have provided the boosters of the Donbas with new ammunition. Republic autonomy may in fact prolong the exploitation of a coal field that, as stated, already has produced more coal than any other field in Europe, and that should be phased out on grounds of human safety and economics. Yet, even substantial investment would only slow the inevitable decline of output from the Donbas. Whether such capital can be found today is doubtful. Substantial new investment in the coalfields, however, can only retard structural change in Ukraine, compounding the long-range problems of the republic.

Summary and Conclusion

As stated at the beginning of this paper, Ukraine historically has been the best-endowed and the most viable of all Soviet regions. Rich resources, favorable climatic conditions, and population potential have combined with the advantages of its location both inside the Soviet Union and in the world. The Soviet regime has drawn heavily on Ukraine's natural endowment, capitalizing on its location inside the USSR and, while it functioned, the Council of Mutual Economic Assistance (CMEA).

That resource-intensive, supply-oriented development policy, however, has saddled the republic with obsolete, environmentally destructive, and mostly unprofitable industries. The policy squandered investment needed for structural change and the improvement of social conditions. It also has turned Ukraine into a region with a severe energy deficit, burdened with nearly the highest fuel costs in the USSR. The increasingly obsolete economic structure and lack of integration into the world market is particularly poignant for Ukraine because in the Soviet Union only the Baltic states and St. Petersburg enjoy similar geographic and infrastructural advantages with respect to the global economy. After natural resources had played out their role in the economic growth of the region, proper use was not made of the potentially more beneficial endowment of location and infrastructure.

The issue of allocation in Ukraine is also important because of equity considerations and consumer welfare. As in the rest of the USSR, the household-municipal economy has been allowed to modernize its energy use to a much smaller degree than other sectors. The meager allocation of electricity, natural gas, and centralized heat, which have forced the consumer to rely on burdensome, polluting, solid fuels, is significant. First, in Ukraine per capita consumption of natural gas and supplies of centralized heat to households and to municipalities are far lower than in the European part of the Russian Federation on the whole, though they are higher than in Siberia, Kazakhstan, or Central Asia. This is so in the cities, despite Ukraine's economic importance, dense population, and the absence of serious physical obstacles (such as mountainous terrain or extensive swamps). Ukraine's milder climate alone is not enough to explain the lag between Ukraine and the rest of the European part of the Russian Federation. Second, the current energy shortage is the result of the extreme resource-intensity of industrial specialization imposed on Ukraine in the central plans. Until recently, these plans included very large interregional and international exports of energy, minerals, an other primary products, among them a significant part of the republic's natural gas for two decades. Such resource transfers without interest or severance payments violate both interregional and inter-generational equity. They represent serious political issues, particularly in multinational federal states.

The Soviet republics and the country's major regions are affected quite differently by the various aspects of perestroika (attempts at modernization, the recent stress on the consumer and the social sphere, the introduction of rent payments and user fees for resources and labor, and the devolution of regional economic rights). The macro-geographic situation of a region and its position in the administrative hierarchy are critical variables in the impact of attempted reform. If the movement towards a consumer-oriented mixed economy makes headway in the USSR, Ukraine should reap substantial advantages from its "resource" of geographic location, infrastructure, and population.

However, even before that and under more tortuous scenarios, republic status and large economic weight surely will place the future of Ukraine into its own hands to a large extent. The July 16, 1990 Declaration of Sovereignty by the Ukrainian Supreme Soviet announces local control over all land, water, air space, and mineral wealth and the exclusive right of their use. In the future, virtually all economic activity is to be controlled by Kiev, and the republic intends to manage its finances, taxes, and budget as well (Mihalisko 1990, 17–18; Baramykov and Nevelev 1990, 8–9).

In and of itself, such autonomy may not much improve efficiency. Indeed, may make it more difficult to phase out some obsolete primary industries and wind down much of the Donbas, as economic logic would dictate. A government in Kiev, however, will have to be far more responsive to regional health, environmental, and social concerns than was Gosplan in Moscow or the CPSU. The Kiev government will be held accountable for interregional resource flows and surely will capitalize on its surplus of food—as it should have capitalized but could not—on its past surpluses of coal, gas, and metallic and chemical minerals.

The creation of a market economy in the vast USSR, whatever geographic shape that country eventually may take, can happen only through hierarchies of cooperative regional markets. A successful economy will be possible only when regions can capitalize on shared values and exercise political control over resources and social arrangements. This is most certainly true in ethnically distinctive regions that are conscious of that distinctiveness. Economic reform agreements now must be hammered out between republics (in the case of the Russian Federation, between regions) concurrently with price reforms, the push towards private ownership, and other measures away from state socialism. Technically, such interrepublic agreements, on which Ukraine and the Russian Federation already have concluded a very general treaty (*Pravda Ukrainy* 21 November 1990, 1), will be terribly difficult to produce.[20] It is unlikely that the treaties will satisfy the abstract criteria of economic efficiency, either. Yet, without such republic/regional perestroika, economic restructuring itself has no chance.

References

Baramykov, E. and A. Nevelev. 1990. "Razvitie mezhrespublikanskikh sviazei v usloviiakh rasshireniia ekonomicheskoi samostoiatel'nosti soiuznykh respublik." *Ekonomika Sovetskoi Ukrainy* 5:3–12.

"Bezopasnost' truda." 1989. *Ugol' Ukrainy* 8:39–42.

Bond, Andrew R. 1987. "Spatial Dimensions of Gorbachev's Economic Strategy." *Soviet Geography* (September):490–523.

Cooper, Caron. 1989. "The Looming Crisis in the Soviet Oil Refining Sector." *PlanEcon Report V* 5 (3 February): 1–12.

Derzhkomstat URSR. *Narodne hospodarstvo Ukraïns'koï RSR. Statystychnyi shchorichnik.* Kiev. Various years.

Dienes, Leslie. 1977. "Minerals and Energy (Chapter 7)." In *The Ukraine within the USSR. An Economic Balance Sheet.* Edited by I. S. Koropeckyj, 155–89. New York.

_____. 1989. "*Perestroika* and the Slavic Regions." *Soviet Economy* 5 (3): 251–75.

Dienes, Leslie and Theodore Shabad. 1979. *The Soviet Energy System. Resource Use and Policies.* Washington.

Dikenshtein et al., eds. 1983. *Neftegazonosnye provintsii SSSR.* Moscow.

[20] With respect to such mutual agreements, Article 10 simply states that the treaty will guarantee that government organs, banks, territorial and municipal bodies, enterprises and other institutions, and individual producers can freely establish direct contractual relationships with their counterparts in other republics.

Dolins'kii, A. A. et al. 1986. "Rozvytok robit po vykorystanniu nyz'kosortnykh palyv," *Vistnik AN USSR* 10:37–41.

Ekonomicheskaia gazeta. Various issues.

Ekonomika i zhizn'. Various issues.

FBIS-SOV (Foreign Broadcasting Information Service-Soviet Union). 1989. *Daily Report* (3 April):50–70.

Fedorshcheva, A. N. and V. A. Alymov. 1986. *Ispol'zovanie osnovnykh fondov v promyshlennosti.* Kiev.

Gavrilenko, M. 1986. "Rasshiriat' mineral'no-syr'evuiu bazu." *Razvedka i okhrana nedr* 12.

Gerasimchuk, N. 1987. "Investitsionnaia politika: napravleniia i problemy perestroiki." *Ekonomika Sovetskoi Ukrainy* 6:6–14.

Goskomstat SSSR. 1988a. *Kapital'noe stroitel'stvo SSSR. Statisticheskii sbornik.* Moscow.

_____. 1988b. *Material'no-tekhnicheskoe obespechenie narodnogo khoziaistvo SSSR. Statisticheskii sbornik.* Moscow.

_____. *Narodnoe khoziaistvo SSSR. Statisticheskii ezhegodnik.* Moscow. Various issues.

Goskomstat USSR. *Narodnoe khoziaistvo Ukrainskoi SSR. Statisticheskii ezhegodnik.* Kiev. Various years.

Gudok (Moscow). Various issues.

HVG, *Heti Vilaggazdasag* (Budapest). Various issues.

Il'in, O. 1989. "Obosnovanie sootnosheniia gosudarstvennukh tsentralizovannykh i netsentralizovannykh kapital'nykh vlozhenii." *Planovoe khoziaistovo* 3:23–32.

Ishchuk, S. I. and L. M. Kiretskii. 1988. "Strukturnye sdvigi v promyshlennom komplekse Ukrainskoi SSR." *Ekonomicheskaia geografiia* 40:69–76.

Izvestiia (Moscow). Various issues.

JPRS-UEA (*Joint Publication Research Service. USSR, Economic Affairs*). Various issues.

Kortus, Bronislaw. 1964. "Donbas and Upper Silesia—A Comparative Analysis of the Industrial Regions." *Geographia Polonica* 2:183–92.

"Krupnye regiony v sisteme narodnogo khoziaistva SSSR. Materialy seminara." 1989. *Ekonomika Sovietskoi Ukrainy* 4:59–65.

Marples, David. 1988. "Working Conditions in Ukrainian Coal Mines Criticized." *Radio Liberty Research* (20 September):1–3.

―――――. 1989. "Emergence of Coal-Mining Crisis in the Donets Basin: Planning and Investment Decisions." Radio Liberty. *Report on the USSR* (11 August):11–12.

―――――. 1990. "Future of Donbas Coal Field Reviewed." Radio Liberty. *Report on the USSR* (May):16–18.

Melent'ev, L. A. and A. A. Makarov eds. 1983. *Energeticheskii kompleks SSSR.* Moscow.

Mihalisko, Kathleen. 1990. "Ukraine's Declaration of Sovereignty." Radio Liberty. *Report on the USSR* (27 July):17–19.

Molod' Ukrainy. 1989. (6 April).

North, Robert N. 1983. "Regional Economic Development in the USSR." *Soviet Natural Resources in the World Economy.* Edited by Robert G. Jensen, Theodore Shabad, and Arthur W. Wright, 97–123. Chicago.

"Novaia informatsiia Goskomstata SSSR." 1990. *Vestnik statistiki* 3:36–53.

Peterson, D. J. 1990. "A Wave of Environmentalism Shakes the Soviet Union." Radio Liberty. *Report on the USSR* (22 June):8–9.

Pravda (Moscow). Various issues.

Pravda Ukrainy (Kiev). Various issues.

Pronin, V. 1986. *Piatiletnii plan energetikov respubliki.* Kiev

―――――. 1989. "Razvitie energetiki Ukrainskoi SSR: problemy i perspektivy." *Ekonomika Sovietskoi Ukrainy* 11:12–20.

Rabochaia tribuna. 1990. (1 June):1.

Sagers, Matthew J. 1990. "Regional Industrialization Levels in 1985 and Recent Regional Trends in Industrialization in the USSR." Washington: U.S. Bureau of the Census, Center for International Research. Manuscript.

―――――. "News Notes." *Soviet Geography.* Various issues.

Sagers, Matthew J., Arild Moe, Milford Green, and Rune Castberg. 1988. "Prospects for Soviet Gas Exports: Opportunities and Constraints." *Soviet Geography* (December):881–908.

Sagers, Matthew J. and Theodore Shabad. 1990. *The Soviet Chemical Industry: A Geographic Perspective.* Washington: American Chemical Society.

Sagers, Matthew J. and Albina Tretyakova. 1987. *USSR: Energy Consumption in the Housing and Municipal Sector.* Center for International Research. Washington: U.S. Bureau of the Census. CIR Staff Paper No. 30.

_____. 1989. *USSR: Trends in Fuel and Energy Consumption by Sector and Fuel. 1970–1980.* Center for International Research. Washington: U.S. Bureau of the Census. CIR Staff Paper No. 36.

Shabad, Theodore. "News Notes." *Soviet Geography.* Various issues.

Sokolov, V. 1989. "Kontseptsiia." *Literaturnaia gazeta,* no. 31 (2 August): 10–11.

Solchanik, Roman. 1990. "Ukrainian Party Congress Supports State Sovereignty." Radio Liberty. *Report on the USSR.* (20 July): 21–22.

Sotsialisticheskaia industriia. Moscow. Various issues.

Starosel'skii, A., L. Kuz'minets and L. Kruteniuk. 1987. "Fondootdacha v chernoi metallurgii." *Ekonomika Sovetskoi Ukrainy,* no. 2 (February): 51–55.

Stroitel'naia industriia. Moscow. Various issues.

Sovetskaia kul'tura. 1986. (22 August):8.

SWB-SU *(Survey of World Broadcast)* (1 April 1989): C/1–4.

TASS and Radio Moscow. Various broadcasts and press releases.

Tereschenko, N. 1986. "Osnovnye napravlenie razvitiia chernoi metallurgii Ukrainskoi SSR v Dvenadtsatoi Piatiletke." *Ekonomika Sovetskoi Ukrainy,* no. 1 (January): 13–20.

Tolz, Vera. 1990. "The USSR This Week." Radio Liberty. *Report on the USSR* (13 April): 25–40.

Treivish, A. I. 1986. "Territorial Concentration of Economy and Population in the European Part of the USSR." *Soviet Geography* (November): 621–37.

Westwood, James T. 1985. "Soviet Maritime Strategy and Transport." *Naval War College Review*, 38, no. 6/sequence 312 (November-December): 42–49.

Zagumennov, M. and N. Sokolova. 1985. "Tendentsii v sebestoimosti dobychi uglia v Ukrainskoi SSR i nekotorye voprosy tsenoobrazovaniia na ugol'." *Ekonomika Sovetskoi Ukrainy* 9:57–60.

Figure 5-1. Share of Amortized Productive Fixed Assets in Ukrainian Industry (in percent of total)

Branch	1970	1975	1980	1985
All industry	28	31	37	43
Electrical power	23	28	33	36
Fuel industries	29	37	43	46
oil refining	21	32	35	54
coal industry	30	37	42	43
Ferrous metallurgy	32	42	44	53
iron ore	26	36	43	53
Nonferrous metallurgy	30	34	32	41
Chemical industries	23	25	33	44
Machine building	30	29	34	40
Building materials	23	31	40	46
Forest, wood products, cellulose, pulp, & paper	29	32	39	42
Glass and porcelain industries	30	33	43	48
Light industries	22	26	31	39
Food industries	26	29	35	39

Source: Gerasimchuk (1987, 5).

Figure 5-2. Shares of Industrial Investment in MBMW and Values Per Capita:
USSR and Republics

Shares of MBMW in USSR and Republics. (Percentages. Total industrial
investment for each period = 100)

	1971–75	1976–80	1981–85	1986–87
USSR	21.9	24.2	24.3	24.6
Russian Federation	24.5	26.0	25.3	25.1
Ukraine	21.8	26.0	27.5	30.0
Belarus	24.9	34.0	34.6	33.4

Per Capita Investment in MBMW
USSR and Republics* (rubles)

	1971–75	1976–80	1981–85	1986–87
USSR	171.6	232.0	266.7	127.7
Russian Federation	225.2	300.1	338.1	165.3
Ukraine	143.3	204.9	240.2	118.9
Belarus	157.9	348.4	337.1	160.4

*Per capita investment computed according to January 1 population estimates for
1974, 1984, and 1987 and the January 17, 1979 census

Source: Goskomstat SSSR (1988a, 53–56); and appropriate years of *Narkhoz SSSR*.

CHAPTER SIX
Capital Formation, Capital Stock, and Capital Productivity

David A. Dyker

Since the inception of the first five-year plan in 1929, gross fixed investment in the Soviet Union has been high as a proportion of national income. For most years the ratio has hovered around the 30 percent mark, which is comparable to those reported for dynamic Western economies such as the West German and Japanese in periods of high growth. To the extent that we can determine in the absence of comprehensive statistics and prices, the Ukrainian picture appears similar to the general Soviet picture. There has been a clear tendency for Ukraine to benefit from this situation, however. Figure 6-1 illustrates this tendency with data from some recent benchmark years. It is not possible to make any precise estimates of savings ratios by Soviet republic, but it is very unlikely that the Ukrainian savings ratio has been lower than the Soviet average, and quite probably it has been higher. Therefore, Ukraine has been a consistent exporter of capital to the rest of the Soviet Union. The Soviet system has, of course, precluded the payment of interest on that capital export. This does not in itself prove that Ukraine has been exploited by the rest of the Soviet Union—to draw any conclusions on that issue would require a complete picture of the Ukrainian balance of payments. The comparative aggregate investment data does, however, raise interesting questions that take us to the heart of the efficiency of the investment process in Ukraine, which is the central theme of this paper. Since proportionately less aggregate fixed investment has taken place in Ukraine, should we look for evidence that Ukraine somehow has obtained better value for each ruble's worth of investment? On the other hand, has the quality of the Ukrainian capital stock suffered in consequence?

Both of these questions will be addressed in this paper. First, however, we must look at the investment dimension in overall systemic terms and try to assess how it has contributed to the general pattern of Soviet-style development. Then we will investigate how the policies of present-day governments, republic and Soviet, aim to restructure that dimension in the future.

The General Systemic Context

It would not be an exaggeration to say that the fixed capital formation sector embodies all the strengths and weaknesses of the Soviet system of centralized planning. In fact, the story of the rise and fall of the Soviet planning system could be told through the investment dimension. Since the inception of the first five-year plan at the end of 1928, that dimension has been dominated by a pattern of extensive investment, within the constraints of broadly defined sectoral priorities. Decisions on project starts have been based on development strategy rather than on any fine calculation of likely returns, and the construction of new projects has been on simultaneous with the patching-up of old, obsolete production capacities, as organizations at all levels have tried to fulfill of exacting output targets. These characteristics alone would have been enough to create numerous problems, which can be summed up in terms of *raspylenie sredstv*—too many projects simultaneously under construction, leading in turn to cost hikes and grossly excessive lead times. This kind of peculiarly Soviet efficiency problem has, however, been exacerbated by secondary characteristics of the system, in particular by organizational/autarkical tendencies at the ministry/enterprise level (Dyker 1983).

It is hardly surprising, then, to discover that the trend in Soviet capital productivity has been uniformly downward from the beginning of the period of central planning (Bergson 1978, 122). Yet there is another side to the coin. In the initial state of Soviet industrialization when there was an abundance of cheap labor and raw materials, extensive investment did provide a powerful impetus to mobilize of those abundant resources to support an extensive development strategy. That, in a nutshell, is why the Soviet economy was able to grow so fast in the absence of any generalized procedures for ensuring investment efficiency.

By the late 1950s and early 1960s, however, the sources of cheap labor and raw materials were drying up, while the growing complexity of the Soviet economy exacerbated perennial cost-efficiency problems in the investment sector. The rate of decline of capital productivity accelerated. This acceleration was briefly halted by the 1965 planning reform, which by introducing a capital charge forced enterprise directors to get rid of some of their extensive collections of equipment. By the early 1970s, as the reforms were abandoned, the accelerated downward trend returned with a vengeance, however. Even more significantly, the rate of growth of total productivity fell to around zero (Greenslade 1976, 279). Investment had ceased to fulfill its traditional role in mobilizing labor and raw materials and had failed to make the necessary transition to mobilize technical progress. One of the most damning features of Gorbachev's perestroika campaign is that absolutely nothing has been achieved in the area of either capital productivity or total productivity. The former continues to fall, the latter, at best, to stagnate (Gregory and Stuart 1990, 370).

The Organizational Efficiency Problem in Ukrainian Perspective

Soviet investment strategy has provided little scope for regional variation. The implementation (and, to a degree, the conception) of investment plans has been entrusted to ministries, usually union ministries in the case of key industrial sectors. The granting of executive powers in the area of infrastructural investment to republican councils of ministers might have been more important if infrastructural investment had carried a higher priority. Collective farm investment—very important for Ukraine—has been formally the business of the kolkhozes, but in practice has been dominated by Moscow just as much as industrial, or sovkhoz investment. Some republics, notably the Central Asian, have been characterized by a distinctive sectoral structure of investment—in the Central Asian case the structure was determined by regional specialization in a specific industrial crop, cotton. That pattern of specialization was as much a decision of Moscow as any of the decisions on key industrial developments of the 1930s, however. Indeed, popular revolt against the excesses of imposed monoculture is one of the main elements in the political turmoil currently unfolding in Central Asia.

For all that, cotton-growing and its supporting sectors such as irrigation, are sufficiently unique to make it dangerous to compare directly investment efficiency indicators between Central Asia and, say, the European Soviet Union. In the case of Ukraine there is no such problem. A major center of traditional heavy industry, a major energy producer, and a key grain-growing area, Ukraine does represent a microcosm of the Soviet economy—for better or worse. So there is no difficulty in directly comparing key indicators of organizational efficiency between Ukraine and the Soviet Union as a whole.

The overall picture, represented in Figure 6-2, is clearly delineated. Over the past 20 years the Ukrainian construction complex has done consistently better than the Soviet average in terms of completing projects and maximizing the active component within total investment. The record of Ukrainian agriculture on completions is particularly good, with volumes of unfinished construction actually being steadily reduced throughout the early and mid-1980s. (Bear in mind that if we compared figures for Ukraine and the rest of the Soviet Union, the contrast would be much sharper.) Gorbachev's ill-advised *uskorenie* policy of the early perestroika period produced a predictable worsening of rates of completion at both Ukrainian and Soviet levels. Interestingly, however, Ukrainian industry seems to have been hit by the *uskorenie* factor as early as 1985, while for the Soviet Union as a whole the main impact came, more predictably, in 1986.

The Construction and Design Sectors in Ukraine

Despite Moscow's dominance in articulating and executing investment plans and despite the typical nature of Ukraine's economic structure, there have been significant differences in levels of organizational efficiency between the republic and the Soviet Union. Does the pattern of organization of design (consultant engineering/architecture) and building in Ukraine explain why?

At first glance, the Soviet construction industry prior to 1986 was as highly centralized as any industrial sector. Bricks-and-mortar construction work was dominated by a number of sectorally specialized ministries: the Ministry of Construction (engineering, light industry, and the food industry), the Ministry of Industrial Construction (chemicals, oil-processing, and petrochemicals), the Ministry for Heavy Industrial Construction (coal and metallurgy), and others. The installation of high-technology and precision equipment, especially imported, was the preserve of the Ministry for Installation and Special Construction Work (Minmontazhspetsstroi,) which possessed a union-wide network of technologically specialized main administrations (*glavki*) and trusts.

In practice, a degree of regional specialization dovetailed into this structure. The main construction ministries worked mainly in the regions dominated by their sectors, so that the Ministry of Industrial Construction operated predominantly in the oil-rich regions of the Volga–Urals, while the Ministry for Heavy Industrial Construction concentrated on Ukraine and southwest Siberia. These were all union-republican ministries, with corresponding republican ministries existing for some, but not all union republics. Even Minmontazhspetsstroi had, not surprisingly, region-specific units at the lowest level.

A 1986 reform effectively reversed the pattern of specialization among the basic, all-union construction ministries. Thus, the Ministry of Heavy Industrial Construction was replaced by Miniugstroi (the Ministry of Construction for the South), the Ministry of Industrial Construction by Minuralsibstroi (the Ministry of Construction for the Urals and Siberia), and the Ministry of Construction by Minsev-zapstroi (the Ministry of Construction for the North and West). The exact territorial coverage of the Ministry of Construction for the South has not been confirmed, but Ukraine must figure very prominently within it. In addition, the 1986 reform created an independent republican ministry of construction for each republic. Thus, since 1986 the Ukrainian Ministry of Construction has played an important role in industrial construction within the republic (Borisovskii 1988). As part of the same package, the Ministry of Installation and Special Construction was transformed into a union-republic basis, giving each republic its own Minmontazhspetsstroi. The old system of intermediate administration based on *glavki* was replaced by a network of territorial and functionally specialized associations. While this reform did represent a real shift towards the territorial principle, it was primarily a rationalization of something that had always been imposed on the building industry by the very nature of its work.

In addition to the major network of building organizations, there have always been numerous small building organizations that were formally subordinate to non-construction organizations. This is a direct result of the general tendency to organizational autarky (Dyker 1983, chapter 4).

The structure of design is much more amorphous than that of construction. There is no Ministry of Design, and design organizations may be subordinate to Gosstroi, the State Construction Committee, or to individual ministries or Councils of Ministers. Since 1965, Soviet government policy towards the sector has been dominated by attempts to bring some rationalization to the sector, such as by building up integrated design-construction associations.

Critiques of design and construction organizations have focused on their excessive concern with fulfilling quantitative targets to the detriment of qualitative, including technological targets (Dyker 1983). This is a universal tendency imposed by the nature of central planning; there is no reason to believe that it might vary in intensity from one region to another. Design and construction also have been characterized by fragmentation and excessive smallness, however, with attendant losses of economies of information and scale, as well as low productivity. Is the situation any better or any worse in Ukraine? Figure 6-3 presents some basic statistics on the two sectors at the Ukrainian and Soviet levels. The picture comes through most clearly in relation to design organizations. There are relatively few *proektnye organizatsii* (design organizations) in Ukraine. Their number has been stable at 15 to 16 percent of the total number of design organizations in the country, lower than Ukraine's contribution to the Soviet national income by any calculation. Around half of these organizations are subordinate to the Ukrainian government (the proportion did rise significantly in 1988). The rest presumably are branches of all-union (mainly Moscow-based) organizations. The picture is more starkly delineated if we look at the volume of design work done by these organizations. In 1970 it amounted to 5.7 percent of the Soviet total. By 1986 the figure had risen to 6.6 percent. (This assumes that comparable prices really are comparable.) Clearly, then, the operating scale of design organizations in Ukraine has been small, regardless of subordination. Perhaps more important, the great bulk of design work for Ukrainian clients has been done by design organizations without so much as an office inside the republic. There is no evidence that this has damaged investment efficiency in Ukraine as such. However, it is interesting that there was a substantial increase in the amount of design work done in Ukraine in 1988, just as the pace of reform began to accelerate.

The pattern in construction is more complicated. As Figure 6-3 shows, Ukraine tends to have a slightly higher proportion of building organizations subordinate to non-construction ministries, but the difference is trivial. Have there been any significant variations in the pattern of scale of operations? Figure 6-4 provides a picture of the size distribution of construction organizations at the republic and all-union level. For all building organizations, the differences are trivial. For building trusts there was a significantly (but not markedly) greater concentration of units in the 18 to 50 million ruble range in Ukraine in 1986. By 1988 this had evolved into a significantly higher share of trusts in the 50-plus million ruble range (*Narkhoz Ukrainy* 1988, 385). Assuming that relatively small Soviet building organizations are of suboptimal size from a scale-economies point of view, which all available evidence on the structure of the Soviet building industry points to, it can be argued that the size distribution of this key subgroup of Ukrainian building enterprises has been nearer the optimum than is the case for the Soviet Union as a whole. Again, if we were to compare Ukraine with the rest of the Soviet Union, we would find this picture much more sharply delineated.

One or two other comparable efficiency indicators for the construction industry are available. If we take the coverage of the brigade system (involving the setting-up of financially autonomous work teams) as an indicator of the extent of decentralizing reform in the period to 1986, we find very little difference between the Ukrainian and Soviet figures. This corresponds to the regional profile of economic policy in relation to construction in the late 1970s and early 1980s. Certain republics—Belarus and Lithuania being perhaps the most prominent—were picked out as laboratories for planning reform in construction. Ukraine was not one of the republics chosen. Again, comparing the cost structure on the republic and the Soviet levels reveals no clue to any Ukrainian lead in efficiency.

Aside from the fact that Ukrainian building organizations may on the average be marginally nearer optimal size than the rest of the Soviet Union, published statistics shed little light on why organizations are better at completing projects than building organizations elsewhere in the Soviet Union. In the end, it may come down to the simple fact that there has always been a de facto Ukrainian ministry of construction.

Investment Efficiency—A Broader Approach

Up to now we have looked only at the efficiency of the investment process narrowly defined, without taking the fundamental issue of project choice into account. Now we will take a wider view, assessing what the Ukrainian economy actually has gotten out of investment activity in the final balance. We will assess, in Soviet terminology, the effectiveness of investment in the republic. For this purpose we utilize the incremental capital-output ratio (ICOR)— a crude indicator, but sanctioned by many years of UN usage. Figure 6-5 presents ICOR trends for Ukraine and the Soviet Union since 1970. The methodological difficulties with these figures are immense.

Purely conceptual problems apart, the calculations are fraught with all the usual Soviet statistical pitfalls. They are based on official Soviet figures for growth in national income, which certainly are inflated, though by how much remains the subject of controversy. The calculations attempt to bridge the gap between figures in comparable prices and figures in current prices. In any event, all the raw data are based on Soviet price weights, which in many cases yield grossly distorted valuations of Soviet goods and assets. On that basis, these ICORs can be taken as only the roughest indication of trends in returns on investment in the republic and at the Soviet level. Thus, the differences that appear between the figures at the two levels for the decade 1971 to 1980 are not significant enough to bear the weight of any real hypothesis. It is interesting that Ukraine does not seem to have shared in the general kick in the ICOR reported for the early 1980s. There is no reason to question the real content of that kick. This is the period in which the policies of the Brezhnev regime finally brought the Soviet economy to a near-standstill in economic growth, while the ratio of investment to national income actually rose slightly. It may be significant that Ukraine did not receive its fair share of the great white-elephant projects of the Brezhnev period—the non-Black Earth Program, the Baikal-Amur Mainline (BAM), and so on. While all these projects were initiated in the 1970s, the slowness of the Soviet investment process ensured that they were still absorbing huge, possibly growing volumes of resources in the early 1980s. In this respect at least, it may have been better to be a step-child than a favorite son in the period of *zastoi* (stagnation).

However, the overwhelming impression from Figure 6-5 is of the staggeringly poor rate of return on investment at both levels throughout the period under consideration. Ukraine may have done better than the Soviet Union as a whole in stopping the ICOR from running away in the early 1980s, but ICORs of 7 to 8 are extremely high by international standards. We should bear in mind that recalculating these ICORs in terms of Western or alternative Soviet figures for growth in national income would more or less double them in each case. In terms of overall investment effectiveness, then, being Ukrainian has not made a great deal of difference. Russia, Ukraine, the Baltic republics, and all the rest of the regions of the USSR have suffered deeply from a system of investment planning that has offered medals to people who spend money and scant respect to those who cut costs and get the job done.

Looking to the Future—The Organizational Legacy

That is all in the past, though. Central planning has been abandoned, and a new treaty of union is in the works that would recognize Ukrainian sovereignty. There would seem to be no major obstacles to building a rational market economy in Ukraine capable of handling the investment and construction sector—with whatever international assistance might be required—to turn the cult of the gross into the cult of the cost-effective.

Of course in practice it is not so simple. Central planning may have been abandoned in the Soviet Union but as yet nothing has taken its place, and the story we read from contemporary plan-fulfillment reports on the investment sector sounds uncannily like the stories we read 10 years ago. Yet, Gorbachev has done something to try to reform the sector. We already have alluded to the ministerial reorganization in 1986. That was part of a series of measures from the middle 1980s that also included attempts, from 1985 on, to increase the size of the average building trust to achieve a better approximation to the optimal scale of operations and provide a sounder basis for transition to full self-financing. At sub-trust level, the collective contract, as developed in agriculture, was programmed to provide a more effective incentive system at the level of the building site (Balakin 1988). As part of the transition from the traditional system of passive banking based on the monopoly of Gosbank and Stroibank (Construction Bank) to a more active, pluralistic system, Stroibank was abolished in

July 1987. The bulk of its business was taken over by a new Bank for Industrial Construction (Promstroibank).

These measures had little impact on patterns of investment activity. The organizational hierarchy of the construction industry remained fragmented and overly complex:

> What they did essentially was to create construction committees in cities and provinces. Under this dispensation the urgent business of the day can only be addressed through the preparation of appropriate decrees and decisions, the determination of staffing levels, salaries and privileges, and also through designation of individuals for specific jobs (as a rule, with even higher salaries, because these committees have the status of all-union ministries). But whenever it comes to any fundamental transformation of production structures, all the enthusiasm of these executives and specialists just disappears, and everything remains as before. (Kaplan 1989, 10)

As of 1989, only 40 percent of the annual volume of construction work in the country was under the jurisdiction of Gosstroi and the main construction ministries (Ivanov 1989, 11). The scale of operations of the average building trust remained at least 25 percent too small. Even where optimal scale was reached, anomalies in the pricing system ensured that many construction organizations continued to post losses, making a transition to full self-financing impossible (Balakin 1988, 62). As if to underscore the degree of indecision on the crucial pricing dimension, the capital charge was abolished for construction organizations in 1986 and then reinstated in 1988 (Timofeev 1989, 79). Success-indicator changes introduced in 1986 abolished the marketable output indicator (a variant of Kosygin's aggregate sales indicator) but set nothing in its place, effectively putting construction organizations back on gross output, the traditional Stalinist success indicator. The pattern of settling accounts between contractor and client was the same: "It changed at some point in the 1960s, was subsequently many times 'perfected,' and in 1986 we arrived, in practical terms, back at the position of 20 to 30 years ago" (*Ogon'* 1989, 13). Again, the old quality coefficients for construction were abolished in 1986 without anything being put in their place (Merkin 1989, 17). The introduction in 1987 of the principle of negotiated prices between client and contractor was a significant step forward, but its impact was dissipated by the inability of the authorities to give the client real power to bargain over things such as lead-times, technology, and so on. (Volosatov 1990, 50–51). Meanwhile, it seems that the degree of "petty tutelage" over building enterprises has not diminished at all. As of 1989, those enterprises still were receiving a total of 6,888 communiques from higher authorities, which required them to complete 160 quarterly forms and 258 more forms of varying frequency (Betrozgov 1989, 72).

While design organizations had been a major target of the Leningrad system, aimed at producing sharp cuts in staffing levels by allowing organizations and their workers to benefit directly in financial terms from such economies (Dyker 1987, 65), they stood accused in 1989 of continuing "to churn out obsolescent design documentation, based on the heaviest possible building elements and the most expensive materials" (Merkin 1989, 15). Design offices remained largely non-computerized (Bulgakov 1989, 29). In 1988, 40 percent of all designs were sent back to the client ministries for correction by *ekspertiza*, the design watchdog organization (Bulgakov 1989, 14). At the same time, the development of integrated design-construction associations still had not really taken off outside the residential building sphere, and this was proving a serious obstacle to the development of the turn-key project approach to investment plan implementation ("O perestroike upravleniia..." 1989, 36). In housing construction itself, the work of design-construction associations reportedly was severely hampered by their subordination to local soviets (Mikhel' 1989, 30). Held back by inadequate legislation and conservative-minded staff members, the "new" investment bank has tended to continue the tradition of Stroibank in its relations with clients— interfering on details and ignoring the big issues of medium- and long-term profitability (Zaichenko and Sharov 1989; Tsypkin 1989). Under the old dispensation the latter had, of course, been strictly the preserve of the planners.

Perhaps even more telling was the failure of the 1986 measures to have any impact on the key interstitial weaknesses of the Soviet investment-planning system. In particular, it seems that the essential nature of planning documents did not change at all:

Unreal title "lines" [properly "Title lists"—the short document that outlines the key technical characteristics of an investment project and provides access to allocation certificates] can be used as the basis for obtaining perfectly real building materials and using them, at least to some extent, on already-started projects for which these materials have been allocated in inadequate quantities...against norms for economizing on use of materials and planned levels of utilization of production capacity in the building and building materials industries of 100 percent and [!] more. (Kolosov 1989, 89)

Again, on the crucial issue of *tekhniko-ekonomicheskie obosnovaniia* (TEO)— feasibility studies:

When some of our economists base their arguments on the market as it exists in capitalist countries, they fail to take account of the fact that that market is based on a comprehensive and wide-ranging informational network, and a complex of highly specialized engineering firms, covering the whole gamut of production technology, and keeping right up to date on all technological innovations, on automation, and on economic trends. This makes it possible for industrial firms to avoid fatal errors in choosing where to invest their capital.... It is vital that Gosplan USSR, together with the State Committee for Science and Technology and the environmental services should work out and have approved at governmental level a fundamentally new methodology for the elaboration of feasibility studies. That task should be entrusted to *engineering firms* [emphasis added]. (Iakovlev 1989, 41, 43)

In September 1989, the Soviet government promulgated yet another set of measures regulating the planning and management of capital investment. The main elements in this new legislation follow:

1. From 1990 success indicators, calculating profit and settling accounts must be based on "finished construction output" (*gotovaia stroitel'naia produktsiia*). For projects with a lead-time of more than a year, finished construction output may be reckoned in terms of operational complexes within the project as a whole. Those with lead times of more than two years may be reckoned in terms of completed buildings or installations.
2. Work in progress must be financed by the construction organizations' own resources and bank credit. Bank credit must be advanced on the basis of the estimated cost of construction, with interest on those credits counted as part of total estimates. Bank credit for construction must be financed on the basis of the funds that clients otherwise would have had to pay in advances, with the banks paying an annual rate of interest of 0.5 percent for the use of these funds.

3. The turn-key approach to project planning must be introduced for residential and infrastructural investment and also brought in selectively in the production-investment sphere. There must be special bonuses for turn-key projects completed on time or ahead of time. Gossnab (State Supply Committee) and Gosplan will work out a special system for supplying materials to turn-key projects.
4. Above-norm volumes of unfinished construction will be penalized at the rate of 6 percent annually. Failure to complete projects on time will incur the same penalty in cases where the finance comes from enterprise funds. In the case of centralized investments, the penalty for missing completion dates is 0.5 percent per month.
5. For design organizations, full payment of completion bonuses will only be made if the project reaches full-capacity production levels within the normed period.
6. The capital charge must be waived for production projects completed ahead of time, that is, for the period up to their planned date of operation, and the funds thus made available will be shared among the organizations involved ('O nekotorykh...' 1989).

This is a disappointing package. It has good elements, but even those mostly derive from the more positive reform attempts of the 1970s. Taken as a whole, the measures are hopelessly fussy and centralist, even for projects financed from enterprise profits, and simply do not address the basic issue of how the market mechanism can be brought into this difficult area. Indeed, the style of the package reeks of Brezhnevite *sovershenstvovanie* (perfecting)— strikingly, that word still appears again and again in contemporary literature on investment and construction problems. It simply ignores the issue of what *radical reform* can mean in the given context.

Has Ukraine fared any better than the Soviet Union as a whole in this respect? As we saw, the republic was not singled out as an investment planning laboratory in the Brezhnev days. Significantly, perhaps, reports on the implementation of the 1986 measures in Ukraine speak ominously of the "further perfecting" of the system (Malyshevskii 1988). More significantly, they bear witness to the continued presence of all the classic problems of Soviet investment planning. In particular, they speak eloquently of the eternal theme of petty tutelage. Here, for instance, is a description of the system of quality and efficiency incentives introduced, under the rubric of the collective contract, in the Chernovitsstroi trust of the Ukrainian Ministry of Construction in 1987:

> The evaluation of each function is carried out on the basis of fractions of a point, e.g. 0.1, 0.15 etc. If a particular indicator is fulfilled, the corresponding point is awarded—if it is not fulfilled, a zero is entered. The basic indicators are: profit, costs, volume of contractual work by technological stages and complexes, labor productivity, growth of labor productivity in relation to growth in wages, design improvements, cost-cutting in relation to contracted price. (Podol'skii 1988, 45)

However laudable these goals, the nightmare of form-filling it implies would be enough to demoralize the most dynamic manager.

Recent reports also confirm the continued prevalence of chronic supply problems—in design as well as construction (Podol'skii 1988, 48; Dubrova 1988, 55). These problems include plans that often bear no resemblance to real production possibilities (Podol'skii 1988, 47) and capital stock that consists, to a substantial extent, of obsolete equipment that has been totally written off but not scrapped (Malyshevskii 1988, 43). As much as 31.9 percent of the total stock of equipment of the Ukrainian building industry comes into this category (Samizdat, 39). As at the Soviet level, part of the reason for the recalcitrance of these problems is the failure of pricing policy to provide building enterprises with the financial basis to renew their capital stock systematically. Thus, in 1987 total investment in the Ukrainian building industry was 9.5 percent *less* than total amortization allowances (Samizdat, 48). Finally, extension of the collective contract system has gone very slowly (Podol'skii 1988, 48). One area where some progress has been made is that of reorganizing production capacities and cutting staffing levels, particularly at the administrative level (Malyshevskii 1988, 42; Velichko 1988, 51). Another is that of uninstalled equipment. Between 1986 and 1987, stocks of uninstalled equipment in Ukraine fell by 8.5 percent (though they still amounted to 13 to 15 percent of total net investment in 1987). This improvement was wholly due to increases in the rate of installation of equipment (Samizdat, 50–54), which must have been the major factor in the marginal improvement in Ukraine's operationalization coefficient in 1987. The general impression is of a system still locked in the patterns of the period of extensive development, however. No specific material on the implementation of the 1989 measures in Ukraine is available, but the 1990 fulfillment reports suggest that nothing much has changed.

What lies behind this sorry tale of reform manqué? In truth the riddle is not so hard to solve. It was naive of Gorbachev (grossly naive of the senior economic advisor at the time, Abel Aganbegian) to believe that they could engineer fundamental reform of the Soviet economy while simultaneously increasing growth rates. In the case under review, pursuing the policy of *uskorenie* necessarily required maintaining extreme pressure on the building industry, which in turn resulted in unrealistic plans, supply blockages, and petty tutelage. Just how much strain *uskorenie* put on the Ukrainian building industry is confirmed by that fact that expenditure on the repair of (superannuated) equipment rose dramatically, from 30.3 percent in 1986 to 58.3 percent in 1987 (Samizdat, 38). The policy of switching the emphasis from the budget to retained profits as a source of investment finance tended, in this context, to increase the tension in the system because it made it possible for enterprise managers, replete with rubles, to bid away resources from budget-financed projects, leaving these projects more vulnerable to overstretch factors than ever.

Looking to the Future—The Capital Stock Legacy

When Soviet leaders talk of the need to reconstruct the Soviet economy they are not, of course, speaking only of a reconstruction of the planning system. The most concrete task of perestroika is to reconstruct a capital stock that has been grossly distorted by 60 years of studied disregard for market criteria in investment decision making, and by a senseless extension of the strategy of extensive growth into the period of labor shortage. Nowhere is this distortion of the capital stock more marked than in Ukraine.

We already mentioned the problem of obsolete equipment, written off but unscrapped, in relation to the building industry. While construction has been infected by this characteristically Soviet disease, it is not its only victim, however. An estimated 24 percent of the total production fixed capital of the republic is superannuated (Samizdat, 42). To put this into perspective, the average service life of production fixed capital in Ukraine is 34 years, 9 years more than the norm (a Soviet norm, which is more than twice corresponding norms of Western industrialized countries). As much as 23 percent of total production fixed capital stock has been in service for more than 20 years (Samizdat, 36). The average age of elements of production fixed capital at the end of 1987 was 11.7 years (Samizdat, 37). To a degree, such average figures understate the extent of the problem, because a significant proportion of the Ukrainian capital stock is retired early, mainly because of quality problems (Samizdat, 43). In 1987, fully 33 percent of total production fixed investment in Ukraine went on major (capital) repair of the existing capital stock, as compared to under 20 percent for the period of 1966 to 1970. It is estimated that about 20 percent of all repairs (3 billion rubles) went on the repair of superannuated equipment (Samizdat, 38). The critical importance of these trends for growth patterns is evident:

> The predominantly extensive mode of development of production demanded high rates of growth of production fixed capital, and these were accompanied by extremely low rates of scrapping.... There is an urgent need to liquidate superannuated fixed capital in the economy, so as to cut out losses on their maintenance, and free resources for the effective exploitation of new capacities which are at present under-utilized *as a result of shortage of labor and materials.* (Samizdat, 33, 50; emphasis added)

This problem is a general Soviet problem. In 1985, the proportion of capital stock written off in the Soviet Union as a whole came to 74 percent of total operationalization of new capacity, compared to 65.4 percent for the United States. It is a particularly serious problem in Ukraine, where the corresponding figure was 85.8 percent. The figure for industry alone in Ukraine was as high as 105.9 percent. (Samizdat, 27-8). Thus, in Ukrainian industry the rate of effective new investment is simply not keeping pace with the rate at which the capital stock is becoming wholly obsolete, whether or not it is being retired from service. The practice of keeping written-off capital stock in service imposes a double burden on the Ukrainian economy. On one hand, it condemns the economy to in-built obsolescence. On the other hand, the funds available for genuine replacement investment have been cut back because of the practice of continuing to impose amortization charges in respect of capital stock fully written off but still in service. Until 1989, capital repairs and renovation were supposed to be financed by ministries out of the funds accumulated at ministerial level on the basis of enterprise depreciation charges, with running repairs treated as a current cost. In practice, the distinction between the two types of repair was treated arbitrarily, leaving the ministries broad scope for the manipulation of aggregate investment flows. A decision made August 13, 1989 abolished the distinction between running and capital repairs, presumably to bring amortization regulations into line with the self-financing package (*Normativy...* 1990). This helps to explain why net investment in production capacities in Ukraine in 1987 was just 10.09 percent of total net investment in production capacities for the USSR as a whole. Ukraine's share in NMP produced in the same year was 16.8 percent (Samizdat, 29). The picture that emerged from looking at gross investment figures is, therefore, strikingly highlighted when we use purer indicators of increments to capital stock.

Looking to the Future—The Prospects for Real Reconstruction

The author of *Samizdat* estimates that it will take at least eight years to eliminate superannuated, obsolete equipment from the Ukrainian economy, assuming that investment ratios in the republic are allowed to fall no further (p. 42), which, given current pressures for improved consumption, may be a fairly optimistic assumption. This estimate relegates the completion of effective reconstruction of the capital stock to the final years of this century. It is important to note that this is a conservative estimate of the likely lead time for comprehensive reconstruction. The *Samizdat* author does not attack the problem of structural distortion in the Ukrainian economy or address the fact that much relatively new capital equipment in the Soviet economy is already obsolete.

Abel Aganbegian, former chief economic adviser to Gorbachev, provides some striking data on the essential problem of obsolescence in the Soviet capital stock as a whole (Aganbegian 1989, 12–13). If plans are fulfilled, which they certainly will not be, the rate of renewal of the total equipment part of the Soviet economy will barely reach the average level for developed industrial countries (6 to 8 percent) over the period of 1986 to 1990. So far, Aganbegian is merely confirming what the Ukrainian *Samizdat* author says. Much more disturbing, a large proportion of the replacement that does take place will simply consolidate the existing East-West technology gap. A survey conducted in 1985 by the Bureau for Machine Building estimated that 71 percent of the equipment produced by the Soviet engineering industry is obsolete. A subsequent study done by the Institute of Economics and Research and Development Forecasting of the Academy of Sciences painted an even more pessimistic picture, though Aganbegian cites no exact figures. If "metal intensity" is used as a crude indicator of obsolescence, the Soviet plan to cut that indicator by 50 percent by the year 2000 would bring the Soviet Union to the contemporary level of metal intensity of the U.S.—by no means the world leader in this dimension. Clearly, restructuring that merely builds in more obsolescence is useless.

On the best assumptions, then, the Ukrainian capital stock is unlikely to arrive at a new, technologically satisfactory balance much before the early years of the next century. Furthermore, the path towards that new balance will be difficult to pick out. Introducing market criteria and market pressures into the investment process is absolutely essential to achieve effective technological up-dating. It would be foolish to believe that the market can do the whole job. The extent of industrial reorganization required is so enormous that it would tax the capacities of the strongest and most sophisticated capital markets in the world to implement it. To make things more difficult, Ukraine has no capital market in place and is unlikely to have one until the bulk of the required reorganization has already been completed. A major role for the state as entrepreneur seems unavoidable. But what kind of state will it be? Will it be a reformed Soviet state? Will it be wholly new, wholly independent Ukrainian state? Or, will it be a sovereign, Ukrainian state within the framework of a new Soviet treaty of union? At present, the last of these is perhaps the most likely scenario. It is vital to begin thinking about how such a confederal arrangement would affect the crucial process of modernizing and rationalizing the role of the state in the economic policy sphere, surely the most important single economic issue in Ukraine, as in every other country of Eastern Europe.

References

Aganbegian, A. 1989. "O kontseptsii sotsial'no-ekonomicheskogo razvitiia na perspektivu," *Izvestiia Akademii nauk SSSR, Seriia ekonomicheskaia* 1.

Balakin, V. A. 1988. "Uglubliat' perestroiku upravleniia i khoziaistvennogo mekhanizma v stroitel'nom komplekse." *Ekonomika stroitel'stva* 1:56–66.

Bergson, A. 1978. *Productivity and the Social System—the USSR and the West*. Cambridge, Massachusetts.

Betrozgov, V. T. 1989. "Problemy razvitiia i povysheniia effektivnosti investitsionnogo kompleksa strany." *Ekonomika stroitel'stva* 10:67–74.

Borisovskii, V. Z. 1988. "Rubezhi ukrainskikh stroitelei." *Ekonomika stroitel'stva* 1:26–35.

Bulgakov, S. N. 1989. "Stroitel'noe proektirovanie—na novyi kachestvennyi uroven'." *Ekonomika stroitel'stva* 12:8–21.

Dubrova, E. P. 1988. "Perestroika v institute." *Ekonomika stroitel'stva* 1:52–55.

Dyker, D. A. 1983. *The Process of Investment in the Soviet Union*. Cambridge.

_____. 1987. "Industrial planning; forwards or sideways?" *The Soviet Union under Gorbachev. Prospects for Reform*. Edited by Dyker. London.

Goskomstat SSSR. 1987. *Narodnoe khoziaistvo SSSR za 70 let*. Moscow.

_____. 1989. *Narodnoe khoziaistvo SSSR v 1988 godu*. Moscow.

Goskomstat USSR. 1987. *Narodnoe khoziaistvo Ukrainskoi SSR za 70 let*. Kiev.

_____. 1989. *Narodnoe khoziaistvo Ukrainskoi SSR v 1988 godu*. Kiev.

Greenslade, R. 1976. "The Real National Product of the USSR 1950–75." In *Soviet Economy in a New Perspective*. Joint Economic Committee, U.S. Congress, Washington.

Gregory, P. and R. Stuart. 1990. *Soviet Economic Structure and Performance*. 4th ed. New York.

Iakovlev, A. M 1989. "Puti korennoi perestroiki upravleniia investitsionnym protsessom v narodnom khoziaistve." *Ekonomika stroitel'stva* 10:40–47.

Ivanov, A. P. 1989. "V mezhotraslevoi nauchno-issledovatel'skoi assotsiatsii ekonomiki stroitel'nogo kompleksa SSSR." *Ekonomika stroitel'stva* 10:4–11.

Kaplan, L. M. 1989. "Osnovnye napravleniia perestroiki khoziaistvennogo mekhanizma v investitsionnogo komplekse." *Ekonomika stroitel'stva* 11:3–11

Kolosov, V. P. 1989. "Organizatsiia upravleniia stroitel'stvom v sisteme mer po sovershenstvovaniiu investitsionnogo protsessa." *Ekonomika stroitel'stva* 10:88–95.

Malyshevskii, G. D. 1988. "Uchimsia schitat' den'gi." *Ekonomika stroitel'stva* 1:41–43.

Merkin, R. M. 1989. "Napravleniia radikal'noi perestroiki investitsionnoi deiatel'nosti i khoziaistvennogo mekhanizma investitsionnoi sfery." *Ekonomika stroitel'stva* 10:12–28.

Mikhel', A. V. 1989. "Sovershenstvovanie khoziaistvennogo mekhanizma kak osnova rosta proizvoditel'nosti truda." *Ekonomika stroitel'stva* 12:27–36.

Normativy kapitalnykh vlozhenii. 1990. Moscow.

Ogon', Ts. G. 1989. "Sistema khozraschetnykh otnoshenii v stroitel'stve trebuet izmeneniia." *Ekonomika stroitel'stva* 11:12–19.

"O nekotorykh merakh po uluchsheniiu polozheniia del v kapital'nom stroitel'stve." 1989. *Ekonomika stroitel'stva* 12:3–7.

"O perestroike upravleniia investitsiiami i sovershenstvovaniia khoziaistvennogo mekhanizma v stroitel'stve." 1989. *Ekonomika stroitel'stva* 10:29–39.

Podol'skii, A. K. 1988. "Chto pomogaet i chto meshaet trestu rabotat' effektivno." *Ekonomika stroitel'stva* 1:44–47.

Samizdat. no date. *Document on Ukrainian investment strategy to the year 2005.*

Timofeev, V. I. 1989. "Sovershenstvovanie khoziaistvennogo mekhanizma v stroitel'stve." *Ekonomika stroitel'stva* 10:74–87.

Tsypkin, G. A. 1989. "Bank: deiatel'nost' i otvetstvennost'." *Ekonomika stroitel'stva* 8:63–68.

United Nations. *Economic Survey of Europe.* Various years.

Volosatov, A. V. 1990. "Dogovornaia tsena. Chto dal'she?" *Ekonomika stroitel'stva* 1:50–54.

Velichko, V. A. 1988. "NPT v novykh usloviiakh khoziaistvovaniia." *Ekonomika stroitel'stva* 1:48–51.

Zaichenko, D. I. and A. N. Sharov. 1989. "Sostoitsia li povorot v deiatel'nosti bankov?" *Ekonomika stroitel'stva* 1:53–65.

Figure 6-1. Ukraine's Share in the Soviet National Income

	Ukraine's share in Soviet NMP A	Soviet gross fixed investment B
1970	18.9	16.0
1980	16.8	14.1
1985	16.7	14.0
1986	16.6	14.2

Source: Goskomstat USSR (1987, 200, 251); Goskomstat SSSR (1987, 122, 324).

Figure 6–2. Investment Efficiency Indicators (1970–1988) *

	1971–75	1976–80	1981–85	1985	1986	1987	1988
Commissionings (*vvod v deistvie*) as a proportion of aggregate investment:							
Ukraine total	95.8	95.4	98.4	95.2	94.2	94.6	92.5
Ukraine industry	92.8	92.8	96.2	90.1	93.9	n.a.	90.5
Ukraine agriculture	95.7	95.9	101.1	99.2	100.9	n.a.	95.8
USSR total	93.5	93.0	96.8	96.2	93.4	95.0	88.2
USSR industry	89.3	90.1	93.8	91.5	87.6	n.a.	81.9
USSR agriculture	93.6	94.6	98.8	97.5	97.6	n.a.	93.4
Equipment as a percentage of total investment:							
Ukraine	30	36	40	41	39	40	40
USSR	29	34	37	38	37	36	36

* Note that these indicators relate solely to the efficiency with which given projects are implemented. They say nothing about the efficiency of project choice itself.

Source: Goskomstat SSSR (1987, 196, 202, 205); *Narkhoz Ukrainy* (1988, 372, 378, 379); Goskomstat SSSR (1987, 318, 326, 328); *Narkhoz SSSR* (1988, 544, 545, 551, 552).

Figure 6–3. The Design and Construction Sectors:
Some Ukrainian-Soviet Comparisons

	1970	1980	1985	1986	1987	1988
Total number of construction organizations						
Ukraine	3,633	4,432	4,488	4,479	n.a.	n.a.
USSR	21,365	31,297	32,376	31,987	n.a.	n.a.
Number of construction trusts (subordinate to construction ministries)						
Ukraine	352	395	398	428	427	422
USSR	2,430	3,222	3,446	3,549	3,520	3,469
Total number of design organizations						
Ukraine	232	272	265	280	284	306
subordinate to the						
Ukrainian CM	111	118	116	137	134	160
USSR	1,520	1,882	1,745	1,728	n.a.	n.a.

Source: Goskomstat SSSR (1987, 210–11); *Narkhoz Ukrainy* (1988, 384, 386); Goskomstat SSSR (1987, 335–36); *Narkhoz SSSR* (1988, 560).

Figure 6–4. Percentage Distribution of Building Enterprises
by Scale of Operation: Ukraine and the Soviet Union (1986)

	Annual planned volume of work in Rb mn			
	<1.2	1.2–3.8	3.8–6.0	>6.0
All building organizations				
Ukraine	22	54	16	8
USSR	20	57	15	8

	<6	6–18	18–30	30–50	>50
Building trusts (subordinate to construction ministries)					
Ukraine	1	44	31	17	7
USSR	4	48	27	14	7

Source: Goskomstat USSR (1987, 210–11); Goskomstat SSSR (1987, 335).

Figure 6–5. Incremental Capital-Output Ratios:
Ukraine and the Soviet Union
(1970–1986)

	1971–75	1976–80	1981–85	1986
Ukraine	6.2	8.2	7.4	8.1
USSR	5.2	7.7	10.2	8.2

Source: Goskomstat USSR (1987, 210–11); Goskomstat SSSR (1987); United Nations various years.

CHAPTER SEVEN
Discussion

Serhii Pyrozhkov

The analysis of resources—the material basis of production of Ukraine's national wealth—is of great importance in the assessment of the republic's economic development. The papers in this section cover a broad range of problems: population and labor force, fuel and energy resources, and the effectiveness of capital investments. Each of the papers submitted, by virtue of the profundity of analysis and the scope of issues examined, merits a separate discussion. It is beyond the limits of this review paper, however, to provide a detailed treatment of the subject of each of the reports.

The general thesis which is shared by the papers consists of the following: Ukraine's rich resource potential, suffering decades of uneconomical utilization, has been substantially depleted and currently presents a serious problem for further economic growth. This thesis was most pronounced in the paper by Dienes. In his opinion, all the essential conditions for economic development existed in Ukraine up to the late 1950s. Both its coal and metallurgy complex and the development of heavy engineering industry exceeded similar complexes in West European countries. Nonetheless, the extensive utilization of fuel and iron ore resources has led to the deterioration of geological conditions, requiring the allocation of a considerable share of capital investments in mining industry in order to maintain the production level of these materials. Resource conditions for oil and gas production have proved to be inadequate in Ukraine. The development of relevant industries has brought about a worsening of the natural habitat and aggravated ecological problems. The industry of the republic has been distorted in the direction of the priority development of heavy industry branches, the share of the light industry being disproportionately low. The situation has been also complicated by the building of atomic power stations.

The shortage of energy resources appears to be an urgent problem facing Ukraine. Outdated and worn-out facilities for the iron and steel and petrochemical industries consume a far greater share of the resources than those optimally required. For instance, energy consumption per ton of steel in Ukraine exceeds that of Japan by 60 percent. The import of various types of fuels from other republics does not meet Ukraine's requirements in energy resources; this has begun to affect adversely the development of agriculture and the needs of the consumer. Gas consumption per capita in Ukraine is lower in comparison with other regions of the European part of the USSR and the Urals.

One must agree with inferences by Dienes that the Soviet Union—in pursuit of hard currency—allocated disproportionately large investments in oil and gas extraction industries instead of utilizing them for modernization of research and development, infrastructure development, and production diversification. After 1970 major investments were allocated primarily to the development of the fuel and energy complex and the Baikal-Amur Mainline (BAM), leaving practically nothing for the development of other sectors of the economy. Attention should be called to the reduction in Ukraine's share in all-union investments. In connection with this, it should be noted that Dienes in his analysis might have examined one more inefficient branch—land reclamation, to which substantial funds were allocated.

The problem of efficiency of capital investments in Ukraine in the context of Soviet economic policy has been considered by Dyker. The author is of the opinion that all strong and weak points of Soviet-type control planning are reflected in the sphere of capital formation. Since the first five-year-plan period a policy of extensive investments has been pursued, not taking into account the productivity of individual projects. Too many projects have been undertaken simultaneously. This has resulted in dissipation of resources and was accompanied by autarkical tendencies of the ministries. Hence, we see low returns on capital investments in the USSR from the beginning of the planning period, which itself was conceived under conditions of relatively great labor availability and extensive raw material resources to ensure the accomplishment of extremely ambitious five- year-plan targets. By the end of the 1950s and the beginning of 1960s, the condition of raw materials and labor availability deteriorated. This led to the urgent task of assessing investments efficiency. Moreover, the mechanism of capital investments did not promote technological progress.

Perhaps excessive attention is devoted by Dyker to the description of the organizational structure of the construction sector in both the USSR and Ukraine; on the other hand, too little consideration is given to the analysis of the capital investment efficiency in various branches of national economy which, strictly speaking, should be the main topic of the paper. I support, however, the author's view concerning the need for radical changes in investment policy, that is, the need to abandon irrational investments in maintenance of worn-out equipment, and instead to direct funds to modern, up-to-date equipment. This is essential for the current economy of Ukraine under conditions of relative labor and material resources shortages.

The analysis of the human factor is of great importance in the evaluation of Ukraine's resources—this is discussed by Clem and Rapawy. The distinctive feature of both papers is the extensive use of current statistical data about the population of Ukraine, permitting a fairly complete presentation of Ukraine's demographic development. The present demographic situation in Ukraine is characterized by low fertility and mortality levels, an insignificant natural growth rate of population, and weak interrepublic migration. Such a state of current demographic processes results in a low natural increment in labor force and an aging of the population.

The papers by Clem and Rapawy could be supplemented with estimates of population losses during the 1930s and 1940s. Although in the past various attempts have been made to quantify these losses in the West, the following estimates by the author were derived on the basis of data recently made available in the USSR. Such estimates are needed because the catastrophic events such as the famine of 1932–1933, the mass repressions of the 1930s to the early 1950s, the Second World War between 1941 and 1945, and the famine of 1947 resulted in population losses, which considerably distorted the population age distribution and induced sharp fluctuations in the future reproduction regime. Computations in this review are based on a simulation of demographic transition and reconstruction of population age distribution. They show that over the period 1929–1939 the population of Ukraine, within its borders existing up to 1939, had lost about 5.8 million people, or 16 percent of that year's population.

During the 1939–1959 period the losses amounted to 8.8 million people or 21 percent of the total population in 1959 (within the present-day territorial borders). Thus, over the period of three decades (1929 to 1959), the population of Ukraine was reduced by 14.6 million people, which is equivalent to a population decline of about 35 percent of the total population according to the 1959 census. Moreover, the losses indicated were caused by the man-made catastrophic events of the 1930s and 1940s, and do not include the normal tendencies of natural movement of population. Estimation of demographic crises of the past proves to be essential not only for the understanding of the present development of the Ukrainian population, but also for demographic forecasting.

In this connection, attention should be called to the demographic projections over the period up to 2025 presented by Clem and Rapawy. My own analysis of long-term population dynamics suggests no grounds for being optimistic about future population growth in Ukraine. Both fertility and mortality are unlikely to change for the better in Ukraine under the present-day economic and ecological situation. This implies that sufficient grounds do not exist for forecasting future population growth as envisaged in the papers presented. Current estimates of the fertility, mortality, and migration hypotheses in Ukraine as well as in the USSR as a whole call for further research.

On the basis of the analysis of papers on resources in Part II, a general inference can be made to the effect that the rich resource potential of Ukraine is inefficiently utilized at present and considerably limits the effective economic development of the republic. A cardinal structural reorganization in allocation of investments, taking into account their productivity and efficiency under conditions of market economy, is needed. The declaration of sovereignty of the republic by the Parliament of Ukraine calls for the solution of a number of serious problems in the national economy related to enhancement of performance of enterprises and rational utilization of the labor force.

Part III: Performance

CHAPTER EIGHT
Gross Social Product and Net Material Product and their Sectoral Structures

Andrii Revenko

Gross national product (GNP) and national income are the most informative macroeconomic indicators. In Western countries the size and structure of these two indicators have been the focus of economic analysis and economic policy for half a century. In the Soviet Union and in Ukraine, on the other hand, these indicators have not played a significant role. Other indicators of economic growth, including the output of the most important goods, have received the most attention in the administratively planned system. Economic planning has focused primarily on the material balances of individual products and their allocation in physical units rather than on an interconnected and integrated system of indexes in money terms. Another deficiency of this type of planning has been the absence of conceptual links between the macroeconomic indicators of the productive and non-productive sectors and the financial and budgetary activities of the state. Nor have these indicators been applied to foreign trade and regional development.

Very few works dealing with national income have been published in the Soviet Union. Recently this has changed, as a result of the transition to a market economy and because the importance and the need for useful macroeconomic indicators has been recognized. New categories, long utilized in the West, are being introduced. Steps also have been taken to release more relevant statistics.

National Income Accounting in Ukraine

The Western reader familiar with the genesis of national income accounting as presented in the well-known work of Paul Studenski may not be as well acquainted with the history of similar research in Ukraine, where several advances in this field have been made.

This history can be divided into three periods, which are separated from each other by 30 years. Original and pioneering works on national income in Ukraine in the mid-1920s probably were more sophisticated than the methods utilized at that time in other countries. In the Soviet Union the theoretical and applied research conducted by the Tsentral'noe statisticheskoe upravlenie (TsSU) statisticians under the direction of Pavel Popov (1926) is well known (although probably less so in the West). Similar research was being conducted concurrently in Ukraine under the leadership of V. S. Myshkis (1927a, 1927b, 1928). Until recently this work was completely unknown even in the Soviet Union. Fortunately, some of its results were presented in recent articles by Nahirniak (1970, 1977a, 1977b). Some of the national accounting methods, proposed by Ukrainians, apparently were more advanced than those utilized in the West at that time (Pakhomova and Revenko 1990). For example, Ukrainian scholars pioneered the product flow method of national income estimation broken down by main economic sectors and type of ownership (Grinshtein 1926, 187).

Unfortunately, the central authorities curtailed research on macroeconomic indicators in the late 1920s and halted it altogether in Ukraine. With the transition to five-year planning, growth indicators, particularly those relating to heavy industry, gained ascendancy over macroeconomic relationships. The growth rates of national income continually increased, but the importance of the indicators themselves diminished with every year. Only recently has it become possible to question this phenomenon openly (Seliunin and Khanin 1987). A good example of the official attitude toward national income estimates is the now well-known but then-secret 1940 report of the Gosplan to the Central Committee of the Soviet Communist Party (TsK KPSS [VKP(b)]) and the central government. It contained detailed information about all branches of the economy but none about national income (Gosplan 1990).

In the second half of the 1950s when important political and economic changes were taking place in the USSR, it became acutely necessary to devise new approaches to estimating macroeconomic indicators. A new, expanded system of balances in the national economy was worked out (Vsesoiuznoe 1959). In 1959 for the first time, an input-output table for the entire Soviet economy was developed. Shortly after, such tables were developed for individual union republics. Methods of estimating national income for the republics by product flow and by end use were established and actual calculations were made for 1956 and 1958. The initial results of these calculations in Ukraine appeared in an important monograph prepared at the Kiev Institute of Economics (Nesterenko 1963).

During the following 30 to 35 years, further work on theoretical and applied macroeconomic issues was discouraged. It was difficult to do any meaningful research in this field, and very few publications on national income estimation, input-output tables, and related problems appeared. Since 1988, increased attention again has been paid to the development and use of macroeconomic indicators. It is important to note that in 1988 a decision was made to begin estimating the annual GNP, quarterly and monthly national income, and, in the near future, the quarterly and monthly GNP. Further, the development of 1989 national income estimates by oblasts (25 oblasts and the city of Kiev in Ukraine) is now in full swing. It is worth mentioning that in the United States, where the GNP has been calculated for 45 years, such calculations for states were published for the first time just recently, in 1988 (Renshaw et al. 1988).

A considerable amount of macroeconomic data is currently being published, although as a result of many years of restrictions, the amount is still much lower than in other countries. For example, in the 1986 statistical yearbook of the United Nations, 54 pages cover the United States, while only one and a half pages are devoted to the Soviet Union and less than a page to the Ukrainian SSR. In addition, in the tables on USSR and Ukraine there are dots instead of numbers for half the data entries, indicating "data not available" (United Nations 1989). New publications contain fairly detailed information about economic ties among union republics (Goskomstat SSSR 1989), and the publication of the volume *Balances of the National Economy of the USSR and the Union Republics* has been announced. Nonetheless, these developments, especially with regard to Ukraine, are still far from satisfactory.

National Income (Net Material Product)—Differing Concepts

National income (in the Soviet sense), called net material product (NMP) in the West, differs from GNP in three ways. First, NMP does not include depreciation. In the United States in recent years, depreciation amounted to 10 to 11 percent of the GNP (*Survey of Current Business* 1987, 5). In the USSR this component of the GNP has been unexpectedly larger: 16.3 percent in 1980 and 19.2 percent in 1988 (Stepanov and Grishin 1989, 43). The inclusion of expenditures on capital repairs in the Soviet definition accounts for some of the difference. This element of depreciation was expected to be dropped as of 1991. The difference also results from so-called double depreciation—the continued inclusion of depreciation allowances of completely depreciated fixed assets.

Second, national income does not include the output of non-productive sectors, which covers expenditures on transportation and communication used by the population and by the non-productive sector itself. These include housing, municipal production, consumer services (beauty salons, photo studios, bath houses), education and health and scientific services. Included in scientific services are independent research and development establishments, research institutions that do not provide manufactured products, and some parts of geological exploration organizations. Culture and the arts, banks, government administration, defense, and party organizations also are covered.

Third, some industries found in the service sector in the United States are not included in the non-productive sphere by Soviet statisticians. Thus, tailoring, shoe repair, dry cleaning, and the repair of automobiles, trucks, appliances, and agricultural machinery are included in the industry sector. In Ukraine, 26.4 percent of all workers (excluding military personnel) were employed in the non-productive sphere in 1988 (*Narkhoz Ukrainy* 1989, 55). This compares to 27.8 percent in the USSR (*Narkhoz SSSR* 1989, 47), while in the United States the figure ranged from 40 to 45 percent.

In converting NMP, according to the Soviet definition, to GNP, the first two components that were just discussed must be added while the third needs to be subtracted from the material production sectors and included into the non-material production sectors.

According to official calculations, in the USSR as a whole the ratio of GNP to NMP was 133.9 percent in 1980 and 140.7 percent in 1989 (*Narkhoz SSSR* 1989, 11–12). Although GNP has not yet been calculated for Ukraine, one can expect a similar relationship, give or take 1 to 1.5 percent. NMP is calculated by three methods: flow of product, flow of income or distribution (which in practice is used only in conjunction with the construction of intersectoral balances), and by end use. The first method is the most accurate and, thus, the one referred to in this chapter.

One should add that in the Soviet Union in 1988 a new indicator was introduced, a modification of NMP-net product of material production of enterprises (henceforth, NPMP). Its value is smaller than that of NMP by the amount of turnover taxes minus budgetary subsidies and international trade balances. The new indicator was created because turnover tax receipts declined as a result of the reduction in the sales of alcoholic products and receipts from the exportation of oil, petroleum-based products, and natural gas.

Macroeconomic Indicators in Constant and Current Price

In Ukraine as in the entire USSR, more macroeconomic indicators in current rubles are now available than at any time in the last 30 years. Of course during inflationary periods, changes in NMP and other indexes in current prices are of limited value. The most useful and widely accepted indicators in these periods would be indexes in constant prices. In the past, Soviet methods of calculating constant price indexes have been criticized in the West, criticism now acknowledged by Soviet statisticians (Kirichenko 1990). Revisions of the existing indexes have now begun.

Using the Soviet methodology, growth rates of national income in the USSR in constant prices are about 1.8 to 2 times as large as those calculated in the West (*Narkhoz SSSR* 1988, 7; Joint Economic Committee 1989, 40). This can be shown on the basis of the growth rate of the GNP for the USSR between 1981 and 1988. According to the calculation by Goskomstat, this rate is equal to 3.77 percent, while Western estimates yielded a rate of 1.91 percent. Thus the Soviet rate is 1.98 times higher than the Western calculation. The following example, taken from official Soviet yearbooks, illustrates the lack of reliability of Soviet indicators. According to this source, the Soviet NMP was 58 percent of the American NMP in 1960. Between 1960 and 1987, NMP in the USSR increased 4.1 times and grew only 2.3 times in the United States. According to this arithmetic, the USSR NMP would have exceeded the American NMP in 1987 by 3 percent. However, the official Soviet yearbook claims that the Soviet NMP is 64 percent of the American NMP (Goskomstat SSSR 1987, 33, 43). In this case, the Soviet calculation produced a rate 1.8 percent higher than the rate obtained in the West. Needless to say, these deficiencies apply also to Ukrainian indexes.

Figure 8-1 summarizes changes in the most important macroeconomic indicators for Ukraine in current and constant prices using Soviet methodology .

It would be impossible to provide estimates of gross social product (GSP) and NMP growth for Ukraine with the help of methodology used in the West and recommended by the United Nations. Nevertheless, a preliminary estimation indicates that between 1956 and 1989, the Ukrainian GSP increased between 2.8 and 3.3 times and NMP between 2.7 and 3.2 times. The value of the official estimates is indeed questionable, since, for example, it implies that the growth of NMP in constant prices has been higher than in current prices.

Relationship between GSP and NMP

In macroeconomic analysis in the USSR, much attention is paid to the relationship between GSP and NMP. Theoretically, GSP should grow at a slower rate than NMP as a result of technological progress. This progress should be reflected in a decrease in intermediate consumption and in an increase in the efficiency of production. As a consequence, the share of NMP in GSP should rise. In practice, however, this has not been borne out and in Ukraine, the reverse actually has been true. GSP in current prices for the entire 33-year period grew at higher rates than NMP, 6.9 times for GSP and 5.5 times for NMP. A similar trend is apparent in the NMP/GSP percentage relationship, as can be seen in the following table.

	1956	1960	1970	1980	1989
Current prices	50.7	48.6	44.9	40.6	39.5
Constant prices	50.9	50.2	47.2	41.9	40.2

Industry has experienced rather sluggish improvements in efficiency both in the USSR and in Ukraine. Nevertheless, some progress has been made. The increasingly unfavorable share of material expenditures in gross value of output and the decline in net output are caused not by inefficiency, but mainly by the rapid rise in the prices of raw materials, energy, and other components of intermediate consumption relative to the prices of all products, including final products. This trend also is reflected in the increase in the proportion of depreciation, resulting from higher growth of fixed assets than of the output of final product. Furthermore, higher prices of intermediate products also are responsible for increases in the shares of those sectors whose intermediate consumption is higher than other sectors (in agriculture, for example, livestock production relative to field production). Finally, the same factor accounts for a marked relative decrease of such components of GSP as the balance of foreign trade, turnover taxes, and budget subsidies.

For comparison, we will now examine the analogous processes in the United States. In the past 20 years, the proportion of intermediate consumption in the gross output decreased from 49.1 percent in 1963 to 45.3 percent in 1983, although there were periods (years of world oil-price increases) when the share of intermediate consumption rose, such as from 46.0 to 47.6 percent between 1977 and 1981 (*Survey of Current Business* 1984, 5; 1987, 51; 1989, 29).

The share of Ukrainian GSP and NMP in the USSR: Totals by Economic Sectors

The GSP and NMP of Ukraine in absolute terms is in second place among 15 union republics. However, Ukraine's shares of the USSR have been declining with respect to these two indicators as well to some other important indicators (Figure 8-2).

This decline can be interpreted in the following way. In the Soviet Union during the postwar period, higher growth rates in GSP and NMP occurred in the republics and regions with relatively lower levels of economic development: Central Asia, Transcaucasus, and the eastern regions of the Russian Federation. Also important is the fact that Ukraine's proportion of the total population of the USSR has decreased; for example, from 20.1 percent in 1956 to 18.0 percent in 1989 (Goskomstat 1988, 8; 1990a, 8–9) . Other factors, such as unfavorable price movements for Ukrainian products, also may help to explain the declining relative importance of this republic.

NMP of Ukraine and Other Union Republics

At present in the Soviet Union, a comparison of the socio-economic development of individual union republics is receiving serious attention. Under the current price-setting mechanism and financial and budgetary policies, the population of every republic feels slighted. This perception is primarily the result of a ministerial approach to regional development that is, in addition, fueled by the current socio-political events in the USSR and throughout the world. The concealment of this issue until now by the authorities and the scarcity of relevant data for research and comparative analyses have certainly contributed to this perception. Recently these constraints have by and large been eliminated, however, facilitating open discussion and reevaluation of these issues. The following list ranks republics by NMP per capita for selected years. As can be seen, Ukraine dropped from fifth among the 15 union republics in 1970 to eighth in 1980 . In 1989 it recovered to sixth place (Liusina and Revenko 1990, 10). It is interesting to compare the development of Ukraine with regard to NMP per capita, for example, with that of its Slavic neighbor Belarus. While the Ukrainian NMP relative to that of Belarus was 1.06 in 1970, it subsequently dropped to 0.90 in 1975, 0.81 in 1980, and 0.76 in 1989 (Liusina and Revenko 1990, 11).

1970	1980	1989
1. Estonia	1. Latvia	1. Latvia
2. Latvia	2. Estonia	2. Russian Federation
3. Lithuania	3. Russian Federation	3. Estonia
4. Russian Federation	4. Belarus	4. Belarus
5.Ukraine	5. Lithuania	5. Lithuania
	6. Armenia	6. Ukraine
	7. Georgia	
	8. Ukraine	

In general, there are significant differences in NMP per capita among the Soviet union republics. In 1989 this indicator was 2.95 times higher for Latvia, the most developed republic, than it was for Tajikistan, the republic with the lowest per-capita NMP. For comparison, and using similar indicators, the most-developed state in the United States had a GNP per capita that was 3.8 times higher than that of the least-developed state in 1986. Excluding the District of Columbia and Alaska, the relationship between the top state (Wyoming) and the bottom state (Mississippi) narrows to only 1.9 (U.S. Department of Commerce 1989, 14, 429).

According to calculations by Illarionov (1990) of the gross value of output per capita in 1986, Ukraine ranked sixth in industry (103 percent of the USSR average), ninth in construction (78 percent), seventh in agriculture (120 percent), fifth in transportation and communication (91 percent), and sixth in retail trade (96 percent). With respect to the productivity of labor, Ukraine ranked sixth in NMP, thirteenth in industry, in last place in construction, seventh in agriculture, fourth in transportation and communication, and thirteenth in retail trade. Ukraine is sixth among republics in the level of fixed capital productivity (the ratio of GSP to the value of fixed assets).

Space considerations do not allow us to analyze adequately the differences in the level of NMP and other macroeconomic indicators between Ukraine and other republics. Most likely all of the following factors come into play: the high proportion of extractive industries (particularly subsidized coal mining) and other branches of heavy industry; a relatively small proportion of light industry and food processing, which nonetheless bear a relatively large proportion of turnover tax; and large subsidies for agriculture.

Productivity in any economy is related to its standard of living. As far as the wages of material production and service workers are concerned, Ukraine ranked eighth among the republics, 90.9 percent of the USSR average, and tenth in terms of wages of collective farm workers (*Narkhoz SSSR* 1988, 81, 83). On the other hand, the cost of living in Ukraine is lower than in the USSR. The prices of many regionally differentiated products, such as vegetables and fruit, are lowest in Ukraine. Also, winter clothing and heating expenditures are lower in Ukraine than in many other regions of the USSR. As a result, the territorial index of the cost of living in Ukraine was estimated at 85.3 percent of that for central regions of the Russian Federation in the mid-1980s. In Western Siberia this index is equal to 112.3 percent, in the Urals 116.7 percent, and in Murmansk Oblast 170.3 percent (Institut ekonomiki 1988, 253).

The construction costs for fixed capital investment in Ukraine also are below the USSR average. For example, if the cost of construction and installation work in Moscow Oblast is assigned 1.00, the corresponding indicator in Ukraine would be 0.97 and in the entire Russian Federation 1.03. The indicators for Asiatic regions are as follows: 1.36 for the Far East, 1.14 for Eastern Siberia, and 1.03 for Western Siberia (Khaikin 1987, 68–69). One cannot dispute Illarionov (1988, 48) who states that "distorted cost proportions lead to unequal assessments of the value of output of goods and services. This leads to distortion of the real magnitude of economic activity and levels of economic development in different regions."

Structure of GSP and NMP by Economic Sectors

Industrial production, construction, and agriculture are the most important sectors of GSP and NMP. Transportation, communication, and retail trade also are included in these concepts. First we will look at characteristics of the indicators in current prices (Figure 8- 3).

In general, there have been rather insignificant structural changes in the Ukrainian economy during the past three decades. Some increases in the industry share of the economy took place alongside a reduction in the construction share and small decline in agricultural share, while the shares of two other sectors remained practically unchanged. The Western reader no doubt will be surprised by the relatively high share of industry and of agriculture in particular and the low share of retail trade in GSP and NMP compared to the distribution in developed countries. In comparison with the USSR, Ukraine's share of agriculture is slightly higher; its share of industry almost the same, and its share of other sectors is slightly lower.

An analysis of the sectoral structure of GSP and NMP also requires an examination of material expenditures of enterprises of material production. In Ukraine, as in the entire Soviet Union, the proportion of these expenditures in GSP and NMP has been increasing, from 0.55 to 0.61 in Ukraine and from 0.55 to 0.59 in the Soviet Union, between 1970 and 1988. Undoubtedly, this inhibits efforts to increase the efficiency of the national economy. To a certain extent this tendency is tied to changes in the types and quality of material resources utilized. In 1988 the level of Ukrainian material consumption expenditures in general and industry and agriculture in particular was somewhat greater than in the USSR.

Structural changes in constant-price GSP and NMP also need to be noted. Interesting differences appear (Figure 8-4). As a result of the change to new prices, the industry's share and the difference between turnover taxes and subsidies decreased while agriculture's share increased. The indicators for agriculture deserve particular attention.

Despite the fact that gross agricultural output grew at a lower rate than gross industrial output, the share of the former in the GSP increased significantly when new prices were introduced (in 1965, 1973, and 1983) . This trend is even more apparent using the net value of output concept; while the share of industrial output declined in 1985 by about 10 percentage points, agriculture's share increased by more than 12 percentage points. An important reason for the change in industry's share is the reduction of turnover taxes minus budgetary subsidies, most of which are included in this sector by the accepted method of accounting. In addition, given such changes, the growth rates of GSP and NMP in new constant prices are, of course, reduced relative to the rates calculated in the old constant prices.

Turnover Tax, Budgetary Subsidies, and Foreign Trade

Turnover taxes and budgetary subsidies account for relatively large shares of the GSP and NMP in the USSR. These taxes and subsidies as well as the Soviet foreign trade balances are calculated differently than in the United States. Since retail prices of final industrial products include turnover taxes, the difference between these two items is included in the gross value output and the net value output. In macroeconomic statistics this tax on a product (minus subsidies) is allocated to the republic in which the product was produced. In financial and budgetary statistics, it is partly allocated to the republic in which it was sold (for example, footwear, textiles, and knitted wear). As of 1991, the tax on all products will be collected at the place of production. To date, in Ukraine the actual magnitude of turnover tax, calculated by the republic Ministry of Finance, is between 2 and 2.5 billion rubles, or 17.5 percent higher than Goskomstat data in 1985 and 7.2 percent in 1989, for example.

Ignoring the political and economic nature of the turnover tax that is being discussed in Soviet economic literature, it is worth noting that the role of the tax is greater in the Soviet Union than the role of turnover taxes in Western countries. Thus in 1984 (prior to the campaign aimed at reducing the production of alcoholic beverages) the turnover tax brought in 102.7 billion rubles, representing 18 percent of NMP or 14 percent of GNP in the USSR (*Narkhoz SSSR* 1988, 409, 548). In the United States, excise taxes accounted in some years for as little as 0.7 percent of GNP in some years. In the USSR, turnover taxes make up a substantial proportion of the retail prices of some products; for example, 94 percent for vodka, 71 percent for jewelry (before the rise in retail prices in 1990), 64 percent for automobiles, 47 percent for synthetic fabrics, 39 percent for refrigerators, and 33 percent for cooking oil (Sengachev 1989, 5).

The proportion of turnover taxes on products produced in Ukraine remained relatively stable between 1970 and 1984, accounting for 16 to 18 percent of NMP. Since then it has declined to about 14 percent. This proportion is about 2 percent lower than in the USSR.

As already mentioned, turnover taxes included in GSP and NMP figures are reduced by the amount of budgetary subsidies. About three decades ago these subsidies were relatively small; they represented about 5 to 7 percent of turnover taxes. They rose to 28 percent of turnover taxes in 1970 and 55 percent in 1983 and by 1989 they even exceeded the level of turnover taxes. The rise in subsidies took place because purchasing prices paid by enterprises increased while officially set retail prices remained largely unchanged. To illustrate, production subsidies to two agricultural products, milk and meat, amounted to 5.3 and 3.4 billion rubles respectively in 1989. Production subsidies to coal mining came close to 3 billion rubles. These and other factors make a radical price reform in the Soviet Union imperative in the near future.

Another characteristic feature of Soviet national income accounting is the treatment of foreign trade balances as a separate component of the GSP and NMP. Until recently this component was not treated as a separate item, but was included under the heading "other monetary accumulation" in the financial section of statistical yearbooks alongside profits and turnover taxes. The size of this component was influenced by world prices of the Soviet Union's most important export product—petroleum. For example, for the USSR this balance amounted to 3.2 billion rubles in 1970, reached a peak of 30.2 billion in 1985, and declined with the decrease of oil prices to 11 billion rubles in 1988 (*Narkhoz SSSR* 1988, 615). Data on the budgetary aspects of foreign trade appeared for the first time in the Soviet yearbook on budgetary statistics in 1989 (Ministerstvo finansov 1989, 7, 16). However, the numbers published there do not completely agree with those included in GSP and NMP.

The Goskomstat of the USSR calculates and distributes the balance of foreign trade component of GSP and NMP by union republics. There is reason to believe that this allocation was undertaken indirectly in earlier years. Since there was no practical need for these data, however, there was no pressure to improve them. Calculating balance of foreign trade volume on the basis of direct statistics with improved methodology only became possible in 1985. Currently, with the transition of union republics to economic sovereignty, the necessity of accurately presenting the republics' foreign trade activity has become particularly acute. It is interesting to note that during recent years, in 1980 and 1985, the foreign trade balance of Ukraine was the sole component responsible for the increase in its NMP.

Finally, Figure 8-5 shows the conversion of NMP into the net product of the material production of enterprises (NPMP) in Ukraine for some recent years.

The Factor-Payment Structure of NMP

The factor-payment structure of NMP in the Marxist sense shows the division of national income between returns to labor and surplus product. In the USSR, interest in this kind of analysis and in comparisons with foreign countries has increased recently. In the past, the lack of data made this kind of research either impossible or imprecise.

In Soviet accounting, several components of returns to labor and surplus product can be isolated. The most important components of the returns to labor are wages of workers in the material production sphere. (Wages and salaries of workers in the non-material production sectors are excluded here, of course.) The second-largest component of returns to labor are payments to collective farm members and items referred to as "bonuses from incentive funds" and "bonuses not included in salaries." The former includes sums that are essentially an element of the redistribution of the net material product because they are part of production costs and must come out of profits. Business travel expenses appear under labor returns in the USSR. (This item is treated as intermediate consumption in the West.) The recent growth in the number of cooperatives involved in material and nonmaterial production has made the establishment of a separate category of labor returns necessary. Finally, a fairly significant element in the returns to labor is the net production of private labor (for example, cultivation of subsidiary plots or the construction of one's own house).

Among the components of surplus value, the largest are profits from sales (excluding bonuses from incentive funds), turnover taxes (minus budgetary subsidies), and the balance of foreign trade. It should be noted that in Soviet practice, surplus product also includes deductions for social security payments to workers, employees, and collective farm workers. Finally, this category includes net profits of collective farms and such other items as deductions into funds for the introduction of new technology, research and development, and geological exploration.

Figure 8-6 presents detailed information on the structure of returns to labor and the surplus product in the Ukrainian NMP for the years for which input-output tables were constructed.

The most important and interesting ratio, the surplus product relative to returns to labor, has increased slightly, by about 1 percentage point, over the past two decades. Among the changes in returns to labor, the decline in the share of payments to collective farm workers caused primarily by the decrease in the number of farm workers is notable. Also, there has been a reduction in the share of the net production of private agriculture and an increase in bonuses out of incentive funds. Within the surplus product there has been a sharp increase (nearly twofold) in the proportion of sales profits and a sharp decline in the share of turnover taxes minus budgetary subsidies (resulting from progressively rising subsidies). Finally, the share of the foreign trade balance has increased significantly.

The ratio between surplus product and returns to labor varies among economic sectors. The ratios in agriculture (particularly prior to recent increases in wholesale prices) and construction are low. This is a result of the relatively low profits in these sectors. Since the profits are not sufficient to finance the replacement and expansion of the capital base, funds accumulated in industry have to be transferred to these sectors. In a market economy, these relationships by sectors probably would be less unequal.

There is no doubt that the ratio of surplus product to returns to labor is higher in Ukraine than in developed Western countries. It is worth remembering that, unlike the definition used in Western countries, returns to labor in our discussion refer only to material production. The returns to labor in non-material sectors (which account for a third to a quarter of the total returns to labor) appear in the surplus product. This obviously distorts this important macroeconomic relationship.

Conclusion

As a result of glasnost in the USSR, the obstacles that had long prevented publication of economic statistics were removed. In the past, secrecy in this area made an analysis of the social and economic situation in Ukraine difficult. It led to false comparisons and conclusions about Ukrainian economic life not only by the population, but even by the leaders. It takes time for publications to reflect the appropriate methodology, provide thoughtful analyses of the social processes and of their consequences, and undertake comparisons with other countries. It is important to realize that the statistical basis for such work is now available and that the first steps have been taken in this direction.

Such macroeconomic analyses are nothing new in Ukraine. As early as the mid-1920s, interesting and original indicators, especially of national income, were estimated there. However, this work remained unknown even in the USSR. Almost 30 years later in the mid-1950s, work on macroeconomic indicators was renewed in the USSR, including Ukraine. Unfortunately, only a few of the more general analyses were worked out and published. The work at that time was limited primarily to the estimation of percentage indicators and often was motivated by political and ideological considerations. These analyses did a poor job examining the existing economic conditions and were not used by the leadership in determining the direction of social and economic development in the USSR.

Ukraine declared its economic sovereignty recently and intends to introduce a free market system soon. At the same time, however, Ukraine suffers from serious economic and social problems. The introduction and further development of macroeconomic analysis— based on the universally accepted system of national accounting of the United Nations—could serve as an effective tool in coping with these responsibilities and problems. A preliminary estimate of 142.2 billion rubles has been made for the Ukrainian GNP in 1989 (Ivanchenko 1990). Yet much remains to be done, such as calculating the structure and utilization of GNP and its relations with finances, budget, and so on. In view of the republic's economic sovereignty, indicators in value and physical terms of its trade relations with other countries and other republics are acutely needed. The improvement of interregional (inter-oblast) development calls for the preparation of macroeconomic indicators on a sub-national level. Finally, a serious problem with political implications is the revision of past growth rates. The results could serve as a basis for a realistic comparison of Ukraine's experience with those of other republics and countries.

References

"Ekonomicheskie vzaimosviazi respublik v narodnokhoziaistvennom komplekse. Vvoz i vyvoz produktsii po otrasliam narodnogo khoziaistva za 1988 g." 1990. *Vestnik statistiki* 3:36–53.

Goskomstat SSSR. 1988. *SSSR i zarubezhnye strany*, 1987. Moscow.

_____. 1990a. *Naselenie SSSR*, 1987. Moscow.

_____. 1990b. *Narodnoe khoziaistvo SSSR v 1989 g.* Moscow.

_____. 1990c. *SSSR v tsifrakh v 1989 g.* Moscow.

Goskomstat USSR. 1990. *Narodnoe khoziaistvo Ukrainskoi SSR v 1989 g.* Kiev.

Gosplan SSSR. 1990. "O predvaritel'nykh rezul'tatakh vypolneniia plana razvitiia narodnogo khoziaistva SSSR za 1940 g." *Izvestiia* 5.

Grinshtein, A. L., ed. 1926. *Kapitaly i natsional'nyi dokhod Ukrainy v 1923–24 gg.* Kharkiv.

Illarionov, A. 1990. "Ekonomicheskii potentsial i urovni ekonomicheskogo razvitiia soiuznykh respublik." *Voprosy ekonomiki* 4:46–58.

Institut ekonomiki AN SSSR. 1988. *Real'nye dokhody naseleniia.* Moscow.

Ivanchenko, I. 1990. "Systema natsional'nykh rakhunkiv ta ïï vykorystannia v statystychnomu obliku i ekonomichnomu analizi." *Ekonomika Radians'koï Ukraïny* 10:21–31.

Joint Economic Committee. 1989. *Gorbachev Changes Course.* Washington, D.C.

Khaikin, G. M. 1987. *Kapital'nye vlozheniia i smetnye tseny: regional'nyi aspekt.* Moscow.

Kirichenko, V. 1990. "Vernut' doverie statistike." *Kommunist* 3:22–32.

Liusina, N. I. and A. P. Revenko. 1990. "Sukupnyi suspil'nyi produkt i natsional'nyi dokhod Ukraïns'koï RSR." *Ekonomika Radians'koï Ukraïny* 11:5–16.

Ministerstvo finansov SSSR. 1989. *Gosudarstvennyi biudzhet SSSR, 1989. Kratkyi statisticheskii sbornik.* Moscow.

Myshkis, V. S. 1927a. "Balans narodnoho hospodarstva ta problemy politychnoï ekonomiï." *Prapor marksyzmu* 1.

_____. 1927b. "Opyt sostavleniia balansa narodnogo khoziaistva Ukrainy za 1923–24 i 1924–25 gody." *Khoziaistvo Ukrainy* 2; 3.

_____. 1928. *Balans narodnogo khoziaistva Ukrainy.* 2 parts, 2nd ed. Kharkiv.

Nahirniak, P. A. 1970. "Uzahal'niuiuchi pokaznyky ekonomichnoho rozvytku v pershomu balansi narodnoho hospodarstva Ukr.RSR." *Istoriia narodnoho hospodarstva ta ekonomichnoï dumky Ukraïns' koï RSR* 4–5:87–101.

_____. 1977a. "Pershi narodnohospodars'ki pobudovy naukovoho vyvchennia sotsialistychnoho vidtvorennia." *Ekonomika Radians' koï Ukraïny* 2.

_____. 1977b. "Pro metodolohichni zasady skladannia pershykh balansiv narodnoho hospodarstva Ukrains'koï RSR za 1923/24–1925/26 rr." *Istoriia narodnoho hospodarstva ta ekonomichnoï dumky Ukraïns' koï RSR* 11:39–48.

Nesterenko, O. O., ed. 1963. *National' nyi dokhod Ukraïns' koï RSR v period rozhornutoho budivnytstva komunizmu.* Kiev.

Pakhomova, T. A. and A. F. Revenko. 1990. "Ischislenie kapitalov i natsional'nogo dokhoda Ukrainy v 20-e gody (Ob odnoi zabytoi razrabotke po balansu narodnogo khoziaistva)." In *Sovershenstvovanie metodov ischisleniia obobshchaiushchikh pokazatelei razvitiia ekonomiki soiuznoi respubliki,* 98–107. Ed. by I. I. Nesterenko. Kiev.

Popov, P. I., ed. 1926. *Balans narodnogo khoziaistva Soiuza SSR, 1923–1924.* vol. XXIX, Moscow.

Renshaw, Vernon, et al. 1988. "Gross State Product by Industry, 1963–1986." *Survey of Current Business* 5.

Seliunin, Vasilii and Georgii Khanin. 1987. "Lukavaia tsifra." *Novyi mir* 2:181–201.

Sengachev, V. K. 1989. "Monolog pro nalog." *Pravitel' stvennyi vestnik* 22:4–5.

U.S. Department of Commerce. 1989. *Statistical Abstract of the United States 1989*. Washington, D.C.

Stepanov, Iu. and A. Grishin. 1989. "Rol' obobshchaiushchikh poka- zatelei planirovaniia v novykh usloviiakh." *Planovoe kho- ziaistvo* 1.

Survey of Current Business. 1984. No. 5.

_____. 1987. Nos. 1 and 4.

_____. 1989. Nos. 2 and 3.

United Nations. 1989. *National Accounts Statistics: Main Aggregates and Detailed Tables, 1986*. Part II. New York.

Vsesoiuznoe soveshchanie statistikov, 4–8 iunia 1957 g. 1959. *Stenograficheskii otchet*. Moscow.

Figure 8-1. Basic Macroeconomic Indicators, Ukraine
(1956–1989)

	1989/1956	1989/1960	1989/1970	1989/1980
Gross social product				
Current prices	691.7	405.3	226.0	144.4
Constant prices	554.1	394.5	204.1	131.2
Produced net material product				
Current prices	538.6	402.6	198.9	140.5
Constant prices	549.3	391.1	1201.2	136.2
Net product of enterprises of material production				
Current prices	683.0	490.9	222.8	170.7
Constant prices	515.1	365.2	192.4	138.6
Material expenditures				
Current prices	849.0	582.9	248.1	147.0
Constant prices	569.3	404.8	210.6	129.5

Source: Liusina and Revenko (1990, 7).

Figure 8-2. Share of the Ukrainian Gross Social Product
and Net Material Product in the USSR by Sectors
(in current prices, percent)

	1956	1960	1970	1980	1988
Gross social product	18.8	18.7	19.0	17.7	17.3
Industry	18.2	17.3	18.9	17.9	18.2
Construction	17.1	18.3	16.8	14.1	13.4
Agriculture	22.6	23.1	21.5	20.7	18.5
Transportation and communication	14.8	15.8	16.5	15.4	13.8
Product turnover*	18.3	17.9	18.5	18.2	17.1
Produced net material product	18.9	17.1	18.9	16.8	16.2
Industry	18.0	17.1	18.5	16.3	17.2
Construction	18.3	19.0	16.7	14.5	13.5
Agriculture	22.1	23.7	22.0	20.5	17.9
Transportation and communication	14.2	15.2	16.4	15.5	13.8
Product turnover*	18.4	18.5	17.9	17.5	17.2

*Includes trade, public eating facilities, procurement of agricultural products, and material-technical supply.

Source: Liusina and Revenko (1990, 9).

Figure 8-3. Sectoral Structure of Ukrainian Basic Macroeconomic
Indicators (1960–1989)
(actual prices, percent)

	1960	1970	1980	1988
Gross social product	100.0	100.0	100.0	100.0
Industry	59.0	63.5	64.1	62.0
Construction	10.5	9.3	7.7	8.3
Agriculture	20.5	18.3	16.5	19.6
Transportation and communication	3.6	3.4	3.8	3.7
Product turnover	3.8	3.2	3.6	3.5
Material expenditures	100.0	100.0	100.0	100.0
Industry	69.5	74.5	73.8	74.6
Construction	10.8	9.4	6.8	7.0
Agriculture	15.2	12.5	15.4	14.0
Transportation and communication	3.0	2.3	2.8	2.8
Product turnover	1.3	1.2	1.1	1.3
Produced net material product	100.0	100.0	100.0	100.0
Industry	47.9	50.0	50.0	42.6
Construction	10.2	9.2	8.9	10.4
Agriculture	26.0	25.3	18.2	28.1
Transportation and communication	4.3	4.8	5.4	5.1
Product turnover	6.4	5.9	7.3	6.9

Source: Liusina and Revenko (1990, 11).

Figure 8-4. The Effect of Price-Index Changes on the Structure of
GSP and NMP for Selected Years
(percent)

	1965		1975		1985	
	1958 prices	1965 prices	1965 prices	1973 prices	1973 prices	1983 prices
Gross industrial product						
Industry	64.6	60.6	67.8	65.3	66.4	61.9
Agriculture	17.2	21.6	13.8	15.9	13.6	19.2
Turnover tax minus						
budgetary subsidies	10.6	8.1	7.4	4.6	4.0	2.2
Net material product						
Industry	55.9	47.4	60.3	51.8	53.8	43.3
Agriculture	21.4	29.3	14.0	20.5	13.4	25.5
Turnover tax minus						
budgetary subsidies	20.9	17.1	16.5	10.9	9.4	5.5

Source: Liusina and Revenko (1990, 12).

Figure 8-5. Produced Net Material Product and Net Product of
Enterprises of Material Production (1960 to 1988)
(in current prices, percent)

	1960	1970	1980	1989
1. Produced net material product	100.0	100.0	100.0	100.0
2. Minus (5+6)	21.9	15.0	21.6	4.8
3. Turnover tax	n.a.	15.8	17.5	18.0
4. Budgetary subsidies	n.a.	-4.5	-5.5	-16.9
5. 3-4	18.6	11.3	12.0	-1.1
6. Foreign trade balance	3.3	3.7	9.6	5.9
7. NPMP (1-2)	88.1	85.0	78.4	95.2

Figure 8-6. Distribution of Ukrainian Net Material Product (1966–1988) (in current prices, percent)

	1966	1977	1988
Net material product	100.0	100.0	100.0
Returns to labor in			
material production	52.3	51.3	51.4
Wages and salaries of			
workers and employees	29.1	31.1	30.9
Bonuses from separate funds	0.4	1.6	2.9
Other monetary payments	1.0	1.2	1.3
Payments to workers of			
collective farms	9.3	7.1	6.6
Net production from			
subsidiary plots	12.5	10.3	9.7
Surplus product	47.7	48.7	48.6
Profits from sales	17.5	22.4	30.5
Turnover tax minus			
budgetary subsidies	16.1	10.1	1.1
Social security payments			
of workers and employees	2.0	2.2	3.4
Social security payments of			
workers of collective farms	0.6	0.7	0.9
Net product of collective			
farms	6.4	3.3	4.2
Foreign trade balance	2.8	6.9	6.4
Other components	2.3	3.1	2.1

Source: Liusina and Revenko (1990, 15).

CHAPTER NINE
National Income of Ukraine: Estimation and Analysis

F. I. Kushnirsky *

New economic and political developments in the Soviet republics are drawing significant attention from the West. In the past, U.S. foreign policy ignored the diversity of Soviet society. Facing the mighty Soviet military machine, Americans did not think much in terms of Soviet republics; in fact, they certainly would have supported any move aimed at the disintegration of the USSR. As the two superpowers entered an era of cooperation and the Soviet military threat subsided, the U.S. increasingly viewed the USSR as a potential stabilizing force in the region, however. Consequently, the U.S. attitude toward secessionist aspirations on the part of Soviet republics took a dramatic turn from supportive to negative. Ironically, however, the U.S. had to face up to the reality that decision-making power in the USSR was rapidly switching from the center to the republics and local governments.

Ukraine, with one-fifth of the Soviet gross national product and population, abundant natural resources, and a well-developed base of industry and agriculture, understandably is the center of attention. The direction of Ukraine's economy will to a large extent determine the direction for other Soviet republics and the country as a whole. After the expectations of the first romantic period of Soviet economic reform faded, it became clear to all involved that there will be no easy solutions. Ukrainian economists, accustomed to awaiting for decisions

*I would like to thank Holland Hunter for valuable comments on an earlier draft of this paper.

to come from Moscow, gradually began to develop their own vision of their economy. This vision is yet to be based on ideas that would facilitate the functioning of a modern economy and its integration into the world market.

The issues that are at the heart of economic reform in Ukraine are discussed in the second part of the paper. In the first part, a methodology for the analysis of economic growth and productivity is developed. Ukraine's growth and productivity have been studied in the West by Koropeckyj (1981, 106–112), using estimates built on data from 1960 to 1975. This paper takes into account the 1959–1988 period and, therefore, can be considered as an extension of Koropeckyj's study. The methodologies differ, however. Koropeckyj's approach is based on the use of a Cobb-Douglas production function while I use the constant elasticity of substitution production function. (For nonspecialists, a production function indicates the maximum output that could be produced for every specified combination of inputs.) The distinction between the two types of production functions and the results based on their use are explained below.

Data: Sources, Meanings, and Reliability

The data on Ukraine's national income, fixed capital stock, and employment used in this study are from official Soviet sources: statistical yearbooks for Ukraine and the USSR. In all, there are 31 observations, with the most current data available for 1980. Let us begin with 1958, the year of the formation of regional economic councils (*sovnarkhozy*).

In Soviet statistics, employment customarily is considered on an average annual basis and is the sum of blue- and white-collar employees (*rabochie* and *sluzhashchie*) and collective farmers (kolkhozniks). Total fixed capital stock (*osnovnye fondy*) includes plants, machinery, transport and service facilities, and livestock. National income is measured as net material product. Fixed capital stock and national income are measured in monetary terms, which presents both methodological and reliability problems. One of the measurement problems results from the fact that national income is usually reported in current prices, with the exception of the 1980–1985 period (plus several previous years). In one exceptional case, Ukrainian national income was reported in 1973 comparable prices. These comparable prices resemble conventional constant-dollar or base-year prices only at the moment when they are first set. For new goods, the first price officially approved is taken as comparable and traced back to the base year.

The values given in 1973 prices were used to reconstruct a time series for Ukraine's national income in combination with reported growth rates. Although the growth rates were measured in comparable prices as well, their base years were not given. In post-World War II Soviet economic history, with periodic revision of base years there were many changes in comparable prices, especially in industry. Because of different base years for industry and agriculture, 1955, 1965, and 1973 prices were used for national income despite more frequent price changes for industry. Comparing the available data in absolute values with estimates drawn from the growth rates for national income shows that most of the growth rates correspond to 1973 prices. It is, therefore, logical to use 1973 prices for national income in this paper. The fixed capital stock data have been expressed on the basis of 1973 prices.

In light of the ongoing critical assessment of Soviet statistics, the reliability of the data on Ukraine's national income, capital stock, and employment is crucial. The least questionable data in these three areas is employment, which, obviously, could not be inflated. Data on national income and fixed capital stock generally could be as distorted as any financial macro-indicator in Soviet statistics. What would be the basis for this distortion?

For decades there was a popular belief among Westerners who did not accept the official information on Soviet economic growth that the Soviets were keeping two parallel sets of books. Otherwise, how would the Soviets themselves know the country's true growth rates? The recent developments have demonstrated that Soviet statisticians never possessed the "true" data, however. Taking advantage of greater openness, many critically thinking Soviet economists seriously damaged the reputation of the official statistical establishment. The greatest challenge to the entire Soviet socioeconomic order came from Khanin and Seliunin (1987). They asserted that Soviet national income rose 6 to 7 times in the 1928 to 1985 period, not about 90 times as officially claimed.

I (1989) tried to reproduce Khanin-Seliunin calculations for Soviet industry based on the description of Khanin's methodology, but the estimates appeared to be closer to the official figures than to Khanin and Seliunin's. In several other studies I also computed real and inflationary components of growth for Soviet machine-building industries. For that purpose, I constructed and compared indices in value terms, in physical units of production, and in technical characteristics of product quality. The results varied for different industries and generally depended on the number of characteristics taken into consideration. The more characteristics I considered, the more my estimates resembled those reported by the Soviets.

The key issue explaining the broad range of these and other recently emerging estimates is, in my view, the treatment of product-quality change. Economists in general are not particularly good on this issue, since the valuation of quality by the consumer is inherently subjective. But in a free economy, consumers' market choices signal whether they accept or reject a change in a product. In response to consumer behavior, a competitive market sets prices by equating the marginal worth of each good's characteristics with its marginal cost. In the Soviet case, the authorities make the determination on quality, using only such "objective" characteristics as capacity, size, weight, or durability. Hence, producing a heavier truck or increasing a tractor's horsepower are treated as improvements.

When the consumer wants small, versatile, and easy-to-operate tractors, those who are critical of official Soviet statistics do not consider increasing horsepower as a quality change. They may be right. Moreover, by not knowing how the consumer values goods and services, the Soviets may even make changes in a product that consumers would consider deterioration. It is possible, however, that some farmers would still desire more powerful tractors. Therefore, even though the critics' estimates are preferable, measures of product quality are dubious when the consumer's valuations are not known. It follows that until a consensus if reached on the "correct" statistics, the official data that we use here are as good (or as bad) as any available alternative.

Theoretical Considerations and Estimation

Production functions relating outputs to a variety of inputs are widely used for estimating economic growth and productivity. However, there is a gap between the theory of production functions and empirical studies based on a priori considerations or statistical tests aimed at better approximation. At the same time, there is a growing realization of the importance of theoretical considerations, with statistical tests still playing a significant, yet not a decisive role.

Production functions were built for Ukraine's economy, for example, by Koropeckyj (1981) for the estimation of productivity growth. They were of the Cobb-Douglas (CD) type. I (1986) also used the CD, as well as linear production functions, as components of the republic's econometric models. There is an assumption associated with the CD specification that may not hold in reality, however. The assumption is related to the elasticity of substitution between the two inputs—labor and capital. The CD function implies this elasticity to be one, namely that the percentage change in the ratio of inputs exactly matches the percentage change in the ratio of productivity. Why is the elasticity of substitution so important? Because it characterizes the ease with which one input can be substituted for another; it generally ranges from zero to infinity. In an extreme case of the input-output (fixed-proportions) production function, there is no opportunity to substitute capital for labor, and the elasticity of substitution equals zero.

The low elasticity of substitution may explain an absurd development in the Soviet planned economy where there is a high demand for investment goods, but, when new plants are finally built, they are greatly underutilized. The new Soviet fixed capital does not differ much from the existing capital stock, which involves manual operations at all stages of production. The paradoxical result of this situation is that new machinery cannot be used without adequate manpower, which, in turn, cannot be provided. (Shortage of manpower is the result of planners' wage and hiring policies.) Even though the inputs may not be used exactly in fixed proportions as in the input-output production function, the elasticity of substitution in this case must be much less than unity, as in the CD function. Otherwise, the problem of the idleness of production capital would not exist in the USSR.

As a matter of fact, Weitzman (1970) found the elasticity of substitution for Soviet industry to be around 0.4; he estimated the constant elasticity of substitution (CES) production function. This function also was used by Desai (1987, 70), who found the elasticity of substitution to be even lower (for five slightly different CES functions in the range of 0.17 to 0.28). However, the low elasticity of substitution was not interpreted appropriately in terms of the inherent backwardness of Soviet technology. The question of the best production function for the Soviet economy thus remains open.

The theory of production functions answers the last question, since all the known types of production functions (CD, input-output, and linear) are partial cases of the CES function. To explain, suppose that in reality data satisfy the CD function but, because of the lack of a priori information, the CES function can only be estimated. In the resulting estimates, the CES function will actually reduce to the partial case of the CD function. In other words, the CES function is specified in the form

$$Q = \gamma \left[\delta L^{-\rho} + (1 - \delta) K^{-\rho} \right]^{-\frac{v}{\rho}} \qquad (9.1)$$

where Q = quantity of output obtainable per period of time, L = quantity of labor used, K = quantity of capital used, γ = scale parameter, $\gamma > 0$; δ = distribution parameter, $0 < \delta < 1$; ρ = substitution parameter, $\rho \geq -1$; v = index of returns to scale (decreasing is v < 1, constant is v = 1, or increasing if v > 1). The substitution parameter ρ is related to the elasticity of substitution σ so that

$$\sigma = \frac{1}{1 + \rho}$$

and, since σ is nonnegative, the indicated condition $\rho \geq -1$ must hold.

The reduction of the CES function happens in the limit as ρ approaches zero (given that v = 1), σ approaches 1, and the CES therefore approaches

$$Q = \gamma L^{\delta} K^{1-\delta} \qquad (9.2)$$

namely, the CD production function. In other alternatives, the CES function can be reduced to the linear production function (as σ approaches infinity) or the input-output production function (as σ approaches zero). Hence, this property of the CES function makes it a family of production functions and, in theory, indicates the best form of the production function.

For example, suppose that the CD is the right production function, but the CES function is estimated, as just discussed. Then, theoretically, ρ will not differ from zero and v from unity, so the reduction of the CES function (9.1) to the CD function (9.2) will take place automatically. The CES function, therefore, is as good as any other production function to which it reduces where we know what function is to be used. If we do not know what function should be used, as is usually the case, the CES function has an advantage of being fairly general and actually leading to a specific production function even without a priori information on the form of the function.

Based on these theoretical considerations, the CES production function was estimated for Ukraine's national income. As indicated in the section on the sources, meaning, and reliability of data, the estimation used official time series from 1958 to 1988. The estimation was performed with the use of the Regression Analysis of Time Series (RATS) package. To secure the nonnegative elasticity of substitution, a constraint was imposed that $\rho \geq -1$. The resulting estimates in the CES function (9.1) are: $\gamma = .39$; $\delta = .87$; $v = 1.65$, and $\rho = 4.03$. All coefficients are significant at the 5 percent level. The explanatory power of the estimated regression is very strong, with the coefficient of determination R^2 close to 1. As for the presence of of serial correlation, the Durbin-Watson test provides inconclusive results.

The value of the distribution parameter $\delta = .87$ just discussed means that labor is responsible for 87 percent of the combined "earnings share" of inputs, and capital is responsible for the remaining 13 percent. The index of returns to scale v exceeding 1 may mean different things. A straightforward explanation would be that the efficiency of newly commissioned capital consistently exceeded the efficiency of the capital replaced. Another, more plausible explanation focuses on the role of the price factor; namely, that its effect on output consistently rose with the rising scale of production. The value of the substitution parameter ρ of 4.03 is equivalent to the elasticity of substitution of .2 (that is, $1/[1 + 4.03]$). This is in agreement with the expectation that the elasticity of substitution of capital for labor is low for Ukraine's economy as well as for the Soviet planned economy in general.

Multifactor Productivity

The measures of multifactor productivity relate output to a given combination of inputs, unlike partial productivity measures of such things as labor productivity. The weights given to each factor are the proportional shares of output that each contributed in a given time period. The inputs are combined in terms of their total cost, as a proportion of total output. Specific measures differ, though, and, as shown below, may produce different estimates of multifactor productivity.

In our study, it is natural to use the estimated CES function discussed in the previous section. For comparison, along with this function, the formula applied to the U.S. economy by the Bureau of Labor Statistics (BLS) of the Department of Labor is used as well. The data and the results of computation are illustrated in Figure 9-1, and the methodology follows.

In supplying the CES function, the weights of labor and capital are .87 and .13, respectively, as given by the distribution parameter δ from the previous section. It is important that these weights are consistent with the other estimates for the CES function: the returns to scale index ν and the substitution parameter ρ. The scale parameter γ does not participate in this computation since it adjusts the growth of factor inputs to the growth of national income. But in the computation of multifactor productivity we do not want such an adjustment, which, in essence, is needed because of the change in multifactor productivity. What we need is the comparison of the two increases—in national income and factor inputs—so that the ratio of the two will demonstrate the effect of the growth of multifactor productivity.

To use the CES function, the average annual rates of growth have to be transformed into an index form (for example, a 1.29 percent rate is equivalent to a 1.0129 index) and inserted into the input part of the CES function (9.1). This yields

$$[.87(1.0129)^{-4.03} + .13(1.0627)^{-4.03}]^{-\frac{1.65}{4.03}} = 1.0311$$

so that the average annual growth rate for factor inputs (as shown in Figure 9-1) equals 3.11 percent. The multifactor productivity average growth index then is obtained as the ratio of the average growth index for factor inputs:

$$\frac{1.0482}{1.0311} = 1.0166$$

Hence, the average annual rate of growth of multifactor productivity for the Ukrainian economy is equal to 1.66 percent. The BLS methodology, which is used for the U.S. economy and also is applied in Figure 9-1 to Ukraine's economy, is based on the application of a straightforward formula:

$$r_M = r_Q - (w_L r_L + w_K r_K) \qquad (9.3)$$

where r_M, r_Q, r_L, and r_K equal the percentage change in multifactor productivity, output, labor, and capital services, respectively, and w_L and w_K equal the share of labor and capital, respectively, in the total value of output ($w_L + w_K = 1$). The labor share is practically estimated as the wages-to-output ratio, and the capital share is then the residual ($1 - w_K$).

The average annual rates of increase of national income, labor, and capital for Ukraine's economy used in this case in Figure 9-1 are the same as in the CES case. What differs is the weights inputs. In the CES case the weights are those estimated in the section on theoretical considerations and estimations and consistent with other parameters. In applying the BLS methodology, I estimated total annual wages of workers and collective farmers (kolkhozniks), plus public consumption. The resulting average ratio of this annual wage bill to Ukraine's national income is equal to .68 for the 1958–1988 period. The capital-services to national-income ratio is consequently .32. Inserting these weights and growth rates from Figure 9-1 into the formula just presented yields the average factor inputs growth rate of 2.88 percent and the average multifactor productivity growth rate of 1.94 percent.

Despite the differences in the methodologies, discussed above, the gap between the average rates of 1.66 percent and 1.94 percent for multifactor productivity could be considered narrow. The results are within a small range. Using the CD function, Koropeckyj (1981) estimated the multifactor productivity for Ukraine measured by national income (net material product) to be equal to 2.6 percent for the 1960–1975 period. Considering the slowdown in Soviet technological progress from 1975 to 1988, that is, the period of this study beyond the period considered by Koropeckyj, the results may at least in part be considered consistent. The difference in the methodologies should have played its role, too.

The Reform Factor

Despite the fact that factors promoting productivity growth and technological change are extremely important, there are periods in nations' histories when these factors by themselves stop playing their usual vital role. Wars and revolutions are examples, as are less-dramatic transformations of societies. Ukraine's economy is undergoing such a transformation, the long-term consequences of which are hard to grasp. The old institutions have already been damaged, while the new institutions have not yet been created. It is clear that the further development of Ukraine's economy will depend on the success of its economic reform.

In the process of estimating the CES production function, I designed a simple test of the effect of reform on Ukraine's economy. The test is "blind," that is, it does not identify any specific developments or effects. Rather, it compares the data for two periods—pre-reform and reform—and answers the question of whether they reflect the same trend. The change, if any, is thus treated as structural and could be either positive or negative. To understand the idea of the test, suppose that a production function is estimated first for the pre-reform period and then, separately, for the reform period. Should changes in productivity, efficiency, or the use of inputs occur in the reform period, the two regressions will turn out to be statistically different. But if no significant change happens, the two regressions will be statistically indistinguishable; hence, one joint regression instead could be run for both the pre-reform and reform periods.

Such a construction allows for the use of a standard F-test. To introduce it, suppose that we have two independent sets of data with sample sizes n_1 and n_2 and two regressions, respectively, with k explanatory variables (including the constant terms). Also define RSS_1 as the residual sum of squares for the first data set, and RSS_2 as the residual sum of squares for the second data set. The sum $RSS_1 + RSS_2$ is the unrestricted residual sum of squares $URSS$ with $(n_1 + n_2 - 2k)$ degrees of freedom. The restricted residual sum of squares $RRSS$ with $(n_1 + n_2 - k)$ degrees of freedom is obtained from the joint regression with the pooled data (the restriction is that the parameters in the two regressions are the same). The F-test then is

$$F = \frac{(RRSS - URSS)/k}{URSS/(n_1 + n_2 - 2k)}$$

From the two separate regressions, estimated $RSS_1 = .02125$ and $RSS_2 = .00056$ so that $URSS = .02125 + .00056 = .02181$ with d.f. = $31 - 8 = 23$. From the regression for the pooled data $RRSS = .02206$ with d.f. = $31 - 4 = 27$. Hence:

$$F = \frac{(.02206 - .02181)/4}{.02181/23} = .066$$

From the F-tables with d.f. 4 and 23, the 5 percent point is about 2.80 and the 1 percent point is about 4.26. Thus at both levels of significance, the hypothesis of stability of the two sets of data cannot be rejected.

Rephrasing the result of the test, the reform factor did not affect the macro-indicators for Ukraine's economy at all. This seems to contradict even the official Soviet position that reform has deteriorated many aspects of Soviet economic life; Ukraine is certainly not an exception. Indeed, taking another look at Ukraine's macro-indicators, according to *Narhosp Ukraïny* (various years), the average annual growth rate for national income was only 3.4 percent in the reform 1985–1988 period, while it averaged 5 percent in the pre-reform 1958–1984 period. Yet such a decline did not occur in just the reform period; it was the continuation of the long postwar trend. As a matter of fact, dividing the whole 1958–1988 period under consideration into three 10-year periods, the average annual growth rates for Ukraine's national income are 6.7 percent from 1958 to 1968, 5.0 percent form 1968 to 1978, and 3.2 percent from 1978 to 1988. The average rate in the reform period, therefore, is in line with these figures. Hence, it seems that reform did not bring any deviations from the trend in Ukraine's economic growth one way or another.

Conclusion: Shifting to the World of Money

It would be logical, in conclusion, to use the methodology suggested in this paper to forecast Ukraine's national income. On one hand, certain assumptions must be made in the process. Basing these assumptions on the existing economic model will certainly date them. On the other hand, it is premature to quantify a model of the future. In any case, the exercise would be rather mechanical. Instead, I prefer to ask what the model of the future should be.

Lenin dreamed of an economy as one factory where proletarians would manage physical commodities without money, the symbol of capitalism and exploitation. For more than seven decades, Soviet planners implemented the world of physical commodities; however, even under planning, money was needed for accounting purposes. The system, though inefficient, worked only because virtually all commodities were involved in the planned distribution process. Attempts to reform the system by planning the distribution of fewer commodities and shifting more decision-making power to enterprises led to rising imbalances, lower physical output, and higher financial incomes and inflation. The 1965 reform caused these types of negative developments, for example, but planners stepped in to reverse the trend. They also would have intervened in the late 1980s, but by then Gorbachev and the reforming forces he unleashed were determined to move ahead. Intervention by planners could stop the excessive rise in incomes and prices and thus balance the economy, but they could not cure the fundamental problems of Soviet economic waste and inefficiency.

Where does this leave Ukraine's economy? To a great extent, the problems of the Soviet economy helped the cause of Ukrainian independence. First, the economic mess made it clear to people in all republics, including Ukraine, that they should take their destiny into their own hands. Second, by the same token it has become increasingly clear that the attempts to impose economic reform in the USSR from a single center are unworkable. Whether the reformers in Moscow will understand this before it is too late is difficult to say. The inertia of over-centralization and the paternalistic attitudes toward the republics are so strong that the reformers in essence are imposing their vision of the new Soviet economic model by the same means used to impose the Stalinist model of central planning.

Ukrainian economists will have to use the greater opportunity now open to them to develop a gradual shift away from planning and the world of physical commodities and shortages that is associated with it. But a shift where? It would be generally beneficial for an integrated economy such as the USSR's to use a common currency, even if the USSR may disintegrate politically. Yet it is the fact of such a disintegration, combined with growing economic hardship, that leaves little chance for a possible strengthening of the ruble. Under these circumstances, Ukraine may have to introduce its own currency, which would bring up the immediate problem of its convertibility into the ruble and other currencies.

Unfortunately, in the USSR money is associated with currency, which always moves there together with wages. When introduced in Ukraine, new monetary aggregates could be similar to those used in the West, with a simplification resulting from the underdevelopment of financial markets. Consequently, at the beginning there could be two monetary aggregates—*M1* and *M2*. The *M1* category would include currency and "checkable" deposits, which incorporate savings deposits of the population (classified in the US as a part of *M2*) and demand deposits of institutions (state enterprises, cooperatives, and private businesses). The *M2* category consists of *M1* along with time deposits, available to both the population and institutions. The system will end up with a privileged position for state enterprises when they obtain money from the state bank to pay wages, frequently regardless of the availability of money in the account. The deposits of the state enterprises are to be transferred to the newly created commercial banks from the state banks, which would assume the responsibilities of a central bank.

The central bank of Ukraine will exercise more regulatory power than, say, the U.S. Federal Reserve. Thus, it will perform the usual functions of a central bank, namely conducting open market sales and purchases of securities, imposing reserve requirements, specifying the terms of bank borrowing and membership, providing check-clearing facilities, insuring deposits, and so on. At the same time, the central bank will have to set ceilings on interest rates paid by banks, regulate bank legal assets and investment policies, stipulate lending practices, and the like.

The world of money is inseparable from two things—incentives and risk. While the Soviet planned economy tried but failed to stimulate incentives, in principle it is unable to introduce risk. From this standpoint, experimenting with new types of collective property (in the form of leasing or buyout) may be even worse than administrative controls. On one hand, bureaucracy restricts wage growth. On the other hand, the Yugoslav experience with self-management proved that, given decision-making power without any economic risk, workers succeed in raising wages but not productivity. The uncontrolled inflation of the last several years of Soviet economic reform demonstrates this case, too.

Since Ukraine's economy is not ready for a large-scale privatization, there must be a clear understanding of priorities. The Soviet reform process has lacked such an understanding. Considering the critical food situation in the USSR and the fact that some 70 percent of raw materials for consumer goods comes from agriculture, it follows that agriculture should have been given the highest priority. Instead, it was once again expected that agricultural performance would gradually improve within the general framework of reform, in response to self-financing, greater independence in production and marketing, more flexible prices, and better material incentives. Yet nothing could resurrect the kolkhoz system.

Shifting to the world of money is impossible with collectivized agriculture in place. Reforming Ukraine's economy will create even greater opportunities for increasing the money supply, while the consumer goods markets simply will have no agricultural raw materials. A typical Soviet argument against private farming is that the peasants do not want to become farmers and work hard. In this case, if they do not want to take land free of charge, why would they be willing to lease it, as a new government program foresees? (As always, the peculiarity of Soviet logic could only compete with that in Alice's wonderland.) Ukraine's economic reform should begin with rural reform, which will be enormously costly, even though probably not as costly as it would be in Russia. Yet without the rural reform, even more resources will keep disappearing, as Seliunin (1989) says, into black holes of the economy.

Privatizing the consumer goods industry would make sense when the rural reform yields an improvement in the supply of food and raw materials. Encouraging private activities prematurely only leads to price increases, as the brief experience of the Soviet cooperative movement has demonstrated. The Soviet reformers are struggling with plans for privatization of existing industrial firms, which primarily would be analogous to big business under the U.S. classification. The competitive U.S. business infrastructure is based on small establishments. Thus, according to the U.S. Department of Commerce (1989, 516), in 1985 there were about 17 million for-profit organizations in the U.S., the bulk of which—12 million—were sole proprietorships in trade and services. By comparison, judging by *Narhosp Ukraïny* (1985, 297, 319, 320), there were some 265,000 state enterprises in trade, catering, and services in Ukraine in 1985. Of course rather than higher numbers, Ukraine's economy needs thousands of efficient, low-cost family businesses in all activities. This is easier said than done. Along with numerous political and bureaucratic impediments, there is strong resentment on the part of the population at the idea of private marketeers becoming rich. Beyond the decades of ideological brainwashing, quite understandable human envy plays a role. Yet, if Ukrainian society rejects the socialist idea of all people being poor to keep some people from being rich, it should gradually accept the capitalist idea that, for all people to live better, some must become entrepreneurial and rich.

Privatizing large-scale industries may take years; moreover, the state may still retain a significant stake in the enterprises. Of the two strategies of denationalization—the Polish "shock therapy" and the Hungarian gradual approach—the latter in my view is more suitable for Ukraine, especially considering that rural reform in Ukraine is yet to come. Ukrainian economists should learn to employ the tools of fiscal and monetary policies to monitor the step-by-step approach to reform, restrict growth of incomes and money supply, keep government spending under control, and provide tax incentives for small private enterprise and farmers. In a modern economy, it is imperative that monetary policy is independent of fiscal policy. Unfortunately, this has not been the case in Ukraine or in the rest of the USSR. Shifting to the world of money thus will require the reeducation of Ukrainian economists. Let us hope that they are ready for the challenge.

References

Derzhkomstat URSR. 1986. *Narhosp Ukraïn'skoï RSR v 1985 r.* Kiev.

Desai, Padma. 1987. *The Soviet Economy: Problems and Prospects.* New York.

Koropeckyj, I. S. 1981. "Growth and Productivity." In *Economics of Soviet Regions.* Edited by I. S. Koropeckyj and G. E. Schroeder, 92–117. New York.

Kushnirsky, Fyodor I. 1986. "Regional Growth in the Soviet Economy: A Model and Analysis." *Journal of Regional Science* 26 (1): 47–62.

————. 1989. *Growth and Inflation in the Soviet Economy.* Boulder, Colorado.

Seliunin, Vasilii. "Chernye dyry ekonomiki." *Novyi Mir* 10 (1989).

———— and Grigorii Kahanin. 1987. "Lukavaia tsifra." *Novyi Mir* 2:192.

U.S. Department of Commerce. 1989. *Statistical Abstract of the United States.* Washington.

Weitzman, M. 1970. "Soviet Postwar Economic Growth and Capital-Labor Substitution." *American Economic Review* 60 (4): 676–92.

Figure 9–1. Average Annual Rates of Increase of Ukraine's National Income, Factor Inputs, and Factor Productivity (1958–1988) (percent)

Income	CES Function	BLS Method
National income	4.82	4.82
Labor	1.29	1.29
Capital	6.27	6.27
Labor weight	87.00	68.00
Capital weight	13.00	32.00
Factor inputs	3.11	2.88
Multifactor productivity	1.66	1.94

Source: *Narkhoz Ukrainy* for different years.

CHAPTER TEN

Ukrainian Industrial Productivity: A Republic-Comparative Analysis

Blaine E. McCants *

Comparing Ukrainian industrial performance to that of other republics in the USSR is not easy. The quantity and quality of industry and industrial output, capital, and labor data released by the USSR State Committee for Statistics (Goskomstat SSSR) and its lineal predecessor, the Central Statistical Administration, challenged outsiders' attempts to compare either static or dynamic inter-republic industrial productivity.

This is not to deny the importance of the work that has been done. Much has been accomplished with the input-output data that is available about the republics. Indeed, the task of carefully reconstructing the data to make republic-level, branch-of-industry comparisons for 1966 and 1972 was immense (Treml 1977; Gillula and Treml 1978; Gillula 1981 and 1982). Interesting comparisons can be made with such data, but these comparisons are limited by two shortcomings: Soviet-administered prices and variations in the composition of industry among the republics.

*This material has been reviewed by the Central Intelligence Agency (CIA) to assist the author in removing classified information, if any. However, that review neither constitutes CIA authentication of material as factual nor implies CIA endorsement of the author's views. The author would like to thank David Kamerling for his helpful comments.

Branch-of-Industry Comparisons: Background

Moscow has long used its central price-setting authority to further a variety of goals, such as transferring income between republics or controlling the profits of enterprises. Thus, the wide regional variations in output/capital and output/labor ratios observed by Gillula and Treml almost certainly reflect differences in regional price levels rather than large variations in the static efficiency of primary resource use. Dynamic efficiency, usually measured as Hicks-neutral technical progress, also is difficult to estimate because input-output data for 1972 were released for only eight Soviet republics (Gillula 1982). To my knowledge, no similar republic-level input-output data have been released for subsequent years.

Dynamic efficiency can be estimated in other ways, however. For example, Cohn (1977) used value-added weights to compare Ukrainian productivity to that of the USSR as a whole for the period of 1960 to 1974. Koropeckyj (1981) used industry data from 1960 to 1975, with Cobb-Douglas production functions, and republic factor return weights to estimate total factor productivity for the USSR and its 15 republics. Here again, however, data limitations make it difficult to get reliable results. Given the pervasive disequilibrium of the Soviet economy, industry factor return shares may reflect poor estimates of actual capital and labor elasticities, and thus may not be the best weights for productivity analysis. The alternative procedure is joint estimation of factor elasticities and technological progress. Unfortunately, econometric estimates of these parameters based on Soviet aggregate industry time series data vary both with model specification and the period under study (Weitzman 1970; Desai 1976 and 1985).

Comparisons of productivity also are affected by the wide variation in the composition of industry among Soviet republics (Gillula and Treml 1978). This is important because the gross value of output (GVO) growth rates in the Soviet Union, especially those of the machine-building and metalworking (MBMW) and chemical branches of industry, have hidden inflation (Greenslade 1972). Aggregate industry output measures incorporate these upward biases, so productivity estimates based on them are overstated.

More important, hidden inflation skews estimates of the relative dynamic productivity of the republics because the MBMW and chemical branches of industry are not located proportionally among Soviet republics. Where the share of MBMW in industrial output is higher, such as in Ukraine, hidden inflation in these two branches tends to overstate dynamic industrial productivity relative to those republics where the share of MBMW in industrial output is lower, such as in the central Asian republics.

The goal of this study is to get a better handle on the relative trends of technical progress among the Soviet republics. This requires a new approach based on expanding the data set used to estimate technical progress. This expansion was accomplished on a republic level by combining input-output, base-year data for various branches of industry GVO with industrial output, capital, and labor growth rates. The result was a cross section of time series data on Soviet industry. This method is not perfect, yet until Goskomstat SSSR sees fit to release official data it seems to be the best way to get relatively reliable estimates of dynamic productivity among the republics.

For this analysis, data on GVO, fixed capital, and labor were assembled for nine major branches of industry for all 15 republics.

The nine major branches of industry tracked were electric power; fuel (oil, gas, coal, and other fuels); metallurgy; chemical; machine-building and metalworking; wood, pulp, and paper industry; construction materials; light industry (textiles, clothing, footwear); and food processing industry. The GVO index series for these major branches were taken from official republic statistical handbooks, such as the *Narkhoz Ukrainy*. The ruble values of output figures in 1966 producers' prices were taken from Gillula and Treml to get common prices for all output series. The output data set was complete, except that Moldova and Armenia lacked a fuel industry, Kyrgyzstan and Tajikistan lacked a chemicals industry, and Belarus, Lithuania, Estonia, Moldova, Armenia, Kyrgyzstan, Tajikistan, and Turkmenistan lacked metallurgical industry.

Combining these types of data can lead to complications. A typical problem, described in Greenslade (1972), is illustrated by electric-power generation and is caused by the fact that the GVO indexes are based on enterprise-level data, but that input-output data are assembled on a commodity basis. Many industrial enterprises have cogeneration facilities. The input-output base includes the value of electricity produced at all facilities, but the GVO index includes only the electricity produced at facilities whose primary function is to produce electricity. One example of specific importance for Ukraine centers on the metallurgical industry. The metallurgy base year includes both ferrous and nonferrous metals; however, the Soviets published ferrous metallurgy indexes only until 1985. After that, they published combined metallurgy indexes, but did not provide sufficient historical detail to construct an index for total metallurgy for the period of 1961 to 1986. The approach chosen was to use post-1985 total metallurgy growth rates to derive the ferrous metallurgy growth indexes, but to use total metallurgy 1966 base-year weights. Additional descriptions of the data and cautionary notes on the errors of rounding and chain-linking indexes of various base years can be found in McCants (1983). GVO growth data for Ukraine are shown in Figure 10-1.

The primary references for the capital stock data for the years 1961 to 1966 and 1968 to 1974 are Gillula (1981) and relevant issues of the *Narkhoz SSSR*. Gillula provides estimates of the end- of-year values of industrial fixed capital by republic by year. The various *Narkhoz SSSR* issues break down the distribution among branches of fixed capital by republic by percentage points. Gillula estimated fixed capital by republic by industrial branch for 1961 and 1974. His methodology was replicated for the intervening years except for 1966, for which no *Narkhoz SSSR* data were available. Data for 1966 were estimated as the average of the relevant 1965 and 1967 estimates. All these capital stock data are valued in 1955 rubles. After 1974 the Soviets stopped publishing such detailed capital stock data. Most republic handbooks continued to publish series on the rate of growth of industrial fixed capital by branch relative to a base year, usually 1970. Growth relative to 1970 was calculated using the fixed capital stock growth rates published in the republic handbooks, using the estimated ruble value as bases. For some republics, however, no capital stock growth series appeared until the mid-1980s and the series, when published, were incomplete. These gaps in the capital stock growth data in the late 1970s and early 1980s were filled by log-linear interpolation. A final potential problem with the capital data is that the published post-1974 capital stock growth rate series apparently was constructed using 1973 capital stock prices. Linking these growth series with their 1970 base values (in 1955 prices) could create very small discontinuities in the 1975 capital stock data. The capital stock growth data for Ukraine are shown in Figure 10-2.

The basic sources for the labor data are Rapawy (1979) for the years 1965 and 1970–1975, and the republic statistical handbooks for other years. Labor data after 1975 were estimated using the growth of output and labor productivity series published in the republic handbooks. Dividing the growth of output series by the labor productivity series gives an implied rate of growth of the labor force. Feshbach (1972) notes the hazards of using this procedure, but there is no attractive alternative. Labor data for Ukraine for 1961 to 1986 are shown in Figure 10-3.

The Basic Model

The model used here is a generalized Cobb-Douglas model in which labor and capital output elasticities are estimated separately for each branch of industry but are assumed to be common among republics. Because Soviet prices are administered, however, relative intercepts are estimated separately for each branch of industry in each republic. The estimated coefficients of the eight major branch-of-industry dummies represent combined price/static efficiency levels of the branch of industry in the Russian Federation relative to that of the electric power branch of the Russian Federation. (This was done purely by convention.) Within each branch, the estimated coefficients of up to 14 republic-branch dummies represent combined price/static efficiency levels relative to that of the major branch of industry's estimated coefficient. The 14 dummies representing electric power in the republics represent combined price/static efficiency levels relative to electric power generation in the Russian Federation, which is picked up by the overall estimate of the intercept.

Trend variables also are used for the MBMW and chemical branches of industry, with the expectation that the estimated parameters for these trends represent their hidden inflation rates. No other adjustment was made for hidden inflation, even though there is a fairly large body of literature on hidden inflation's effects on Soviet comparable-price capital stock series. For example, Nove (1981) and I (1987) find less cause for concern. Any rate of hidden inflation in capital stock will cause estimates of residual technical progress to be understated. However, no adjustments for hidden inflation have been made to the capital stock data in the following regressions, since rates of hidden inflation in industrial fixed capital stock are not likely to vary greatly among Soviet republics.

One adjustment is made to the fixed capital data. Weighted annual averages of the end-of-year capital stock values are used in the following regressions. They are used because Soviet commissionings tend to be bunched toward the end of the year. The weighted annual average value used for fixed capital is

$$K(t) = K(t-1) + 0.35(K(t) - (K(t-1)))$$

That is, weighted capital equals capital stock at the beginning of the year plus 35 percent of the increment. This is the formula used by Gosplan as its measure of the average value of fixed capital available annually (Tretyakova 1977).

Modeling Dynamic Productivity Differences Among Republics

The direct way to estimate the relative rates of technical progress among the republics is to model separate trend rates of technical progress for each republic. However, such trend rates may be misleading because the years they are based on include the years of the great Soviet industrial slowdown (Schroeder 1985). Schroeder observed abnormally large energy shortages, transport bottlenecks, and planning errors that created system-wide shocks and resulted in an extended, perceptible drop in the USSR's trend rate of industrial productivity. A simple way to reflect the sharp kink in trend rates of technical progress observed in the mid-1970s is to estimate common levels of technical progress across republics and branches for each year relative to 1961. Because of the great Soviet industrial slowdown, it would be nice to estimate dynamic trend rates of technological progress across the republics simultaneously with industry-wide estimates of technical progress relative to a base year. However, a model with 15 republic time trends and dummy variables for each out-year is overspecified.

The solution used is to run the model twice. The first run uses 15 republic dummy time trends, thus estimating relative dynamic productivity rates among the republics. The second run uses 14 republic dummy time trends as well as 25 dummy variables for the years 1962 to 1986. These trends capture technical progress in each year relative to 1961. The republic for which the time trend is excluded is that republic with the mean estimated time trend of the first run; in this case, Armenia. The resulting estimated coefficients of republic time trends in this second run represent trend rates of technical progress relative to that of Armenia.

The model used in the first run is shown in equation a; the model used in the second run is shown in equation b.

(a)

$\log(\text{output}) = \text{intercept} + a_{\text{branch}} * \log(\text{labor}) + b_{\text{branch}} * \log$ (average capital)

        + Time trend for machinery + time trend for chemicals

        + Dummy variables for eight major branches of industry

        + Dummy variables for up to 14 republics for each of nine branches of industry

        + Time trend for each republic

        + Error

where a_{branch} and b_{branch} are output elasticities estimated separately for each of the nine major branches of industry.

(b)

$\log(\text{output}) = \text{intercept} + a_{\text{branch}} * \log(\text{labor}) + b_{\text{branch}} * \log(\text{average capital})$

        + Time trend for machinery + time trend for chemicals

        + Dummy variables for eight major branches of industry

        + Dummy variables for up to 14 republics for each of nine branches of industry

        + Time trend for each republic except Armenia

        + Dummy variable for each year, 1962–1986

        + Error

where a_{branch} and b_{branch} are output elasticities estimated separately for each of the nine major branches of industry.

Due to space constraints, only abridged results of model *b* are shown in Figure 10-4. Coefficients for 114 dummy variables for up to 14 republics for each of the nine branches of industry are estimated, but not provided. no republic dummy in the machine-building, construction materials, or food-processing branches of industry was statistically significant; however, all but two of the remaining 72 dummy variables for the other six branches of industry were statistically significant.

The results of model *b* then were tested for simple global heteroscedasticity (that is, to see if the variance of the disturbance term was related to the size of the observation), using a procedure outlined in

Thiel (1971): The log of the squared residuals from equation *b* were modeled as the dependent variable against the predicted values of equation *b*. The predicted outputs of this model were exponentiated, squared, and inverted and used as weights for a subsequent run of model *b*. As seen in Figure 10-5, heteroscedasticity exists to a significant degree. however, as also seen by the abridged results of the weighted version of model b, shown in Figure 10-6, the parameter estimates changed only slightly.

Industrial Technical Progress and Ukraine

From the preceding modeling exercises, it appears that Ukraine is one of the underperforming Soviet republics, along with the Russian Federation and most Central Asian republics. Ukraine's negative trend rate of relative technical progress is statistically significant in disaggregated models, when dummy variables are used to account for differences in relative price/static efficiency levels among branches of industry by republic.

These findings for Ukraine have not changed much from Koropeckyj's earlier ranking of comparative republic industrial productivity for the years 1960 to 1975, even though the time period Koropeckyj considered was before the time of the great Soviet industrial slowdown. In that study, Ukraine's trend of productivity was slightly less than the all-union average. For purposes of comparison, Koropeckyj's estimates of the trend of productivity levels in the republic have been normalized in comparison with his estimate of the USSR's trend productivity level. These are contrasted with this study's estimates of relative republic productivity trends, taken from Figures 10-4 and 10-6. These results are shown in Figure 10-7.

The reasons for Ukraine's performance are speculative. The first would be the "rust belt" or traditional industries' effect alluded to by Cohn (1977). Western market economies faced (and are still facing) a painful transition and disruptions when moving out of heavy industries such as old-line machine building and ferrous metallurgy and into higher-technology industries. A cursory look at the history of U.S. and Western European steel and coal industries attests to this.

If anything, Soviet central planners and politicians seem less willing to bite the bullet and close redundant and inefficient steel mills and coal mines than their Western counterparts. It appears that instead they continue to pour capital into existing facilities and technologies, regardless of the rate of return. In this respect, central planning has been less beneficial for Ukraine, in a purely technical sense, than for the more rapidly progressing republics such as Belarus (Sager 1985), where some industrial evolution appears to have occurred. Ukraine's economic plan for 1990 naturally called for a faster transformation to higher technologies, but this refrain is both often played and often ignored throughout the Soviet economy.

Far more speculative reasons for Ukraine's relatively uninspired economic performance could be related to adverse trends in worker demographics or education, pollution, or alcohol consumption. Unfortunately, data that can support such speculation are unavailable.

Conclusion

These modeling exercises indicate that Ukraine has suffered a relative deterioration in its technological base over the past decades. There is, perhaps, one bright spot on the horizon. The economic and political changes now underway in the Soviet Union should offer republics far greater autonomy in making investment and other economic decisions. To the extent that Ukraine's poor economic performance was caused by bad decisions made in Moscow, Ukrainian decision-makers of all types now will have the chance to show their mettle. They certainly face a challenge.

References

Cohn, Stanley H. 1977. "Economic Growth." In *The Ukraine Within the USSR: An Economic Balance Sheet*. Edited by I. S. Koropeckyj, 67–83. New York.

_____. 1981. "A Comment on Alec Nove 'A Note on Growth, Investment, and Price Indices.'" *Soviet Studies* 33 (2): 296–99.

Desai, Padma. 1976. "The Production Function and Technical Change in Postwar Soviet Industry: A Reexamination." *American Economic Review* 66 (3): 372–81.

_____. 1985. "Total Factor Productivity in Postwar Soviet Industry and its Branches." *Journal of Comparative Economics* 9 (1): 1–23.

Feshbach, Murray. 1972. "Soviet Industrial Labor and Productivity Statistics." In *Soviet Economic Statistics*. Edited by Vladimir G. Treml and John P. Hardt, 195–228. Durham, North Carolina.

Gallik, Dimitri M., Barry L. Kostinsky, and Vladimir G. Treml. 1983. "Input Output Structure of the Soviet Economy: 1972." *Foreign Economic Report no. 18*, U.S. Department of Commerce, Bureau of the Census. Washington, D.C.

Gillula, James W. 1977. "Input-Output Analysis." In *The Ukraine within the USSR: An Economic Balance Sheet*. Edited by I. S. Koropeckyj, 193–234. New York.

_____. 1981. "The Regional Distribution of Fixed Capital in the USSR." *Foreign Economic Report no. 17*, U.S. Department of Commerce, Bureau of the Census (March). Washington, D.C.

_____. 1982. "The Reconstructed 1972 Input Output Tables for Eight Soviet Republics." *Foreign Economic Report no. 18*, U.S. Department of Commerce, Bureau of the Census. Washington, D.C.

_____ and Vladimir G. Treml. 1978. "Comparison of the Structure of Production by Soviet Republics." *Duke University/University of North Carolina Occasional Papers on Soviet Input-Output Analysis*, 55–56.

Greenslade, Rush V. 1972. "Industrial Production Statistics in the USSR." In *Soviet Economic Statistics*, 155–94. Edited by Vladimir G. Treml and John P. Hardt. Durham, North Carolina.

Koropeckyj, I. S. 1981. "Growth and Productivity." In *Economics of Soviet Regions*. Edited by I. S. Koropeckyj and Gertrude Schroeder, 92–117. New York.

McCants, Blaine E. 1983. *An Econometric Study of Soviet Industry by Republic and Major Branch of Industry, 1961–1980*. Ph.D. Dissertation, Duke University.

_____. 1987. "Projecting Soviet Energy Requirements Using a Vintage Capital Model." *Journal of Comparative Economics* 11 (4): 572–83.

Nove, Alec. 1981. "A Note on Growth, Investment, and Price-Indices." *Soviet Studies* 33 (1): 142–45.

Rapawy, Stephen. 1979. "Regional Employment Trends in the USSR: 1950–1975." In *Soviet Economy in a Time of Change 1*, 602–17. Joint Economic Committee. Washington, D.C.

Sagers, Matthew J. 1985. "The Soviet Periphery: Economic Development of Belorussia." *Soviet Economy* 1 (3): 261–84.

Schroeder, Gertrude. 1985. "The Slowdown in Soviet Industry, 1976–1982." *Soviet Economy* 1 (1): 42–74.

Thiel, Henry. 1971. *Principles of Econometrics*. New York.

Treml, Vladimir G., ed. 1977. *Studies in Soviet Input-Output Analysis*. New York.

Tretyakova, Albina. 1977. "Labor and Capital in the Soviet Union by Republic." *Duke University Occasional Papers on Soviet Input-Output Analysis*, 20. Translated by James W. Gillula. Edited by Vladimir G. Treml.

Weitzman, Martin. 1970. "Soviet Postwar Economic Growth and Capital-Labor Substitution." *American Economic Review* 60 (4): 676–96.

Wiles, Peter. 1982. "Soviet Consumption and Investment Prices, and the Meaningfulness of Real Investment." *Soviet Studies* 34 (2): 289–95.

Figure 10-1. Growth of Gross Value of Output for Ukraine
by Major Branch of Industry
(1970 = 100)

	1961	1962	1963	1964	1965	1966	1967	1968	1969
	1970	1971	1972	1973	1974	1975	1976	1977	1978
	1979	1980	1981	1982	1983	1984	1985	1986	
Electric	40.7	46.4	53.2	58.9	64.9	68.8	71.4	82.5	92.2
power	100.0	109.0	115.0	125.0	132.0	142.0	153.0	158.0	163.0
	170.0	175.0	172.0	178.0	180.0	192.0	205.0	205.0	
Fuel	65.3	69.2	73.0	78.2	82.6	85.1	88.4	90.9	95.0
industry	100.0	104.0	108.0	112.0	114.0	117.0	119.0	122.0	122.0
	122.0	122.0	120.0	122.0	124.0	128.0	128.0	130.0	
Chemicals	28.3	33.5	39.1	45.3	52.9	59.8	68.3	77.2	86.8
	100.0	112.0	122.0	136.0	153.0	169.0	186.0	197.0	207.0
	214.0	224.0	238.0	244.0	257.0	267.0	276.0	290.0	
Metallurgy	59.5	64.5	68.3	73.9	79.4	84.1	89.7	92.9	95.2
	100.0	104.0	107.0	112.0	117.0	122.0	127.0	128.0	128.0
	129.0	127.0	126.0	126.0	131.0	133.0	136.0	142.0	
Machine	35.6	41.5	47.0	51.9	56.8	63.6	72.2	80.1	89.8
building	100.0	111.0	124.0	140.0	158.0	175.0	193.0	211.0	229.0
	245.0	259.0	273.0	285.0	303.0	325.0	349.0	376.0	
Wood and	59.9	60.5	63.4	68.6	71.4	73.6	78.6	85.0	91.4
paper	100.0	108.0	113.0	120.0	127.0	134.0	139.0	144.0	149.0
	149.0	153.0	161.0	169.0	179.0	187.0	194.0	203.0	
Construction	49.5	53.2	55.9	60.8	66.7	73.3	80.0	86.7	92.0
materials	100.0	109.0	116.0	124.0	132.0	139.0	144.0	147.0	148.0
	147.0	146.0	147.0	148.0	155.0	161.0	162.0	169.0	
Light	48.3	50.5	52.4	53.7	55.6	61.7	71.7	81.1	90.6
industry	100.0	107.0	111.0	117.0	122.0	130.0	137.0	143.0	151.0
	157.0	162.0	167.0	167.0	171.0	174.0	177.0	179.0	
Food	57.3	61.4	61.9	64.5	76.3	79.4	84.0	89.3	95.4
processing	100.0	103.0	107.0	113.0	120.0	127.0	122.0	130.0	133.0
	134.0	130.0	133.0	140.0	147.0	150.0	151.0	156.0	

Figure 10-2. Growth of Ukrainian Industrial Fixed Capital Stock
by Major Branch of Industry
(1970 = 100)

| | 1961 | 1962 | 1963 | 1964 | 1965 | 1966 | 1967 | 1968 | 1969 |
| | 1970 | 1971 | 1972 | 1973 | 1974 | 1975 | 1976 | 1977 | 1978 |
	1979	1980	1981	1982	1983	1984	1985	1986	
Electric	33.4	37.9	45.2	49.6	57.9	63.9	71.1	80.5	91.4
power	100.0	112.3	123.0	133.0	152.8	144.0	153.0	163.0	172.0
	176.0	184.0	197.0	205.0	215.0	232.0	242.0	258.0	
Fuel	54.3	61.8	66.8	72.2	76.1	79.5	82.6	88.5	93.8
industry	100.0	105.2	111.2	116.5	122.0	131.0	139.0	145.0	151.0
	161.0	171.0	180.0	190.0	200.0	211.0	222.0	233.0	
Chemicals	26.7	36.0	42.6	47.5	55.0	61.6	69.0	75.8	86.6
	100.0	111.8	119.6	132.4	131.0	163.0	174.0	183.0	203.0
	236.0	251.0	260.0	271.0	283.0	308.0	325.0	339.0	
Metallurgy	45.2	54.4	59.0	64.5	69.3	73.7	78.4	84.7	91.7
	100.0	104.4	107.5	115.1	121.9	134.0	141.0	150.0	158.0
	165.0	175.0	181.0	190.0	199.0	207.0	217.0	220.0	
Machine	42.3	47.7	52.2	57.7	61.0	68.2	76.1	82.6	92.1
building	100.0	110.2	122.3	132.9	151.6	162.0	179.0	195.0	214.0
	232.0	252.0	273.0	294.0	315.0	338.0	362.0	387.0	
Wood and	53.9	60.1	70.1	73.1	79.6	81.0	82.2	83.8	92.0
paper	100.0	101.1	108.2	116.9	133.4	147.0	156.0	166.0	175.0
	185.0	194.0	202.0	231.0	242.0	254.0	270.0	285.0	
Construction	49.4	53.5	59.3	65.1	70.8	74.7	78.8	83.9	90.4
materials	100.0	105.9	113.3	122.5	126.8	150.0	157.0	165.0	173.0
	179.0	185.0	190.0	201.0	211.0	221.0	231.0	236.0	
Light	34.7	33.8	41.2	49.4	56.0	62.5	69.7	78.4	86.0
industry	100.0	107.9	115.5	133.2	138.8	153.0	168.0	183.0	198.0
	207.0	216.0	229.0	237.0	247.0	257.0	270.0	279.0	
Food	53.0	51.8	60.4	67.0	79.1	83.1	83.3	88.5	96.1
processing	100.0	106.7	114.2	124.8	129.9	146.0	154.0	164.0	173.0
	180.0	187.0	197.0	207.0	216.0	226.0	236.0	248.0	

Figure 10-3. Industrial Personnel in Ukraine
by Major Branch of Industry
(1000s)

	1961	1962	1963	1964	1965	1966	1967	1968	1969
	1970	1971	1972	1973	1974	1975	1976	1977	1978
	1979	1980	1981	1982	1983	1984	1985	1986	
Electric	59	67	72	76	80	85	90	94	99
power	104	103	106	100	103	107	108	109	109
	111	113	115	117	122	122	127	126	
Fuel	598	599	599	600	600	606	597	589	581
industry	572	558	538	522	517	527	536	549	567
	586	596	602	623	633	637	637	636	
Chemicals	124	140	157	173	189	205	222	238	255
	271	282	286	294	304	314	323	328	332
	337	341	345	344	345	346	348	333	
Metallurgy	401	414	426	439	454	467	477	488	498
	508	503	496	494	494	488	492	493	485
	485	485	481	489	489	483	483	478	
Machine	1,280	1,391	1,503	1,614	1,725	1,818	1,910	2,003	2,095
building	2,188	2,272	2,343	2,441	2,520	2,587	2,673	2,732	2,799
	2,867	2,921	2,957	2,998	3,027	3,065	3,104	3,140	
Wood and	268	275	283	291	298	300	302	303	305
paper	307	310	311	312	311	319	321	320	320
	322	320	321	324	327	328	329	331	
Construction	342	345	349	352	356	370	385	399	414
materials	428	437	442	447	451	454	460	456	456
	456	456	453	452	458	456	450	455	
Light	533	551	570	589	607	649	688	727	766
industry	805	821	828	831	836	844	855	866	874
	872	869	867	867	860	849	843	833	
Food	470	489	508	527	546	562	578	593	609
processing	625	627	638	643	653	656	657	671	676
	681	677	681	689	686	684	679	672	

Figure 10-4. Model with Time Trends Normalized Relative to Armenia

Model: 1b.			SSE	46.294673	F RATIO	3946.91
			DFE	3016	PROB>F	0.0001
Dep var: Log(Output)			MSE	0.015350	R-SQUARE	0.9958

Variable		DF	Parameter Estimate	Standard Error	T Ratio	Prob>|T|
Intercept		1	1.526466	0.238313	6.4053	0.0001

Elasticities

Variable		DF	Parameter Estimate	Standard Error	T Ratio	Prob>|T|
El. power	labor	1	0.105301	0.055148	1.9094	0.0563
	capital	1	0.616267	0.025065	24.5863	0.0001
Fuels	labor	1	1.107484	0.061864	17.9019	0.0001
	capital	1	0.312618	0.023112	13.5260	0.0001
Chemicals	labor	1	0.569820	0.061076	9.3298	0.0001
	capital	1	0.321245	0.030215	10.6321	0.0001
Metallur	labor	1	0.645655	0.111766	5.7769	0.0001
	capital	1	0.214708	0.036240	5.9247	0.0001
Machinery	labor	1	0.578243	0.077255	7.4849	0.0001
	capital	1	0.355933	0.066269	5.3711	0.0001
Wood & p	labor	1	0.944244	0.070804	13.3361	0.0001
	capital	1	0.242758	0.024959	9.7264	0.0001
Con mats	labor	1	0.796481	0.086466	9.2115	0.0001
	capital	1	0.216995	0.033185	6.5389	0.0001
Light in	labor	1	0.500685	0.079722	6.2804	0.0001
	capital	1	0.220724	0.030127	7.3264	0.0001
Food pr	labor	1	0.733798	0.115814	6.3360	0.0001
	capital	1	0.168481	0.038872	4.3343	0.0001
Chemicals trend		1	0.013726	0.002677	5.1259	0.0001
Machinery trend		1	0.017340	0.004605	3.7650	0.0002

Industry dummy variables

Variable	DF	Parameter Estimate	Standard Error	T Ratio	Prob>|T|
Fuel industry	1	−3.229527	0.458688	−7.0408	0.0001
Chemicals	1	0.748793	0.328873	2.2768	0.0229
Metallurgy	1	1.552592	0.582521	2.6653	0.0077
Machine building	1	0.238557	0.487440	0.4894	0.6246
Wood and paper	1	−1.915197	0.473421	−4.0454	0.0001
Construction mat	1	−0.399714	0.419384	−0.9531	0.3406
Light industry	1	2.799387	0.472908	5.9195	0.0001
Processed foods	1	1.876272	0.583828	3.2137	0.0013

(cont'd.)

Tajikistan	1	−0.012016	0.001796133	−6.6900	0.0001
Kazakhstan	1	−0.011567	0.001713952	−6.7486	0.0001
Kyrgyzstan	1	−0.011284	0.001785658	−6.3194	0.0001
Ukraine	1	−0.008857	0.001713357	−5.1697	0.0001
Russian Fed.	1	−0.007169	0.001757277	−4.0798	0.0001
Turkmenistan	1	−0.004254	0.001754571	−2.4249	0.0154
Uzbekistan	1	−0.003358	0.001695505	−1.9808	0.0477
Estonia	1	−0.002544	0.001813254	−1.4035	0.1606
Georgia	1	0.000829	0.001729478	0.4797	0.6314
Latvia	1	0.001605	0.001784452	0.9000	0.3682
Azerbaijan	1	0.003712	0.001703704	2.1793	0.0294
Moldova	1	0.007143	0.001813403	3.9393	0.0001
Belarus	1	0.009906	0.001744486	5.6786	0.0001
Lithuania	1	0.010142	0.001741860	5.8225	0.0001

Annual dummies (technical progress relative to 1961)

Y1962	1	0.019144	0.016127	1.1871	0.2353
Y1963	1	0.037950	0.016891	2.2467	0.0247
Y1964	1	0.073105	0.018029	4.0548	0.0001
Y1965	1	0.114499	0.019247	5.9488	0.0001
Y1966	1	0.160303	0.020673	7.7541	0.0001
Y1967	1	0.209886	0.022124	9.4868	0.0001
Y1968	1	0.249984	0.023786	10.5097	0.0001
Y1969	1	0.276991	0.025652	10.7981	0.0001
Y1970	1	0.331849	0.026953	12.3120	0.0001
Y1971	1	0.381882	0.028786	13.2664	0.0001
Y1972	1	0.405804	0.030514	13.2988	0.0001
Y1973	1	0.445156	0.032267	13.7962	0.0001
Y1974	1	0.485694	0.033982	14.2928	0.0001
Y1975	1	0.535036	0.035763	14.9607	0.0001
Y1976	1	0.557223	0.037390	14.9032	0.0001
Y1977	1	0.573599	0.039023	14.6991	0.0001
Y1978	1	0.589112	0.040724	14;4658	0.0001
Y1979	1	0.599149	0.042401	14.1305	0.0001
Y1980	1	0.609514	0.043980	13.8588	0.0001
Y1981	1	0.625395	0.045512	13.7412	0.0001
Y1982	1	0.632514	0.047137	13.4187	0.0001
Y1983	1	0.648499	0.048776	13.2956	0.0001
Y1984	1	0.664627	0.050375	13.1936	0.0001
Y1985	1	0.675447	0.051980	12.9943	0.0001
Y1986	1	0.698216	0.053582	13.0307	0.0001

Figure 10-5. Testing for Global Heteroscedasticity

Model:	Heteroscedasticity	SSE	18359.3	F RATIO	245.73
	2	DFE	3196	PROB>F	0.0001
Dep var:	log(residuals)	MSE	5.74446	R-SQUARE	0.0714

Variable	DF	Parameter estimate	Standard error	T ratio	PROB>|T|
Intercept	1	−3.913921	0.150511	−26.0042	0.0001
Predicted values	1	−0.358788	0.022888	−15.6759	0.0001

Figure 10-6. Weighted Model 1b, with Time Trends Normalized
Relative to Armenia

Model:	1b-weighted		SSE	804.903209	F RATIO	5782.08
			DFE	3016	PROB>F	0.0001
Dep var:	Log(Output)		MSE	0.266878	R-SQUARE	0.9971

Variable		DF	Parameter estimate	Standard error	T ratio	PROB>|T|
Intercept		1	1.313333	0.242078	5.4253	0.0001
Elasticities						
El. power	labor	1	0.083526	0.056704	1.4730	0.1408
	capital	1	0.653926	0.025361	25.7848	0.0001
Fuels	labor	1	1.082395	0.064725	16.7230	0.0001
	capital	1	0.353613	0.021954	16.1070	0.0001
Chemical	labor	1	0.584348	0.060251	9.6986	0.0001
	capital	1	0.360497	0.031593	11.4105	0.0001
Metallur	labor	1	0.700275	0.099465	7.0404	0.0001
	capital	1	0.234824	0.032330	7.2633	0.0001
MBMW	labor	1	0.537055	0.065148	8.2436	0.0001
	capital	1	0.403196	0.058757	6.8620	0.0001
Wood & p	labor	1	0.986372	0.070510	13.9890	0.0001
	capital	1	0.289955	0.023965	12.0990	0.0001
Con mats	labor	1	0.803140	0.082274	9.7617	0.0001
	capital	1	0.264264	0.031320	8.4375	0.0001
Light in	labor	1	0.478053	0.064323	7.4321	0.0001
	capital	1	0.269267	0.026102	10.3158	0.0001
Food pro	labor	1	0.764287	0.096155	7.9485	0.0001
	capital	1	0.212957	0.033424	6.3713	0.0001
Chemical trend		1	0.013360	0.002624	5.0910	0.0001
Machinery trend		1	0.019130	0.004189	4.5658	0.0001
Kazakhstan		1	−0.012343	0.001534954	−8.0410	0.0001
Tajikistan		1	−0.010734	0.001735437	−6.1852	0.0001
Kyrgyzstan		1	−0.009691	0.001694922	−5.7182	0.0001
Ukraine		1	−0.008250	0.001468588	−5.6177	0.0001
Russian Fed.		1	−0.006705	0.001477246	−4.5389	0.0001
Uzbekistan		1	−0.005117	0.001534570	−3.3349	0.0009
Turkmenistan		1	−0.004963	0.001689365	−2.9382	0.0033

(*cont'd.*)

Figure 10-6. Weighted Model 1b, with Time Trends Normalized
Relative to Armenia *(cont'd.)*

Model:	1b-weighted	SSE	804.903209	F RATIO	5782.08
	DFE	3016	PROB>F	0.0001	
Dep var:	Log(Output)	MSE	0.266878	R-SQUARE	0.9971

Variable	DF	Parameter estimate	Standard error	T ratio	PROB>|T|
Estonia	1	−0.001820	0.001712686	−1.0630	0.2879
Latvia	1	0.000904	0.001678398	0.5387	0.5901
Georgia	1	0.002441	0.001603370	1.5225	0.1280
Moldova	1	0.003809	0.001692172	2.2514	0.0244
Azerbaijan	1	0.005589	0.001572774	3.5536	0.0004
Lithuania	1	0.005897	0.001615587	3.6506	0.0003
Belarus	1	0.007996	0.001557574	5.1337	0.0001

Figure 10–7. Average Annual Rates of Industrial Productivity
by Republic Relative to a Mean Productivity Rate
(percent)

	Koropeckyj (1960–75)	Figure 10–4 (1961–86)	Figure 10–6 (1961–86)
Kyrgyzstan	−2.2	−1.1	−1.0
Kazakhstan	−1.8	−1.2	−1.2
Uzbekistan	−1.2	−0.3	−0.5
Turkmenistan	−1.1	−0.4	−0.5
Armenia	−0.9	0.0**	0.0**
Azerbaijan	−0.7	0.4	0.6
Ukraine	−0.3	−0.9	−0.8
Lithuania	0.0	1.0	0.6
Russian Fed.	0.1	−0.7	−0.7
Estonia	0.3	−0.3**	0.2**
Moldova	0.5	0.7	0.4
Georgia	0.7	0.1**	0.2**
Belarus	1.0	1.0	0.8
Latvia	1.1	0.2**	0.1**
Tajikistan	2.1	−1.2	−1.1

Notes: ** signifies that this trend is not statistically significant in relation to productivity in the mean republic.

The erratic behavior of productivity in Tajikistan may be related to a substantial, but unexplained, discontinuity in Tajikistan's published MBMW fixed capital stock series, post-1980.

CHAPTER ELEVEN
Ukrainian Agriculture

Elizabeth Clayton

Within the USSR, Ukrainian agriculture provides an exceedingly valuable and relatively underdeveloped resource for meeting the Soviet Union's perennial food problems. The land is rich and fertile, with contours that facilitate mechanized farming; the labor force is well-trained; and the infrastructure is adequate for expansion. Despite these advantages, Ukrainian agriculture has not received full Soviet support for developing this natural wealth. Nevertheless, it is not clear that an independent Ukrainian agriculture could provide significant exports to either other republics or the world market. This paper explores some of the alternative courses of action that might provide such a foundation.

The Resource Base

Building on a long-standing agricultural tradition, Ukraine has melded its agricultural resources—land, labor, and capital—into a powerful productive force. As the second-largest republic in the Soviet Union, it has both scale and expertise. It is useful to examine agricultural resources before exploring the opportunities for price and other reforms that would improve and extend productivity. In this paper, only the basic resources of land and labor will be discussed; manufactured inputs, while indisputably important, require solid ties to industry and are outside this paper's scope.

Land

Ukrainian land, the predominant input to agriculture, is inherently very productive. Its topography is flat to gently rolling and well suited to mechanized farming; its climate is relatively moderate and warm;

and two-thirds of its soils are the fertile chernozems.[1] Through the years, the quantity of agricultural land has gradually diminished through erosion and degradation, but above all through loss to cities, mining, industry, and large hydroelectric projects. Between 1955 and 1987, agricultural land fell 2.4 million hectares (5.5 percent; about 6 million acres), with the greatest losses between 1960 and 1970.[2]

The land lost is often not easy or inexpensive to replace. First of all, 86 percent of Ukrainian farmland is already in production and little remains for further exploitation. The little farmland that remains requires significant investments to overcome excess or deficient water supply. Drainage projects transform marginal boglands into crop areas, and irrigation schemes modify yield variability in basic crops. The investment strategies have often foundered on imperfect engineering and implementation and are increasingly expensive, but in general have added to Ukrainian wealth in land. In 1987, of total sown area in Ukraine, 89 percent was unimproved, 6 percent was irrigated (most by overhead sprinklers), and 5 percent was drained. In 1984, 44 percent of vegetables, 14 percent of fruit, and 17 percent of feed corn were produced on improved land. Each year some 200,000 unimproved hectares are improved by irrigation or drainage, some to replace land that has been degraded or otherwise lost to production.

With the loss of land, Ukrainian economists, deploring the ease of Soviet eminent domain, have led a movement to introduce artificial land prices based on cadastral surveys. Although their significant work has had little effect in relocating production and stemming the land loss, it provides a benchmark for comparing land wealth in Ukraine and the Soviet Union because it provides differentiated prices for different qualities of land. Using synthetic prices that reflect the marginal cost of adding agricultural land (Loiter 1984, 165) and evaluating Ukrainian land by use (for annual and perennial crops, hay, and

---

[1] A world-wide study (Linneman et al. 1979, 47, 69) rated Ukrainian farmland as "moderately high" in productivity, ranking it 4 on a scale of 1 (extremely high) to 10 (extremely low). In terms of ruble value of production per hectare, in 1987 the range was between the Transcarpathia Oblast (3,710 rubles per hectare) and Mykolaïv Oblast (911 rubles per hectare), and the republic average was 1,493 rubles per hectare. Since prices were differentiated by product and region, this measure is dependent upon the structure of production.

[2] Data in the text, unless otherwise noted, are taken wholly from Soviet and Ukrainian statistical yearbooks, which are referenced in the bibliography.

pasture) and improvements (natural, irrigated, and drained), it can be shown that the Ukrainian land devoted to annual crops is 15 percent of unimproved land but 24 percent of the Soviet Union's total value of unimproved land; 13 percent of total irrigated land but 24 percent of its value; and 13 percent of drained land but 29 percent of its value. Other land uses show a similar pattern.

Since all Soviet land is nationalized, its use has been determined by the national plan, which leaves little to local option. In general, the Ukrainian crop specialties—winter wheat, sugar beets, and feed corn—are well-suited to the land, the climate, and natural advantages, but the pricing structure of planning, as will be discussed, has not fostered specialization or made it attractive in the contemporary economy.

Land tenure arrangements in Ukraine follow the Soviet pattern that was established by collectivization during the 1930s. Collective farms have slowly given way to state farms, but remain the dominant organizational form. There were 27,000 collective farms and 2,500 state farms in 1985, the latter specializing primarily in sugar beets, fruits and vegetables, and meat. Both types of socialized farms are large— almost 4,000 hectares in average size. The private sector in Ukraine—the household plots that supplement both farm and city diets—are, on the other hand, very small. In 1984, they comprised 5 to 6 percent of agricultural land use. In 1987, despite the small land area, they produced significant quantities of potatoes, vegetables, meat, and animal products. Like the private sector in other republics, however, the output of this sector has slowly declined in importance. The number of households with animals is decreasing, as is total output from the sector. Only the production of vegetables and pork has remained stable. This experience suggests a weak base for establishing a privatized agriculture.

To be productive, agricultural land requires roads to transport agricultural inputs from industry to farm and agricultural outputs from farm to city. The lack of roads, a perennial complaint throughout the USSR, has affected Ukraine slightly less than other republics, since the ratio of road length to area served is higher than other republics. As early as 1980, all of its socialized farms were connected by paved roads to a regional administrative center, and all of its sub-units to their farm centers. This advantage benefited not only productive capacity, but the population's ability to receive the medical care, shopping, and education provided by a larger population center.

Labor

When agriculture is developing rapidly, the agricultural labor force declines noticeably as people are replaced or made more productive by purchased inputs and capital. In recent years, Ukraine has experienced this phenomenon; the agricultural labor force declined by 19 percent between 1970 and 1987. The decline was particularly rapid among collective farmers, whose numbers in the same years dropped by 31 percent. The exodus also has meant that Ukraine's share of the Soviet Union's total agricultural labor force declined—from 26 percent to 21 percent.

Not all departing farmers leave the countryside. Many are housewives who leave paid employment, and the share of women in Ukraine's collective farm labor force has dropped below 50 percent. Occasionally a rural exodus during development creates other employment in rural communities, but this apparently has not happened in Ukraine. The total Ukrainian rural population dropped by 20 percent (4.3 million people) between 1970 and 1987.

There are several main reasons for migrating from the countryside. First, agricultural labor in the Soviet Union has long been a low-status occupation. Second, agricultural wages cannot compete with industrial pay. Finally, rural living conditions are often deplorable. Even with money in hand, the farmers find the stores to be few and badly stocked. Each of these points will be illustrated in turn.

The low status of farm work results from several factors, such as the work itself, the sexual composition of the labor force (women's work often has a lower status), and the average education of workers. Recently it has become possible to separate these factors. Drawing on a survey of Soviet emigrants to the United States, Swafford (1987) has documented the low social status of farm workers by separating the effects of ethnicity, party membership, and education. Holding constant party membership, ethnicity, and education, farmers were found to have almost the lowest status among 24 occupations—only mail carriers were lower. Education, as expected, raises the social status of farming but does not entirely mitigate the occupation's reputation. In addition, education often offers an opportunity to escape the countryside.

Low agricultural wages are an important component of social status and, in addition, have a weight of their own. In 1984, an average collective farmer received 129 rubles per month (153 rubles on a state farm), while an average industrial worker received 195 rubles, more than half again as much. Furthermore, Ukrainian farmers are paid less than the national average. In 1987, average monthly farm earnings (adjusted for the structure of employment in state and collective farms) in Ukraine were 163 rubles; in the Soviet Union, 185 rubles. Ukrainian earnings were only 88 percent of the national average, a position virtually unchanged since 1970.

Despite their relatively low level, agricultural wages in both the republic and the nation have more than doubled in the last decades and the rates of increase have been the same in both. Supported by significant agricultural price increases, farm wages have risen faster than industrial wages in an attempt to improve conditions in the countryside.

New money, however, does not necessarily improve rural living conditions, which often are primitive and unattractive. Investment in the rural housing fund has expanded, but it comes primarily from individuals and not from the government, as is usual in urban centers. Ukraine has a particularly large share of private rural housing; it was 89 percent in 1987 and 92 percent in 1980. The national shares were 70 percent in 1987 and 77 percent in 1980. The emphasis on private housing indicates few amenities, which are reserved for public construction, but it also signifies more space: Ukrainian rural housing provides each inhabitant with 15 square meters, while the national average for the rural population is only 13 square meters.

Other amenities, such as schools, entertainment, village roads, and medical care, also are lacking. Peterson (1990) and Newhauser (1990), however, show that Ukrainian infant and maternal mortality rates are lower than the national average. Furthermore, there is a tendency to close up or consolidate facilities for amenities as the population dwindles. The number of libraries, for example, declines each year, although the number of library books increases.

The agricultural labor situation, in the Soviet Union on the whole, as in Ukraine, represents a particular strength. With increasing production, more is produced with fewer people, who are living better. By no means is their circumstance enviable, but on the average there has been progress.

Technical Efficiency

Technical efficiency refers to the use that is made of existing inputs, without regard for their price and value. (Economic efficiency, on the other hand, incorporates these values and is discussed in the next section.) Koopman (1989), by estimating translog production functions, has ranked Soviet republics by the technical efficiency with which they use their existing resources. Two of his findings are of particular interest here. First, agricultural land contributes 55 percent of marginal incremental agricultural output, which is an exceedingly high value. Labor, the other important input, contributes 56 percent. Fertilizer, which augments land, contributes 26 percent; livestock and machinery have a negative impact. These findings indicate the particular importance of Ukrainian land and labor policy, a point made also by Stebelsky (1987).

Second, Koopman also finds that Ukraine uses its existing inputs at a level of 93.5 per cent of technical capacity, exceeding the Soviet average of 92.6 percent and the U.S. average of 91.5 percent. This record is exceeded by five other Soviet republics (in descending order: Georgia, Lithuania, Moldova, Belarus, and Estonia), but it is nonetheless impressive. Koopman suggests but does not document the potential gains that might accrue from institutional reforms in pricing and organization. Although Koopman's conclusion regarding technical efficiency is surprising when one considers the Soviet Union's food shortages and slow agricultural growth, the restrictive nature of his model should be kept in mind. He analyzes the use of existing inputs, but not their growth. In his view, the Soviet economy has achieved a static efficiency in using what it has but not a dynamic efficiency that would bring strong agricultural development and first-class modernization. Only systemic reform can achieve those goals.

Agricultural Output and Prices

The output of Ukrainian agriculture includes both crops and the products of animal husbandry. In the republic as a whole, 53 percent of revenue in 1987 came from animal products (meat, milk, eggs, and wool), and the remainder from crops.[3] Generally, the share devoted to

---

[3] Unless otherwise noted, all data include production from both the socialized and the private sectors.

each is about equal; only in L'viv Oblast is there an obvious specialization, in animal husbandry, which provided 61 percent of total oblast agricultural revenue in 1987. Animal husbandry, of course, relies on crops for feed supplies.

Meat production in Ukraine increased 29 percent between 1970 and 1987, lagging behind national growth, which was 35 percent. During the first half of the 1970s, pork was the dominant meat; by 1987, it had given way to beef, which now comprises 48 percent of meat production. In the USSR, beef was the dominant product in both periods. Although poultry production increased during this period, the growth in Ukraine (80 percent) was less than in the nation (134 percent). The growth of meat production indicates no particular natural advantage for Ukraine, which ranks about average in feed per unit of meat and average weight at slaughter.

In 1987, Ukraine supplied 24 percent of the Soviet Union's beef, 23 percent of its pork, and 22 percent of its poultry products. Most of these products (72 percent in 1987) were distributed through the state procurement system, a practice that prevails throughout the Soviet Union. The procurement system buys from both socialized farms and the private sector; in Ukraine, the private sector's share of output was 30 percent, a somewhat larger share than the Soviet Union's average. Much private-sector meat, statistically, must have entered the state distribution network.

Production of milk and milk products in Ukraine has grown relatively slowly, but a growing share has entered the state procurement system. Accordingly, the share of private production and marketing has decreased. This parallels the national trend. Much of the growth apparently has gone into cheese production; between 1970 and 1984, for example, cheese production increased 77 percent while the production of milk and dairy products as a whole increased only 22 percent. Egg production has grown similarly and increasingly entered distribution by way of the procurement system.

The dominant crop in Ukraine is grain, whose yields have exceeded the union growth rates. The republic excels in the production of winter wheat, whose yields exceed the union average by more than 25 percent; and of barley, similarly a high-yield crop. Ukraine also is a major producer of corn, whose yields match the union average. Barley has been a particularly successful feed-grain crop, with a growing share of national production and good growth in yields. Ukraine retains prominence in sugar beet production, producing more than half of the Soviet total, most of which enters the procurement system. It is also productive in growing oilseed crops (sunflower, flaxseed, and linseed).

Soviet demand for fruits and vegetables, except potatoes, is expected to grow rapidly in the next decades. The share of Ukrainian land devoted to these crops is small—they are labor-intensive and the republic has lost labor—but it is growing slowly. The structure is slow to change. Each year Ukraine grows fewer and fewer potatoes, the traditional vegetable, but it provides a larger and larger share of union potato production. With yields only slightly higher than the union average, Ukraine in 1987 supplied 25 percent of the Soviet Union's crop. Of that, more than half (58 percent) came from the private sector.

Vegetable production has grown to meet, but not match, demand. As with potatoes, a significant share (30 percent) comes from the private sector, but this share is smaller than the union average (37 percent). In the socialized sector, greenhouse production is important, but still on a small scale, and irrigated land often is used for field crops. Yields are very close to the Soviet average.

The structure of production can be analyzed only with the help of prices to add together such disparate products as barley and eggs. The Soviet agricultural price system has been well described and analyzed elsewhere; both Bornstein (1987) and Brooks (1990) provide an excellent overview and appraisal of recent agricultural price changes. It is useful to compare prices in Ukraine and in the Soviet Union in general (Cook 1989, 10).[4]

Soviet agricultural prices are differentiated by republics and zones to capture differential land rent. The purpose is equitable; the state wishes to reward comparable farmers in a similar manner. The prices, however, reflect neither consumer demand nor the relative costs of production, and they discriminate against areas such as Ukraine that have good cropland.

---

[4] These price data are derived from a Soviet source and include only the prices received by collective farms. They also include payments above the norm for quality, timeliness, and over-quota production.

The revenue loss that comes from differentiated zonal pricing can be estimated by re-calculating the annual agricultural revenue in Ukraine with Soviet prices and comparing it to that calculated with Ukrainian prices. In 1987, Ukrainian farms would have earned at least 4 billion rubles more if they had been paid union prices instead of their own zonal prices, and this is an underestimate (see Figure 11-1). Some critical exclusions affect this estimate. First, some products are omitted. The prices for oilseeds, fodder, and poultry, for example, were not available for the calculation. Second, the prices were paid only to collective farms, not state farms, whose prices often are higher. (State farm output, however, is included.) Finally, no estimate was made of the effect of higher prices on output because under the current planning system, it would have no meaning. These exclusions in each case would increase the estimate. Nevertheless, the calculation offers an estimate of potential gains to Ukraine from using union prices in a union market.

More interesting for future agricultural development is the relative effect of price differentials. The gains to Ukraine from union pricing are highest in grain and meat. These two products alone at the Soviet prices would have contributed 59 percent of the additional 4 billion rubles. Furthermore, if the gains from crop production are adjusted for the share of land area devoted to the crop, by calculating gains per hectare, the revenue prospects are bright indeed for vegetable production directed toward the Soviet market.

High revenues, however, do not imply great profitability, which requires a knowledge of costs. In Figure 11-2, the collective farm price and cost (*sebestoimost'*) for selected agricultural products in Ukraine are shown, along with profit calculations. The Soviet measure of cost includes only current expenditures; in using these statistics, a rule of thumb is that 35 percent profitability is a farm's break-even point. Field crops, particularly grain and sugar beets, have been the most profitable. Vegetables and animal products have not earned enough to reach the break-even point. Overall, in 1987 Ukraine achieved a 26 percent profitability (4.6 billion rubles), somewhat more than the Soviet average of 24 percent but below the break-even point.

Proportional price increases of 32 percent announced during the summer of 1990 should ameliorate some low profitability, but they will not change Ukraine's relative position and are unlikely to encourage more output. Demikhovskii (1990), writing from Kharkiv, states that higher prices in 1990 have increased profitability in wheat from 133 percent to 476 percent in his area, but he deplores the fact that the money cannot buy more inputs, especially forage, to increase output. He describes the outcome of a Soviet plan to sell grain for foreign exchange that could be used to buy inputs: only two farms in his area, selling 406 tons of grain, could take advantage of the program. Higher state prices have yet another drawback: they attract production from the collective farm market to state procurements, which is a substitution but not an increase of output. Latul (1990), writing from Mykolaïv Oblast, documents how farmers transferred from collective farm market sales to state procurements when that price became more favorable.

Distribution of food products, in other words getting production from the farm to the consumer, was a high priority of the Soviet government in the 1980s. As noted, the Ukrainian road network is better than the union average. As a consequence, Ukraine fares best of all Soviet republics in meeting established norms of food consumption (Stebelsky 1990, 75).

Within the republic, however, there are distributional inequities. Iazynina and Kozachenko (1989), comparing production and consumption in each Ukrainian oblast, find that per-capita production exceeds consumption in all oblasts except those with major cities, but that per-capita consumption is much lower than the republic average in several forest-steppe oblasts (where production also exceeds consumption). The forest-steppe oblast population consumes less food than its neighbors because it sends so much to urban centers. The authors blame the planning system, which serves only urban consumption and completely ignores the rural consumer, who has less purchasing power.

Prospects for the Year 2000

The prospects for Ukrainian agriculture, as for the rest of the economy, depend on the outcome of the Gorbachev reforms. The first reform is in place. In May 1990, the ownership of land and other natural resources passed to the republic governments, who now hold title to the most important agricultural input. So far, they have made few changes in the way that land is allocated to users and to uses. The users remain the collective and state farms, who may subcontract land to other users but may not sell or otherwise alienate it and must meet the obligations placed on them by central planning.

Land ownership was accompanied by a political reform, as Ukraine declared its status as a sovereign state with the powers to issue currency, create its own armed forces, and engage in international trade. Although the power of the new Ukrainian political entity is unknown, some of its intentions can be ascertained from initial announcements (*"Prioritety—selu"*). Ukraine wants to retain agricultural labor, invest more, and receive compensation for environmental degradation.

The fact that agricultural labor has been steadily leaving the countryside is an issue that the new government must face. Most authors decry the flight from the land and seek remedies to keep people in rural areas. A few would encourage the out-migration as an indicator of agricultural development, but the general flight from the land has a demographic component that makes the first view more realistic: the best and most able, the young and well-educated workers, are those who choose to leave.

Wages alone will not keep workers in the countryside, but they are an important factor. In general, the data show that farm incomes have risen faster than urban incomes. Zastavnyi (1988), however, suggests that the data showing the convergence of family income in urban and rural areas glosses over some real and important differences. In particular, he points out that the government provides and maintains housing in the city but that the family must provide its own in the countryside. Furthermore, the family's cost is greater than the government's cost, because it must buy materials on an open market. He also suggests that the private income earned in rural areas from garden plots is at the expense of leisure, of which the city dweller enjoys more. When Zastavnyi recalculates urban and rural income with adjustments for these differences, the statistic that estimated farm income at 90 percent of urban income drops to 68 percent of urban income. Such a difference is a powerful incentive to migrate.

An unusual program, which has increased one farm's labor force, provides urban amenities to make the countryside more attractive to farm labor (Ulanchuk 1988). In addition to excellent wages, the collective farm offers modern housing equivalent to that in urban areas, entertainment facilities, and other urban services. It also has established close ties to the pedagogical institute and local schools to encourage students to become agricultural professionals. It has given them land, tractors, a greenhouse, and after-school jobs. The result is an ever-growing and high- quality labor force on that particular farm.

Since the collective farm financed the necessary investments, the ability to replicate this program to develop and retain high-quality farm labor obviously depends on farm profitability. The farm has taken on the combined functions of a company town and a municipal government. Rarely is it possible for the regular municipal government to provide these services. Obligations have shifted to local levels, but the authority and power of taxation have not accompanied them. The result may be the eventual demise of weaker farms, followed by new obligations to employ or otherwise support the labor that is released. This sequence of events, which has afflicted all agricultural systems during modernization and development, may face Ukraine if it is to move forward.

By and large, private Ukrainian entrepreneurs have not seized upon the opening of agriculture. In an article in *Sel' skaia zhizn'* titled "Fermer, gde ty?" ("Farmer, where are you?") (1990), several reasons are given. First, the farm that rents out land retains its obligations to supply products to the state; therefore it transfers the obligations to subcontractors. The private farmers can choose neither their product nor their buyer. Second, the collective or state farm often rents only the marginal land and retains the best for itself. One farmer received land that had been abandoned for 20 to 30 years and was wholly overgrown, but he would have no secure stake in the ownership if the land were cleared. Third, the authority to allocate land is not yet clear: some might want land, but not to farm. Kuzyk (1988), for example, notes that tourism is more profitable than farming in the Carpathian region; no program at this point allows a shift to a more profitable alternative, especially outside farming. Finally, no law regulates land rental obligations on either side of the contract and the sides are unequal in power as well.

The priorities of the new Ukrainian government (*"Prioritety—selu"*) include a shift of investment resources from industry to agriculture. They note that agriculture provides 34 percent of the republic's income but receives only 20 percent of state investment, that each week two villages in the republic disappear from the map, and that in one year, in 3,000 villages not one child was born. The priorities emphasize increasing and improving the agricultural labor force rather than improving the land.

Land improvement is a missing link in increasing Ukrainian agricultural output, but the republic and local governments seem unable to envision a scale and direction for such a program. Government acknowledges the wealth inherent in land, for the republic seeks recompense for environmental degradation from both erosion and radioactivity. It envisions, however, no major projects. There are successes that can be emulated and high-value prospects: Kostochka (1988) discusses the productive effects of no-till farming that also preserves the soil. Poplavskaia (1988) analyzes the allocation of investments between low-cost and high-cost farms. Simonenko (1988) would allocate far more to storage, processing, and infrastructure (roads). Pilot projects and demonstrated successes are unmistakable, but the will and power to broaden the initiative are weak. Furthermore, success in production demands a genuinely integrated market without differentiated regional price subsidies. Incentives and infrastructure that will support change are needed. To enter the European or world market, Ukraine must accustom itself to those diverse systems, too. Ukraine is well situated to make these moves, but must become accustomed to painful change.

The solutions to agricultural deficiencies can never be whole and unified in the way that central planning once promised. That system, however, has not brought success in recent years. "Muddling through," which has brought prosperity elsewhere, may be the brightest prospect if the lofty dreams of the past can be forsaken.

References

Bornstein, Morris. 1987. "Soviet Price Policies." *Soviet Economy* 3 (September): 96–134.

Brooks, Karen. 1990. "Soviet Agricultural Policy and Pricing under Gorbachev." In Gray, *Soviet Agriculture*, 116–29.

Cook, Edward C. 1988. "Deriving Soviet Agricultural Producer Prices." *CPE Agriculture Report* 1 (November-December): 8–13.

_____. 1989. "USSR: Collective Farm Producer Prices by Republic." *CPE Agriculture Report* 2 (March-April): 10–13.

Demikhovskii, N. 1990. "Net rezona..." *Sel'skaia zhizn'* (3 August):1.

"Fermer, gde ty?" 1990. *Sel'skaia Zhizn'* (2 July):1.

Goskomstat SSSR. 1988a. *Sel' skoe khoziaistvo SSSR*. Moscow.

_____. 1988b. *Narodnoe khoziaistvo SSSR v 1987 g.* Moscow.

Goskomstat USSR. 1985. *Narodnoe khoziaistvo Ukrainskoi SSR v 1984 g.* Kiev.

Gray, Kenneth R. 1990. *Soviet Agriculture: Comparative Perspectives*. Ames, Iowa.

Iazynina, R. and T. Kozachenko. 1989. "Territorial'naia differentsiiatsiia proizvodstva i potrebleniia produktov pitaniia v Ukrainskoi SSR." *APK: Pkonomika, Upravlenie* 11:23–28.

Koopman, Robert B. 1989. *Efficiency and Growth in Agriculture: A Comparative Study of the Soviet Union, United States, Canada, and Finland*. Washington: U.S. Department of Agriculture (ERS) Report AGES 89–54, October.

Kostochka, I. 1988. "Intensifikatsiia agrarnogo sektora v usloviiakh uskoreniia nauchno-tekhnicheskogo progressa." *Ekonomika Sovetskoi Ukrainy* 2:52–57.

Kuzyk, S. 1988. "Ob effektivnosti razvitiia turisma v karpatskom regione." *Ekonomika Sovetskoi Ukrainy* 10:56–59.

Latul, I. 1990. "Shchedrost'—za chei schet?" *Sel'skaia zhizn'* (26 July):2.

Linneman, Hans. 1979. *MOIRA: Model of International Relations in Agriculture*. Amsterdam.

Loiter, M. N. 1984. *Prirodnye resursy i effektivnost' kapital'nykh vlozhenii*. Moscow.

Mickiewicz, Ellen. 1990. "Ethnicity and Support: Findings from a Soviet-American Public Opinion Poll." *Journal of Soviet Nationalities* 1 (Spring): 140–47.

Newhauser, Kimberly. 1990. "New Statistics on Maternal Mortality in the Soviet Union." *Report on the Soviet Union* 2 (6 April): 6–8.

Peterson, D.J. 1990. "Understanding Soviet Infant Mortality Statistics." *Report on the Soviet Union* 2 (6 April): 4–6.

"Prioritety—selu." 1988. *Sel' skaia zhizn'* (4 August):2.

Poplavskaia, Zh. 1988. "Resursnyi potentsial i effektivnost' ego ispol'zovaniia." *Ekonomika Sovetskoi Ukrainy* 4:57–60.

Simonenko, S. 1988. "Struktura kapital'nykh vlozhenii v agropro-myshlennyi kompleks Ukrainy." *Ekonomika Sovetskoi Ukrainy* 12:78–79.

Slider, Darrell. 1990. "Soviet Public Opinion on the Eve of the Elections." *Journal of Soviet Nationalities* 1 (Spring): 155–62.

Stebelsky, Ihor C. 1987. "Institutional Constraints on Land Management in the Ukraine." Working paper.

————. 1990. "Soviet Food Imbalances and their Prospective Amelioration." In Gray, *Soviet Agriculture*, 68–93.

Swafford, Michael. 1987. "Perceptions of Social Status in the USSR." in *Politics, Work, and Daily Life in the USSR: A Survey of Former Soviet Citizens*. Edited by James R. Millar, 279–300. Cambridge.

Ulanchuk, V. 1988. "Opyt formirovaniia trudovogo potentsiala kolkhoza." *Ekonomika Sovetskoi Ukrainy* 3:78–79.

Waedekin, Karl-Eugen, ed. 1990. *Communist Agriculture: Farming in the Soviet Union and Eastern Europe*. London and New York.

Zastavnyi, F. 1988. "Netraditsionnye podkhody k otsenke urovnia zhizni gorodskogo i sel'skogo naseleniia." *Ekonomika Sovetskoi Ukrainy* 11:61–67.

Figure 11–1. Gains to Ukrainian Agriculture
if National Prices Were Received

Product	Unit	Prices (rubles/ton)		Revenues (mil. rubles)		Gain	Gain/ hectare
		(1)	(2)	(1)	(2)	Gain	hectare
Grain	th.T.	150	171	7,527	8,581	1,054	68
Sugar beets	th.T	42	48	2,087	2,386	298	179
Potatoes	th.T.	146	150	2,754	2,829	75	51
Vegetables	th.T.	137	166	1,111	1,346	235	459
Beef	th.T.	2,422	1,982	4,800	5,300	500	N/A
Pork	th.T	1,911	1,469	2,807	3,285	477	N/A
Milk	th.T	348	23,655	8,232	9,557	1,325	N/A
Eggs	m.sh.	86	17,425	1,499	1,551	52	N/A

Source: Prices (1986), collective farm: Cook (1988). (1) = Ukrainian prices; (2) = national prices. th.T = thousand tons. m.sh. = million units.

Production and land area from various statistical yearbooks (not shown) were used to calculate revenues and gain.

Figure 11-2. Price, Cost, and Profitability for Selected Collective
Farm Products: Ukraine and Soviet Union (1987)

Product	Cost (r/T)	Price (r/T)	Profitability (%)
Grain	68	150	121
Sugar beets	30	42	40
Potatoes	126	146	16
Vegetables*	124	137	10
Beef	2249	2422	8
Pork	2124	1911	-10
Milk	290	348	20
Eggs (000)	79	86	9

* Hothouse only

Source: Costs from Goskomstat (1988a, 448). Prices from Figure 11–1.

CHAPTER TWELVE
Discussion

Holland Hunter

The four papers at this session add significantly to our understanding of key issues in Ukrainian economics. Revenko offers a thoughtful account of how Ukrainian economists, under constrained research conditions, have estimated the republic's gross product. Clayton's paper evaluates the current situation and development potential of Ukrainian agriculture, and McCants' describes his efforts to create an enlarged data set and use it to test inter-republic differences in factor productivity. Finally, Kushnirsky's paper combines a sophisticated new computation for the growth of Ukrainian national income with a challenging new essay on how Ukrainian economic reform should be conducted.

Revenko's account of Ukrainian research on defining and estimating the republic's output in various coverages shows how basic research can proceed independently in different places at the same time. Ukrainian economists and statisticians have been working for more than 60 years with little contact with researchers in Moscow and Leningrad and with almost no contact with Western economists studying similar problems. Original Ukrainian contributions from the 1920s demonstrate the wealth of scientific talent devoted to studying the wealth of nations.

The original work directed by Pavel I. Popov in Moscow during the 1920s took place at a time when the conceptual and statistical study of national income was in its infancy in the United Kingdom and U.S. Only later were major Western landmarks in this area of study completed. The major contributions included Simon S. Kuznets, whose two-volume treatise (Kuznets 1938) codified basic theory and offered detailed annual estimates; Wassily W. Leontief, who formulated a new system of input-output accounts and applied it to U.S. data

(Leontief 1941); and Richard A. Stone, who extended parts of the theory and applied it to the United Kingdom (Stone 1954).

This pioneering work in theory and data-gathering led to the elaborate framework of national accounts in the United Nations' system of national accounts (United Nations 1968), which laid out both a Western-style and a Soviet-style approach to income and product estimates. In one or the other of its two variants, this framework is now employed all over the world.[1]

In the West, initial attention focused on the income side of the accounts, with detailed estimation of the product side following a few years later. In the USSR, on the other hand, researchers concentrated their attention on flows of material product, beginning with Popov's national balance of 1923–1924. Similarly, extending the national accounts to the state level began in the United States in 1957 with the publication of the Department of Commerce volume, *Personal Incomes by State, 1929–1954*.

U.S. estimation of product detail at the state level is quite recent, however. In Ukrainian research, as Revenko indicates, estimates at the oblast level started with the product side of the accounts. This difference in priorities may result from the fundamental differences between a planned economy and a market economy.

An additional early landmark has only recently been uncovered. Issued by TsUNKhU in October 1932 in Moscow, its 500 copies were "for official study only." This remarkably detailed presentation of estimates for the years 1928, 1929, and 1930 is now available in an English translation as *Materials for A Balance of the Soviet National Economy, 1928–1930* (1985).[2]

This landmark has facilitated the recomputation of the 1928–1940 Soviet record of output expansion, based on Western reconstructions of primary Soviet data. A just completed study generally supports and confirms the Western estimates, while adding some new results. It makes use of an internally consistent 12-sector inter-industry model calibrated to fit the historical record and also tests the impact of alternative policies (Hunter and Szyrmer 1992).

---

[1] A detailed discussion of both variants is available in Stone (1970).

[2] The original volume included explanatory essays by A. Petrov and A. Pervukhin and the edited translation includes a detailed and informative introduction by the editors as well as a useful foreword by Richard Stone.

National accounts data for the USSR from 1950 to 1980, including detailed estimates of the Soviet GNP and disaggregated indexes of industrial production, agricultural production, and household consumption, along with methodological discussion are available in a detailed volume published in 1982 (U.S. Congress 1982). It provides a solid starting point for basic research on the postwar economy.

Turning to definitional and conceptual issues concerning Soviet national accounts, I start with the question of so-called "nonproductive" economic activity. Economic reform in Ukraine and the USSR can benefit greatly if statisticians and policy makers in general recognize that this term *non-productive* is highly misleading and should be abandoned.

For Marx and Engels, creating tangible commodities deserved to be recognized as productive, while the activities of traders who merely "bought cheap and sold dear" was morally suspect and added nothing useful to the value of produced commodities. For more than a century, therefore, non-material output has been castigated as "unproductive" in the Soviet Union. Borderline activities such as transportation have troubled Marxist philosophers and statisticians for many decades (movement of freight, for example, is said to be productive, but movement of people is not). Revenko illustrates the dilemmas in discussing their treatment in Ukrainian research.

Obviously, however, modern science and technology have altered the structure of economic life to create a wide range of nonmaterial activities and outputs that are highly productive. Health care, scientific research, education, and the arts, for example, are essential components of an advanced society. Perhaps less universally recognized but equally prominent, the labor force in an advanced society includes millions of people employed as public or private paper-shuffling bureaucrats and working in a myriad of other services (including the military). Are they all useless?

Modern technology has lowered real unit costs in agriculture, transportation, and manufacturing, thus permitting a larger share of our now-higher incomes to consist of intangible output in the form of all these services. This intangible output (including scholarly output) is genuine, and the income earned in producing it is recognized in most countries as legitimate and morally acceptable. Boundary-value problems remain, of course; Kuznets suggested long ago that the legality or illegality of an activity provides a practical criterion within each society.

In Ukraine and the USSR generally, these kinds of economic activity have always been present and have been given grudging recognition. Recently, their share of output and employment has grown, and it is to be expected that effective economic reform will expand their share still more. Perhaps this healthy trend can be encouraged if those who define and estimate the national accounts abandon the label "non-productive," with its connotation of secondary status, and focus their attention on the many different problems of measuring the output of the services sector. Already there appears to be a shift in emphasis, signaled by the fact that since 1988, the publication *Narkhoz SSSR* has been placing a large section on social indicators before its section on industry, reversing a practice going back to 1929.

Revenko discusses the central issue of accounting for the contribution of fixed capital to the production of the national product. In classic Western terms, depreciation is supposed to account for the annual contribution by a long-lived physical asset to production over the period of the asset's useful life, and the sum to be depreciated is normally taken to be the original historical price paid for the asset. Among the many difficulties in this area, three stand out. If the price of a replacement for the asset rises over time, depreciation charges will not fully cover the cost of replacing the asset when it wears out. Second, technological advances may erode the economic value of the asset long before its physical usefulness has ended. Third, a decline in the demand for the output made by the asset may shrink the actual current value of an asset far below its historical cost. All three of these difficulties are serious problems under current Ukrainian conditions.

Asset values now are a major issue in connection with privitization, especially if it involves joint ventures with foreign firms. Several questions arise in this regard. How meaningful are the book values recorded in official accounts? How can future earning power best be estimated? How should kolkhoz officials and potential land-leasers estimate proper payments for the use of land? Ukrainian national accounts specialists can help clarify questions regarding asset valuation.

A related issue concerns regional differences in construction and production costs. Revenko (citing Ilarionov) refers in this connection to "distorted cost proportions [that] lead to unequal assessments of the value of output of goods and services." McCants refers to regional price-setting by Moscow in pursuit of goals other than efficient resource use, leading to wide variations in output/capital and output/labor ratios. Clayton criticizes Soviet agricultural prices as reflecting "neither consumer demand not the relative costs of production" and illustrates the impact of distorted prices on Ukrainian agriculture.

Regional differences in climate and resource endowment give rise to unavoidable differences in construction and production costs. The fundamental question is how these differences are reflected in incomes and prices. If construction and living costs are higher in northern and eastern regions of the USSR than in Ukraine while agricultural costs in Ukraine are lower, for example, theory says that in the long run people should migrate and industry should relocate in various ways that will tend to equate incomes. At the same time, reciprocal trade flows will tend to reduce surpluses and shortages. In theory, differential rents should tend to capture the remaining returns attributable to nonreproducible and nonmovable factors of production.

But in the short run, the existing structure of relative asset values, prices for goods and services, and earning-rates for all the factors of production is likely to reflect government taxes, subsidies, tariffs, and legal restrictions, as well as many forms of collusive restriction organized by capital and labor. The theoretical economist can visualize a set of economic relationships in which all this interference has been stripped away, leaving an interregional equilibrium in which the location of people and economic activities maximizes total output and incomes. Interregional exports and imports would reflect long-run comparative advantages, and all possible gains from trade would be captured.

Does this vision provide a standard by which prices and values should be judged? Can an inter-sectoral and interregional model of this kind be built and calibrated empirically to fit Ukraine or the whole USSR? Not quickly or easily, of course, but this is the ultimate challenge facing Ukrainian economists and national-accounts researchers.

One specific question in this area concerns Ukraine's agricultural potential and the geographic pattern of Ukraine's agricultural exports. For centuries, Ukrainian agricultural output has moved north to population centers less able to grow goods cheaply. Before World War I, Ukraine also made substantial agricultural exports to the outside world (mainly southern Europe). One wonders about the long-run implications of this record for agriculture's future role in Ukrainian foreign and domestic trade.

Can an autonomous Ukraine expect to continue agricultural exports to northern centers like Saint Petersburg and Moscow? On what terms? Are there markets for Ukrainian agricultural output? Europe is now plagued with agricultural surpluses fostered by national subsidies; what would be the comparative-cost situation if these protections were removed? Are there promising markets for Ukrainian agricultural exports to other continents? Would the exportable products be field crops or livestocks products? Research on these questions by Ukrainian economists clearly is necessary, as an extension of the work that Revenko alludes to concerning treatment of external transactions in Ukrainian national accounts.

As McCants and Kushnirsky mention, hidden inflation is an important issue complicating the measurement of output growth and input productivities. A chronic upward drift of prices and wages pervades the world economy, but in the USSR, including Ukraine, it has taken a special form for many decades. State-controlled legal prices remain almost constant for long periods, punctuated by substantial increases every seven years or so. At the same time administered prices on individual products, especially in the machine-building and metal-working (MBMW) sector, are frequently adjusted upwards, usually under cover of a supposed improvement in quality or as the price of a supposedly new product.

Some Western researchers are trying to test Soviet MBMW output indexes by applying base-period prices to individual products or product categories and summing the results. These researchers have long concluded that the official series contain a considerable amount of hidden inflation, which overstates the growth of output and exaggerates the productivity of labor and capital. McCants points out that comparisons among the republics are affected by the size of the MBMW sector in each republic; a republic's relatively high output growth rate may to some extent merely reflect its large MBMW sector. Kushnirsky reports his research on the extent of hidden inflation in official measures of MBMW, noting the importance of quality improvements in accounting for a large part of the aggregate price rise. If alleged quality improvements are accepted as genuine, much of the hidden inflation disappears. He emphasizes the indeterminacy of all efforts to pinpoint quality changes, and thus the difficulty of identifying precise estimates of hidden inflation.

The issue is less important now than it was when the USSR was claiming rapid growth in output closely related to military strength. The official index for MBMW output in 1989 was only 2.5 percent above the 1988 index (Goskomstat 1990, 335), and the 1990 index may well show a decrease. If recently there has been appreciable hidden inflation, then the correct, uninflated series must involve an even earlier leveling off and decline in the output of this sector.

Official output indexes based on 1913, 1928, or 1940 have long been replaced in Western understanding by indexes growing out of the work of Abram Bergson and his co-workers (Bergson 1961). He found that Soviet GNP (in ruble factor cost of 1937) rose about 2.4 times from 1928 to 1950. Western output indexes for the USSR covering postwar decades tend to match fairly closely those presented in the 1982 Joint Economic Committee volume mentioned earlier, which indicates that the Soviet GNP in 1970 prices grew from 1950 to 1980 about 3.9 times. Despite their different price bases, chaining these two series together indicates that the Soviet GNP in 1980 was about 9.5 times as large as in 1928, which at 3 percent annual growth between 1981 and 1985 would imply a 1985 level about 11 times the 1928 level. Kushnirsky refers to the calculation by Khanin and Seliunin in 1987, calculating that "Soviet national income rose 6 to 7 times in the 1928–1985 period, not about 90 times as officially claimed." The Khanin-Seliunin computations have not yet been published in detailed form, and Kushnirsky reports his difficulty in replicating their results without access to their underlying methodology. It seems obvious, nevertheless, that while the Seliunin-Khanin estimate for 1928–1985 Soviet output growth may be somewhat low, it is clearly in the same ball park as the linked Bergson-JEC calculation, and very far indeed from the traditional Soviet claim. While it may have limited relevance, moreover, it is interesting to find that the GNP of the United States increased roughly five-fold from 1929 to 1985 (in 1982 dollars), according to the U.S. Department of Commerce, Bureau of Economic Analysis (*Economic Report* 1988, 250). The overall extent of output expansion for the U.S. is not very different from the USSR figure estimated by Seliunin and Khanin.

If the new head of the USSR State Committee for Statistics, Vadim Nikitovich Kirichenko, is able to implement the reforms he called for in an article (Kirichenko 1990), the long-standing claim that Soviet output growth has been extraordinarily rapid may be reconsidered.

Kirichenko's article criticizes past practices affecting economic relations among the republics. These practices led to a "division of labor that formed in the national economy over many decades independent of the will of of the republics themselves," Kirichenko said. He criticized "the imperfection of the correlation of prices on raw material resources and finished products, the irrational turnover tax mechanism, and the payment of subsidies on meat and dairy products, as well as other goods."

Kirichenko mentioned statistics on commodity flows among republics, evidently alluding to the data first appearing in *Vestnik statistiki* (1989, no. 3) and again in the 1989 *Narkhoz SSSR*, but cautions that these data reflect the distortions he criticizes. He added that the USSR State Committee for Prices has analyzed interregional flows revalued in world prices, and he offered tantalizing tidbits of information on how republic exports to and imports from the outside world in 1988 would have appeared at world prices. His next paragraph is worth quoting in full:

> But of course the main task of improving regional statistics is by no means to calculate who "owes" what to whom. This question cannot be resolved without a normally functioning internal market. Calculation in world market prices is an analytic technique that is not without merit, but its significance should not be exaggerated. As long as internal prices are divorced from them, it is necessary to make too many conditional assumptions. Instead of engaging in fruitless discussions over the redivision of the public pie, it is much more important to develop balance statistics at the regional level, including a balance of the social product, a balance of fixed capital, the largest fragments of the summary fiscal balance, and of all the most important summary indicators of socioeconomic development—national income, net output of enterprises in the material production sphere, gross national product, overall volume of consumption of material goods and services, and general indicators of effectiveness of social production. Only in this way can the development of regional self-management and self-financing be placed on a sound information base.

Kirichenko's long list of data, much of which is already compiled (though in faulty prices) at republic and even oblast levels, includes a cryptic reference to "the largest fragments of the summary fiscal balance." Does this refer to the kind of data on government budgets and long-term bank credits available now in *Narkhoz SSSR?* If so, much more is needed. The closing section of Kushnirsky's paper is especially relevant here.

Kushnirsky reminds us that price stability is a crucial element of successful economic reform and that it is chiefly threatened by uncontrolled increases in the money supply associated with a large government deficit. The deficit in turn is closely linked to burgeoning cash payments of wages and salaries by state employees, together with bank credits for enterprises to subsidize their losses from below-cost sale of output. He recommends that the USSR adopt stricter controls over government spending linked to tighter monetary controls over both cash in circulation and bank deposits.

One central aggregate (*M1*) would cover cash in circulation plus the checking accounts of individuals. A larger aggregate (*M2*) would add to *M1* the savings accounts (time deposits) of individuals and institutions and also would cover the demand deposits of state enterprises, cooperatives, and private businesses. Changes in the first aggregate primarily would reflect the decisions of the general public, while changes in the larger aggregate would also reflect the policies of government fiscal and monetary authorities. Kushnirsky moves the demand deposits held by enterprises from *M1* (as defined in the United States) over to *M2* to stress the need for greater attention to and tighter control over this comprehensive measure of the money supply in the USSR.

As these papers show, there is a substantial agenda for scholarly work that can contribute to economic progress for the Ukrainian economy. Its central technical goal would be to define and estimate a correct set of relative prices for the services of land, capital, and labor in Ukraine. Correct prices would send signals to all buyers and sellers, guiding them toward income-maximizing and cost-minimizing choices that in the long run would serve to promote equitable and efficient use of the economy's resources.

Ukrainian national accounts can be extended and enriched in many ways to benefit Ukrainian economic reform. As Revenko suggests, the breakdowns estimated at the republic level can be brought down to the oblast level, following the path taken in many other countries, to the extent that statistical resources become available. The cadastral land surveys referred to by Clayton could form part of the foundation for a more efficient Ukrainian agriculture. McCants' use of combined cross-section and time series data for the 15 Soviet republics could be used to monitor the comparative performances of 25 Ukrainian oblasts, using data available in Ukrainian research centers. Productivity trends can be analyzed more fully if CES production functions, following Kushnirsky's approach, are estimated for Ukrainian agriculture as well as industry. Estimating factor productivity in the services sector is much more difficult, but perhaps Ukrainian economists will find new approaches. In all these ways and more, the ideas and results offered in these four papers might be used to stimulate Ukrainian progress.

References

Bergson, Abram. 1991. *The Real National Income of Soviet Russia Since 1928*. Cambridge, Massachusetts.

Goskomstat SSSR. 1990. *Narodnoe khoziaistvo SSSR v 1989 g.* Moscow.

Economic Report of the President. 1988. Washington.

Hunter, Holland and Janusz M. Szyrmer. 1992. *Faulty Foundations: Soviet Economic Policies, 1928–1940*.

Kirichenko, Vadim Nikitovich. 1990. "Vernut' doverie statistike," *Kommunist* 3:22–32. [Translated in *Problems of Economics* (September): 38–54.]

Kuznets, Simon S. 1941. *National Income and Its Composition, 1919–1938*. New York.

Leontief, Wassily W. 1941. *Structure of American Economy, 1919–1929*. Cambridge, Massachusetts.

Stone, Richard A. 1954. *Measurement of Consumers' Expenditure and Behaviour*. Cambridge.

_____. 1970. *Mathematical Models of the Economy and Other Essays*. London.

United Nations, Statistical Office. 1968. *A System of National Accounts*. Studies in Methods, series F, no. 2, rev. 3. New York.

U.S. Congress, Joint Economic Committee. 1982. *USSR: Measures of Economic Growth and Development, 1950–80*. Washington.

U.S. Dept. of Commerce, Office of Business Economics. 1954. *Personal Incomes by State, 1929–1947*. Washington.

Wheatcroft, S. G. and R. W. Davies, eds. 1985. *Materials for A Balance of the Soviet National Economy, 1928–1930*. Cambridge.

Part IV: Welfare

CHAPTER THIRTEEN
Living Standards in Ukraine: Retrospect and Prospect

Gertrude E. Schroeder

When I assessed the matter of living standards in Ukraine some 15 years ago (Schroeder 1977, 84–108), I lamented that the paucity of published data permitted only a general evaluation of this important subject. With the advent of glasnost under Gorbachev, however, considerably more information was released after 1985. Although the volume and quality of the data compare poorly with the statistical output of Western governments, the newly released data allow assessments of how various groups within the republic have fared. In particular, we now can consider the relative position of urban versus rural residents and can examine regional differences within Ukraine.

The first section of this paper describes the levels and trends in personal incomes between 1971 and 1989. The second section deals with the levels and trends in total per capita consumption and its major components. In the third section, we describe the disintegration of consumer markets that has occurred in Ukraine and throughout the Soviet Union since 1985. Finally, we consider what may be in store for Ukrainian workers and consumers in the 1990s.

Personal Incomes

Several sets of data relating to personal income in Ukraine are presented in Figure 13-1. The wages of the state labor force (white- and blue-collar workers) comprise the largest component of total money income in Ukraine, about 70 percent. Between 1971 and 1989, average monthly wages in Ukraine increased at an average annual rate of 3.4 percent, a little more slowly than in the Russian Federation

(3.9) and the USSR (3.6). Thus, Ukraine's relative position deteriorated over the period: in 1989, average monthly wages were 85 percent of those in the Russian Federation and 91 percent of the USSR average, whereas in 1970 the corresponding levels were 91 and 94 percent. Although complete data are lacking, the cost of living in Ukraine may be lower than in the Russian Federation (Kuznetsova and Shirokova 1987, 76). Average wages rose 3.0 percent annually during the 1970s, 2.3 percent annually between 1981 and 1985, and 5.8 percent annually during the period of 1986 to 1989. In 1989, they rose by 9 percent (*Pravda Ukrainy* February 2, 1990). Ukraine's ranking among all republics in regard to average wages changed from 9th to 8th between 1971 and 1988.

Workers in all branches of the economy shared in these wage gains, but not equally. The fastest gains were made in state agriculture, where wages rose by a total of 94 percent between 1971 and 1988; in contrast, wages in health care rose only 53 percent (*Narkhoz Ukrainy* 1988, 43–44). In general, wages increased considerably faster in the so-called "productive" branches than in the "nonproductive" (service) branches. State white- and blue-collar workers residing in rural areas fared better than their urban counterparts in terms of gains in average wages for the 1971–1987 period, according to recently released data; thus, the rural/urban wage gap was reduced during that period. Average wages in rural areas were 82 percent of those in urban areas in 1970 and 90 percent in 1987. The rural/urban wage gap is somewhat wider and was reduced more slowly in Ukraine than in either the Russian Federation or the USSR as a whole. In Ukraine in 1987, 87 percent of the state labor force worked in cities and 13 percent worked in rural areas; the corresponding shares in 1970 were 85 percent and 15 percent.

The largest group employed in rural areas consists of collective farmers, who numbered 3.5 million in 1989, compared with 5.4 million in 1970. Their earnings in the socialized sector comprised about 10 percent of total money incomes in Ukraine in 1988. As elsewhere in the Soviet Union, wages of collective farmers have been rising much faster than those of both the state labor force as a whole and of workers on state farms. Between 1971 and 1988, collective farm wages rose at an average annual rate of 5.3 percent, compared with 3.1 percent and 4.0 percent for the other two groups, respectively. Thus, the differentials between earnings of collective farmers and those of the state labor force were rapidly reduced. In 1970, collective farmers' average wages were 58 percent of those of the state labor force and 69 percent of those of state farmers; in 1988, these gaps had narrowed to 84 percent and 86 percent relative to the two groups, respectively. Wages of collective farmers in Ukraine are below those in the Russian Federation as well as in the USSR as a whole. In 1989, earnings of Ukraine's collective farmers were 81 percent of the average wages of farmers in the Russian Federation and 90 percent of the average for the USSR. In 1970, the ratios were 85 and 89. Ukraine's ranking among all republics in terms of wages paid to collective farmers changed from 12th to 10th during the 1971–1988 period.

Figure 13-2 presents data on average wages of the state labor force and of collective farmers by oblast. The data are grouped into the three large economic regions that have been used for planning purposes by Soviet authorities. Regional differentials in wages among the state labor force are fairly narrow in Ukraine. In 1988, average monthly wages ranged from 175 rubles in Chernivtsi Oblast to 217 in Donets'k Oblast. Relative to the average for Ukraine, the range of average monthly wages was a narrow 88 to 108 rubles. In view of the uniformity of application of Soviet government-determined wage scales, procedures, and policies, these narrow differences are to be expected within a republic such as Ukraine, where regional wage coefficients do not apply. the inter-oblast differentials that do exist mainly reflect differences in their rural-urban character and their economic structures. Judging from the change in the range alone, differentials have narrowed since 1970. Also, the unweighted coefficient of variation fell from 0.086 in 1970 to 0.060 in 1988. Among the three economic regions, the highest average wages are found in the relatively urbanized Donets'k-Dnieper region (with 42 percent of the total population in 1988), followed by the south region (with 8 percent), with the much more rural southwest region, with half the population, ranking third. The ranking of the three regions was the same in 1988 as in 1970.

As one would expect, the inter-oblast differentials in earnings of collective farmers are much wider than those for state workers. In 1988, average earnings of collective farmers ranged from 140 rubles per month in Volhynia Oblast to 207 rubles in Crimea Oblast. Much of this disparity reflects differences in the compositions and prices of farm output. Differentials among the oblasts were much narrower in

1988 than in 1970. The differentials in 1970 ranged from 66 percent to 161 percent of the republic average, while in 1988 the range was only 83 percent to 123 percent. The unweighted coefficient of variation fell from 0.24 to 0.12 during that period. Collective farm wages were highest in the southern region and lowest in the southwest region in both 1970 and 1988.

Recently released data permit another perspective on personal income in Ukraine. These data, derived from annual surveys of the incomes of a sample of families, are also presented in Figure 13-1. Incomes are defined to include wages of all family members from work in the state sector and in the socialized sector of collective farms, earnings in money and in kind (valued at state retail prices) from private agricultural activities, money from social consumption funds (pensions, aid, stipends, subsidies for passes to vacation resorts, pioneer camps, and child care facilities), and other incomes, such as interest on savings deposits. Income is expressed per family member per month and given separately for families of white- and blue-collar workers in the state sector and for collective farm families. In Ukraine, the average family size for state workers was 2.91 members in 1975 and 2.84 members in 1988; corresponding figures for collective farm families were 3.30 and 3.27. Wages made up 82.1 percent of the total income of state worker families in 1970 and 78.3 percent in 1988, while earning from private plots were 2.8 percent and 2.4 percent, respectively (*Narkhoz Ukrainy* 1988, 53–54). In contrast, wages from work in the socialized sector of the farms comprised 42 percent of the total income of collective farm families in 1970 and 52.2 percent in 1988, while private plots provided 35.9 percent of the total family income in 1970 and 26.7 percent in 1988.

Given the dominant role of wages in family income, it is not surprising that the trends shown by data on total incomes per family member are similar to those already described with respect to trends in wages alone. The differentials in income between state worker families and collective farm families are somewhat smaller, and the reduction in the gap has proceeded a little more slowly than was the case for wages alone. However, the data on family incomes show that the income of state collective farm families was almost the same as that of collective farm families in 1988, rather than considerably higher, as indicated by data on average wages, total per capita income of both state workers and collective farm families in Ukraine exceeded the national average in 1988, as they did in 1975. Per capita family income of both groups, however, was below that of families in the Russian Federation in both years. Ukraine ranked fifth in the level of per capita family income of state workers in 1975 and sixth in 1988; the republic ranked seventh in both years in levels of per capita family income of collective farmers.

Up to now, the discussion has been in terms of changes in nominal wages and income. To assess progress in raising living standards, however, one needs a measure of the change in real incomes after allowing for inflation. The official index of retail prices published by Ukrainian statistical authorities shows a total increase of only 10 percent in the 1971–1988 period, most of which is attributable to increases in the prices of alcoholic beverages. Since this index measures changes in the prices of selected products on official price lists and not the prices people actually pay, it understates the rate of price change. Its use to deflate nominal income would lead to the conclusion that real income had increased virtually at the same rate as money income since 1970. To learn what at least a minimum adjustment for actual inflation might reveal about real progress, we can employ an "alternative" retail price index developed for the USSR. This index, an implicit measure reflecting the difference between the values of total retail purchases in the USSR, measured in current prices and in constant prices, shows an increase in prices of 46 percent during the 1971–1988 period. When this deflator is used, real wages of state workers increased by only 1 percent annually during the period, and per capita incomes of state worker families rose by 1.1 percent annually. Corresponding figures for collective farmers are 3.1 and 2.4 percent.

Newly released data also permit an initial assessment of the distribution of personal incomes by income class. There are two sets of data: one pertains to average monthly wages of state workers and employees taken from periodic wage surveys (*Narkhoz Ukrainy* 1988, 45), and the other gives a distribution of total per capita monthly incomes of the entire population in 1988 obtained from the regular government surveys of family budgets (*Narkhoz SSSR* 1988, 82 and 94). According to the latest wage survey, conducted in March 1986, 5.4 percent of all state workers in Ukraine received wages of less than

80 rubles per month; 18 percent received 100 rubles or less, and 5.9 percent had wages above 300 rubles per month. In April 1968, 35 percent of workers had monthly wages below 80 rubles, 56.9 percent earned 100 rubles or less per month, and only 0.8 percent received more than 300 rubles per month. As might be expected from the republic's relatively lower average wages, the proportion of workers with wages below 80 rubles in March 1986 was larger in Ukraine than in the Russian Federation and in the USSR as a whole; conversely, the proportion of workers with wages above 300 rubles was smaller.

A much more revealing picture of the degree of inequality is provided by the data from family budget surveys on total per capita income in 1988 in the USSR and the republics. In Ukraine, 8.1 percent of the population (4.2 million people) had a per capita income of less than 75 rubles per month. The semi-official poverty line for the USSR is set at 78 rubles per month, and some economists argue that it should be at least 100 rubles. Nearly one-fourth of the Ukrainian population (12.8 million people) had incomes of less than 100 rubles per month in 1988; 14.2 percent (7.3 million) had incomes above 200 rubles per month. The proportion of the population with incomes below 100 rubles per month is smaller in Ukraine then in all other republics except the Russian Federation, Belarus, and the Baltics. Conversely, the proportion with incomes above 200 rubles per month is smaller in Ukraine than in any other republic except for the five Central Asian republics, Azerbaijan, and Moldova.

Pensioners fare poorly in Ukraine compared to the rest of the population. In 1988, Ukraine's 12.6 million pensioners, three-fourths of whom were old-age pensioners, received an average monthly pension of 75.2 rubles (*Narkhoz Ukrainy* 1988, 59–60). This compares with an average pension of 85.1 rubles in the Russian Federation and 80.4 rubles in the USSR as a whole. In Ukraine, state old-age pensioners received an average of 92.7 rubles, while collective farm pensioners received an average of only 52.5 rubles. In 1987, 36.6 percent of all state pensioners and 89 percent of all collective farm pensioners had pensions of less than 60 rubles per month. Even though many pensioners supplement their pensions with income from jobs and from their private plots, the incidence of poverty among them is probably very high.

Consumption

The best overall measure of trends in living standards is an index of real per capita consumption, which is derived from gross national product accounts and measures changes in real expenditures for all the goods and services households purchased, plus government current expenditures on education and health care. I have devised such an index for the republics that is designed to be comparable in concept to a similar measure derived separately for the USSR as a whole as part of the measurement of economic growth (Schroeder 1981, 118–56). The index does have problems—stemming largely from data availability—but I think it much more accurately reflects real trends than does the official index published by the Soviet government, which is intended to assess progress in raising living standards. The official index, labeled "Real Per Capita Incomes of the Population," measures household income spent on purchases of material goods and services plus government expenditures on materials for education and health care. The deflator rests mainly on the official retail price index, which significantly understates the rate of price change.

My estimates of the relative level and rates of growth of per capita consumption in Ukraine are shown in Figure 13-3 for the period of 1971 to 1988. Throughout that period, living standards in Ukraine remained below the USSR average and much farther below those in the Russian Federation. In both comparisons Ukraine's position improved appreciably during the 1970s, but much of the gain in relative position was lost during the 1980s. In 1988, per capita consumption in Ukraine was 96 percent of the USSR level and 88 percent of the Russian Federation level. Among all the republics, Ukraine ranked fifth in 1970 and seventh or eighth in 1988. These relative levels for Ukraine given by my estimates are close to those shown by recently published official data on levels of real incomes per capita in the republics.

According to my measures, real per capita consumption increased at an average annual rate of 1.6 percent between 1971 and 1988, or by about one-third. In contrast, the official measure records a gain of two-thirds, or 2.9 percent, annually during the period. Both measures show much slower gains during the 1980s than in the first half. The official index was not published for 1989. Both the official index and my methodology probably would show real growth, but the relatively small quantitative improvement might not have been perceptible to the population because of rising inflation and the explosive rise in money incomes of 10.8 percent (*Pravda Ukrainy* 2 February 1990).

Data from the family budget surveys provide some information about how the pattern of family expenditures on consumption has changed as incomes have increased (*Narkhoz Ukrainy* 1988, 53–54). Data are given separately for families of state white- and blue-collar workers and for collective farm families. The trends and relative shares are about what one would expect. As incomes have risen for both groups, the share of consumption expenditures spent on food and beverages falls, and the share spent on nonfood goods rises. But little change has occurred in the share of services, which should be expected to rise. The likely explanation is that they simply are una-vailable, a reflection of the relative backwardness of the service sector in general. As is to be expected from their relatively lower incomes, collective farm families devote larger shares of their total outlays to food and beverages than do families of state workers. The following tabulation provides the data, expressed as shares of total family expen-ditures after deducting taxes and similar payments and additions to savings. Family expenditure patterns for both groups in Ukraine are close to the pattern for the USSR as a whole.

	State worker families		Collective farm families	
	1970	1988	1970	1988
Food and beverages	49	42	54	46
Nonfood goods	33	39	32	35
Services	12	12	5	6
Other	6	7	9	13

Although data on retail sales are available by product category, those data have a number of shortcomings as indicators of consump-tion in the republics, their urban and rural residents, and their adminis-trative subdivisions. Nonetheless, the general picture is similar to that provided by a variety of other data, including the data on incomes just described. In per capita retail sales of both food and beverages and nonfood products, sales in Ukraine in 1988 were below levels in the Russian Federation as well as the national average. In addition to retail sales data, a variety of physical data pertaining to a number of aspects of people's consumption and levels of living have been pub-lished. The available data are assembled in Figure 13-4.

Food

Data are available on per capita consumption of ten foods expressed in kilograms or units. As can be observed from the data given in Figure 13-4, per capita consumption of the so-called "quality foods"—meat and dairy products, vegetables, and fruits—has increased markedly between 1971 and 1988. Conversely, per capita consumption of potatoes and bread products has declined, a normal pattern of development as income levels rise. Per capita consumption of meat and dairy products in Ukraine generally has remained a little above the national average, but consistently below levels in the Russian Federation. Ukraine's per capita consumption of vegetables, potatoes, and grain products has been appreciably higher than in the Russian Federation and the USSR as a whole, however. Per capita consumption of most quality foods remains well below the recommended dietary norms.

Consumer Durables

Figure 13-4 provides data on household stocks of eight standard consumer durables. Possession of these consumer durables improved rapidly over the period, but especially during the 1970s. Thus, nearly all Ukrainian families now have a television set, whereas less than half had one in 1970. In that year, only about one quarter of families had a refrigerator, but in 1988 nearly nine-tenths of all families owned one. With regard to that symbol of the modern world—the automobile—a miniscule 2 percent of families had a car in 1970, but by 1988, 16 percent of all families had a car. This was very low by Western standards, but reflects significant progress nonetheless. For nearly all the durables listed, the percentage of Ukrainian families possessing them remained below the shares in both the Russian Federation and the USSR, but only by a few percentage points. For cameras and for automobiles, the percentages were the same in Ukraine as the national average. In 1988, car ownership in Ukraine was either equal to or slightly higher than in the Russian Federation, depending on which source is used for data for Ukraine.

Telephones

The USSR has been woefully backward in providing its population with another major symbol of modernity—a home telephone. Only recently have data been released on this matter. The published data are shown in Figure 13-4, expressed per 1,000 people. When these data are recalculated as percentages of all families having telephones, we learn that in 1980 only about 21 percent of urban families and 4 percent of rural families in Ukraine had a telephone. By 1988, about 35 percent of urban families and about 9 percent of rural families had home telephones. Generalizing from the data for all the republics, we can conclude that telephone ownership in Ukraine is a little above average for urban families and somewhat below average for rural families. The same conclusion holds in a comparison with the Russian Federation.

Housing

The lack of available housing is a major grievance throughout the USSR, and Ukraine is no exception. At the end of 1980, 1.7 million families and individuals were on waiting lists for better housing, provided either through the state or the housing cooperatives (*Narkhoz Ukrainy* 1988, 110); at the end of 1988, that figure had grown to 2.4 million persons. Although housing space per capita has grown steadily, it was not until the early 1970s that urban housing space per capita in Ukraine reached the minimum standard for health and decency set by the Soviet government in 1928. During the 1971–1988 period, with the share of investment in housing rising from 14 to 16 percent of the total, urban housing space measured in square meters per capita rose by 3.5 square meters, or 28 percent. Although data for rural housing are available only since 1980, rural housing may have improved more rapidly than urban housing since 1970. Ukraine has been somewhat better-supplied with urban housing than the USSR as a whole and the Russian Federation. Among all the republics, Ukraine ranked fifth in both 1970 and 1988 in this area. Undoubtedly, one reason for its relative superiority is the larger share of privately owned housing in the total; investment data reveal that people prefer to purchase larger units when they use their own funds. In 1988, 32 percent of urban housing in Ukraine was privately owned, compared with 22 percent and 16 percent in the USSR and the Russian Federation, respectively. Rural housing space per capita in Ukraine also exceeds that in the Russian Federation and the national average; in 1988, Ukraine ranked seventh among all republics. Rural housing, 88 percent of which is privately owned in Ukraine, is much more spacious on a per capita basis than is urban housing—32 percent larger in 1988.

When measured by living space rather than total space, the rural margin is 48 percent.

The supply of amenities for urban housing also has improved considerable since 1970. For example, in that year 80 percent of urban housing had running water and 76 percent had indoor plumbing; in 1988, these shares had reached 94 and 92, respectively. For the most part, urban housing in Ukraine is somewhat better suppled with amenities than in the Russian Federation or the USSR as a whole. Although there are only partial data, rural areas are woefully lacking in housing amenities. The data available pertain to the stock of public housing owned by collective farms. In 1986, 31 percent of such housing (measured in square meters of living space) had running water, 21 percent had plumbing, 18 percent had baths, and only 7 percent had hot water (Vashchukov and Esipenko 1988, 189). These shares were significantly lower than those for kolkhozes in the Russian Federation and for the USSR. Overall, the situation is similar for housing owned by state farms, but the availability of amenities for privately owned housing—the vast bulk of the total in rural Ukraine—is much poorer than for publicly owned rural housing. Virtually all housing is now supplied with electricity, however.

Housing conditions vary considerably among economic regions and oblasts in Ukraine. In general, the oblasts of the Donets'k-Dnieper region fare best in regard to both urban and rural housing space per capita, and the south region fares worse. Even so, there is significant variation within regions. In 1988, Luhans'k Oblast, with 17.5 square meters of space per capita, ranked at the top with regard to urban housing, and Volhynia and L'viv oblasts ranked lowest, with 14.2 square meters per capita. Vinnytsia Oblast had the highest per capita rural housing space (25.1 square meters), and Crimea Oblast was lowest, with 15.2 square meters. Both urban and rural housing space per capita increased in all oblasts between 1980 and 1988, but there was little change in their rankings.

Child-Care Facilities

Since virtually all women of working age are employed, availability of child-care facilities is a critically important ingredient in family welfare in Ukraine. Information about the availability of permanent day-care facilities is published; these are supplemented by seasonal facilities, for which there are no data pertaining to Ukraine. The data, expressed in terms of place in permanent facilities as percentages of the relevant age groups, are presented in Figure 13-4. They show that marked progress has been made since 1970, especially in rural areas. There, the percentage of children who could be accommodated tripled, while the share in cities rose by only 19 percent. Even with these gains in 1988, 30 percent of urban children and 55 percent of rural children could not be accommodated. Ukraine has been above the national average in child-care facilities for all children of the relevant age group, but ranks far behind the Russian Federation. In 1988, Ukraine had places for 61 to 62 percent of its children, compared with 71 percent in the Russian Federation. Ukraine ranked sixth among all the republics on this measure in 1988. In Ukraine, as elsewhere in the USSR, there are long waiting lists to get children into child-care facilities, but at the same time complaints about their quality are widespread.

Health Care

Judging from the three standard indicators that the USSR and the republics routinely use to measure their progress in improving health care for the population, Ukraine has made steady and appreciable gains since 1970 (Figure 13-4). The number of doctors per 10,000 people has risen by more than half, the number of mid-level medical professional personnel by nearly one-third, and the number of hospital beds by close to one-fourth. Ukraine has consistently remained behind the Russian Federation on all three measures, close to the national average with respect to health care personnel, and somewhat above that average for hospital beds. Among all the republics in 1988, Ukraine ranked sixth in provision of doctors, eighth in provision of mid-level medical personnel, and fourth in the supply of hospital beds. Availability of health care professionals and facilities varies greatly among oblasts in Ukraine, with more-rural oblasts far more poorly supplied than urban oblasts. In 1988, for example, there were 62.7 doctors and 144.1 mid-level professionals per 10,000 population in Crimea Oblast, compared with 32.7 doctors per 10,000 people in Chernihiv Oblast and 99.1 in Transcarpathia Oblast. Kirovohrad Oblast was best supplied with hospital beds and Transcarpathia Oblast least well supplied.

Despite all this apparent progress, health care in Ukraine, as elsewhere in the Soviet Union, is considered to be in a state of crisis. A major national program to provide remedies was launched in 1988 and is being implemented in Ukraine. The program attacks the problems on a broad front, with a critical component simply the upgrading of the sector's priority in investment and budgetary funding. The bulk of health care is financed through the budget of Ukraine. Budgetary allocations for that purpose rose from 60 rubles per capita in 1987 to 66 rubles per capita in 1988, with further increases from these meager levels being projected. The Chernobyl disaster has been a particularly onerous burden on the health care system in the republic. In November 1989, the Ukrainian Council of Ministers announced another major program to attack the health care problem through preventive approaches (*Pravda Ukrainy* 16 November 1989). The decree has the grandiose title "Comprehensive Program for the Preventive Treatment of Diseases and the Development of a Healthy Life-Style for the Ukrainian SSR Population to the year 2000."

Educational Attainment

The level of education in Ukraine rose steadily and markedly between 1970 and 1986, the latest year for which data have been published (Figure 13-4). The number of persons per 1,000 in the population age ten and over with at least some secondary education increased by 41 percent, while educational attainment at that level among the labor force rose by 34 percent. In 1986, the levels in Ukraine were slightly below and somewhat above levels in the USSR with regard to the overall population and the labor force, respectively. In that year, Ukraine ranked seventh among all the republics in general educational attainment and sixth in educational attainment of the labor force; its ranking in 1970 was fifth on both measures.

Disintegration of the Consumer Market

When Mikhail Gorbachev became General Secretary of the Communist Party of the Soviet Union (CPSU) in March 1985, he inherited an economy with a consumer sector in a chronic state of malaise, with shortages, queues, and black markets prevalent in varying degrees throughout the Soviet Union. Nonetheless, the retail markets were functioning after a fashion. After more than five years of perestroika, consumer markets are close to total disintegration in Ukraine, as elsewhere. This parlous state of affairs is mainly the result of a string of serious policy mistakes made by the central government and implemented in all the republics. These mistakes wreaked havoc on both the supply and the demand sides of the consumer market.

To combat the worsening social problems associated with rapidly rising alcoholism, in May 1985, Gorbachev launched a draconian anti-drinking drive intended to bring about a rapid reduction in the population's consumption of alcoholic beverages. The campaign entailed sharply reducing state production of alcoholic beverages, closing many liquor stores, curtailing the hours liquor was sold in retail stores, and steeply increasing alcohol prices. In Ukraine, state production of vodka and similar beverages fell by 15 percent between June and December 1985, 35 percent in 1986, and 17 percent in 1987. Production of all other types of alcoholic beverages also dropped sharply, and production of fruit and berry wines was virtually eliminated. Even though the price of alcoholic beverages rose by 39 percent between 1985 and 1987, the cutback in supplies deprived the retail stores of several billions of rubles in potential sales. As a result of this campaign, per capita consumption of legal alcoholic beverages in Ukraine fell from 6.8 liters per capita (measured in pure alcohol) in 1980 to 5.8 liters in 1985 and to 2.9 liters in 1987 (Goskomstat SSSR 1989c, 150). Total per capita consumption fell much less, however, because a booming illegal production took up some of the slack. Besides the cutback in liquor sales, there were runs on the stores to buy sugar and products containing alcohol that could be used to produce homebrew (*samogon'*). Although this misguided approach to the problem of alcoholism was reversed in 1988, much damage had already been done to retail trade supplies. Although sales of alcoholic beverages rose sharply in 1988 and 1989 (by 28 percent in the latter year), sugar continued to be rationed throughout Ukraine.

Another policy error that affected the supply of consumer goods between 1985 and 1988 was the central government's decision to substantially cut back the imports of consumer goods, which are costly and highly prized, and whose share in retail sales had been rising. This decision was made in response to hard currency balance-of-payment problems stemming from the fall in the world price of oil, the USSR's principal source of foreign exchange. Again, retail stores were deprived of billions of rubles of potential sales in the USSR as a whole; there are no specific data for Ukraine. Despite grandiose programs and near-frantic efforts to boost domestic supplies of other goods and services to replace the lost sales of alcoholic beverages and imported products, these efforts failed. Although production of all consumer goods in Ukraine, measured in current retail prices, rose by 30 percent between 1985 and 1988, much of this gain reflected higher prices. In Ukraine, the situation was complicated by the mediocre performance of agriculture, where the growth of output averaged only 2.2 percent annually.

While these policy errors served to restrain the growth of supplies, other developments were creating sharply rising demand. The most critical factor was the increase in the growth of the population's money incomes. In Ukraine, total money incomes rose at an estimated average annual rate of about 3.5 percent from 1981 to 1985, but between 1986 and 1989 the rate grew to an estimated 5.5 percent. Incomes rose 10.8 percent in 1989 and by 15 percent in the first half of 1990 compared with the corresponding period in 1989 (*Pravda Ukrainy* 2 February and 31 July 1990). Since wages of the state labor force make up the bulk of money incomes, their rapid growth—by 25 percent during 1986 to 1989—accounted for most of the increase in total incomes. The wages of collective farmers rose by 31 percent, however, and the high earnings of members of the fast-growing cooperatives (more than 400 rubles per month in 1989) contributed to the fast rise in the population's money incomes. The wage explosion resulted mainly from the general wage reforms that began in 1987 and from the economic reforms launched in 1988 that focused on expanding the autonomy of enterprises. While according enterprises much more leeway, however, the reforms did little to impose hard budget constraints on them. Under conditions of growing excess demand that prevailed, the enterprises were able to raise product prices and manipulate product mixes in the interest of higher profits. These funds, in turn, could be used to pay bonuses to workers. Competition for scarce labor from the cooperatives provided additional incentive to offer bonuses. The government's efforts to limit the growth of wages through assorted administrative controls proved unsuccessful. Curiously, the government itself mandated large increases in pensions and other benefits.

Thus, the classic situation of far too much money chasing too few goods was created, with all of its adverse consequences. Under the Gorbachev administration, the mismatch between the growth of money incomes and that of real goods and services has increased greatly. According to my estimates, money incomes in Ukraine rose twice as fast as real goods and services between 1981 and 1985, but nearly five times as fast between 1986 and 1989. This adverse trend has greatly exacerbated inflationary pressures. Open inflation has accelerated from around 2.2 percent between 1981 and 1986 to 6 percent or more in early 1990 (Marples 1990, 13). Collective farm market prices rose by 3 percent in 1988, 6 percent in 1989, and 16 percent in the first half of 1990 compared with the first half of 1989. The degree of repressed inflation also has risen markedly. One indicator of this is the behavior of the increments to the population's deposits in state savings banks. Between 1981 and 1985, the population added an average of 3.1 billion rubles to savings accounts; the increment was 6.3 billion rubles in 1988 and 8.5 billion rubles in 1989. No doubt cash holdings also increased, but there are no data on such holdings. Repressed inflation has fueled black markets, spawned a proliferation of special distribution channels that bypass the ordinary retail outlets, and fostered corruption and economic crime. In early 1990, the Presidium of the Supreme Soviet of Ukraine issued an edict providing stiff penalties for "abuses" in the trade network—speculation, illegal sales of alcohol, and the like (*Pravda Ukrainy* 10 March 1990). The government's reports on economic performance in 1989 and the first half of 1990 amply document the rising crime rate.

Still another development has exacerbated the situation on the demand side. That factor is the population's behavior in response to public discussion about possible major retail price increases and a monetary reform. The public discussion about retail price reform stems from repeated statements in speeches given by political leaders, as well as an explicit provision in the 1987 economic reform decrees that no action on the matter will be taken without a full public discussion of the issues involved. At present, retail food prices are heavily subsidized, and the prices of products such as vodka, clothing, and consumer durables include large turnover taxes. Also, as the population's money has risen compared to the supply of goods and services, a so-called "ruble overhang" has become a frequent subject of comment in the press, with monetary reform often suggested as a way to eliminate the overhang. Consumers have responded by hoarding goods and denuding the stores of almost everything they can find. Well-publicized shortages of particular products, such as soap and detergents, have produced similar responses. As a consequence of such hoarding, retail inventories reported in days of turnover in Ukraine have fallen from 91 days in 1985 to 69 days in 1988 (*Narkhoz Ukrainy* 1988, 77). A further drop probably occurred in 1989. Finally, after the unveiling in May 1990 of the central government's proposal to triple the price of bread on July 1, 1990 and to raise other consumer prices sharply beginning in 1991, people in Ukraine, as elsewhere, went on a buying spree ("Rising food prices" 1990; *Pravda Ukrainy* 27 May 1990). The Supreme Soviet in Ukraine voted not to implement the proposed price increases, which have been postponed by the USSR legislature.

Prospects

After five years of economic perestroika, the consumer sector in Ukraine is in a terrible state. The section dealing with the population's welfare in the report on plan fulfillment in 1989 is a litany of woes (*Pravda Ukrainy* 2 February 1990). The report laments: the consumer market remains "strained"; sugar is rationed everywhere; meat is hard to find in some regions; the supply of fish worsened; demand is not met for a long list of food products; many kinds of shoes, clothing, socks, and knitwear are sold only intermittently and with long lines resulting; soap and detergents are still being hoarded, absorbing one-third of the supply; returns and repairs under warranty occurred with regard to one-third of tape recorders sold, one-sixth of television sets, one-seventh of washing machines, and one-fourteenth of refrigerators. At the end of the year, one-sixth of all urban families were on a waiting list for better housing. The report for the first half of 1990 suggests that the situation has worsened (*Pravda Ukrainy* 31 July 1990).

Although real (quantitative) per capita consumption has continued to rise under Gorbachev, the gain has been so small as to be almost imperceptible to consumers and scarcely enough to maintain work incentives, let alone strengthen them. In terms of people's perceptions, the small quantitative improvement in living standards has been swamped by rising inflation, both open and repressed, and by the progressive deterioration of the consumer goods market. A recent article emphasizes these points for Ukraine, especially as they apply to low-income families. The author argues that the real standard of living of such families has been declining in recent years (Moskvin 1990, 13–21). Plan fulfillment reports for 1989 and the first quarter of 1990 state that the miners' strikes in Ukraine in 1989 resulted in a loss of more than 2 million man-days of work, work discipline is deteriorating, "the prestige of conscientious work is falling," and labor turnover is rising. Although the chairman of the Ukrainian Council of Ministers declared in early 1990 (*Pravitel'stvennyi vestnik* 1990, 5) that "overall, the economic situation in the republic is not so bad," the average consumer no doubt disagrees, considering himself or herself to be less well-off and the general economic situation to be deteriorating.

The growing disarray in the consumer sector has led to a major policy shift—a decision to sharply upgrade the priority for consumption and development of social infrastructure in the plans for production and allocation of investment. Also, many defense plants are to be converted to consumer goods production. The Ukrainian government's plan for 1990 calls for an increase of 5.3 percent in consumer-related industrial production (Group B), compared with only 3 percent for heavy industry (Group A) (*Pravda Ukrainy*, 2 December 1989). Markedly high targets are set for growth in retail sales (8.7 percent) and paid services (13.1 percent), and for completions of housing, schools, child care facilities, hospitals, and clinics. Judging from the results for the first half, these ambitious targets probably will not be met. In any case, the key to the success of this "supply-side" approach to stabilizing consumer markets is the extent to which the government succeeds in reducing the growth of incomes. The omens are not good so far.

Over the longer term, the fortunes of consumers in Ukraine will depend on the overall performance of the republic's economy. Regardless of Ukraine's future relationship with Moscow, the republic will need a large amount of new investment to modernize the capital stock of its aging industries, to create new industries, to clean up the devastated environment, and to improve the social and production-related infrastructure. Urgent though the needs may be, stemming as they do from many decades of neglect, the strong current reorientation of resource allocation toward consumption will mean fewer resources for investment and threatens long-term economic growth, as a Ukrainian economist forcefully argued recently (Heiets' 1990, 15–24). With a reduced rate of capital formation and an essentially stable labor force, economic growth is bound to slow unless productivity improves substantially. Such a breakthrough in productivity is expected to come ultimately from fundamental reform of the economic system in the direction of marketization for such reforms have yet to be finalized at the union or republic level. In the meantime, the numerous measures taken by the central government to try to stabilize the economy, especially the consumer market, are not accomplishing their objectives. All this bodes ill for consumers and workers in Ukraine in the near term. Even if the current crisis in consumer markets is alleviated somehow and truly radical economic reforms are introduced, the payoff in terms of a rapid improvement in living standards will not come quickly. The legacies of many decades of socialist central planning are awesome, as attempts to reform Eastern European countries are revealing.

Similar considerations bear on any assessment of the prospects for an upsurge in living standards in Ukraine under a different set of political-economic relationships with Moscow. Their shape has yet to be determined. At present (1988), enterprises producing 56.2 percent of total industrial production in Ukraine are subordinated to national ministries in Moscow (*Narkhoz Ukrainy* 1988, 236). How the recently adopted "Declaration of State Sovereignty" (*Pravda Ukrainy* 17 July 1990) will be implemented in Ukraine remains to be seen, as does how the population of Ukraine will respond to whatever new arrangements are finally determined. But an "economically sovereign" or an "independent" Ukraine will inherit the terrible economic legacies of six decades of diktat and mismanagement from the center. Thus, the short-term prospects for appreciably raising living standards are not auspicious.

References

Goskomstat SSSR. 1987. *Narodnoe khoziaistvo SSSR za 60 let*. Moscow.

_____. 1988. *Trud v SSSR*. Moscow.

_____. 1989a. *Narodnoe khoziaistvo SSSR v 1988 godu*. Moscow.

_____. 1989b. *Sotsial'noe razvitie SSSR. Statisticheskii sbornik*. Moscow.

_____. 1989c. *Torgovlia SSSR. Statisticheskii sbornik*. Moscow.

_____. 1990. *Biudzhety rabochikh, sluzhashchikh i kolkhoznikov v 1975–1988 gg. Sbornik materialov po dannym biudzhetnyk obsledovanii*. Moscow.

Goskomstat USSR. 1981. *Narodnoe khoziaistvo Ukrainskoi SSR v 1980 godu.* Kiev.

_____. 1989. *Narodnoe khoziaistvo Ukrainskoi SSR v 1988 godu.* Kiev.

Heiets', V. 1990. "Proportsiia 'nahromadzhennia-spozhyvannia' i stratehiia rozvytku ekonomiky Ukraïns'koï RSR." *Ekonomika Radians'koï Ukraïny* 1:15–21.

Kuznetsova, N. P. and L. N. Shirokova. 1987. *Raionnoe regulirovanie zarabotnoi platy.* Moscow.

Marples, David. 1990. "Poverty and Hunger Becoming Widespread in Ukraine." Radio Free Europe/Radio Liberty. *Report on the USSR* (4 May):13–15.

Moskvin, O. 1990. "Analiz tendentsiï zminy rivnia naselennia URSR." *Ekonomika Radians'koï Ukraïny* 2:13–21.

Pravda Ukrainy (Kiev). Various issues.

Pravitel'stvennyi vestnik. 1990. No. 12.

"Rising Food Prices Stir Panic Buying in Soviet Markets." 1990. *New York Times* (26 May):1, 5.

Schroeder, Gertrude E. 1977. "Consumption and Personal Incomes." In *The Ukraine Within the USSR.* Edited by I. S. Koropeckyj, 84–108. New York.

_____. 1981. "Regional Living Standards." In *Economics of Soviet Regions.* Edited by I. S. Koropeckyj and Gertrude E. Schroeder, 118– 156. New York.

Vashchukov, L. I. and D. A. Esipenko, eds. 1988. *Kolkhozy SSSR. Kratkii statisticheskii sbornik.* Moscow.

Figure 13–1. Measures of Personal Incomes in Ukraine
(1970, 1980, 1985, 1988)

	1970	1980	1985	1988	1970	1988
	Rubles per month				Percent of USSR level	
Average wages of state employees	115.2	155.1	173.9	199.8	94.4	90.9
Urban	118.4	158.6	177.0	NA	93.7	NA
Rural	97.4	133.6	154.4	NA	91.1	NA
Wages of collective farmers	66.6	103.6	135.6	167.5	88.9	92.1
Wages of state farmers	95.9	135.0	162.0	193.7	94.9	91.2
Total personal income per family member						
All state employees	88.0	123.0	141.0	156.0	NA	102.0
Collective farmers	62.0	96.0	125.0	139.0	NA	114.8
State farmers	NA	103.0	120.0	138.0	NA	NA

Notes and Sources: Wage Data: *Narkhoz SSSR* 1988 (81, 83). Goskomsat SSSR (1988, 156–57). Family Income Data: These data are obtained from annual surveys of family budgets. Total income include incomes in money and in kind from private agricultural activity, as well as money income from all other sources. Data for Ukraine are given in *Narkhoz Ukrainy* 1988 (52). Data for the USSR are given in Goskomstat SSSR (1990, 47, 243).

Figure 13-2. Indicators of Regional Differences in Personal Incomes in Ukraine (1970, 1980, 1988)

	Average monthly wages of state workers (rubles)				Average monthly wages of collective farmers (rubles)			
	1970	1980	1988	Percent change	1970	1980	1988	Percent change
Ukraine	**115**	**155**	**200**	**74**	**67**	**104**	**168**	**151**
Donets'k-Dnieper Region								
Dnipropetrovs'k O.	122	163	205	68	83	124	185	123
Donets'k O.	130	174	217	67	93	128	199	114
Kharkiv O.	116	159	204	76	79	123	199	152
Kirovohrad O.	107	150	194	81	81	126	178	120
Poltava O.	107	151	198	85	63	120	184	192
Sumy O.	103	164	194	88	68	107	169	149
Luhans'k O.	131	171	213	63	86	122	200	133
Zaporizhzhia O.	119	160	203	71	93	125	191	105
Southwest region								
Cherkasy O.	103	143	190	84	71	115	182	156
Chernihiv O.	100	140	178	78	54	92	147	172
Chernivtsi O.	101	135	175	73	60	93	155	158
Ivano-Frankivs'k O.	101	141	188	86	44	87	147	234
Khmel'nyts'kyi O.	99	139	183	85	57	86	145	154
Kiev O.	115	156	210	83	66	108	182	176
L'viv O.	109	148	192	76	50	84	148	196
Rivne O.	101	139	181	79	54	82	142	163
Ternopil O.	98	135	178	82	57	86	157	175
Transcarpathia O.	104	142	186	79	52	94	155	198
Vinnytsia O.	100	138	178	78	60	94	157	162
Volhynia O.	102	139	181	77	58	74	140	141
Zhytomyr O.	101	137	179	77	47	83	150	219
South region								
Kherson O.	108	150	190	76	96	132	179	86
Crimea O.	116	154	195	68	108	149	207	92
Mykolaïv O.	111	151	198	78	86	121	192	123
Odessa O.	117	155	195	67	73	109	165	146

Source: Narkhoz Ukrainy (1988, 46, 48).

Figure 13–3. Relative Levels and Growth of Per Capita Consumption
in Ukraine (1970–1988)

	1970	1980	1985	1988	1971–80	1981–85	1986–88
	Relative levels				Average annual rates of real growth		
Ukraine	100.0	100.0	100.0	100.0	2.0	1.5	0.6
Russ. Fed.	110.8	118.3	114.1	114.3	2.6	0.8	0.6
USSR	103.6	108.3	104.2	103.6	2.4	0.7	0.4

Source: These measures are revised and updated versions of those given in Schroeder (1981, 118–56). The methodology described there has been revised to convert the Soviet published index of per capita real incomes (used to update the base year ruble estimate for 1970) to current prices. The official retail price index was used to do so. In the original procedure, I had assumed that the official index of real incomes was essentially a current price measure.

Figure 13–4. Physical Indicators of Living Standards in Ukraine
(1970–1988)

	1970	1980	1985	1988
Food consumption, kilograms per capita				
Meat	49.0	61.0	66.0	68.0
Milk products	311.0	351.0	350.0	366.0
Eggs (units)	156.0	239.0	276.0	285.0
Fish	15.9	16.7	18.5	18.7
Sugar	41.4	51.8	46.5	49.7
Vegetable oil	7.4	10.0	10.5	10.7
Potatoes	156.0	133.0	139.0	120.0
Vegetables	103.0	115.0	124.0	128.0
Fruits	48.0	44.0	56.0	56.0
Bread products	155.0	146.0	138.0	140.0
Stocks of durables per 100 familes				
Watches and clocks	386.0	489.0	510.0	525.0
Radios	55.0	71.0	85.0	85.0
Television sets	48.0	80.0	92.0	98.0
Tape recorders	6.0	22.0	33.0	42.0
Cameras	23.0	29.0	34.0	35.0
Refrigerators and freezers	26.0	79.0	88.0	89.0
Washing machines	44.0	65.0	65.0	65.0
Sewing machines	45.0	54.0	55.0	55.0
Automobiles	2.0	10.0	14.0	17.0
Home telephones per 1000 people				
Urban	NA	64.0	85.0	106.0
Rural	NA	13.0	18.0	27.0
Housing, m^2 per capita				
Urban	12.2	14.2	15.2	15.7
				(9.8)
Rural	NA	16.7	18.6	20.7
				(14.5)
Child care places,				
percent of age group	38	57	59	62
Urban	59	70	68	70
Rural	15	34	40	45

(*cont'd.*)

	1970	1980	1985	1988
Health care personnel and facilities per 10,000 people				
Doctors	27.7	36.5	41.4	43.1
Mid-level personnel	86.9	103.1	111.4	115.5
Hospital beds	107.9	125.4	131.5	133.7
Educational attainment per 1,000 people	494	630	699	NA

Notes and Sources:
Food consumption: *Narkhoz Ukrainy* (1988, 73).
Stocks of durables: Ibid., Goskomstat (1989c, 37–42).
Home telephones: Goskomstat (1989b, 347).
Housing: *Narkhoz Ukrainy* (1980, 5, 253).
Narkhoz Ukrainy (1988, 119). Figures in parentheses for 1988 refer to living space rather than total space. Goskomstat (1989b, 100).
Child care: *Narkhoz Ukrainy* (1988, 140).
Health care: Ibid., 170, 172, 176.
Education: Data refer to persons 10 years of age and older who have had some higher or secondary specialized education. Goskomstat SSSR (1987, 525). The data pertain to the years 1970, 1979, and 1986.

CHAPTER FOURTEEN
Regional Aspects of Ukraine's Economic Development

Mariian Dolishnii

The equalization of economic development and the protection of the environment have become pressing global concerns. It is important that positive steps toward the resolution of these problems be taken by all nations, because these issues often transcend national boundaries. The amelioration of economic inequality should extend to the regional level within individual nations. By the same token, the geographical specificity of environmental destruction requires appropriate countermeasures starting at the lowest levels of government.

Ukraine holds a prominent place among European nations— indeed in the world as a whole—with respect to its area and population. Regional problems have played an important role in the country's history. An analysis of the regional aspects of Ukraine's economic development merits particular attention. The purpose of the present paper is to examine this issue in recent years. The discussion includes an analysis of the existing system of economic regionalization, unfavorable demographic trends, interregional economic and social inequality, and the regionally unbalanced development of the manufacturing sector. Particular emphasis is placed on the union authorities' harmful policies that led to the current catastrophic condition of the environment. I conclude with suggestions for reforms that are urgently needed to assure the further development of the Ukrainian economy.

Improving the System of Economic Regionalization

Economic regionalization is the direct result of the geographic division of labor. Its objective is to facilitate the efficient performance of the entire economy. Since individual economic sectors develop at different rates, these changes, in turn, determine the structure of economic regions. Therefore, continuous adjustments in economic regionalization are required. The Ukrainian economy would benefit from an improvement in its regional system at the present time. The existing development of territorial industrial complexes and the pattern of geographical population distribution should serve as the basis for the necessary changes. I believe that Ukraine's regionalization would be enhanced if its three large economic regions—Donets'k-Dnieper, the Southwest, and the South—were subdivided into a number of subregions. These new subdivisions should be given the appropriate status within the republic's administrative system. In the future, these smaller regional bodies could themselves be subdivided in response to new characteristics which inevitably emerge in the process of development.

I propose that the Donets'k-Dnieper economic region should be divided into three subregions: Donets'k, Dnieper and Kharkiv. The coal-mining complex forms the basis of the highly urbanized Donets'k subregion. Other industries found in this important Ukrainian industrial center currently include highly developed ferrous metallurgy, energy generating, chemicals production, and machine-building. The economy of the equally well industrialized Dnieper subregion depends foremost on its metallurgical complex. Also of considerable importance to this region are the machine-building, chemical, and electric generating industries. The Kharkiv subregion, situated in the northern part of the Donets'k-Dnieper region, specializes in machine-building, light industry production, and food processing. This subregion, with the large industrial agglomeration of the city of Kharkiv at its core, is also known for its efficient agricultural sector.

The southwest economic region should be subdivided into four subregions: Kiev, Carpathia, Podillia, and Polissia. The large industrial agglomeration of the Ukrainian capital with its highly developed manufacturing constitutes the heart of the Kiev subregion and the entire country. The subregion as a whole has such industries as extensively developed and diversified machine-building, shipbuilding, chemical industry, electric generation, light industry, and food processing. Geographically dispersed food processing (sugar refining, fruit and vegetable preserving), machine-building, light industry, and chemical branches dominate the industrial structure of the Podillia subregion. In the Carpathia subregion the most important industries include oil and gas refining, wood products, sulfur extraction, kaoline production, machine-building, light industry production, and food processing. In addition, the resorts in Morshyn and Truskavets' are well known throughout the Soviet Union. The L'viv industrial complex plays an important role in this subregion. Various types of machine-building, tool manufacturing, electrical equipment, light industry, and food processing enterprises are located there. The oblasts of Ivano-Frankivs'k and Chernivtsi are gradually developing their industrial potential. Industrial development lags somewhat in the Polissia subregion. Machine-building, chemicals, and light industry are located there alongside such traditional branches as wood products, pulp and paper, and construction materials.

Two subregions would make up the south economic region: the Black Sea and the Crimea. The main industries of the Black Sea subregion, ship-building, farm equipment, food processing, wine making, fish processing, and sugar refining, are technologically comparable to the same industries in the developed countries of the world. The development of extractive industries such as iron-ore mining and the quarry industry, as well as wine making, food (particularly fish processing), and the vacation industry distinguish the Crimea subregion.

The delineation of these subregions is required in order to create a geographically determined administrative system with appropriate agencies in Ukraine's government. These authorities could then facilitate the efficient economic development of the subregions, while taking into consideration such specific characteristics as geographical location, the availability of natural resources, local environmental conditions, population distribution, and other demographic characteristics. These factors would then be used in determining the future growth of the subregions during the transition of the present economic system in Ukraine to a market economy.

Socio-Demographic Indicators

The foundation of every country is its population. The population represents the source of the country's labor potential and hence of its production. A country's future social and economic growth depends on the size and quality of its labor force. Since Ukraine has experienced many political upheavals during the twentieth century, its demographics demand special attention. One need only mention the major disruptions of this century—the First World War and the subsequent civil war, the tragic famine of 1932 and 1933, the repressions of 1937 and 1938, the Second World War, and the massive postwar deportation from Western Ukraine—to underscore the need for such special attention. The effects of these human losses on the economic dynamics of Ukraine have thus far been inadequately analyzed for the nation as a whole, not to mention, in the context of its regional framework.

The population censuses of 1959, 1970, 1979, and 1989 reveal a steady worsening of demographic indicators for Ukraine as a whole, its regions, and its oblasts. All the indicators of variables contributing to Ukraine's population growth have decreased during the postwar period. Between 1960 and 1988 the population growth declined from 13.6 to 2.3 persons per thousand. Across oblasts the growth varied from 8.5 to 20.4 persons per thousand in 1960 while in 1988 this variation ranged between a scant 1.8 and 9.1 per thousand. In the western oblasts the corresponding figures for these two years were 21.6 to 27.3 persons per thousand and 2.8 to 9.1 per thousand. In L'viv oblast the natural rate of population growth declined sharply, by a factor of five, over the past twenty years (*Narkhoz Ukrainy* 1988, 15.). Obviously, such weak population growth adversely affects the growth rate of the labor supply.

The birth, death, and natural growth rates per thousand in the republic and by oblasts for 1988 are presented in Figure 14-1. The data indicate large variations in the natural population growth of the three large economic regions, oblasts—and even within oblasts' administrative regions—as well as between urban and rural areas. Urban areas have experienced increases in population growth in comparison with rural areas. The migration of young people from the countryside to the cities is responsible for the aging of the rural population and thus for increases in the death rate and declines in the birth rate. For this reason the natural growth rate of the rural population of the republic as a whole as well as of all of its oblasts, with the exception of the Crimea, fell well below that of urban areas.

The differences in the levels of natural growth of the rural and urban population of particular oblasts are in some cases relatively large. Accordingly, the natural growth rate of the urban population of the republic amounts to 5.0 percent while that of the rural population is −1.9 percent. The same trend can be observed in all of the Donets'k-Dnieper oblasts. The natural growth rate of the rural population was positive in only six of the thirteen oblasts of the southwest region—but it still was lower than that of urban population. The entire south region also experienced a positive rural population growth. Only in the Crimea subregion, however, did the growth rate of the rural population exceed (slightly) that of the urban population.

Figure 14-2 shows the total number of administrative units (*raions*) in individual Ukrainian oblasts and the number of those units whose population declined, broken down by urban and rural residents. In the oblasts of the Donets'k-Dnieper region and the Kiev and Podillia subregions more than 50 percent of all *raion*s registered negative natural population growth. Catastrophic environmental conditions may have in part contributed to this dismal record. The highest indicators of population growth are found in the Carpathia, Black Sea, and Crimea subregions.

The aforementioned pervasive tendencies in Ukraine's population growth are indeed disturbing. They not only characterize reproductive trends, but also attest to the socioeconomic, ecological, psychological, medical, and other conditions which prevail in the republic. To appreciate the meaning of the statistics it is useful to compare Ukraine to the other union republics. Ukraine's demographic picture has been progressively worsening relative to them. Ukraine, with a birth rate of 14.5 per thousand, ranks last among the republics. The union average stands at 18.8 per thousand. Ukraine shares with Estonia second place among the republics with respect to death rate, but comes in last with respect to the natural rate of population growth.

In addition to the natural growth of the Ukrainian population, internal migration processes, primarily between urban and rural areas, are also of interest. Increased employment opportunities and the enormous differences in working and living conditions between rural and urban areas are often cited as the reasons for the population migration from the countryside to the cities. The pendulum migration of part of the rural population, that is, the daily commuting for work or education to the cities, also affects the availability of labor in the countryside. The regions with agro-industrial complexes are especially negatively affected by this phenomenon. An analysis of statistical data indicates that 9.2 percent of the rural population of the republic engages in such short-term migration.[1] In Kiev Oblast 13.3 percent of the rural population are commuters; in Kharkiv Oblast, 13.4 percent; and in L'viv Oblast, 19.9 percent. For the years 1971 to 1980 the number of rural dwellers in the republic who commuted to cities on a daily basis increased by 35.6 percent. The deterioration of the demographic and employment situation in rural areas is likely to cause a further increase in the population flight to the cities. In years to come this is apt to depress the already low growth of agricultural production in the republic. It should be emphasized that young people make up the overwhelming majority of rural migrants, the group from which new ranks of agricultural experts and innovators are expected to be drawn.

Manufacturing

This section offers an analysis of the most important technical and economic indicators which characterize the manufacturing and socio-economic potential of specific subregions. The relevant data are presented in Figure 14-3.

The level of industrial development in Ukrainian regions varies markedly. The Donets'k-Dnieper region, which produces 53 percent of Ukraine's industrial output, is the most industrialized region. It should be noted that although enterprises of union and union-republic subordination account for 56 percent of all industrial enterprises in Ukraine, they account for 69 percent in this region. The percentage of these types of enterprises in some of the region's oblasts is as follows: Donets'k, 73 percent; Luhans'k, 74 percent; Dnipropetrovs'k, 74 percent; and, Zaporizhzhia, 72 percent. The fuel industry, machine-building, and metal working are the dominant branches in the industrial structure of this region. Although 79 percent of the Donets'k-Dnieper region's population is urban, this important manufacturing region nevertheless supplies a notable 35.5 percent of Ukraine's

---

[1] Based on Gosplan information.

agricultural output. Agriculture however plays just an auxiliary role, concentrated primarily on suburban plots, where vegetables, berries, orchard fruits, and livestock are produced. Given the high population density, the value of agricultural production per person is only 84 percent of the republic average. Among the region's oblasts the lowest values of this indicator can be found in Donets'k Oblast, 52 percent; Luhans'k Oblast, 60 percent; and, Dnipropetrovs'k Oblast, 71 percent. Unlike the rest of the region, in the northeastern oblasts of Kharkiv, Poltava, and Sumy, highly developed machine-building and metalworking enterprises, which supply the energy, transportation, and agricultural equipment industries, coexist alongside an efficient and relatively large agricultural sector.

The southwest region is characterized by developed tool making and machine-building, mining and extractive industries, woodworking, light industry, and food processing as well as diversified agricultural production (with the exception of the Carpathia subregion). In contrast to the Donets'k-Dnieper region, enterprises controlled by Moscow are not as important in this region—they produce only 44 percent of its industrial output. The southwest region covers nearly half of the republic's territory, while its population density falls below the republic average. The Carpathia subregion, whose oblasts account for only 9.4 percent of the republic's territory, contrasts sharply with the rest of the southwest region. While neither manufacturing nor agriculture are especially developed in this region, the resort and tourist industry is of unionwide importance thanks to its rich natural endowments. The subregion's high population density, 112 people per thousand square meters, accounts largely for the relatively low level of agricultural output per capita.

The south economic region, best known for its health spas and resort industry, also boasts highly developed manufacturing industries such as machine-building, metalworking and equipment for the agro-industrial complex, and a highly developed transportation industry, particularly ship-building. In addition, the diverse agricultural sector produces grains, vegetables, fruits, berries, and grapes.

As Figure 14-4 indicates, the welfare of Ukraine's population varies substantially among the republic's regions. The following three welfare indicators are used: material well-being, housing availability, and health care.

Material Well-being

The number of kilometers of paved roads per thousand square kilometers serves as an indicator of the level of the development of social infrastructure in an economic region. Differences in this indicator over regions are fairly small—235 to 250 kilometers per 1,000 square kilometers (of territory in the region). The best network of paved roads traverses the Podillia and Carpathia subregions, 327 and 325. kilometers per 1000 square kilometers, respectively.

The volume of savings serves as a reasonable proxy for the financial well-being of the population. The highest level of savings is found among the populations of the Kiev and Black Sea subregions, while the lowest among the population of the Carpathia subregion. Earned income remains the primary source of population income. In the year under consideration it varied little across regions for manufacturing and service workers ranging from 180 rubles per month in the Podillia and Polissia subregions to 215 rubles per month in the Donets'k subregion. More significant differences in average income emerge from interregional comparisons of the incomes of collective farm members. Kolkhozniks in the Donets'k, Dnieper and Crimea subregions earn the highest monthly income, about 190 to 200 rubles per month. In the western subregions, of Podillia, Polissia and Carpathia they receive 25 percent less, from 140 to 150 rubles monthly.

Housing Availability

Housing availability is an important determinant of material well-being. This indicator is highest for the residents of Donets'k, Dnieper and Podillia, particularly in rural areas where on average each inhabitant occupies 22 to 25 square meters. Residents of the Crimea and Carpathia subregions have to endure the worst housing availability, averaging from 15 to 17 square meters per person. The waiting-list system varies in certain respects from region to region. In the Donets'k-Dnieper economic region, for example, relatively more people await government housing than cooperative housing, while in the southwest economic region those waiting for cooperative housing make up the greater share.

Health Care

The quality of health care is best assessed by the number of qualified doctors per 10,000 persons. The Kiev and Crimea subregions enjoy the highest ratio of doctors, 49.8 and 62.7 per 10,000 persons, respectively. The residents of the Podillia and Polissia subregions live with below average ratios of doctors, 36.9 and 32.8 per 10,000 persons, respectively. In terms of the availability of hospital beds little variation exists among regions.

The Environment

The extensive development of industry, agriculture, and other economic sectors have taken a heavy toll on Ukraine's environment, rendering the issue of environmental protection of critical importance. Selected data on Ukraine's environmental conditions are presented in Figure 14-5. It must be stated at the outset that the republic's history of exploiting its natural resources can only be characterized as a chain of theoretical and practical miscalculations and decisions of central planners, all of which have culminated in ecological catastrophe.

Air pollution is a particularly acute problem in Ukraine. Manufacturing establishments yearly emit nearly 11 million tons of harmful substances into the atmosphere. One-third of these emissions comes from motor vehicle exhausts. On a per capita basis all emissions amount to 0.22 tons per year. In other republics this indicator is relatively low; for example, in Belarus it stands at 0.12 tons per year, in Moldova at 0.11 tons, and in Latvia at 0.07 tons (cf. Goskomstat SSSR 1989, 88). Furthermore, the level of filtering of harmful emissions in Ukraine—only 75 percent—falls far below world standards. In addition, Ukraine utilizes only 46 percent of its recyclable hazardous waste as opposed to 49 percent in the USSR as a whole. Such cities as Mariiupil', which emits 786 thousand tons of pollutants per year into the atmosphere; Kerch, with 375 thousand tons; Kamians'k, with 337 thousand tons; Makiïvka, with 319 thousand tons; and, Zaporizhzhia, with 287 thousand tons head the list of the most polluted cities in the Soviet Union (*Narkhoz Ukrainy* 1988, 196–97).

An unwarranted concentration of water-utilizing industries has developed in Ukraine. As a result of natural, climatic, and social changes, the scarcity of water which characterized the republic historically anyway has turned into a water crisis. In 1988 the republic used 68 billion cubic meters of water, 81 percent of which was used for industrial porposes (*Narkhoz Ukrainy* 1988, 191). A significant amount of water, 7.9 billion cubic meters, is used for irrigation (Goskomstat SSSR 1989, 75). The growth in industrial and consumer demand for water has led to an increase in waste streams, reaching a volume of over 2.4 billion cubic meters in 1988. Only 62 percent of waste water produced is filtered, and, to make matters worse, new water treatment facilities are being built at a slow rate. The oblasts which have achieved the highest levels of waste water treatment, close to 90 percent, include Transcarpathia, Kiev, L'viv, Volhynia, Kharkiv, Cherkasy, and Chernivtsi (*Narkhoz Ukrainy* 1988, 192). The largest resources of underground water reservoirs (aquifers) are found in the southwest economic region with 12 cubic kilometers per year, followed by Donets'k-Dnieper with 7 cubic kilometers per year, and the southern region with 2 cubic kilometers per year (Goskomstat SSSR 1989, 64). The southern and southeastern oblasts utilize these waters most intensively. Economizing on fresh water can only be achieved once purified water is effectively utilized.

While the dismal picture of water utilization applies to all of Ukraine, it is particularly bleak in the industrial zones of the Donets'k-Dnieper and the south economic regions. In these regions, pollution of small rivers and the Black and Azov Seas has reached crisis proportions. In the Donets'k-Dnieper economic region the concentration of heavy industry, with its inadequately processed emissions into the atmosphere and water has caused this condition. Certain urban agglomerations in the Donets'k and Dnieper subregions can be declared virtual disaster areas. It is no wonder that this region takes first place among all regions of the USSR for its level of pollution and environmental destruction. The southwest region holds second place for its concentration of manmade destruction, especially because of its emission of hazardous wastes into the atmosphere. The chemical and petrochemical industry exerts no less a deleterious impact on the environment, especially in the Carpathia subregion. On the other hand, the south region is affected most by the pollution of its rivers and and the contamination of its soil. The disastrous ecological consequences of the Chernobyl catastrophe obviously compound the environmental destruction in the contaminated zone and require immediate remedial action.

The Carpathia subregion (L'viv, Ivano-Frankivs'k, Transcarpathia, and Chernivtsi oblasts) is one of the most colorful areas in Ukraine. It has a beautiful natural setting and popular vacation spots. But its natural endowments are being threatened by industrial development. A group of industries extensively utilizing natural resources (mining, fuel, timber, pulp and paper, chemicals) continues to play a significant role in the economic structure of the region's manufacture. Under Soviet conditions this industrial mix has become counterproductive to the efficient utilization of natural resources and the protection of the environment in general. The ecological situation, however, differs from oblast to oblast. Thus, the amount of hazardous waste emissions into the atmosphere in Ivano-Frankivs'k Oblast, 46.5 tons per square kilometer, greatly exceeds the level of this indicator in such oblasts as Transcarpathia with 12.2 tons per square kilometer, and Chernivtsi with 17.9 tons per square kilometer. The volume of emissions of hazardous substances in L'viv oblast, 30.5 tons per square kilometer, approximates the republic average of 29.0 tons per square kilometer.[2]

The development of the timber industry, concentrated in the Carpathian Mountains, has been particularly irrational. Plans demand a certain amount of logging without regard to established norms of environmental protection. Nearly 25 percent of all forests have been poisoned by hazardous substances, while in some areas this proportion is now 50 percent, sometimes reaching as high as 80 percent. In addition, tens of thousands of hectares of Carpathian forests were cut down when oil and natural gas pipelines and high voltage electrical lines were laid from the USSR to the Central European countries. As a result forests now cover only 55 percent of the Carpathian Mountains. In general, the vegetative cover which stabilizes the ecological system has shrunk by 25 percent (Goskomstat SSSR 1989, 110–17).

Conclusion

The above analysis attests to the critical need for fundamental changes in the branch and territorial structure of the Ukrainian economy. Without such changes Ukraine's political and economic independence cannot be safeguarded. To conclude, I will outline some of the most urgently needed reforms.

A large share of the basic branches of industry in Ukraine are of union and union-republic subordination, particularly mining and machine-building, the prices of whose products are centrally determined. As a result, Ukraine's resources are inefficiently utilized and its role in the economic system of the USSR is misrepresented. The

---

[2] Calculated on the basis of "Povitria" f. no. 2-TP of the Ukrainian Gosplan.

Ukrainian government should therefore acquire ownership of all of its industry from the central authorities. The introduction of a national currency is essential to the successful transition to market economics. This step would facilitate the adoption of a more realistic pricing system. Such changes would enable the economy of the republic to protect itself from intrusions by central, Moscow-based ministries and protect Ukraine from the further depletion of its natural wealth. Also, drastic measures should be taken to ameliorate the ecological conditions and prevent further environmental destruction. Under these conditions, Ukraine would be able to address the issue of the unequal development of certain oblasts and regions. Furthermore, the conversion of the military-industrial complex to civilian uses may free a significant share of resources from arms output for the production of consumer goods. All this leads to the conclusion that rational regional development and an efficiently run economic structure demand the implementation of the "Declaration on Political and Economic Sovereignty of Ukraine," as proclaimed recently by Ukraine's Supreme Soviet.

References

Goskomstat SSSR. 1989. *Okhrana okruzhaiushchei sredy i ratsional'noe ispol'zovanie prirodnykh resursov v SSSR.* Moscow.

Goskomstat USSR 1989a. *Narodnoe khoziaistvo Ukrainskoi SSR v 1988 godu.* Kiev.

_____. 1989b. *Obshchie itogi estestvennogo dvizheniia naseleniia v 1988 godu.* F. no. I-A. Kiev.

Figure 14-1. Regional Reproduction Rates in Ukraine (1988)
(per 1000 population)

Administrative and Territorial Unit	Birth Rate			Death Rate			Natural Increase		
	Urban	Rural	Total	Urban	Rural	Total	Urban	Rural	Total
Ukraine	**14.6**	**14.1**	**14.5**	**9.6**	**16.0**	**11.7**	**5.0**	**-1.7**	**2.8**
A. *Donets'k-Dnieper Economic Region*									
I. *Donets'k subregion*									
1. Luhans'k Oblast	13.3	14.6	13.4	10.8	18.0	11.7	2.5	-3.4	1.7
2. Donets'k Oblast	12.9	13.1	13.0	11.0	14.9	11.4	1.9	-1.8	1.6
II. *Dnieper Subregion*									
1. Dnipropetrovs'k Oblast	14.1	14.7	14.2	10.2	18.0	11.4	3.9	-3.3	2.8
2. Zaporizhzhia Oblast	14.3	14.4	14.3	9.6	17.0	11.3	4.7	-2.6	3.0
3. Kirovohrad Oblast	15.7	12.0	14.2	10.7	18.7	13.9	5.0	-6.7	0.3
III *Kharkiv Subregion*									
1. Kharkiv Oblast	13.8	12.2	13.5	10.9	17.8	12.4	2.9	-5.6	1.1
2. Poltava Oblast	14.4	12.6	13.6	9.9	19.3	13.9	4.5	-6.7	-0.3
3. Sumy Oblast	15.0	10.0	13.1	10.4	19.6	14.0	4.6	-9.6	-0.3
B. *Southwest Economic Region*									
I. *Kiev Subregion*									
1. Kiev	14.6	x	14.6	8.2	x	8.2	6.4	x	6.4
2. Kiev Oblast	16.5	14.2	15.7	8.3	17.4	12.7	8.2	-3.2	3.0
3. Chernihiv Oblast	14.9	9.7	12.5	9.6	19.8	14.3	5.3	-10.1	-1.8
4. Cherkasy Oblast	15.9	10.8	13.5	9.4	17.4	13.7	6.5	-6.6	-0.2

II. Podillia Subregion									
1. Vinnytsia Oblast	15.4	12.0	13.6	8.5	18.2	13.8	6.9	-6.2	-0.2
2. Khmel'nyts'kyi Oblast	17.1	11.4	14.1	7.7	18.0	13.1	9.4	-6.6	1.0
3. Ternopil' Oblast	17.6	13.8	15.4	7.6	16.2	12.6	10.0	-2.4	2.8
III. Carpathia Subregion									
1. L'viv Oblast	15.1	16.4	15.6	7.7	14.5	10.4	7.4	1.9	5.2
2. Ivano-Frankivs'k Oblast	16.6	17.0	16.8	7.3	12.8	10.4	9.3	4.2	6.4
3. Chernivtsi Oblast	15.6	16.9	16.4	8.1	12.4	10.6	7.5	4.5	5.8
4. Transcarpathia Oblast	17.1	19.2	18.3	7.7	10.3	9.2	9.4	8.9	9.1
IV. Polissia Subregion									
1. Zhytomyr Oblast	16.2	12.4	14.4	9.0	16.4	12.5	7.2	-4.0	1.9
2. Rivne Oblast	18.3	16.8	17.5	7.0	13.0	10.2	11.3	3.8	7.3
3. Volhynia Oblast	18.4	16.1	17.3	7.6	15.1	11.3	10.8	1.0	6.0
C. South Economic Region									
Black Sea Subregion									
1. Odessa Oblast	13.1	16.5	14.5	10.1	16.1	15.1	3.0	0.4	1.4
2. Mykolaïv Oblast	15.4	15.6	15.5	9.9	14.7	11.5	5.5	0.9	4.0
3. Kherson Oblast	15.7	15.5	15.6	10.2	11.9	10.8	5.5	3.6	4.8
II. Crimea Subregion									
1. Crimea Oblast	14.5	15.4	14.8	9.5	10.0	9.6	5.0	5.4	5.2

Source: Based on data from Goskomstat USSR (1989b).

Figure 14-2. Administrative and Territorial Units of the Republic Experiencing Negative Growth of the Population (Urban and Rural Regions and Districts, 1988)

Administrative and Territorial Unit	Number of Administrative Units in a Region		Number of Administrative Units in a Region			
	Total	Including Negative Population Growth	Urban		Rural	
			Total	Including Negative Growth	Total	Including Negative Growth
A. *Donets'k-Dnieper Economic Region*						
I. *Donets'k Subregion*						
1. Luhans'k Oblast	18	12	18	5	18	14
2. Donets'k Oblast	18	12	16	6	18	12
II. *Dnieper Subregion*						
1. Dnipropetrovs'k Oblast	20	16	20	6	20	17
2. Zaporizhzhia Oblast	18	9	17	3	18	13
3. Kirovohrad Oblast	21	17	18	3	21	20
III. *Kharkiv Subregion*						
1. Kharkiv Oblast	25	24	20	9	25	24
2. Poltava Oblast	25	25	22	4	25	24
3. Sumy Oblast	17	17	16	8	17	17
B. *Southwest Economic Region*						
I. *Kiev Subregion*						
1. Kiev	—	—	—	—	—	—
2. Kiev Oblast	26	15	24	1	25	24

3. Chernihiv Oblast	22	21	22	6	22	22
4. Cherkasy Oblast	20	19	18	2	20	20
II. *Podillia Subregion*						
1. Vinnytsia Oblast	26	23	25	1	26	26
2. Khmel'nyts'kyi Oblast	20	17	20	1	20	20
3. Ternopil' Oblast	16	9	16	—	16	15
III. *Carpathia Subregion*						
1. L'viv Oblast	20	—	20	1	20	5
2. Ivano-Frankivs'k Oblast	14	—	14	—	14	—
3. Chernivtsi Oblast	10	1	10	—	10	1
4. Transcarpahtia Oblast	13	—	13	—	13	—
IV. *Polissia Subregion*						
1. Zhytomyr Oblast	22	14	21	1	22	17
2. Rivne Oblast	15	4	15	—	15	6
3. Volhynia Oblast	15	4	15	2	15	8
C. *South Economic Region*						
I. *Black Sea Subregion*						
1. Odessa Oblast	26	5	24	2	26	7
2. Mykolaiv Oblast	19	5	19	1	19	10
3. Kherson Oblast	18	1	17	1	18	3
II. *Crimea Subregion*						
1. Crimea Oblast	15	—	13	1	15	—
Total for Ukraine	**479**	**270**	**453**	**64**	**479**	**325**

Source: Based on data from Gosplan, Ukraine.

Figure 14-3. Ratio of Territorial Development in National Economy for 1989
Selected Socioeconomic Indicators by Regions, 1989

	1	2	3	4	5	6	7	8	9
A. *Donets'k-Dnieper Econ. Region*	36.6	42	79	99	53	69	35.5	3.913	0.788
I. *Donets'k Subregion*	8.9	16.8	89	154	21.1	73	8.2	4.101	0.483
1. Luhans'k Oblast	4.4	5.5	86	107	7.4	74	3.3	4.100	0.560
2. Donets'k Oblast	4.4	10.3	90	201	13.7	73	4.9	4.101	0.441
II. *Dnieper Subregion*	13.9	13.9	77	86	19.0	70	13.5	4.188	0.911
1. Dnipropetrovs'k Oblast	5.3	7.5	83	122	11.2	74	5.3	4.578	0.666
2. Zaporizhzhia Oblast	4.5	4.0	76	77	5.9	72	4.3	4.513	1.002
3. Kirovohrad Oblast	4.1	2.4	60	50	1.9	46	3.9	2.419	1.527
III. *Kharkiv Subregion*	13.9	12.4	89	76	13.5	59	13.5	3.363	1.053
1. Kharkiv Oblast	5.2	6.2	79	102	7.3	64	5.0	3.623	0.753
2. Poltava Oblast	4.8	3.4	50	61	3.5	55	5.1	3.174	1.412
3. Sumy Oblast	3.9	2.8	62	60	2.7	51	3.6	3.012	1.223
B. *Southwest Econ. Region*	44.5	43	55	83	35.1	39	47.1	2.512	1.022
I. *Kiev Subregion*	13.5	14.5	69.5	91.7	13.8	43.8	45.5	2.512	1.022
1. Kiev	0.1	5.0	100	3253	5.8	58	—	3.535	—
2. Kiev Oblast	4.7	3.8	54	69	3.0	38	6.1	2.484	1.525
3. Chernihiv Oblast	5.3	2.7	53	44	2.4	27	4.7	2.739	1.602
4. Cherkasy Oblast	3.5	3.0	53	73	2.6	37	4.7	2.707	1.477
II. *Podillia Subregion*	10	9.0	44.4	75.9	6.3	29.2	12.9	2.164	1.352
1. Vinnytsia Oblast	4.4	3.7	44	73	2.6	28	5.6	2.123	1.407

	(1)	(2)	(3)	(4)	(5)	(6)	(7)	(8)	(9)
2. Khmel'nyts'kyi Oblast	3.4	2.9	47	74	2.2	38	4.1	2.269	1.281
3. Ternopil' Oblast	2.3	2.3	38	85	1.5	18	3.3	2.095	1.354
III. Carpathia Subregion	9.4	12.3	49.3	112.0	10.0	44.0	9.4	2.449	0.718
1. L'viv Oblast	3.6	5.3	59.0	126	5.1	53	3.9	2.981	0.684
2. Ivano-Frankivs'k Oblast	2.3	2.8	42.0	102	2.2	41	2.1	2.416	0.721
3. Chernivtsi Oblast	1.3	1.8	42.0	116	1.2	24	1.8	2.036	0.943
4. Transcarpathia Oblast	2.1	2.4	41.0	98	1.5	32	1.6	1.884	0.621
V. Polissia Subregion	11.6	7.3	49.4	53.8	5.0	28.0	9.2	2.103	1.175
1. Zhytomyr Oblast	5.0	3.0	53	52	2.1	26	4.0	2.234	1.241
2. Rivne Oblast	3.3	2.3	45	58	1.6	29	2.5	2.154	1.046
3. Volhynia Oblast	3.3	2.0	49	53	1.2	29	2.7	1.858	1.221
C. South Econ. Region	18.9	15.0	68.0	71.0	12	42	17.4	2.474	1.099
I. Black Sea Subregion	14.3	10.0	64.8	60.3	8.3	43.7	12.7	2.520	1.178
1. Odessa Oblast	5.5	5.1	66.0	79	3.9	40	5.5	2.338	0.398
2. Mykolaiv Oblast	4.1	2.6	66.0	54	2.2	52	3.5	2.611	1.260
3. Kherson Oblast	4.7	2.4	61.0	44	2.2	41	3.8	2.809	1.473
II. Crimea Subregion	4.5	4.8	70.0	91	3.1	47	4.7	2.003	0.932
1. Crimea Oblast	4.5	4.8	70.0	91	3.1	47	4.7	2.003	0.932
Total for Ukraine	**100**	**100**	**67**	**86**	**100**	**56**	**100**	**3.079**	**0.935**

Codes for columns: (1) Percent of total territory of Ukraine; (2) Percent of total population of Ukraine; (3) Percent of regional population that is urban; (4) Population density (persons/km²); (5) Percent of total Ukrainian industrial output; (6) Percent of all industrial enterprises subordinated to union and/or union-republic organs; (7) Percent of total Ukrainian agricultural output; (8) Industrial output (millions of rubles per capita); (9) Agricultural output (millions of rubles per capita). *Source: Narkhoz Ukrainy* (1988, 11, 240, 299).

Figure 14-4. Selected Indicators of Population Welfare (1988)

Administrative and Territorial Unit	1	2	3	4	5	6	7	8	9	10
A. Donets'k-Dnieper Economic Region										
I. Donets'k Subregion	15.8	15.0	16.6	26.5 : 16.9	11.0	368	459	240	15.3	250.0
II. Dnieper Subregion	13.9	15.0	15.4	12.7 : 14.4	13.8	521	570	183	14.0	236.5
III. Kharkiv Subregion	12.3	12.9	13.5	13.3 : 12.6	18.6	697	695	264	13.5	245.2
B. Southwest Economic Region										
I. Kiev Subregion	14.4	14.0	13.2	11.4 : 12.3	20.6	544	963	429	16.8	236.2
II. Podillia Subregion	8.9	9.9	11.2	7.2 : 9.4	5.8	791	504	259	9.3	326.7
III. Carpathia Subregion	12.3	9.4	13.0	11.6 : 12.7	11.7	464	1,028	414	9.7	325.0
IV. Polissia Subregion	7.3	7.1	11.9	4.7 : 7.6	3.7	596	537	280	6.8	240.7
C. South Economic Region										
I. Black Sea Subregion	10.0	12.1	13.9	10.5 : 10.3	12.3	688	540	270	9.9	238.9
II. Crimea Subregion	4.7	4.6	16.1	3.1 : 3.8	2.5	533	536	150	4.7	243.3

	11	12	13	14	15	16	17
A. Donets'k-Dnieper Economic Region							
I. Donets'k Subregion	14.9	40.2	16.6	23.1	5.3	17.8	12.5
II. Kharkiv Subregion	11.9	41.7	12.5	12.5	11.8	13.0	11.9
III. Dnieper Subregion	13.8	42.3	14.4	16.5	10.3	15.8	11.8
B. Southwest Economic Region							
I. Kiev Subregion	16.9	49.8	14.5	15.3	15.2	16.4	17.5
II. Podillia Subregion	7.7	36.9	9.2	5.4	16.8	6.5	8.7
III. Carpathia Subregion	12.3	42.9	11.3	8.5	16.3	9.4	11.5
IV. Polissia Subregion	5.6	32.8	7.4	5.0	10.3	5.7	8.9
C. South Economic Region							
I. Black Sea Subregion	10.1	43.5	9.7	9.2	9.8	8.8	7.3
II. Crimea Subregion	6.8	62.7	4.4	4.5	3.2	5.5	9.9

Codes for columns: (1) Percent of total population of Ukraine; **Public Education:** (2) Percent of children attending full-time preschool establishments; (3) Enrollment per teacher; (4) Percent of work-force with specialized training (1970 : 1988); (5) Percent of students enrolled in post-secondary schools; **Consumption:** (6) Expenditures for food (rubles/person); (7) Expenditures for non-food consumer goods (rubles/person); (8) Expenditures for light industry goods (rubles/person); (9) Percent of rubles in savings deposits (per capita); (10) Hard surface roads (km/1000km²); **Public Health:** (11) Percent of all Ukrainian doctors; (12) Medical doctors per 10,000 population; (13) Hospital beds per 10,000 population; **Housing:** (14) Urban housing space (percent of Ukrainian total); (15) Rural housing space (percent of Ukrainian total); (16) Percent of population awaiting state housing; (17) Percent of population awaiting cooperative housing.

Source: *Narkhoz Ukrainy 1988* (11, 31, 133–34, 140, 148, 56, 283, 394, 169–70, 175, 112, 115, 110).

Figure 14-5. Selected Ecological Indicators by Region (January 1, 1989)

Regions, districts	1	2	3	4	5	6	7	8	9	10
Ukraine	**17,511.7**	**100**	**29.0**	**2,634.0**	**100**	**516.0**	**197,527**	**100**	**58,780**	**100**
A. Donets'k-Dnieper Economic Region										
I. Donets'k Subregion										
1. Luhans'k Oblast	1,379.1	7.9	51.7	337.6	12.8	200.9	8,932	4.5	2,120	3.6
2. Donets'k Oblast	3,410.8	19.5	128.7	242.7	9.2	5.9	22,798	11.5	3,989	6.8
II. Dnieper Subregion										
1. Dnipropetrovs'k Oblast	2,921.4	16.6	91.6	929.5	35.3	188.3	37,609	19.0	3,775	6.4
2. Zaporizhzhia Oblast	990.9	5.6	36.4	167.7	6.4	50.2	3,751	1.9	1,462	2.5
3. Kirovohrad Oblast	408.6	2.3	16.6	38.0	1.4	6.0	5,495	2.8	1,059	1.8
III. Kharkiv Subregion										
1. Kharkiv Oblast	763.6	4.4	24.3	322.1	12.2	6.2	3,431	1.7	1,453	2.5
2. Poltava Oblast	491.2	2.8	17.1	9.4	0.4	5.0	6,997	3.5	675	1.2
3. Sumy Oblast	280.1	1.6	11.8	59.7	2.3	0.9	4,812	2.4	2,846	4.8
B. Southwest Economic Region										
I. Kiev Subregion										
1. Kiev Oblast	911.8	5.2	31.6	39.0	1.5	7.9	5,482	2.8	3,359	5.7
2. Chernihiv Oblast	276.8	1.6	8.7	0.7	0.02	—	7,280	3.7	3,079	5.2
3. Cherkasy Oblast	374.6	2.1	17.9	4.6	0.18	—	5,161	2.6	2,194	3.7
II. Podillia Subregion										
1. Vinnytsia Oblast	490.1	2.8	18.5	21.6	0.8	0.6	4,532	2.3	1,734	2.9
2. Khmel'nyts'kyi Oblast	333.7	1.9	16.2	12.8	0.5	0.2	3,752	1.9	1,496	2.5
3. Ternopil' Oblast	257.2	1.5	18.6	5.9	0.2	2.0	5,398	2.7	2,320	3.9

	(1)	(2)	(3)	(4)	(5)	(6)	(7)	(8)	(9)	(10)
III. Carpathia Subregion										
1. L'viv Oblast	665.5	3.8	30.5	107.7	4.1	5.2	15,439	7.8	2,884	4.9
2. Ivano-Frankivs'k Oblast	645.7	3.7	46.5	69.0	2.6	14.7	4,391	2.2	2,349	4.0
3. Chernivtsi Oblast	144.7	0.8	17.9	1.3	0.05	0.4	1,020	0.5	308	0.5
4. Transcarpathia Oblast	156.4	0.9	12.2	17.0	0.6	0.9	885	0.4	372	0.6
IV. Polissia Subregion										
1. Zhytomyr Oblast	284.6	1.6	9.5	45.6	1.7	0.9	15,677	7.9	4,876	8.3
2. Rivne Oblast	228.2	1.3	11.4	15.7	0.6	0.2	7,693	3.9	2,922	4.9
3. Volhynia Oblast	181.7	1.0	9.0	10.1	0.4	—	10,590	5.4	5,090	8.7
C. South Economic Region										
I. Black Sea Subregion										
1. Odessa Oblast	456.4	2.7	14.0	119.7	4.5	5.6	3,118	1.6	1,765	3.0
2. Mykolaïv Oblast	325.5	1.8	13.2	21.3	0.8	6.6	3,685	1.9	1,826	3.1
3. Kherson Oblast	309.9	1.7	10.9	5.4	0.2	1.7	3,349	1.7	2,546	4.3
II. Crimea Subregion										
1. Crimea Oblast	814.1	4.6	30.1	39.1	1.5	10.8	6,255	3.2	2,186	3.7

Codes for columns: **Atmosphere:** (1) Emissions of poisonous substances (thousand tons); (2) Percent of Ukrainian emissions; (3) Emissions of poisonous substances (tons/km²); **Water resources:** (4) Discharges of contaminated sewage water (million cubic meters); (5) Percent of Ukrainian discharges; (6) Discharges of unpurified water (million cubic meters); **Land resources:** (7) Hectares of cultivated land; (8) Percent of Ukrainian cultivated land; (9) Hectares of exhausted land; (10) Percent of Ukrainian exhausted land.

Source: Based on data from Derzhpryroda Ukraïny for 1988.

CHAPTER FIFTEEN
Environmental Conditions

Craig ZumBrunnen

Geographically, Ukraine possesses the richest composite natural-resource base of any Soviet republic in terms of energy resources, industrial minerals and raw materials, agricultural land, natural beauty, and hospitable climate. Unfortunately, Ukraine also contains some of the world's most disturbed and polluted air, water, and land resources. It should not be surprising, therefore, that environmental and natural resource problems are high on the agendas of various Ukrainian Popular Front political groups, such as Rukh, which supports reform and Ukrainian independence (cf., "Ukrainian 'Front' Stirs Media Furor" 1989, 1–5; Tsikora 1990d, 27; Odinets and Tikhomirov 1989a, 26–27; and Drozd 1990, 24–25). At the same time, local chapters of the Green Movement and other nongovernment environmental organizations have been springing up across Ukraine over the past four or five years (Levicheva 1990, 5–8, 28). Environmental issues apparently played decisive roles in the 1989 Ukrainian political campaign to elect republic representatives to the first All-Union Congress of People's Deputies. Several recent Soviet newspaper articles suggest that candidates espousing environmentally conscious political themes received strong voter support during the 1990 elections in local soviets, municipal soviets, and the Ukraine Republic Parliamentary elections. Granted, these candidates usually were also able to capitalize on citizen grievances against local Communist Party officials and their candidates. Many of these grievances, however, were directly related to environmental problems and the chronically poor response to them by local-, district-, oblast-, and republic-level governments, and by ministry and Party bureaucrats. Popular Front and Green Movement candidates ran well, not only in the more nationalistic western part of Ukraine, but also in the more "russified"

Eastern Ukraine (cf. Tsikora 1990b, 29–30; Tsikora 1990a, 29; Derimov 1990, 13; Tsikora 1990d, 13; Odinets and Tikhomirov 1989b, 20–21; Baklanov 1989a, 3).

The true, or operational glasnost era can be linked directly to the events surrounding the Chernobyl nuclear power accident in 1986 and its aftermath. Since then, increasing candor has led to the publication of numerous hard-hitting, investigative reports, scientific investigations, and debates about a wide range of environmental and ecological problems throughout the USSR. This chapter draws heavily upon two official publications that contain previously unavailable environmental and natural-resource management data: *Doklad sostoianie prirodnoi sredy v SSSR v 1988 godu* (Report on the State of the Environment in the USSR in 1988), hereafter *Doklad* (1989), and *Okhrana okruzhaiushchei sredy i ratsional' noe ispol' zovanie prirodnykh resursov v SSSR: statisticheskii sbornik* (Protection of the Environment and the Rational Use of Natural Resources in the USSR: Statistical Handbook), hereafter *Okhrana* (1989).[1] A third source of useful official Soviet statistical information about environmental protection consists of the "*Okhrana prirody*" data series published since 1986 in the *Narkhoz SSSR* annual statistical handbook series.

Drawing upon these documents and a number of other scientific and journalistic accounts, an environmental portrait of Ukraine, varying in geographic scale and detail, can be created. First, Ukraine's pollution and environmental problems will be compared with those of other economic regions in the USSR to place Ukraine's problems in an all-union context. Availability of data limits the size of the brushes that can be used to compose our multi-layer environmental picture. The environmental layers that will be presented are air pollution and air quality, water use and water quality, land resource conditions, and the human and environmental consequences of the Chernobyl accident. Ukrainian and national expenditures on environmental protection also will be discussed. This chapter concludes with a cursory discussion and evaluation of some of the implications of perestroika, or economic restructuring for environmental protection in Ukraine and the USSR.

---

[1] For a panel discussion of these two important Soviet publications, see Bond et al. (1990, 401–468).

Environmental Conditions: Ukraine vs. the USSR

Data from the Laboratorii monitoringa prirodnoi sredi i klimata (Laboratory for Monitoring the Natural Environment and Climate) of the newly created Goskomgidrometa SSSR (State Committee on Hydrometeorology) and the USSR Academy of Sciences have been used by the Soviets to create rank-order estimates by degree of pollution and environmental degradation for all 20 Soviet economic regions (Figure 15- 1). Each of the regions has been ranked on six indices of pollution and environmental disruption. Because of various ties in these rankings, none of the six indices numerically traverse the entire range from 1 (worst pollution and/or degradation level) to 20 (lowest pollution and/or degradation level). The rankings for "pollution of rivers and water shortages," for example, only extend from 1 through 12, and the rankings are the same for several regions.

Despite these limitations of ordinal data estimates, Figure 15-1 provides a very informative regional overview of the relative levels of environmental disruption and pollution of Ukraine compared to the rest of the Soviet Union. To emphasize Ukraine's rankings, its three economic regions, the Donets'k-Dnieper, Southwest, and South, are listed twice. First, they are listed together in descending order of overall environmental disruption, with the Donets'k-Dnieper economic region the most environmentally disturbed and the South the least. Second, they are ranked with the other 17 Soviet economic regions based on the index of Aggregate Human Impact, which appears to be the best single index in ranking the overall regional environmental degradation. Unfortunately, as Figure 15-1 shows, these official data paint a grim portrait of the current environmental conditions in Ukraine. For instance, the Donets'k-Dnieper region ranks worst in three areas, air pollution per unit of total area (tied with the Urals), pollution of rivers and water shortages, and aggregate human impact. In fact, this part of the heavily industrialized and urbanized Eastern Ukraine is undoubtedly the most severely environmentally degraded region in the entire Soviet Union, with the heavily industrialized Urals second overall. Only the Urals rank worse than the Donets'k-Dnieper region when the two air pollution indices are combined.

High levels of air pollution and acid rainfall are behind the Donets'k-Dnieper's relatively high index for forest damage (4th), especially since the region's natural vegetation is more steppe than forest. Even the more rural and less industrialized Southwest economic region fares no better than eighth place overall in terms of aggregate human impact. The estimate that only the Donets'k-Dnieper and Urals regions are worse than the Southwest economic region in air pollution per unit of total area is distressing and somewhat surprising. Given the extensive areas affected by radioactive contamination from the Chernobyl accident in both Belarus and the Southwest economic regions, it seems surprising that they are ranked as low as fifth and seventh, respectively, in terms of soil contamination and soil erosion. More likely, this merely suggests how very serious soil contamination and erosion are in other Soviet regions, such as Moldova, Central Asia, Kazakhstan, and chernozem (black earth) soil regions. The South, which even includes the balmy resort climes of the Crimean peninsula, ranks no better than twelfth in terms of human impact. More disturbing, however, are this region's relatively high degrees of air pollution per unit area (sixth), water pollution and shortages (fifth), and soil contamination and erosion (fifth). Finally, since neither the Southwest nor the South has much forested area, their ranks of fifteenth and seventeenth, respectively, in terms of forest damage is of little solace.

In summary, it is clear from official Soviet data that Ukraine overall is one of the most severely environmentally disturbed regions of the entire Soviet Union, especially the Donets'k-Dnieper economic region. Next, examining some of Ukraine's air-quality problems will present a more-detailed geographical portrait of the republic's disturbing environmental conditions.

Atmospheric Pollution and Air Quality

The general quality of Ukraine's atmosphere can be assessed from at least three perspectives. First, published emission levels of atmospheric pollutants can be studied. While this information can reveal the geographical patterns of atmospheric discharges, it can not be used alone to indicate regional patterns of air quality, however. This is because air quality is a dynamic function of both the airborne discharge of contaminants and local environmental conditions, such as prevailing wind speed and direction, atmospheric stability characteristics, and topographic relief patterns. Second, published ambient air-quality statistics, especially over urban areas, can be examined to obtain a more accurate portrait of air pollution severity. Third, other published accounts of air pollution problems can be used. All three sets of sources are utilized in this section.

The Obshchegosudarstvennoi sluzhby nabliudenii i kontrolia zagrazheniia prirodnoi sredy (OGSNK; State Environmental Pollution Monitoring and Control Service) was established in the mid-1960s. Composed of subdivisions of the Soviet State Committee on Hydrometeorology, the USSR Ministry of Public Health, and the laboratories of industrial enterprises, its mission is to monitor, assess, and predict pollution levels and to provide information to interested organizations. At first, OGSNK monitored only dust, sulfur dioxide, carbon monoxide, and nitrogen dioxide. Atmospheric concentrations of 80 different substances currently are monitored in urban areas, with 8 different components measured systematically in each city. In 1965, the Soviet air-quality monitoring network consisted of only 45 cities, with a total of 86 air-monitoring stations. By 1988, the network had expanded to include 534 cities with 1,167 monitoring stations. Standards for maximum permissible pollution-emission levels (MPE) for each source and enterprise are established to prevent contamination levels from exceeding the maximum permissible concentrations (MPC) established by the Soviet Ministry of Public Health (*Doklad*, 8–10). Presumably, OGSNK collected the air-quality data published in *Doklad* (1989) and *Okhrana* (1989) that are used in the following analysis.

In 1988, 15 Ukrainian cities ranked within the worst 104 Soviet cities with regard to total measured emissions of air-borne contaminants (Figure 15-2). Other sources suggest that the city of Horlivka should be added since pollutant gases in its atmosphere commonly exceed the MPC's of other pollutants by factors of 10 to 30 (Lisovenko and Trach 1989, 28– 29). In terms of Ukraine's area (2.7 percent of the USSR) and the fraction of the total Soviet urban population that these 15 heavily industrialized Ukrainian cities represent (5.2 percent in 1989), it is not surprising that they account for a high, but slowly declining fraction of total Soviet stationary source discharges (7.1 percent in 1985 and 6.9 percent in 1988). Looking at the share these 15 cities had in the total urban population of the 104 cities studied, about 14 percent in 1989 ("O predvaritel'nykh itogakh" 1989, 1-3.), their combined share of stationary source emissions is high— 19.6 percent in 1988, and actually has grown from 19.1 percent in 1985. Only the nonferrous-polymetallic-mining and smelting city of

Noril'sk, located in the far northern part of East Siberia, discharged a greater quantity of atmospheric contaminants than Kryvyi Rih, a major Ukrainian iron and steel center (*Okhrana*, 22–24). The worst 8 of the 15 cities plus Ienakiieve are centers of ferrous metallurgy. The other six are major petroleum refining or chemical industry centers. Thermal power-plant smokestacks are point sources in or near all 15 of these cities (Glavnoe upravlenie geodeziia 1984, 132–51, 192–93). The data in Figure 15-2 indicate that 12 of the 15 cities have reported steady absolute reductions in their annual airborne discharges from stationary sources. At this point, it would be speculative to attribute the recent general reduction in the discharge of harmful substances from stationary sources to improved pollution-abatement efforts or to selective cutbacks in industrial outputs that were made recently. Of the three exceptions, Kremenchuk, Sivers'kodonets'k, and Lysychans'k, only Lysychans'k reported higher emissions in 1988 than in 1985. Despite these positive trends in the absolute reduction of emissions, the relative ranking of nine of these cities became worse among the 104 Soviet cities. Four improved their relative ranking and two, Makiïvka and Sivers'kodonets'k, remained the same.

Figure 15-3 supports a strong correlation between city population size and autotransport discharge levels. As listed, 13 Ukrainian cities rank among the 100 worst Soviet cities in terms of the quantity of harmful atmospheric discharges from autotransport sources. The *Doklad* (1989) volume also lists Kharkiv as having between 150,000 to 300,000 metric tons per year of vehicular emissions (*Doklad* 1989, 66.). Furthermore, in terms of both absolute discharge and relative levels, Ukraine's positions were worse in 1987 than in 1986. Of the 13 cities, only Cherkasy improved its relative rank (increased rank number) from 1986 to 1987. Nine of the twelve non-Ukrainian cities listed in the group of the 17 worst cities reported absolute reductions in their emissions between 1986 and 1987, whereas 11 of the 13 Ukrainian cities are reported as actually having *increased* their harmful autotransport emissions. In this regard, Donets'k, Odessa, Zaporizhzhia, and Sivers'kodonets'k had the largest increases. Although the 100 cities overall had a measured reduction of 225,500 metric tons, or 2.9 percent, between 1986 and 1987, the Ukrainian cities experienced a 40,700 metric ton, or 4.2 percent, increase in their autotransport discharges. How should these short-term trends be interpreted? On the one hand, it seems possible that the auto-exhaust emissions in Ukraine are getting worse. On the other hand, even if this is true, different interpretations are possible. First, these increases may reflect a deterioration in the maintenance of Ukraine's cars, trucks, and buses. Second, it may represent a general increase in autotransport numbers and usage in Ukraine. Third, both of these factors may apply. At the same time, the last row in Figure 15-3 suggests that the 13 Ukrainian cities actually discharge slightly less harmful substances from auto-transport (13.1 percent in 1987) than would be expected based solely on their combined share of population (13.6 percent in 1989).

The discussion so far has focused only on the magnitude of harmful airborne discharges. When examining ambient air quality, the concentrations of atmospheric pollutants also must be assessed. For the Soviet Union as a whole, the average, monitored urban levels of sulfur dioxide (SO_2), carbon monoxide (CO), and nitrogen oxide (NO) concentrations remain within the Soviet MPC sanitary norms. The average concentrations of dust, phenol, ammonia (NH_3), and nitrogen dioxide (NO_2) somewhat exceed the MPCs; while average carbon disulfide (CS_2), benz(o)pyrene and formaldehyde levels (both of which are carcinogens) exceed their MPCs by factors of 3 to 4 (*Doklad* 1989, 11-13).

Okhrana's (1989) statistics include recent average atmospheric concentration data on the four key substances—dust, sulfur dioxide, carbon monoxide, and nitrogen dioxide—for 14 Ukrainian cities (Figure 15-4). In Figure 15-4, all concentration values that exceed the MPCs for the respective substances are in boldface. With reference to their MPCs, dust and nitrogen-dioxide levels are the most problematic and carbon monoxide the least. This may reflect the relatively low levels of automobile usage in Ukraine (and the USSR in general) compared to that in the United States.

Goskompriroda has developed an atmospheric pollution index, *indeks zagriazheniia atmosfery* (IGA), based on the sum of the five highest municipal pollutant concentrations based on their risk classification. *Doklad* (1989) contains an alphabetical list of the worst 68 Soviet cities according to this IGA for 1988 (*Doklad* 1989, 20–23). As shown in Figure 15-5, 12 of these 68 cities are in Ukraine. In terms of ambient air quality, air pollution is especially severe in many of the heavily industrialized cities and towns of the Donets'k-Dnieper economic region of Eastern Ukraine, especially in Kharkiv, Luhans'k, Donets'k, Dnipropetrovs'k, and Zaporizhzhia oblasts. Of the 12 Ukrainian cities experiencing the highest air-pollution levels, all but Kiev and Odessa are located in this region. As shown in Figure 15-5, the most common contaminants include benzopyrene, which is carcinogenic, formaldehyde and phenol (also suspected of being carcinogens), ammonia, hydrogen fluoride, nitrogen dioxide, and dust. Coal-using industries, such as metallurgical coke-chemical plants, steel mills, and thermal power plants, are major sources of high levels of sulfur dioxide, dust, unburned hydrocarbons, and other harmful substances. In particular, the air quality in the cities of Dnipropetrovs'k and Zaporizhzhia is reported to be among the worst in the USSR. The 1988 Ukrainian documentary film *Hostages* contains many graphic scenes of the highly polluted industrial landscape of Zaporizhzhia and tragic, grotesque scenes of deformed human babies, whose medical problems are said to be the result of the severe air contamination that hangs over this major manufacturing center of ferrous metallurgy, chemicals, and semi-conductors. Average phenol concentrations in Lysychans'k (four times the MPC) and Sivers'kodonets'k (three times the MPC) were reported as being the highest of any monitored Soviet cities. Furthermore, these two Ukrainian chemical-industry centers were tied for the dubious distinction of having the highest average formaldehyde concentrations (10 times the MPC) in 1988 (*Doklad* 1989, 23). Airborne metals are also major contaminants. For example, in Odessa the highest average monthly concentration of cadmium was three times the MPC. In Kamians'k the average annual manganese concentration was three to five times the MPC (*Doklad* 1989, 14). Finally, of the 15 Soviet cities listed as having higher death rates attributed to air pollution, three are in Ukraine, namely, Kremenchuk, Rivne, and Cherkasy (*Doklad* 1989, 23). Even the air quality of the famous Crimean resort city of Yalta has become alarmingly bad (Savin 1989, 29).

In summary, of the entire Soviet Union, probably only the Urals has worse air-quality conditions than the Donets'k-Dnieper region of southeast Ukraine. Furthermore, as noted previously, even the Southwest and South economic regions of Ukraine fare poorly in terms of air pollution per unit area. Ukraine's environmental conditions with respect to water quality are not much, if any, better.

Water Use and Quality

Fresh Water Supply and Use

Ukraine is situated almost entirely within the drainage basins of the Black Sea and Sea of Azov system. For its relatively small size and limited water resources, Ukraine's waters are used intensively. The high population density, heavy industrial development, and, until recently, government's low priority on environmental protection have resulted in chronic and very serious water pollution throughout Ukraine, with surface-water shortages in some places. For instance, in 1988, 9 percent of all Soviet fresh water withdrawals came from Ukrainian sources (All-Union Institute 1990, 12). Furthermore, although the Dnieper, Ukraine's major drainage system, is the tenth-longest river in the Soviet Union (2,200 km) and eleventh in terms of the area of its drainage basin (with 504 thousand km^2; cf. Glavnoe upravlenie geodeziia 1984, 206), rising non-returned or consumptive water use within the basin is creating water-supply problems for many of the cities, industries, and agricultural facilities within the Dnieper basin (All-Union Institute 1990, 15).

Regional and sectoral breakdowns of Soviet and Ukrainian water use in 1988 are contained in Figure 15-6. The first two columns reveal that Ukrainian municipal water use is slightly below the Soviet average on an annual per capita basis (87 versus 92 m^3/capita). The tragic irony in the Soviet resource-pricing scheme or "free use" doctrine is that some of the least well-endowed water-resource regions in the Transcaucasus and Central Asia actually have the highest per capita municipal water usage. Not surprisingly, the arid Central Asian republics dominate the irrigation and rural water-supply figures. Compared to Ukraine's share of industrial output, its industrial water use is low. In other words, the large demand for water for industrial use, combined with modest fresh water supplies have forced planners to invest in recirculating-recycling industrial water-supply systems. In this regard it seems as though water scarcity or a mass balance perspective has yielded the same "rational" water-resource investment strategy as a scarcity pricing scheme would have. More specifically, only the smaller industrial bases of Belarus and Armenia have higher shares (84 percent) of fresh-water industrial use savings attributed to systems for recirculating and recycling the industrial water supply (81 percent for Ukraine). Nearly 25 percent of the total Soviet capacity in such systems is located in Ukraine (see Figure 15-6). Unfortunately, these positive responses often went hand-in-hand with massive and potentially ecologically harmful water-diversion schemes (cf. "Responsibility to Nature" 1987, 18–19; Lukyanenko 1987, 215–16; Drobotov 1988, 15–17; Pastukhova 1989, 22; Manucharova 1990, 33-34; Manucharova and Kornev 1990, 30-31). On a positive ecological note, a resolution calling for the suspension of the highly controversial Volga-Don water diversion canal project was adopted by a *Gosplan* committee of experts in March 1990. This happened after more than 100 million rubles had been spent, even though permission for the project has never been granted (Manucharova 1990, 33–34). Such behavior has been typical of the ministry in charge of water-diversion projects, the "new" Ministry of Water Resources Construction, formerly the Ministry of Land Reclamation and Water Management. On February 7, 1990, *Izvestiia* published a scathing attack on the mode of operation of this ministry signed by five prominent Soviet People's Deputies active in the Soviet environmental protection movement, S. Zalygin, A. Kazannik, V. Tokhonov, A. Iablokov and A. Ianshin. Of relevance here is that although both the large, proposed Danube-Dnieper and Volga-Don diversion canals supposedly have been halted, the angry deputies claim that "massive environmental alteration" activities of the ministry will just move elsewhere, such as Siberia. There is no real guarantee that they will not try to reinstate the Ukrainian projects later (Zalygin et al. 1990, 29–30).

Fresh Water Quality Problems

The biological, chemical, and physical pollution levels of Soviet surface waters are monitored on 2,206 sources by 3,173 observation stations. Hydro-chemical laboratories measure up to 106 water quality indices, including some 40 specific contaminants. Water samples are taken daily, every 10 days, every month or quarterly both upstream and downstream from effluent sources and at varying distances from them depending on the type of monitoring station. Maximum permissible concentration (MPC) standards, which vary by intended water use, such as fish-spawning reservoirs, industrial, potable, and household use, are applied to these monitored waterways (*Doklad* 1989, 54).

Water pollution problems are pervasive throughout Ukraine, but are most severe in the heavily industrialized Donets'k-Dnieper region. In relative terms, the South and Southwest economic regions fare better, with 10 of the 20 Soviet economic regions appearing to be in worse shape with respect to water pollution (and/or water shortages; cf. *Okhrana* 1989, 8). Overall, more than 30 million metric tons of pollutants were discharged into Soviet water bodies and reservoirs in 1988. These pollutants included 15 million tons of chlorides, 11 million tons of sulfates, 2.09 million tons of suspended matter, 1.75 million tons of organic matter, 57,500 tons of petroleum products, 23,500 tons of detergents, and 82 tons of pesticide (*Doklad* 1989, 66). Unfortunately, these data on pollutant mass do not appear to have been published by region.

Selected, limited geographic data on volumetric discharges into water bodies are presented in Figures 15-7 and 15-8. For example, of the reported 162.9 cubic kilometers of sewage, collected drainage, and other waste waters discharged in the Soviet Union in 1988, 152.4 cubic kilometers were discharged into surface waterways. At the all-union level, the waste discharged into surface waterways by economic sector (in cubic kilometers) were industry (including thermal power), 79.4; agriculture, 52.7; communal economy, 19.6; and other sectors, 0.7 cubic (All-Union Institute 1990, 15; *Okhrana* 1989, 77–79). For Ukraine alone the 1988 figure for total waste-water disposal was 19.6 cubic kilometers and for discharges into surface waterbodies, 18.7 cubic kilometers. These waste volumes amount to 12.0 percent and 12.3 percent, respectively of the national totals just noted. This means Ukraine's figures are high in relation to the republic's share of area (2.7 percent) but low in relation to its share of total Soviet population (18 percent). Clearly, Ukraine lags far behind the national average in the fraction of its effluents that receive treatment prior to discharge, 40 percent compared to the national average of 70 percent. On the other hand, only 18.6 percent of Ukraine's slightly more than 2.6 cubic kilometers of *polluted* effluent was discharged untreated, compared to the national average of 28.1 percent (see the last three columns in Figure 15-7).

The data in Figure 15-8, while sketchy and puzzling, are nonetheless rather disturbing. First, although the total volume of sewage water discharged in the USSR more than doubled, between 1985 and 1988 the absolute volume of untreated sewage declined by more than 16.5 percent and the percent of the flows being discharged without treatment improved markedly, declining from 46.2 percent to 17.3 percent. This strong union improvement is not apparent in the published point-source data for the listed Ukrainian cities. Especially troubling is the lack of treatment or low levels of treatment at urban coastal locations and cities along the Dnieper River. No additional information was found pertaining to the wide fluctuations at Kamians'k and Dnipropetrovs'k.

According to Goskompriroda, the most polluted waterways in the entire Soviet Union include several in Ukraine. Small rivers in Donets'k Oblast, such as the Kalmiius, the Kryvyi Torets', the Lower Krynka, and the Bulavynka, have toxic substance concentrations 5 to 7 times their MPCs (Lisovenko and Trach 1989, 29). Among them are the Western Buh, the Dniester, and the Danube. The non-Ukrainian waterways in this ill-fated group are the rivers and lakes of the Kola Peninsula, the lower reaches of the Amur River, the rivers of Sakhalin Island, and the Don, which flows into the Azov Sea. Pollutant concentrations in all these rivers exceed the MPCs by ten-fold. Since the mid-1980s, pollutant-concentration levels have been increasing for ammonium nitrate, phenols, and oil products in the Dniester; for ammonium nitrogen, oil products, copper, and zinc salts in the Danube; and for nitrates, copper salts, and formaldehyde in the Don River. Copper salts and oil products exceed their respective MPCs by 5 to 7 times in the Kuban basin (*Doklad* 1989, 56). In a highly publicized industrial-environmental accident in 1988, a slug of 4.5 million cubic meters of salty brine poured out of a sludge-storage pond at a Stebnyk industrial facility in L'viv Oblast and resulted in massive fish kills and contamination of the Dniester all the way to the Black Sea (Petrashkevich 1988, 29). Extensive eutrophication has taken place in the water reservoir network in the Black Sea basin, especially in the relatively flat terrain along Dnieper River. Also, reservoir filling has elevated water tables and altered the surrounding environment, often damaging formerly productive agricultural lands (*Doklad* 1989, 68). Small waterways and the groundwater in the vicinities of the ferrous metallurgical installations at Kryvyi Rih, Zaporizhzhia, Dnipropetrovs'k, and Mariiupil' have been severely polluted by phenols, cyanides, and other chemicals as a result of highly inefficient waste water treatment plants (*Doklad* 1989, 71). A short 1988 Ukrainian film, *Zhuba* (The Dying Rivers) documents the absolutely deplorable conditions of the thousands of small Ukrainian rivers that provide the water supply for three-quarters of the villages and half of the cities of Ukraine.

Marine and Coastal Pollution Problems

The magnitude of the water pollution problems of the Sea of Azov and the Black Sea coasts are so severe that Goskompriroda's *Doklad* (1989) spotlighted them in a section on "Regional Ecological Problems" (*Doklad* 1989, 143–47). The shallow and previously biologically rich and commercially productive Sea of Azov has experienced serious problems from industrial and municipal waste water contamination and increased levels of salinity since the early 1970s. The Sea of Azov's shallowness (average depth: 8 meters), combined with the high-organic-waste loads being dumped into it from its coastal cities and polluted tributaries creates chronic eutrophication problems, especially in the Gulf of Taganrog. Long-term fresh-water flows into the Sea of Azov amounted to about 42 cubic kilometers annually, including 13 from the Kuban, 28 from the Don and about 2 from the numerous small rivers. These fresh water inflows were sufficient to keep the salinity in the Gulf of Taganrog between 6 and 7 grams per liter (salinity of open oceans is 35 grams per liter). Eighty percent of the sea had a salinity of less than 10 grams per liter and the highest salinity (12 grams per liter) was in the Kerch' area.[2]

Significant reductions in the fresh-water inflows began in 1948 with the filling of the first of several reservoirs on the Kuban' and Don rivers. The largest of these include the Tsimliansk hydrologic works on the Don and the Nevinnomyssk, Federov, Krasnodar, and the nearly finished Tikhov hydrologic works on the Kuban'. An additional Don hydrotechnical works, the Temizhbesk, is under design. When the Tsimliansk works were completed in 1952, it cut off all the spawning grounds of the white sturgeon, 75 percent of the sturgeon spawning grounds, and 50 percent of the starred sturgeon and herring spawning grounds. Continuing gross water withdrawals for irrigation use of fresh, but not necessarily pure, water from the two major rivers flowing into the Azov Sea, the Don and Kuban', amount to nearly 71 percent of their combined multi-year runoff (*Okhrana* 1989, 66–67). These high levels are a primary cause of the Sea of Azov's ecological deterioration. They have resulted in an increase in the Sea of Azov's salinity by more than 40 percent since the 1950s. Current annual

---

[2] For more complete discussions of the Sea of Azov problems, see Mote and Zum-Brunnen (1977, 744–59); and Marti and Parkovich (1976, 21–34).

inflows total approximately 31 cubic kilometers, which is an improvement over the fresh water discharges in the late 1970s when the Sea of Azov appeared to have a steadily increasing salinity level with a dynamic salinity level destined to approximate that of the Black Sea (17.6 grams per liter; cf. *Doklad* 1989, 143–44; and Mote and Zum-Brunnen 1977, 744–59.). This elevated salinity combined with the sea's pollution has resulted in dramatic, negative impacts on the Sea of Azov's food chain. For example, zooplankton biomass (160-250 milligrams per cubic meter) has dropped below the level necessary for anchovy feeding (400 grams per cubic meter), fish catches have dropped by 60 to 90 percent, non-commercial Black-Sea jellyfish invade during the low water periods, and hydrogen sulfide zones develop in the summer, producing massive fish kills (*Doklad* 1989, 143–44; Savin 1989, 29).

Goskompriroda appears to be quite forthright in publishing quantitative pollution data. Keeping in mind that the current inflow amounts to 31 cubic kilometers, Goskompriroda's 1988 data show that industrial facilities along the coastline emptied more than 1.24 cubic kilometers of waste water into the Sea of Azov, of which 0.158 million cubic meters were untreated and more than 82 million cubic meters were inadequately treated. Furthermore, the Don River discharged 9.368 cubic kilometers of waste water, of which 1.451 cubic kilometers was polluted, and the Kuban' discharged 4.093 cubic kilometers of waste water, of which 1.212 cubic kilometers was polluted, into the Sea of Azov. Kerch Bay is polluted by waste water containing iron, arsenic, and manganese compounds from the Kerch' iron-ore enrichment complex. Nitrogen and phosphorus compounds are released from meat- and fish-processing enterprises. Petroleum products enter the bay from the discharge of bilge water and a ship-repair facility. Petroleum products (one to three fold MPC) contaminate the shipping lanes in the Kerch Strait, Taganrog Gulf, oil drilling areas in the shelf zone, the northwestern part of the sea, and the three commercial fishing regions of Iasensk, Arabat, and Temriuk Bays. Monitoring data from the Azov Scientific Research Institute for Fisheries indicate that the concentration of pesticides in the sea increased five-fold between 1983 and 1987, and 1988 data reveal even more alarming pesticide levels. For instance, the weighted average concentrations of stable chlorinated organic pesticides multiplied 17-fold in the sea as a whole and 27-fold in the Gulf of Taganrog in 1988 (Lukyanenko 1989, 29–

30). According to the Soviet water pollution index (WPI). the open waters of the Sea of Azov are classified as being moderately polluted. Other WPI classifications of Azov coastal environs include: *contaminated*, Berdiansk Bay; *polluted*, outer harbor of the port of Mariiupil', Kerch Inlet, the northern part of Kerch Bay; *moderately polluted*, the Gulf of Taganrog, the Don River delta, and Kamysh-Burunsk Bay; *clean*, Kuban' beach, the Temriuk Peninsula, the branch of Protok, and the liman straits (*Doklad* 1989, 145).

Despite repeated warnings and special government anti-pollution resolutions, the conditions of the Azov Sea continue to deteriorate. In the summer of 1988, *Izvestiia* cited pesticide and fertilizer residues as being as alarming as untreated or poorly treated urban and industrial wastes. Swimming beaches were closed along the entire Azov Sea shoreline in Donets'k Oblast (Lisovenko 1988, 29).

The Black Sea receives about 266 cubic kilometers of fresh water inflows annual, primarily from the Danube (132 cubic kilometers), the Dnieper (54 cubic kilometers), and the Dniester (10 cubic kilometers). The most serious and widespread pollution problem of the Black Sea stems from hydrogen sulfide. Ninety percent of the Black Sea is now affected by this rising area of toxic hydrogen sulfide. Ferrous metallurgy and chemical plants, along with municipal wastes, represent the primary pollution sources for the Black Sea. Between 1935 and 1985 this toxic zone has accelerated its rise towards the surface from a rate of 3 centimeters per year to 2 meters per year. Now the average depth of this toxic zone is only 80 meters. In 1988, industrial and commercial enterprises of the major cities and resorts dumped 848.1 million cubic meters of waste water into the Black Sea. Of this amount, the estuarine region of the Danube received 262.3 million cubic meters (92 percent of which was untreated). The Dnieper-Buh estuarine region received 202.5 million cubic meters (4 percent untreated). The northwestern region of the sea received 166.1 million cubic meters (11 percent untreated). The southern Crimean coastal sites discharged 34.5 million cubic meters. In addition, 0.8 million cubic meters were emptied into Sevastopil' Bay in Crimea. Elsewhere along the Black Sea coastline, 156.3 million cubic meters (3 percent untreated) of waste water entered the sea from Krasnodar Krai and 25.6 million cubic meters (18 percent untreated) from along the Georgian shoreline. This waste water is reported to have contained the following pollutants: 7,600 tons of copper, 2,800 tons of total nitrogen, 1,500 tons of ammonia nitrogen, 900 tons of petroleum products, 900 tons of iron, 700 tons of total phosphorus, and 200 tons of surfactants (*Doklad* 1989, 145–46).

In comparison to the volume of the Black Sea, of course, these quantities seem minor. However, overall the coastal pollution levels in the Black Sea substantially exceed the ambient levels, and in comparison to their MPCs, many of the pollutants create severe coastal pollution problems. For instance, surfactant concentrations (10 to 32 times their MPC) and phenol concentrations (30 to 52 times their MPC) have repeatedly been measured in the waste water discharge regions for the Odessa and Ochakiv municipal storm drains. Accidents are common at sewage treatment and pumping stations (*Doklad* 1989, 146). Odessa beaches have been closed periodically because of violations of health standards for both hydro-chemical and bacteriological factors. Odessa, Astrakhan, and Kerch' have all had cholera outbreaks in recent years (Yegorov 1987, 28). Throughout the monitored regions of the sea, average surfactant concentrations doubled between 1987 and 1988 and reached 2 MPC level in the resort city of Yalta. Oil slick contaminant has commonly been observed along the coastlines of the Crimean Peninsula and the Caucasian coastline from Anapa to Batumi. For example, the reported total oil slick areas on the sea surface for individual months in 1988 were as follows (in square kilometers): January, 2,653; April, 4,794; June, 367; August, 156; and December, 361. Water quality in many coastal ports, including Sevastopil' Bay, and in the Dnieper-Buh estuary is particularly poor. The worst water quality is claimed to be in the northwestern portion of the sea, where concentrations of petroleum products, phenols, and synthetic surfactants all exceed their MPCs (*Doklad* 1989, 146).

The Black Sea constitutes a major international resource and body of water. In recognition of this and the "common property" nature of the sea, the Soviet Union is cooperating to develop a draft convention with the bordering states of Bulgaria, Romania, and Turkey (*Doklad*, 1989, 147).

Land Resource Conditions

Soil Erosion, Soil Contamination, and Disrupted Lands

As noted, Ukraine accounts for 2.7 percent of the territory of the Soviet Union. It accounts for 4.6 percent, or 48.6 million hectares of the Soviet Union's land, 41.8 million hectares of which are currently being used for grazing, hayfields, and field crops. Because much of Ukraine consists of rolling lands covered with easily erodible loess, it is not surprising that parts of Ukraine along with regions of Moldova and Kazakhstan have major soil erosion problems (*Okhrana* 1989, 92–93). Wind deflation is a more significant problem in the more arid southern and southeastern portions of Ukraine, while water erosion problems dominate the western half of the republic. Some portions of the northwest and northeast Ukraine are significantly affected by both wind deflation and water erosion (see, e.g., Figure 24 in *Doklad* 1989, 85.).

Soil contamination in Ukraine results from two logical sources: (1) excessive fertilizer and pesticide application and (2) water- and wind-transported pollutants from industry, especially ground contamination at industrial sites. Ferrous and nonferrous centers are especially problematic in this regard. For example, high soil-pollutant concentrations have been identified at distances of up to 20 kilometers from Horlivka and Kostiantynivka in Donets'k Oblast. Maximum lead (Pb) concentrations in Kostiantynivka have been measured that are 50 times the MPC. Manganese concentrations in the soils around Alchevs'k average six times the MPC, with a range up to 18 MPC. Other Ukrainian cities whose soils have manganese concentrations exceeding the MPC standard include Kamians'k, Dnipropetrovs'k, Donets'k, Ienakiieve, Kryvyi Rih, and Mariiupil' (*Doklad* 1989, 88–89).

Because of the mining of several minerals, ores, and coal, Ukraine has relatively large amounts of disturbed lands. These disturbances are of three major types: (1) removal and destruction of topsoils associated with open-pit mining, (2) the covering of land with discarded mine tailings and slag heaps from underground mining activities, and (3) disturbances by pipeline construction. Figure 15-9 presents a regional summary of the inventory of disturbed lands and the reclamation backlog. In terms of the land area reclaimed in 1988 (columns 2 and 3) Ukraine trailed only the much larger Russian Federation. Column 6 reveals that Ukraine has the second-shortest backlog time, 2.4 years, of any Soviet republic for the "*otrabotannye*" portion of the backlog. Given the intensive mining activities and the density of energy pipelines in Ukraine, it is not surprising that Latvia, Estonia, and Belarus are the only regions having larger relative fractions of their areas disturbed. On a positive note, the last column in Figure

15-9 reveals that despite Ukraine's relatively large areas of disturbed lands, the fact that it took the third-shortest time to eliminate its backlog of disturbed lands indicates that Ukraine is actually one of the Soviet Union's most active regions in terms of (disturbed) land reclamation.

Nature Preservation and Protection

Given the natural agro-climatic conditions of the greater Ukraine and its natural vegetation patterns, Ukraine is not suffering severe negative impact from anthropocentric forest damage, except in the Donets'k-Dnieper region (see Figure 15-1) where, presumably, air pollution and acid rain are the causes. Nonetheless, Ukraine does have some other types of forestry problems. Examples include the oak moth in the Crimea and the widespread juniper moth in central Ukraine (*Doklad* 1989, 111).

Figure 15-10 lists all of Ukraine's nature preserves, protected hunting areas, and national nature parks (*zapovidnyks*). Overall, in 1988 the Soviet Union had 164 such preserves encompassing 21.597 million hectares and 19 national nature parks covering 1.779 million hectares (the total USSR territory was 2,240,220,000 hectares). In 1988, the Soviet Union had 183 of the three types of preserves listed in Figure 15-10 and Ukraine had 18, totaling 366,000 hectares, or 1.56 percent of the preserved land of the USSR. Huge preserves in Siberia make the Russian Federation preserves dominant in total area, 19.385 million out of 23.376 million hectares, or 82.9 percent. On the other hand, Ukraine's expenditures on the preserves, 5.8 million rubles, which seems an incredibly small amount, equals 13 percent of the entire Soviet operating budget for preserves.

Chernobyl: The Human and Environmental Consequences

Chernobyl has become the most notorious and tragic symbol of this environmental degradation. The long-term environmental repercussions and costs associated with the Chernobyl accident constitute a true catastrophe on a global scale. From a human health and safety perspective, land, water, food chains, and their products may well remain seriously contaminated and uninhabitable, undrinkable, and inedible possibly for decades to come over extensive areas—not just Ukraine. According to V. Komarov, the deputy chief engineer of the Ministry of Atomic Energy's Kombinat Production Association,

"Today, no matter how morally difficult it is to admit it, the radiation situation in Chernobyl is such that full-fledged human life cannot be resumed there for decades" (Levada 1988, 28–29). The Goskompriroda *Doklad* (1989) devotes slightly more than seven pages of the report to consideration of the radiation conditions in the country. Nearly all of the discussion focuses on the Chernobyl accident, and three radiation isopleth maps are included (*Doklad* 1989, 41– 48). The most important and relevant information in the Goskompriroda report is reproduced here. However, not everybody by any stretch of imagination agrees with the relatively optimistic assessments of *Doklad* (1989). Other reports leave the distinct impression that the situation is considerably more serious than the Goskompriroda report suggests. The most stark news has been a continuing series of news releases charging an official cover-up of the Chernobyl nuclear accident and clean-up.[3]

According to Goskompriroda, at least 2,200 weather stations take daily radiation readings and 80 stations record atmospheric aerosol concentrations. Several dozen stations collect precipitation and inland and ocean water samples in order to regularly measure tritium, strontium-90, and cesium-137 concentrations. According to the *Doklad* (1989) radiation levels in the regions of Ukraine, the Russian Federation, and Belarus that were originally contaminated by the April 1986 Chernobyl accident, stabilized in 1988 and have since shown downward trends. Except for the relatively highly contaminated regions in Homel', Mahilaŭ Kiev, Zhytomyr, and Briansk oblasts, which still have elevated radiation levels, all other areas of the

---

[3] For example, see the following series of multi-item translations in the *CDSP*, which over time become less and less optimistic in their assessment of the entire Chernobyl episode and the candor and speed with which officials have responded to the events: "Chernobyl: A One-Year Progress Report" (1987); "Why Do Nuclear Safety Problems Persist?" (1988); Tsikora (1988); "Chernobyl Hasn't Solved All its Problems" (1988); "Pre-Chernobyl Safety Erosion Detailed" (1988); "How Likely Is Another Chernobyl?" (1988); "Chernobyl Radiation Raises New Concerns" (1989); Kolinko (1989); Baklanov (1989b); Baklanov and Illesh (1989); Diomidova (1989); "Confessions of a Chernobyl Veteran" (1989); Simurov and Ultyonok (1989); "Who'll Pay the Bill" (1989); "In the Politburo of the CPSU Central Committee" (1989); "Politburo Reviews Chernobyl Cleanup" (1989); Tsikora (1990c); "Chernobyl: Has Impact Been Downplayed?" (1990); "Chernobyl: A New Cleanup Program Is Set" (1990); "News Hotline: What Will the Defense Ministry Answer?" (1990).

USSR are reputed to have radiation levels essentially equal to the ambient levels (*Doklad* 1989, 41–42).

Nonetheless, radioactive contamination over substantial areas still remains a severe technical, ecological, political and social problem in the five regions just mentioned. To briefly review the events of April 1986, the radioactive cloud of particles released by the explosions and fire at Chernobyl spread in a westerly direction, producing narrow bands of contamination across the terrain. By April 26 and 27 the radioactive material moved as a plume in a northwesterly direction, which shifted to an east by northeast trajectory by April 28 and 29. Finally, by April 29 and 30 the plume's trajectory again shifted, this time to south by southeast. Although the majority of the radioactive particles were precipitated during the first four to five days after the event, "hot" spots continued to develop throughout the month of May (*Doklad* 1989, 42). The total estimated quantity of radioactive emissions from Chernobyl is still the subject of controversy. The State Committee on Hydrometeorology and the Environment's official estimate of the total Chernobyl emissions of 50 million curies has been challenged by an estimate of 1 billion curies made by specialists of the All-Union Atomic Power Station Research Institute, and other estimates range up to 6.4 billion curies (*Moskovskie novosti* 1989, 8–9).

Extensive areas have been affected by the Chernobyl accident. In the first few days after the event, approximately 200,000 square kilometers had radiation readings higher than 0.2 mr/hr (milliroentgens/hour). For comparison, natural background radiation levels in Kiev, for example, are reported to be 0.014 mr/hr (Kolinko 1989, 22). The data in Figure 15-11, adapted from tables provided by Iuri A. Izrael, Chairman of the USSR State Committee on Hydrometeorology and originally published in *Pravda* on April 17, 1990, are disturbing given the extensive areas with high levels of contamination from which people were *not evacuated*.

About 10,190 square kilometers have been contaminated with a cesium-137 level about 15 Ci/km^2 or higher. Excluding the resettlement zone, about 640 populated centers and more than 230,000 people were located in this cesium-137 contaminated zone. Figure 15-11 clearly reveals that the Belarus was the region that was hurt the most by radiation fallout from Chernobyl. A map compiled by the USSR Supreme Soviet Commission on Ecology and the Rational Use of Resources plotting areas of intensive radiation contamination (defined as 40 curies/km^2 or more) indicates that the bulk of the contamination extended northward from Chernobyl into the Belarus (*New York Times* 1990a, 4). The last three columns of Figure 15-11 show that more than half of these high-contamination zones lie outside of the evacuation zone. About 4 million people are said to be living in areas contaminated by fallout (levels not specified). More than 2 million of them are in Belarus, or 20 percent of its population (Marples 1990a, 27; *New York Times* 1990c, 4). Some 12 million hectares, or approximately 15 percent of the combined territory of Ukraine and Belarus, are being specifically monitored for high radiation levels (Marples 1990b, 9–14). Iodine-131 deposition and air pollution was registered in the following regions of the European USSR during May 1986: in Belarus at Berestia, Hrodno, Minsk, and Mahilaŭ; in the Baltic region at Vil'nius, Kaliningrad, Klaipeda, and Riga; and in Ukraine at Kiev, Kryvyi Rih, Zaporizhzhia, Donets'k, L'viv, Poltava, Rivne, Vinnytsia, and Ivano-Frankivs'k. Goskompriroda's report claims these iodine-131 levels were short-lived and posed no health danger (*Doklad* 1989, 46-47). Aerial reconnaissance of radiation levels in the European USSR identified several other contamination zones in addition to the primary zone of high radiation surrounding Chernobyl. These zones are as follows: west of the primary zone in the vicinity of Pinsk and Rivne; south of the primary zone near Bila Tserkva and Kaniv; southwest of the primary zone around Ivano- Frankivs'k; northeast of the primary zone at the junction of Mahilaŭ, Homel', and Briansk oblasts; south of Orel'; around Plavsk, south of Tula; zones along the southern coast of the Gulf of Finland; far to the north in the Kola Peninsula; and in the Caucausus (*Doklad* 1989, 46–47.).

One of the major concerns has been radioactive contamination of water resources, especially in the string of Dnieper reservoirs. The Prypiat' river basin clearly had high radioactive contamination levels. Goskompriroda claims that β-activity in the Kiev reservoir's water during the first two months after the accident ranged between 1 to 6 x 10^{-9} Ci/l, within the standard (10^{-8} Ci/l). Downstream in the Kremenchuk reservoir, the stronium-90 concentration level in May 1986 was about 5 x 10^{-12} Ci/l, only about a hundredth of the MPC. Testing of bottom sample sediments from the various Dnieper reservoirs in mid-May 1986, not surprisingly, revealed a steep, steady decline in radiation levels downstream, diminishing by a factor of tens and hundredths for specimens from the southern Kiev reservoir and Kaniv reservoir compared to the bottom deposits in the Kiev reservoir near the mouth of the Prypiat' River. Again, according to the Goskompriroda report, the measured radionuclides in Ukrainian waterways have been below the expected and modelled levels (*Doklad*, 1989, 47–48). In a more recent account, however, A. Volkov, head of the Institute of Land Reclamation's Laboratory for Problems of the Polesie Lowland is quoted as claiming:

> The Pripyat has been virtually ruined, and along with it the entire Pripyat Basin, 122,000 square kilometers in all—it can be used only as an ecological reserve. Today, the waters of the Pripiat and the Sozh and of their tributaries, the Nevsich, Iput, Besyad, Braginka, Kolpita, and Pokot, are carrying radioactive silt into the Dnepr (*sic*). The Kiev Reservoir is gradually turning into a 'time bomb.' The water is clean, but all the silt 'glows,' and there is already 60 million tons of it. The entire cascade of power stations on the Dnepr (*sic*), right down to the Black Sea, is seriously threatened. And 40 million people live in this region!
>
> Two other problems give me no rest. ...All the timber in the affected districts is radioactive. It cannot be used for furniture, for construction, or even for firewood. And the peat 'glows,' too. Where are people going to get fuel?
>
> The so-called 'burial grounds' simply horrify me. I have not seen a single one built according to all the rules—with concrete walls, with a concrete roof. As a rule, they are large pits the walls and bottoms of which are covered with polyethylene film. After two or three years, groundwater will wash unimpeded over the radioactive waste and flow into the rivers and lakes.
>
> Several times I have been in the 'dead zone,' which has been turned into a dump where everything is heaped— equipment, clothing, furniture. The homes that have been abandoned there without supervision 'glow' like candles. The fires that break out there in overly dry peat bogs aggravate the tragedy. Smoke carries the radiation great distances (Matukovsky 1990, 1–4).

The continuing impact on residents in the vicinity of Chernobyl and on those involved in the clean up has been tremendous. In the first few days after the accident, more than 500 people were hospitalized in Moscow and Kiev with suspected radiation sickness. In addition to the three people killed in the initial explosion, 28 of the acute radiation-sickness cases soon became fatalities (Odinets and Pokrovsky 1988,

23). Supposedly, extensive measurements were made immediately and served as the basis for evacuation decisions, which have been widely criticized as being too little, too late (cf. Izrael 1990a, 8–9; Dolganov 1990, 10; Izrael 1990b, 10). People residing in areas enclosed by isolines above 5 mr/hr were evacuated. Children and pregnant women were temporarily resettled if the radiation measurements exceeded the 3 to 5 mr/hr figure that was used to delineate the on-going monitoring zone. In the first year, 186 population centers with 116,000 inhabitants were evacuated from the resettlement zone. Of these evacuees, 90,000 were from 75 Ukrainian population nodes, 25,000 were from 107 Belarussian centers, and 1,000 were from four populated areas of the Russian Federation. Fourteen Belarussian and two Ukrainian villages were undergoing "re-evacuation" when the *Doklad* (1989) was being drafted, and approximately 10 additional settlements in the southern region of the 30-km radius resettlement zone supposedly were safe for return settlement (*Doklad* 1989, 46). In October 1989, *Pravda* printed a story claiming that the Belarus alone needed to relocate 100,000 people at a price of 17 billion rubles, or 7 billion rubles more than the entire republic's annual budget. This staggering task and its cost have prompted republic officials to make international appeals for assistance (*Pravda* 1989, 3; *New York Times* 1990a, 4)

Official figures reveal the lost power, clean up, and relocation costs had amounted to more than 8 billion rubles by early 1988, of which 900 million was paid out in various forms of compensation and benefits, and 4 billion in direct costs of the accident. Approximately 540 million were collected from citizen contributions ("In the Politburo of the CPSU Central Committee" 1988b, 19–20.). Other reports indicate that the direct losses alone tallied 4 billion (Baklanov and Illesh 1989, 27). In early May 1990, The Soviet Parliament voted to allocate 26 billion rubles to aid the victims of Chernobyl through evacuations, better benefits to the soldiers and workers involved in the cleanup, and more thorough medical checkups. A Ukrainian Deputy, Iurii Shcherbak, reckons when the value of lost farmland, agricultural production, and water supplies are included, the total direct and indirect costs of the cleanup will be a staggering 415 billion rubles (Bogert 1990, 31). As of mid-1988, 696,000 people who have either lived, worked, or are living in this "special zone" or are currently living in contaminated territory had undergone medical examination (Salyamon 1990, 31–32; Zaikin 1989, 20; Odinets and Pokrovsky

1988, 23). The chairman of the Belarus Children's Fund reported that in September 1987, the Soviet Council of Ministers transferred from Chernobyl Charity Account No. 904 more than 65.8 million rubles in individual donations to the Ministry of Atomic Energy to compensate it for the Chernobyl accident rather than dispensing the money to the human victims of the accident. In October 1989, the USSR Fund for Social Inventions made a 100,000 ruble donation to set up a new public organization, the Chernobyl Alliance, to monitor the safety at existing atomic power plants through a commission of independent experts.[4]

Several press reports claim that significant numbers of deaths from radiation sickness and elevated levels of spontaneous abortions, stillborns, and birth defects have occurred in the affected areas. Some Soviet observers claim the direct radiation fatalities from Chernobyl now total around 300 (*New York Times* 1990b, A6). The 1988 Soviet documentary film *Mikrofon* (Microphone) contains graphic footage documenting the effects of radiation on children, especially major birth defects. Physicians addressing a conference at the Soviet Embassy in Washington, D.C., in April 1990 admitted that 150,000 people were suffering from thyroid ailments linked to their exposure to radioactive iodine, a claim that clearly undercuts the *Doklad* (1989) assertion that the radioactive iodine releases were too low to cause any health problems (*New York Times* 1990d, A1). The number of deaths from childhood leukemia at one Minsk hospital has increased from one or two deaths per year to one to two per week. Childhood leukemia rates from parts of Ukraine also are reported as two to four times the norm *(New York Times* 1990d, A1). Given the incubation time for radiation-linked diseases, especially carcinomas, it may be well into the next century before the final toll of Chernobyl can be known.

Nuclear power itself may well be a casualty of the Chernobyl accident. In addition to all the newly published concerns about impending energy shortages (cf. Marchuk 1989, 31–32; Khodzhayev 1990, 32–33), there are even stronger concerns about nuclear safety.[5]

---

[4] Personal interview with members of the Fund for Social Invention, Leningrad, December 1989.

[5] For example, see the two previously cited series of translated articles in CDSP: "Pre-Chernobyl Safety Erosion Detailed" (1988, 13–16); and "Why Do Nuclear Safety Problems Persist?" (1988, 9–11).

So far, a number of planned or partially completed nuclear stations have been halted indefinitely, including the proposed Crimean station, and a facility at Odessa. In addition, in March 1990, the Ukrainian Republic Supreme Soviet passed a resolution calling for shutting down the Chernobyl stations in stages by 1995, and for halting the further expansion of the Khmel'nyts'kyi, Rivne and other nuclear power plants located in Ukraine ("Ecology Is a Nationwide Concern" 1990, 31; Marples 1990c, 27; Sagers 1990, 306–313).

Expenditures for Environmental Protection

From 1985 to 1988, total Soviet expenditures for environmental protection increased from 9.13 billion rubles to 11.11 billion rubles. In 1988, the total Soviet expenditure was allocated in five major categories. Slightly more than half, or 5.84 billion rubles, was used for current maintenance and operating expenses for environmental protection facilities and equipment at industrial, agricultural, transport, and other enterprises and organizations. Water-protection uses received more than 70 percent of the funds, or 4.13 billion rubles, atmospheric protection 1.16 billion rubles, protection of land from industrial pollution 370 million rubles; and land reclamation 170 million rubles. Capital repair expenditures amounted to 840 million rubles, with 480 million going to waste-water treatment equipment and installations and about 350 million to pollution-abatement structures and equipment at stationary sources of air pollution. Expenditures for operating *zapovidnyks* (nature preserves) and parks, and for wildlife protection amounted to 190 million rubles and those for forestry 1.12 billion rubles. State capital investment in environmental protection and rational use of natural resources were estimated at 3.122 billion rubles (*Okhrana* 1989, 9). Unfortunately, no geographically disaggregated data about these expenses have been published except the republic-level data listed in Figure 15-12.

As indicated in Figure 15-12, out of the total 1988 Soviet capital investment of 3.122 billion rubles in environmental protection and "rational" resource use, water resource use and protection, atmospheric protection, and land use and protection measures accounted for nearly 90 percent, or 2.801 billion rubles. The last two columns in Figure 15-12—each republic's percentage of total population in the 1989 Soviet census and percentage of the total Soviet area—have been included for comparative purposes. Clearly, the Russian Federation received the lion's share of all such capital investments, 59.6 percent, which is a relatively high share with respect to its population but a low share with respect to its share of total Soviet land area. Ukraine received 16.2 percent of these capital investment funds, which is slightly low in respect to its population (18.0 percent), but relatively high compared to its fraction of Soviet territory (2.7 percent). In fact, only Moldova and Armenia received higher amounts relative to their areas. On the other hand, in comparison to their relative population sizes, the Russian Federation, Kazakhstan, and the three Baltic republics fared better than Ukraine in these capital investments.

Limited republic-level data also are available to study these investments in terms of physical capacity enhancements and not just ruble-investment figures. For example, in 1988 Ukraine commissioned 1.092 million cubic meters per day of new waste-water treatment capacity or 21 percent of the Soviet total. Ukraine was only able to expand its recirculating water supply systems by 923,000 cubic meters per day, which represented only 6 percent of the new Soviet capacity in 1988, while the Russian Federation's new capacity amounted to 88.1 percent of the total. On the other hand, as Figure 15-6 showed, the low-water endowment of Ukraine had already forced the Soviet central planners to invest so heavily in these recirculating systems that only Belarus and Armenia had larger water reuse capacities as a share of their respective republic's industrial water use. Finally, Ukrainian smokestacks were able to cleanse an additional 4.2 million cubic meters per hour of exhaust gases as a result of newly commissioned air pollution abatement equipment in 1988. This new capacity amounted to 16.3 percent of total Soviet new capacity in 1988. While certainly not keeping up with the need for such air pollution protection facilities in Ukraine, the republic clearly made more progress relative to most other Soviet republics, especially Lithuania, Latvia, Armenia, Georgia, and Turkmenistan, all of which added no new air purification capacity in 1988 (*Okhrana* 1989, 152).

Summary and Conclusions

From this overview of the environmental conditions, problems, and challenges in Ukraine, it seems safe to draw some specific conclusions. Unfortunately, these conclusions do not augur well for Ukraine's environment. First, the evidence unquestionably and unfortunately indicates that environmental deterioration is occurring at a truly alarming rate and on a widespread scale in Ukraine. All the evidence points to the conclusion that the Donets'ke-Dnieper economic region of Eastern Ukraine is the most ecologically disrupted region of the entire Soviet Union, especially when considering the deleterious human impact. The Urals probably would rank second.

The reasons for this are both simple and complex. First, the drive for rapid industrial and agricultural development as called for and articulated by the Soviet/Stalinist economic system led to increasing demands for energy, water and raw material extraction, production, consumption, and waste disposal. Second, political decisions to invest disproportionately in dirty heavy industries at the expense of environmentally less-damaging light industries and consumer sectors exacerbated the effects of the ecologically harmful energy and raw material extraction and production processes. Third, the manifold environmental crises in Ukraine—as elsewhere in the Soviet Union—are a corollary of the Soviet emphasis on the expansion of productive industrial activities as opposed to investments in such non-productive activities as training ecological and environmental pollution-prevention specialists, environmental research, and the development of efficient technical pollution-prevention and abatement equipment. Fourth, the maxim of production maximization under the Soviet model of extensive growth policies obviously produces deleterious ecological consequences as severe, and in all likelihood more severe than capitalism's profit maximization one. Fifth, all post-Stalin Soviet leaders implicitly recognized this situation, but their efforts to respond by transferring to intensive growth and modernization campaigns have been doomed from the start by the Soviets' irrational administrative pricing structures and property rights institutions. These structures and institutions have produced both chronically and acutely inefficient resource uses throughout Ukraine's economy.

Unfortunately, from an environmental perspective the social-economic transformations currently underway in Ukraine and the Soviet Union pose as many questions as they solve. For example, the pervasive and serious nature of environmental problems in Western countries makes it foolhardy to think that the efforts by Ukrainian reformers to change to a market-based economy will result in anything more than a rather anemic improvement of Ukraine's ecological and resource-use problems. The global nature of environmental problems provides a persuasive argument that certain human economic activities and values,—not different institutional structures and arrangements—are the cause of environmental degradation. Nonetheless, the importance of institutions and an educated, ecologically sensitive populous should not be understated. In this potentially positive regard, the new Goskompriroda (State Committee on the Environment) currently is actively trying to elaborate environmental impact statements (EIS) methods and regulations, but has as yet unclear authority and is severely underfunded given its monumental task of protecting the natural environment. The committee also is trying to grapple with the task of training more environmental specialists.[6]

The most acute and chronic environmental-deterioration problems in Ukraine are those associated either directly or indirectly with the management of air and water resources. This is true even of the Chernobyl disaster. Yet, in fact, these two fluid resources universally take on the difficult management attributes of common property resources and all their associated "free rider" and "market failure" problems. In 1975, at a joint Soviet-American symposium on the use of mathematical models to optimize water quality management, I argued for the introduction of economically efficient auto-regulatory methods of pollution control, such as effluent changes and taxes, and ironically, was opposed by U.S. Environmental Protection Agency (EPA) regulatory officials (ZumBrunnen 1979, 186–216).

Currently, Ukraine has sound environmental regulations and legislation on paper. Unfortunately, 20 years of National Environmental Policy Act (NEPA) laws and regulations in the United States have clearly demonstrated that environmental laws and regulations alone simply do not work. The new risk is that as Ukraine seeks more autonomy and decentralization, its relatively new and weak legal-regulatory strategies for environmental protection also will be discarded or compromised before market-oriented, self-regulatory pollution control

---

[6] Personal interviews with Goskompriroda officials in Moscow, November and December, 1989.

structures can be introduced. Sadly, but surely, if Ukrainian leaders look westward for help in solving their many environmental deterioration problems, they will get little guidance in finding efficient, market-based, self-regulating pollution control strategies. Nonetheless, Soviet plans also call for "shifting the management of environmental protection activities from administrative to predominantly economic methods over the next few years" ("In the Politburo of the CPSU Central Committee" 1988a, 18).

Currently, throughout Ukraine, the Soviet Union, and Eastern Europe two different constellations of reform forces and processes seem to be struggling to fill the vacuum left by the rapid demise of Stalinism. Initially, many of the nascent democratic fronts and groups such as Rukh had strong Green or environmental-protection agendas. These Green groups played significant and catalytic roles in bringing down the Stalinist systems. The goal of these democratic-reform movements has been to transform long-subjugated people and governments into voting citizens and democratically elected civil societies. The other forces of reform, of which Gorbachev represents the prime example, seem to be seeking a technologic and technocratic revolution that will enable their economies to compete in global markets. So far, it seems that the modest Western aid that was made available has been in the form of financial, technical, and managerial assistance that primarily serves these technologic and technocratic goals. The West seems to be less willing and able to assist in the more difficult task of developing stable, pluralistic, competitive political institutions and systems. While it is true that new market competition would force old, inefficient, polluting factories in Ukraine to close, scarce capital-investment funds also could hinder their restructuring into non-polluting enterprises. Furthermore, it seems likely that environmentalists will be hard pressed to compete with the inevitable fears engendered by rising market prices and the specter of widespread unemployment. As the Ukrainian and Soviet economies continue to unravel, so will reliable deliveries of coal, oil and natural gas to Ukrainian factories and apartments. As the large government subsidies for housing, utilities, and food disappear (long used to fulfill the "Communist social contract" of low-cost daily living costs for Ukrainians as well as most Soviet citizens), the promises of democracy and a market economy will be seriously tested.

Twenty years of research dealing with environmental problems, mostly those of the Soviet Union, have persuaded us that clear, firm, and guaranteed private-property rights are an absolutely essential first step for protecting the environment from degradation. Currently, this first step seems more than a little wobbly at best. Although private property rights are still alive, a careful political and economic examination of the various land reform and ownership debates, the laws surrounding the *kooperativ* movement, and so on suggests something very deformed and distorted may be developing (cf., Dolganov and Stepovol 1990b, 24; "The Law on Property in the USSR" 1990, 21–25; "Principles of Land Legislation" 1990, 22–28, 36; and Dolganov and Stepovol 1990a, 7.) Although they are necessary, rational markets and guaranteed property rights unfortunately by themselves are not anywhere near sufficient to address and correct Ukraine's environmental-deterioration problems. In other words, restrictions imposed by the republic's geography, human landscapes and infrastructures, and human values, including most forms of nationalism, all constitute formable constraints on what can be done, where, how well, and how quickly it can be done to heal the deep environmental wounds of the present-day Ukraine.

References

All-Union Institute of Scientific and Technical Information. 1990. *State of the Environment in the USSR, 1988. Abridged Version of the Official Report.* Moscow.

Baklanov, N. 1989a. "Affirmation of Democracy." *Current Digest of the Soviet Press* (hereafter, CDSP) 41 (13): 3.

_____. 1989b. "Chernobyl: Information Versus Rumors." *CDSP* 41 (9): 22–23.

_____ and A. Illesh. 1989. "At the Station, In the Zone, and Nearby. Several Interviews Three Years After the Chernobyl Tragedy." CDSP 41 (18): 27– 28.

Bogert, Carroll, 1990. "Chernobyl's Legacy." *Newsweek* (7 May): 30–31.

Bond, Andrew R., et al. 1990. "Roundtable Discussion of the State of the Soviet Environment at the Start of the Nineties." *Soviet Geography* 31 (6): 401–68.

"Chernobyl: A New Cleanup Program Is Set." 1990. *CDSP* 42 (18): 5–8.

"Chernobyl: A One-Year Progress Report." 1987. *CDSP* 39 (17): 1–4.

"Chernobyl: Has Impact Been Downplayed?" 1990. *CDSP* 42 (13): 1–5.

"Chernobyl Hasn't Solved All its Problems." 1988. *CDSP* 40 (17): 13–14.

"Chernobyl Radiation Raises New Concerns." 1989. *CDSP* 41 (7): 10–14.

"Confessions of a Chernobyl Veteran. Written from a Hospital Bed." 1989. *CDSP* 41 (24): 31–32.

Derimov, M. 1990. "Our Parliamentary Correspondents Report: What's Happening at the Session?" *CDSP* 42 (20): 13.

Diomidova, G. 1989. "So As Not to Die One by One. Or, Why the Estonian Chernobyl Committee Was Created." *CDSP* 41 (22): 22–23.

Dolganov, V. 1990. "Izvestia Report of Izrael Testimony at Hearing on Chernobyl Suggests That Radiation Findings, Evacuation Needs Went Unheeded by Government." *CDSP* 42 (18): 10.

_____ and A. Stepovoi. 1990a. "Property Law Is Adopted: Concern Voiced over Large Number of Absentee Deputies: A Joint Committee on Combatting Crime is Formed." *CDSP* 42 (9): 7.

_____. 1990b. "The Third Session of the USSR Supreme Soviet: Whom Our Land Belongs To." *CDSP* 42 (8): 24.

Drobotov, V. 1988. "Ecological Situation: The Volga's Groans." *CDSP* 39 (50): 15–17.

Drozd, V. 1990. "On Our Way to the Elections: Under Their Own Flag." *CDSP* 41 (51): 24–25.

"Ecology Is a Nationwide Concern." 1990. *CDSP* 42 (7): 31.

Glavnoe upravlenie geodeziia i kartografii pri Sovete Ministrov SSSR. 1984. *Atlas SSSR*. Moscow.

Goskomstat SSSR. 1989. *Okhrana okruzhaiushchei sredy i ratsional' noe ispol' zovanie prirodnykh resursov v SSSR. Statisticheskii sbornik*. Moscow.

Gosudarstvennyi komitet SSSR po okhrane prirody. 1989. *Doklad sostoianie prirodnoi sredy v SSSR v 1988 godu.* Moscow.

"How Likely Is Another Chernobyl?" 1988. *CDSP* 40 (42): 1–6.

"In the Politburo of the CPSU Central Committee." 1988a. *CDSP* 40 (1): 18.

_____. 1988b. *CDSP* 40 (2): 19–20.

_____. 1989. *CDSP* 41 (44): 25.

Izrael, Iu. A. 1990a. "Chernobyl—1990." *CDSP* 42 (18): 8–9.

_____. 1990b. "Izrael Protests That His Meaning Was Distorted in the Izvestia Report, Says Findings Were Not Ignored, Evacuation Was Carried Out Promptly." *CDSP* 42 (18): 10.

Khodzhayev, M. 1990. "In the Mirror of Science: Where Do We Go from Here?" *CDSP* 42 (7): 32–33.

Kolinko, Vladimir. 1989. "Radioactive Echo. Peasants' Farm Plots in the Ukraine After the Chernobyl Accident." *CDSP* 41 (9): 22.

Kryvarchuk, A., director and writer; and Ia. Leizerovysh, cameraman. 1988. *Zhuba (The Dying Rivers).* Documentary film.

"The Law on Property in the USSR." 1990. CDSP 42 (12): 21–25.

Levada, Aleksandr. 1988. "Writer's Notes: Will Chernobyl Survive?" *CDSP* 40 (40): 28–29.

Levicheva, Valentina. 1990. "Nedelya Offers Up-to-Date Catalogue of Regional Popular Fronts, Local Associations, Political Discussion Clubs, Incipient Parties, Myriad Religious, Cultural, and Environmental Groups." *CDSP* 42 (8): 5–8, 28.

Lisovenko, N. [Losovenko, N.] 1988. "When a Sea Chokes." *CDSP* 40 (29): 29. [Translated from *Izvestiia* (23 July 1988): 8.]

_____ and V. Trach. 1989. "Gas Mask for a City. Purifiers Installed, But They Can't Clean the City's Air. What to Do?" *CDSP* 41 (40): 28–29.

Lukyanenko, V. 1987. "Problems and Opinions: Don't Let the Caspian's Resources Shrink." *CDSP* 39 (24): 215–16.

_____. 1989. "Ecology: The Drama of Water." *CDSP* 41(32): 29–30.

Manucharova, Ye. 1990. "Returning to What Was Printed: From a Sea of Lies to a Field of Rye." *CDSP* 42 (12): 33–34.

_____ and V. Kornev. 1990. "Events, Facts, Opinions: In the Name of the Volga. Sentence Pronounced Against the System That Generates 'Projects of the Century' That Are Ruinous for People and Nature." *CDSP* 42 (24): 30– 31.

Marchuk, A. 1989. "Letter for the Day: And What Will We Do without Light?" *CDSP* 41 (34): 31–32.

Marples, David. 1990a. "The Medical Consequences of Chernobyl'." *Radio Liberty Report on the USSR* (9 March):27.

_____. 1990b. "A Retrospective of a Nuclear Accident." *Radio Liberty Report on the USSR* (20 April):9–14.

_____. 1990c. "Ukraine Declares Moratorium on New Nuclear Reactors." *Radio Liberty Report on the USSR* (12 October): 27.

Marti, Iu. Iu. and D. Ia. Parkovich. 1976. "Vodokhoziaistvennye problemy azovskogo i kaspiiskogo morei." *Vodnye resursy* 3:21–34.

Matukovsky, N. 1990. "Catastrophe. What the Lessons of Chernobyl Teach." *CDSP* 42 (13): 1–4.

Moskovskie novosti. 1989. (15 October): 8–9.

Mote, Victor and Craig ZumBrunnen. 1977. "Anthropogenic Environmental Alteration of the Sea of Azov." *Soviet Geography: Review and Translation* 18 (10): 744–59.

New York Times. 1990a. (24 April): 4.

_____. 1990b. (27 April): A6.

_____. 1990c. (28 April): 4.

_____. 1990d. (28 April): A1.

"News Hotline: What Will the Defense Ministry Answer?" 1990. *CDSP* 42 (27): 24.

"O predvaritel'nukh itogakh Vsesoiuznoi perepisi naseleniia." 1989. *Izvestiia* (28 April): 1–3.

Odinets, M., and A. Pokrovsky. 1988. "Rumors. Notes from the Scientific Conference 'Medical Aspects of the Accident at the Chernobyl Atomic Power Station'." *CDSP* 40 (22): 23.

Odinets, M., and I. Tikhomirov. 1989a. "En Route to Renewal. Notes from the Plenary Session of the Ukraine Communist Party Central Committee." *CDSP* 41 (42): 26–27.

_____. 1989b. "Preparing for Elections." *CDSP* 41 (48): 20–21.

Pastukhova, Ye. 1989. "Specialists' Arguments That Went Unheeded." *CDSP* 40 (50): 22.

Petrashkevich, Ales. 1988. "Baikal Movement: Salt in the Wound." *CDSP* 40 (10): 29.

"Politburo Reviews Chernobyl Cleanup." 1989. *CDSP* 41 (45): 18–20.

Pravda. 1989. (26 October): 3.

"Pre-Chernobyl Safety Erosion Detailed." 1988. *CDSP* 40 (20): 13–16.

"Principles of Land Legislation Published." 1990. *CDSP* 42 (13): 22–28, 36.

Radio Liberty Report on the USSR. 1990a. (9 March): 27.

_____. (27 April): 27.

"Responsibility to Nature. Greater Attention Must Be Paid to Ecological Problems." 1987. *CDSP* 39 (2): 18–19.

Sagers, Matthew J. 1990. "News Notes." *Soviet Geography* 31 (4): 278–320.

Salyamon, L. 1990. "A Special Zone in Medicine. More About the Health of Chernobyl Victims." *CDSP* 42 (5): 31–32.

Savin, A. 1989. "Saving Our Home." *CDSP* 41 (18): 29–30.

Simurov, A., and A. Ultyonok. 1989. "Echoes of Chernobyl: The Belorussian Zone." *CDSP* 41 (30): 33–34.

Tsikora, Sergei. 1988. "The Aftermath of Chernobyl. Echo of Earlier Warnings." *CDSP* 40 (6): 22–23.

_____. 1990a. "The Election Campaign Is Under Way: Elections in Latvia and Estonia; Run-Off Elections in the Russian Republic, the Ukraine, and Belorussia: Kiev." *CDSP* 42 (11): 29–30.

_____. 1990b. "The Election Campaign Is Under Way: First Deputies Named," *CDSP* 42 (10): 29–30.

_____. 1990c. "In Republic Governments: Chernobyl—Emergency Measures Again." *CDSP* 42 (1): 30–31.

————. 1990d. "News Hotline: New Masters of the Ukraine's Capital." *CDSP* 42 (20): 13.

————. 1990e. "News Hotline: Official Recognition of Rukh." *CDSP* 42 (6): 27.

"Ukrainian 'Front' Stirs Media Furor." 1989. *CDSP* 41 (37): 1–5.

"Who'll Pay the Bill for Chernobyl?" 1989. *CDSP* 41 (30): 35.

"Why Do Nuclear Safety Problems Persist?" 1988. *CDSP* 39 (49): 9–11.

Yegorov, Aleksandr. 1987. "Yury Shcherbak on What Chernobyl Prohibited." *CDSP* 39 (44): 28.

Zaikin, V. 1989. "Chernobyl Alliance Unites Concerned Individuals." *CDSP* 41 (45): 20.

Zalygin, S. et al. 1990. "Letter to the Editors: Water Entangled in the Nets of the Water Resources Ministry." *CDSP* 42 (6): 29–30.

ZumBrunnen, Craig. 1979. "Vliianie geografo-ekonomicheskikh faktorov na sistemy upravleniia kachestvom vody." In *Ispol'zovanie matematicheskikh modelei dlia optimizatsii upravleniia kachestvom vody. Trudy Sovetsko- Amerikanskogo simpoziuma, Tom I*, 186–216. Leningrad.

Figure 15-1. Rank Ordering of Soviet Economic Regions by Degree of
Pollution and Environmental Degradation.[1]

Region	Air pollution per unit of total area	Air pollution per unit of urban area	Pollution of rivers and water shortages	Damage to forests	Soil contamination and soil erosion	Aggregate human impact
Ukraine						
Donets'k-Dnieper	1	5	1	4	4	1
Southwest	2	11	6	15	7	8
South	6	17	5	17	5	12
Donets'k-Dnieper	1	5	1	4	4	1
Urals	1	1	2	3	9	2
Trans-Caucasus	3	15	3	10	2	3
Central	4	6	3	6	10	4
Volga	4	8	1	12	6	5
Central-Chernozem	6	9	4	14	3	6
Central Asia	11	14	2	11	2	7
Southwest	2	11	6	15	7	8
North Caucasus	5	12	2	14	6	9
Moldova	7	20	3	16	1	10
Belarus	8	13	5	13	5	11
South	6	18	5	17	5	12
Baltic	6	19	6	9	8	12
North	12	2	8	2	12	13
Kazakhstan	10	4	7	18	4	14
Northwest	9	10	9	7	13	15
East Siberia	12	3	11	1	15	15
West Siberia	13	7	10	5	14	16
Volga-Viatka	14	15	4	18	11	17
Far East	15	17	12	8	15	18

[1] Based on estimates of the Laboratory for Monitoring the Environment and
Climate of Goskomgidrometa SSR and AN SSSR.

Source: Goskomstat SSSR (1989, 8).

Figure 15-2. Discharge of Harmful Substances from Stationary Sources into the Atmosphere of Ukrainian and Other Selected USSR Cities (1000 metric tons)

City	1985	1987	1988	Change 1985–88	1985 Rank	1987 Rank	1988 Rank
Noril'sk	2,518.0	2,400.1	2,343.7	–174.3	1	1	1
Kryvyi Rih	**1,314.2**	**1,290.0**	**1,252.7**	**–61.5**	**3**	**2**	**2**
Temirtau	1,064.0	998.9	917.6	–146.4	4	3	3
Magnitogorsk	904.1	871.4	849.0	–55.1	6	6	4
Novokuznetsk	1,001.9	892.9	833.0	–168.9	5	5	5
Mariiupil'	**814.3**	**785.8**	**777.2**	**–37.1**	**7**	**7**	**6**
Ekibastuz	1,336.0	917.4	744.1	–591.9	2	4	7
Kamians'k	**370.4**	**337.0**	**315.7**	**–54.7**	**18**	**17**	**15**
Moscow	411.0	369.1	311.8	–99.2	15	15	16
Makiivka	**375.0**	**318.8**	**306.6**	**–68.4**	**17**	**19**	**17**
Dnipropetrovs'k	**354.3**	**321.2**	**296.3**	**–58.0**	**21**	**18**	**20**
Zaporizhzhia	**302.1**	**286.9**	**267.0**	**–95.1**	**25**	**24**	**22**
Alchevs'k	**369.1**	**251.4**	**243.2**	**–125.9**	**19**	**28**	**24**
Avg. for 104 cities	244.8	225.8	210.3	–34.5	52	52	52
Donets'k	**208.1**	**192.8**	**178.2**	**–29.9**	**35**	**34**	**33**
Kremenchuk	**174.9**	**194.2**	**167.7**	**–7.2**	**41**	**33**	**35**
Lysychans'k	**120.5**	**132.2**	**130.8**	**10.3**	**53**	**50**	**46**
Ienakiieve	**136.5**	**120.8**	**115.2**	**–21.3**	**48**	**53**	**53**
Odessa	**124.5**	**105.6**	**87.8**	**–36.7**	**52**	**57**	**63**
Kiev	**99.2**	**93.7**	**70.5**	**–28.7**	**60**	**62**	**69**
Cherkasy	**64.4**	**62.4**	**54.3**	**–10.1**	**77**	**77**	**76**
Sivers'kodonets'k	**29.3**	**30.1**	**24.2**	**–5.1**	**98**	**96**	**98**

	1985	1987	1988	
Total of 15 listed Ukrainian cities	4,856.9	4,522.9	4,287.4	Ukraine = 2.7% of USSR area, 18%total USSR population and
In % of 104 cities	19.1	19.3	19.6	18.3% of total USSR urban
In % of USSR Total	7.1	7.0	6.9	population in 1989.
Total 104 USSR cities	2,5454.0	2,3485.0	2,1866.5	
Avg. for 104 cities	244.8	225.8	210.3	
USSR Total	**68,344.9**	**64,295.7**	**61,716.2**	

Source: Goskomstat SSSR (1989, 22–24). *Note*: Ukrainian cities are in boldface type.

Figure 15–3. Discharge of Harmful Substances from Autotransport into the Atmosphere of Different Cities
(1000 tons)

City	Population 1989 × 10^3	1986	1987	Change 1986–87	1986 Rank	1987 Rank
Moscow	8,967	861.8	841.5	−20.3	1	1
Leningrad	5,020	365.8	371.9	6.1	2	2
Tashkent	2,073	272.0	310.8	38.8	4	3
Baku	1,757	338.9	297.8	−41.1	3	4
Tbilisi	1,260	257.4	269.6	12.2	5	5
Kiev	**2,587**	**231.3**	**233.2**	**1.9**	**6**	**6**
Yerevan	1,199	179.3	175.3	−4.0	7	7
Alma-Ata	1,128	172.7	164.8	−7.9	8	8
Omsk	1,148	148.8	143.4	−5.4	9	9
Odessa	**1,115**	**128.4**	**135.4**	**7.0**	**14**	**10**
Donets'k	**1,110**	**122.9**	**135.3**	**12.6**	**15**	**11**
Novosibirsk	1,436	129.6	127.8	−1.8	13	12
Ufa	1,083	131.3	126.4	−4.9	12	13
Gor'kii	1,438	139.3	125.6	−13.7	11	14
Minsk	1,589	118.6	125.0	6.4	18	15
Dnipropetrovs'k	**1,179**	**119.9**	**122.6**	**2.7**	**17**	**16**
Zaporizhzhia	**884**	**105.7**	**120.3**	**14.6**	**23**	**17**
Kryvyi Rih	**713**	**79.0**	**79.2**	**0.2**	**33**	**29**
Cherkasy	**290**	**52.3**	**44.9**	**−7.4**	**52**	**55**
Mariiupil'	**517**	**39.1**	**38.4**	**−0.7**	**62**	**61**
Kamians'k	**282**	**23.2**	**24.4**	**1.2**	**77**	**74**
Kremenchuk	**236**	**23.9**	**24.2**	**0.3**	**76**	**75**
Sivers'kodonets'k	**131**	**11.5**	**18.2**	**6.7**	**92**	**86**
Lysychans'k	**127**	**12.6**	**13.8**	**1.2**	**90**	**90**
Alchevs'k	**126**	**11.3**	**11.9**	**0.6**	**93**	**92**
Total 100 USSR cities	68,245	7,851.4	7,625.9	−225.5		
Total for 13 listed Ukrainian cities	9,297	961.1	1,001.8	40.7		
Avg. for 13 listed Ukrainian cities	715.2	73.9	77.1	3.2		
Share of 13 Ukrainian in 100 USSR cities	13.6%	12.2%	13.1%	0.9%		

Source: Goskomstat SSSR (1989, 25–27); and "O predvaritel'nykh itogakh" (1989, 1–3).

Figure 15-4. Average Concentration of Polluting Substances in the Atmosphere of Different Ukrainian Cities
(In mg/m^3; figures in boldface equal or exceed MPCs.)

City	Dust (s.s.) 1985	Dust (s.s.) 1987	Dust (s.s.) 1988	SO$_2$ 1987	SO$_2$ 1988	CO 1985	CO 1987	CO 1988	NO$_2$ 1985	NO$_2$ 1987	NO$_2$ 1988
Alchevs'k	**0.5**	**0.4**	**0.3**	**0.07**	**0.06**	**4**	**3**	**3**	...	**0.10**	**0.09**
Cherkasy	**0.2**	**0.2**	0.1	**0.08**	**0.06**	1	**3**	**3**	**0.04**	**0.06**	**0.06**
Dnipropetrovs'k	**0.3**	**0.2**	**0.2**	0.02	0.02	1	1	1.5	**0.05**	**0.05**	**0.04**
Donets'k	**0.9**	**0.7**	**0.5**	0.03	0.02	2	2	2	**0.07**	**0.07**	**0.10**
Kamians'k	**0.5**	**0.3**	**0.3**	**0.14**	0.01	2	2	1	**0.06**	**0.04**	**0.05**
Kiev	**0.2**	0.1	0.1	0.01	0.01	1	1	1	**0.05**	**0.12**	**0.07**
Kremenchuk	**0.2**	**0.2**	**0.2**	0.02	0.02	**5**	**5**	**3**	0.03	**0.07**	**0.05**
Kryvyi Rih	**0.4**	**0.4**	**0.4**	**0.22**	0.03	2	2	2	**0.11**	**0.07**	**0.08**
Lysychans'k	**0.4**	**0.3**	**0.2**	**0.15**	**0.18**	1	1	1	**0.07**	**0.05**	**0.07**
Makiïvka	**0.5**	**0.6**	**0.5**	**0.17**	0.03	1	2	2	0.03	**0.04**	**0.05**
Mariiupil'	**0.2**	**0.2**	**0.2**	**0.12**	0.02	1	1	1	**0.06**	**0.04**	**0.04**
Odessa	**0.5**	**0.4**	**0.4**	**0.08**	**0.06**	2.6	2	2	**0.07**	**0.07**	**0.08**
Sivers'kodonets'k	**0.5**	**0.3**	**0.2**	**0.17**	**0.20**	1	1	1	**0.05**	**0.06**	**0.06**
Zaporizhzhia	**0.2**	**0.2**	**0.2**	0.03	0.04	1	1	1	0.03	**0.13**	**0.10**
MPCs	**0.15**	**0.15**	**0.15**	**0.05**	**0.05**	**3.0**	**3.0**	**3.0**	**0.04**	**0.04**	**0.04**

Source: Goskomstat SSSR (1989, 28–31); and *Doklad* (1989, 11).

Figure 15–5. List of Ukrainian Cities with the Highest Atmospheric
Pollution Levels (1988)

City	Relevant Atmospheric Pollutants
Alchevs'k	BP, nitrogen dioxide, dust
Dnipropetrovs'k	Formaldehyde, BP, dust, ammonia
Donets'k	BP, dust, pheno, ammonia
Kamians'k	BP*, formaldehyde, phenol, ammonia
Kiev	BP, formaldehyde, carbon disulfide, nitrogen dioxide
Kryvyi Rih	BP, formaldehyde, dust, nitrogen dioxide
Lysychans'k	Formaldehyde, phenol, ammonia
Makiïvka	BP, carbon disulfide, dust, phenol
Mariiupil'	BP, formaldehyde, hydrogen fluoride, ammonia
Odessa	BP, formaldehyde, hydrogen fluoride, phenol
Sivers'kodonets'k	BP, formaldehyde, phenol, ammonia
Zaporizhzhia	BP, nitrogen dioxide, formaldehyde, phenol

* BP–Benz(o)pyrene

Source: *Doklad* (1989, 20–22).

Figure 15-6. Portrait of Soviet and Ukrainian Water Use (1988)

Region	Municipal Water Use	Irrigation and Rural Supply		Fresh Water Intake for Industrial Use		Fresh Water Savings from Reuse	
(10^6m^3)	(m^3) (cap.)	Fresh water (10^6m^3)	Sewage & drainage water irrigation (10^6m^3)	Total (10^6m^3)	Potable (10^6m^3)	Total (10^6m^3)	As share of total indust. use (%)
USSR Total 26,380	92	15,2467	2,275	107,163	9,461	274,018	72
Ukrainian SSR 4,473	**87**	**7,868**	**196**	**16,363**	**1,250**	**68,064**	**81**
RSFSR 14,273	97	22,319	278	58,054	5,293	164,776	74
Belorussian SSR 651	64	388	1	1,681	225	8,987	84
Uzbek SSR 1,986	101	46,216	687	6,575	715	6,630	50
Kazakh SSR 1,237	75	24,398	413	7,493	654	12,294	62
Georgian SSR 659	122	1,282	0.0	1,182	184	1,048	47
Azerbaijan SSR 640	92	8,726	11	3,023	288	1,861	38
Lithuanian SSR 302	82	126	3	3,150	69	3,148	50
Moldavian SSR 248	58	729	4	2,663	93	857	25
Latvian SSR 218	81	76	0.0	358	82	502	58
Kirghiz SSR 365	62	1,907	347	678	169	670	50
Tadzhik SSR 494	98	10,590	289	621	163	922	60
Armenian SSR 591	180	2,434	0.0	520	118	2,694	84
Turkmen SSR 214	61	18,162	46	2,095	87	596	22
Estonian SSR 129	82	45	0.0	2,707	71	969	26

Source: Compiled and computed from Goskomstat SSSR (1989, 72–76).

Figure 15-7. Waste Water and Polluted Effluent Data for 1988
(in millions of m^3)

Region	Waste water disposal Total	Retention ponds, evaporation, filtration fields	Sub-surface disposal	Discharge of Waste Water into Surface Waterways				
				Total	Total effluent subject to treatment (%)	Polluted volume Total	un-treated	inade-quately treated
USSR Total	162,878	9,385	1,137	152,356	70	28,646	8,062	20,584
Ukrainian SSR	**19,646**	**849**	**79**	**18,718**	**41**	**2,634**	**489**	**2,145**
RSFSR	76,317	2,494	1,009	72,814	84	23,323	6,366	16,957
Belorussian SSR	2,084	172	3	1,909	7	63	0.0	63
Uzbek SSR	26,686	1,284	1	25,401	42	349	25	324
Kazakh SSR	9,040	1,492	13	7,535	55	340	47	293
Georgian SSR	1,551	102	0	1,449	51	317	262	55
Azerbaijan SSR	4,501	35	18	4,448	58	349	273	76
Lithuanian SSR	3,405	44	0	3,361	73	326	125	201
Moldavian SSR	2,959	33	0	2,629	32	91	2	89
Latvian SSR	570	0.0	0	570	70	257	114	143
Kirghiz SSR	1,432	235	0	1,197	7	14	9	5
Tadzhik SSR	4,020	44	0	3,976	31	91	17	74
Armenian SSR	783	0.0	0	783	49	295	291	4
Turkmen SSR	6,720	2,597	13	4,110	—	0.0	—	—
Estonian SSR	3,164	4	5	3,159	39	39	42	155

Source: Compiled and computed from Goskomstat SSSR (1989, 77–79).

Figure 15-8. Discharge of Polluted Waste Water
(Without Purification and Inadequately Purified) into Waterways
from Municipal Sewer Systems of Different Ukrainian Cities

Location	1985			1987			1988		
	Total	Untreated	%	Total	Untreated	%	Total	Untreated	%
Total from municipal economies of the USSR (in million m³)	5,807	2,684	46.2	9,217	2,568	27.9	12,948	2,240	17.3
From selected Ukrainian cities (in 1,000 m³)									
Zaporizhzhia	52,926	52,926	100.0	50,392	50,392	100.0	50,200	50,200	100.0
Sevastopil'	11,739	3,396	28.9	3,678	3,678	100.0	3,460	3,460	100.0
Mariiupil'	—	—	—	782	782	100.0	462	462	100.0
Kamians'k	11,520	11,520	100.0	6,343	6,343	100.0	31,373	—	—
Alushta	451	—	—	653	—	—	659	—	—
Poltava	2,920	2,920	100.0	6,441	6,441	100.0	5,218	4,457	85.4
Mykolaïv	25,859	2,870	11.1	19,310	2,684	13.9	16,931	2,600	15.4
Odessa	201,300	6,000	3.0	123,430	5,430	4.4	99,122	3,200	3.2
Dnipropetrovs'k	31,599	21,399	67.7	19,554	7,563	38.7	159,992	1,182	0.7
Other Black & Azov basin cities (in 1,000 m³)									
Bendery	13,566	7,853	57.9	25,341	6,851	27.0	25,555	—	—
Kishinev	1,648	—	—	28,170	—	—	22385	—	—
Tiraspol'	37	37	100.0	449	44	9.8	—	—	—
Novorossiisk	5,082	3,837	75.5	2,255	2,014	89.3	1,592	1,203	75.6
Rostov-na-Donu	199,125	38,525	19.3	170,820	30,020	17.6	172,711	25,939	15.0
Taganrog	35,251	35,251	100.0	35,291	—	—	35,291	—	—

Source: Derived from Goskomstat SSSR (1989, 34, 35)

Figure 15–9. Reclamation Backlog on Disturbed Land in the USSR (1988)

Region	Total Land Area (%)	Area reclaimed (1988)		"Otrabotannye"* component of disturbed land, 1/1/89		Years required to eliminate backlog	Total area of disturbed land 1/1/89 (1000 ha.)		Years required to eliminate backlog—all disturbed lands
		1000 ha.	%	1000 ha.	%		1000 ha.	%	
USSR Total	100.0	155.0	100.0	678.7	100.0	4.4	1,890.8	100.0	12.2
Ukrainian SSR	**2.7**	**24.1**	**15.5**	**58.7**	**8.6**	**2.4**	**197.5**	**10.4**	**8.2**
RSFSR	76.2	103.4	66.7	422.5	62.3	4.1	1,179.6	62.4	11.4
Belorussian SSR	0.9	8.9	5.7	44.4	6.5	5.0	119.9	6.3	13.5
Uzbek SSR	2.0	1.6	1.0	25.4	3.7	15.9	51.8	2.7	32.4
Kazakh SSR	12.1	10.7	6.9	69.1	10.2	6.5	167.0	8.8	15.6
Georgian SSR	0.3	0.4	0.3	0.9	0.1	2.2	2.7	0.1	6.8
Azerbaijan SSR	0.4	1.1	0.7	16.4	2.4	14.9	20.7	1.1	18.8
Lithuanian SSR	0.3	1.2	0.8	13.5	2.0	11.2	32.4	1.7	27.0
Moldavian SSR	0.2	0.5	0.3	1.4	0.2	2.8	3.1	0.2	6.2
Latvian SSR	0.3	1.0	0.6	13.3	2.0	13.3	44.0	2.3	44.0
Kirghiz SSR	0.9	0.4	0.3	1.3	0.2	3.2	6.6	0.3	16.5
Tadzhik SSR	0.6	0.4	0.3	3.1	0.5	7.8	6.2	0.3	15.5
Armenian SSR	0.1	0.1	0.1	2.0	0.3	20.0	8.2	0.4	82.0
Turkmen SSR	2.2	0.6	0.4	1.9	0.3	3.2	4.5	0.2	75.0
Estonian SSR	0.2	0.6	0.4	4.8	0.7	8.0	46.6	2.5	77.6

* Land disturbed in mining and pipeline construction but no longer used in the day-to-day operations of the appropriate industrial enterprises.

Notes: Includes lands scarred or polluted from surface and underground mining and pipeline construction; covered by spoil, enrichment tailings, or industrial slag; or comprised of abandoned industrial areas.

Source: Abstracted from Goskomstat SSSR (1989, 98).

Figure 15–10. Ukrainian *Zapovidnyks* (Nature Preserves) (end of 1988)

Name of Preserve	Location (Oblast)	Year Organized	Area 100 ha.	Number of Protected Species		
				Animals	Birds	Plants
"Askania-Nova"	Kherson	1921	33.3	57	213	1,729
"Dianisky Plavni"	Kherson, Odessa	1981	14.9	22	212	563
Kanevs'ka	Kiev	1923	2.0	49	240	832
Karadags'ka	Crimea	1979	2.9	42	200	1,100
Karpats'ka	Ivano-Frankivs'k, Transcarpathia	1968	12.8	50	141	898
Luhans'ka	Luhans'k	1968	1.6	43	151	1,037
"Mys Mart'ian"	Crimea	1973	0.2	29	146	500
Poliss'ka	Zhytomyr	1968	20.1	39	174	604
Rostoch'e	L'viv	1984	2.1	33	117	793
Ukrains'ka Stepnoi	Donets'k, Luhans'k, Sumy	1961	2.8	30	129	926
Chornomors'ka	Kherson	1927	57.0	44	300	624
Ialtins'ka	Crimea	1973	14.5	33	91	1,363
Protected Hunting Areas						
Azovo-Sivashs'ka	Kherson	1957	30.1	6	230	240
Dniprovsko-Teterevs'ka	Kiev	1967	30.5	16	15	11
Zaless'ka	Kiev	1957	15.0	15	17	160
Krims'ka	Crimea	1923	43.0	37	250	1,180
National Nature Parks						
Karpats'ka	Ivano-Frankivs'k	1980	50.4	50	110	1,100
Shats'ka	Volhynia	1981	32.8	30	219	825

Source: Goskomstat SSSR (1989, 122–27).

Figure 15–11. Areas Contaminated with Cesium-137 from the Chernobyl Accident (km²)

Republics	Contamination Range (curies/km²) 5–15			Contamination Range (curies/km²) 15–40		
	Total Area	Excluding Evacuated Zones	Evacuated Zones	Total Area	Excluding Evacuated Zones	Evacuated Zones
USSR Total	17,880	17,130	750	7,090	6,050	1,040
Ukrainian SSR	**1,960**	**540**	**1,420**	**820**	**350**	**470**
Belorussian SSR	10,160	9,830	330	4,210	3,640	570
RSFSR	5,760	5,760	0	2,060	2,060	0

Republics	Contamination Range (curies/km²) 40+		
	Total Area	Excluding Evacuated Zones	Evacuated Zones
USSR Total	3,100	1,670	1,430
Ukrainain SSR	**640**	**200**	**440**
Belorussian SSR	2,150	1,160	990
RSFSR	310	310	0

Source: Adapted from Izrael (1990a, 8–9).

Figure 15–12. State Capital Investment in Measures for Environmental Protection and Rational Use of Natural Resources by Union Republics (1988)

	Protection & Rational Use of Water Resources		Protection of Atmosphere		Protection & Rational Use of Land		Total State Capital Investment in All Environmental Protection and Rational Resource Use Measures			
	Million Rubles	% of Total	Million Rubles	% of Total	Million Rubles	% of Total	Million Rubles	% of Total	% Pop.	% Area
USSR Total	2,091	100.0	317.0	100.0	393.0	100.0	3,122	100	100	100
Ukrainian SSR	**311**	**14.9**	**31.0**	**9.7**	**85.0**	**21.6**	**505**	**16.2**	**18.0**	**2.7**
RSFSR	1,332	63.7	203.0	64.0	190.0	48.3	1,862	59.6	51.4	76.2
Belorussian SSR	73	3.5	11.0	3.5	6.0	1.6	91	2.9	3.6	0.9
Uzbek SSR	53	2.5	20.0	6.3	32.0	8.2	105	3.4	6.9	2.0
Kazakh SSR	109	5.2	40.0	12.5	9.0	2.1	252	8.1	5.8	12.1
Georgian SSR	20	0.9	1.0	0.4	25.0	6.3	50	1.6	1.9	0.3
Azerbaijan SSR	14	0.7	1.0	0.3	11.0	2.7	26	0.8	2.5	0.4
Lithuanian SSR	44	2.1	0.1	0.0	2.0	0.6	48	1.5	1.3	0.3
Moldavian SSR	20	1.0	1.0	0.4	20.0	5.1	42	1.3	1.5	0.2
Latvian SSR	39	1.9	0.6	0.2	0.02	0.0	40	1.3	0.9	0.3
Kirghiz SSR	8	0.4	1.0	0.3	2.0	0.6	11	0.4	1.5	0.9
Tadzhik SSR	11	0.5	3.0	1.1	5.0	1.3	22	0.7	1.8	0.6
Armenian SSR	22	1.0	0.5	0.2	4.0	1.0	27	0.9	1.1	0.1
Turkmen SSR	13	0.6	1.0	0.2	1.0	0.5	15	0.5	1.2	2.2
Estonian SSR	22	1.1	3.0	0.9	1.0	0.2	26	0.8	0.5	0.2

Source: Adapted from Goskomstat SSSR (1989, 148–50); "O predvaritel'nykh itogakh (1989, 1–3); Glavnoe upravlenie geodeziia (1984, 204–205).

CHAPTER SIXTEEN
Discussion

Alan Abouchar

The three papers in this panel provide informative insights into the welfare of Ukrainians. They focus on environmental factors and social variables, which are not easily quantified in money terms, as well as the more conventional variables of consumption and income. Two of the authors conduct much of their presentation on a comparative intra-union basis, but they leave unasked explicit questions of historic exploitation and abuse. These questions have been developed in several other papers of this conference and are frequently the subject of investigation today.

The picture painted by these authors—especially Dolishnii and ZumBrunnen—is not a pretty one. The high levels of pollution and environmental degradation are an unattractive subject; it is not easy to apologize for the damage done or mitigate the blame for it by reference to possible achievements in income growth, which do not appear to have been astounding in any event. Environmental wreckage, moreover, has a ring of finality, especially in low-income countries where resources are in too short supply to be diverted to improvement of the environment. But precisely because the picture is so bleak, it behooves us to ask how it came to pass that the most resource-rich region of its size in the USSR reached such a state, and what are the implications of this state for Ukraine's future.

The three papers in this panel are all very solidly researched, but the overall picture benefits from a more comparative perspective. I will bring a few such matters to bear below. In the section "Some Larger Issues" I will compare today's Ukraine with a Ukraine which might have existed had it never confederated into the Soviet Union. I will then outline possibilities for future growth and development in Ukraine.

Gaining Perspective

The situation presented by Dolishnii, ZumBrunnen, and Schroeder seems desperate, but perhaps viewed in a wider scope it might be less desperate than it initially appears. I would not criticize the authors' basic choice of subjects or their selection of sources. For this, other researchers should long be grateful. For the most part, I simply would draw attention to some other aspects of the situation which the authors have not addressed, in order to gain perspective on the Ukrainian state of affairs.

Schroeder's income and consumption data suggest an unequal treatment of putative equals. This explains an average real consumption in this resource-rich region that is 8 to 10 percent below the all-union and Russian Federation averages (Figure 13-3); 25 percent of the population below the semi-official poverty line; or consumption/ownership levels of individual consumer goods below the Russian Federation or all-union levels.

Many factors are to blame. But the first question to ask is whether the consumption does truly reflect welfare levels. Schroeder notes that regional wage coefficients may play some role in explaining the 8 to 10 percent differences. But regional wage differentials also reflect incentives and bear on the welfare sacrifices that must be made to attract workers in the first place. These sacrifices may take psychological forms of personal isolation and family disruption, but these are after all "real" and do constitute variables in modern consumer utility optimization theory. They also may reflect the higher living costs associated with climates less hospitable than those in Ukraine. The same considerations must be maintained in any analysis of gains from trade among the republics.

ZumBrunnen's ecological disruption data are disturbing. Figure 15-1 is probably the most trenchant indictment of disregard for the environment. I believe, though, that the situation presented in Figure 15-1 may look worse than it is, owing to the way that the ranks appear (that is, reducing the best rank to be assigned—the highest number—by the total number of tied items, less the number of tied ranks). Most no doubt would instinctively compare the rank of 5 which is assigned to the South for river and water pollution through the *Okhrana* procedure with the number 20. This would suggest that 75 percent of the regions do better and that southwest Ukraine is among the 25 percent worst regions in this respect. But in fact only eight regions did perform better than the South (that is, had rank number 6 or higher). Instead of 75 percent of the regions doing better, only 40 percent did. Only six regions did better than the Southwest with regard to river and water pollution.

In terms of total air pollution, the South, whose rank of 6 at first suggests that 70 percent of the regions fare better, actually is in better standing: since it is tied with two others, and since there are several other ties between regions which are worse, only 50 percent of the regions did better, while 35 percent did worse.

While ZumBrunnen's degradation levels do attempt to take account of several variables, such as urbanization (Figure 15-1), the inferences which one might normally draw from the high degradation levels should be qualified in other ways as well. This is especially true for the Donets'k-Dnieper subregion. Information from the Ukrainian National Economy yearbook presented by Dolishnii permits us to consider several additional variables. Industrial production per capita in this region is 60 to 100 percent higher than in the other two Ukrainian regions and oblasts; population density is considerably higher than in the other regions, with the Donets'k subregion being especially high. The whole region produces over one-third of the agricultural output of Ukraine. Some region has to be the worst in the country in terms of environmental degradation; it should come as no surprise that this economically extremely active region of Ukraine attains this distinction.

To recognize the foregoing, of course, is not to give carte blanche to polluters to do their worst, and ZumBrunnen is undoubtedly right in advocating that water use be priced. Also, while it is almost certainly true that uncharged-for water has irrationally hastened the problems of Uzbekistan by stressing water-intensive agriculture, we should be careful not to assume automatically that all water use is somehow excessive, or that investment in water recycling for industrial water use is irrational. In view of the dreadful water giveaways to agriculture in California and its dominant use in Nevada for tourist-oriented activities, such as golf courses built in the desert (which make use of water at prices far below the cost of providing it, not to speak of the economic rent), we in the United States should be doubly wary of our criticism of the Soviets.

There are other details in the grim picture which ZumBrunnen paints which might offset its total impact. For example, the atmospheric discharge by the 15 Ukrainian cities which are among the 104 worst cities cited in his source account for 19.6 percent of the combined pollutant emission of these 104 cities. While this is somewhat disproportionate to variables such as relative population size, it is certainly in the same ballpark (Figure 15-2). Other measures might also be interpreted more sympathetically. The high proportion of industrial water reuse, 81 percent, seems commendable when contrasted with the national reuse percentage of 72 percent (Figure 15-6).

Finally, we can be heartened by the expenditure plans to arrest ecological deterioration, which are presented in the penultimate section of ZumBrunnen's contribution. The 16.2 percent share of total all-union investment in remedial/protective measures which is allotted to Ukraine is nearly proportional to population. If one allows that the picture is not as dark as seems to emerge from ZumBrunnen's data sources, this level of expenditure may well be appropriate, in relative terms, to the present damage levels (taking account of the needs elsewhere as well).

The interesting paper by Dolishnii provides a great deal of detailed information on intra-Ukraine regional variation of environmental disruption, provision of social services, and income levels. His tables lead one to wonder about total Ukrainian income, availability of services, consumption, and degradation levels, which would be useful for further intra-union comparisons.

Some Larger Issues

What lessons for the central topic of the day—separation of republics, or, at least, secession of Ukraine—does this session on Ukrainian welfare have to offer? To pose this question is to ask whether Ukrainians would be better off on their own, and this in turn raises the question of whether they would be better off today if they had always been independent, instead of being incorporated into the USSR in 1922.

To answer the question in the affirmative would be to suggest that unification was somehow the cause of degradation. Given the environmental damage that we see around us today in both the first world and the third, it is hard to see any reason to say that a different form of government and independence from Moscow would have changed things? How would it?

An independent Ukraine would surely have embarked on an industrialization course every bit as fervent as the one followed. Perhaps some mistakes would have been avoided, for example the tenacious attempt at cotton agriculture for a decade before World War II in spite of appalling yields and harvests. Other errors, however, might well have been committed, for example even more intensive development of Donbas steel production in response to the pressure of Soviet demand through unrestricted international trade at freely determined market prices. Instead, this was partly replaced before the war by production at the newly developed Ural-Kuznetsk Complex.

To suggest that a free market price system could somehow have optimized pollution surely demonstrates faith beyond reason in that system: even today, in the West, we find it hard to price pollution in a socially optimal way, either because people remain unready to accept the concept of license to do harm or simply because entrenched interests are too powerful to be denied.

What of the more traditional economic criteria, those which are susceptible to monetary measurement? What would have been the effect of independence on the level and rate of growth of consumption, for example? Or, better, a more aggregated measure such as total gross national product (GNP)[1] which would recognize the value of longer-term production activities like investment? In spite of the various ambitious efforts of scholars to measure these magnitudes, I believe the results are inconclusive. For example, would an independent Ukraine have pursued as strait (and I do mean "strait") a path as the one which was followed which would ultimately yield greater production potential, or would it have gone directly for consumption, settling for lower levels and possibly even more disastrous wartime results.

To continue in the vein of a more inclusive measure, one must consider the welfare of "expatriate" Ukrainians, the second most populous group of extra-republic temporary and permanent residents in the USSR. What would have become of them?

---

[1] We should remind ourselves of the distinction between GNP and gross domestic product (GDP), the latter including profits generated by external capital and excluding profits generated externally by domestic capital. The differences in a fledgling economy could be sizeable and the independent economy would presumably be more interested in the former than the latter.

Another thought emerging from these concerns is the possible contradiction in employing the incremental capital-output ratio (ICOR) as a guide to regional investment allocation. Such a course environmentally would be more disruptive since investments having little production potential, as is typical for environmental remedial-works, would raise the ICOR and using it as a guide would give short shrift to republics or regions seeking to correct environmental decay.

Conclusion

What then are we to conclude from this cursory attempt to review and tie to a larger question the three well-researched and factually informative papers in this session.

The papers do not show Ukraine to be the rich uncle, distressingly exploited and drained, that separatist argument depicts. With its continuing advantages of climate, agriculture and mineral resources, and high-quality labor force, it should continue to prosper, especially in a federated union with new-found determination for republic decentralization (with respect to, for example, banking and tax distribution).[2] That the tide of environmental concern is rolling across the union presages commitment to improvement throughout the union. There is no reason to expect that this would be easier to achieve outside the union than inside.

One of the two sponsors of the present symposium is Temple University in Pennsylvania. There may be a lesson for us today in the soubriquet of that state—the "Keystone State." It was adopted to reflect the way that Pennsylvania seemed to fit as a keystone into the map of early America, but it also portended a greater ambition to serve as a fundamental building block for the new nation. Certainly in resources and population Pennsylvania was a major constituent in the new nation. In many ways Ukraine also appears like a keystone on the map—although it serves as the base of the building blocks rather than

---

[2] The new legislation on banking and taxes has been published in recent issues of *Ekonomika i zhizn'*. Banking legislation accords far greater rights to the republics regarding formation of republic national banks to parallel the new Gosbank which is to act more like a western central bank, as well as respecting commercial bank chartering and supervision ("Zakon SSSR o gosudarstvennom banke SSSR" 1990). The new sales tax legislation calls for a 30/70 division between the union and the republics ("Polozhenie o poriadke ischisleniia i uplaty naloga s prodazh" 1991).

at the top of an arch. Its human and physical resources suggest the same metaphor for it, *kraeugol'nyi kamen'*, with the same hope for prosperity and freedom that was Pennsylvania's when it cast its lot with the unified colonies.

References

Goskomstat SSSR. 1989. *Okhrana okurzhaiushchei sredy i ratsional'noe ispol'zovanie prirodnykh resursov SSSR. Statisticheskii sbornik.* Moscow.

"Polozhenie o poriadke ischisleniia i uplaty naloga s prodazh." 1991. *Ekonomika i zhizn'* 7:17.

"Zakon SSSR o gosudarstvennom banke SSSR." 1990. *Ekonomika i zhizn'* 52:16–17.

Part V: External Relations

CHAPTER SEVENTEEN
Ukraine's External Trade

Tetiana Pakhomova and Serhii Mischenko

The issue of the economic independence of Ukraine (as well as other republics of the Soviet Union) is the focus of heated political and academic debate. Ukraine's economic relations with the outside world constitute an important part of the problem. How well balanced is the so-called "interrepublic exchange" (flow of goods, factors of production, and services between the republics)? How efficient is the existing division of labor? What is the current status of Ukraine's foreign trade and how should it develop? Answers to these questions are being sought both by scholars and politicians.

It must be noted that issues of foreign trade performance at the level of the individual republic until recently were outside the framework of official statistical publications and studies. Statistical data on this subject, when officially published, were treated in terms of the standard cliché "beneficial cooperation between parts of a unified national economic complex." Comparisons of per capita indicators between republics were forbidden and no comprehensive data on intra-union flows of goods and incomes were open to public access. Even the majority of researchers in the republics had no access to existing statistical information, since data on interrepublic exchange and foreign trade were collected by the USSR Central Statistical Agency (TsSU, presently Goskomstat). Upon processing this information Goskomstat passed on to the republics' statistical agencies only the resulting figures of each republic trade balance to be used in obtaining such macroeconomic indicators as net material product (NMP). Statistics on imports and exports, and financial results of foreign trade by republic were considered to be classified material.

This state of affairs hampered any serious research effort in the field, though several more detailed studies were prepared at the Economic Research Institute of Gosplan and the Institute for Social and Economic Studies of Foreign Countries—both in Kiev. Unfortunately, such studies were not available to the public.

A good illustration of the situation can be the fact that the local Ukrainian statistical reference source, *Narkhoz Ukrainy*, had no chapter—in fact no data at all—on the foreign economic relations of Ukraine until the final issue published in 1990. A small annual booklet on the foreign trade of the republic published by the state statistical agency became available as a nonclassified source of information only in 1990. More thorough and much more critical appraisals of Ukraine's position with respect to the rest of the world have been made by Western scholars. Their research efforts recently have intensified.

The purpose of the present report is to interpret, on the basis of newly available statistics, Ukraine's trade relations with other republics and third countries. We argue here that the structure and performance of foreign trade are strongly determined by trade with the rest of the Soviet Union, which is very important to Ukraine in scope and influence. Both trade sectors bear the marks of the deep structural disproportions of and price aberrations in Ukraine's economy. Moreover we stress that widely discussed ideas and proposals to make a radical shift in the republic economy, reorienting its trade and other economic links to the outside world, must address the formidable task of developing a rational economic system and restructuring an economy which has been designed for 70 years to suit the needs of the Soviet Union.

Recent Developments in Statistical Coverage

Political and economic changes in the Soviet Union have started the painful but rewarding processes of decentralizing economic decision making on the one hand, and liberalizing foreign trade on the other. It is expected that beginning January 1, 1991 the Ukrainian government will take over from the central government in Moscow such functions as issuing export-import licenses, setting product quotas, registering joint ventures with foreign partners, as well as setting up its own customs office.

These developments call for a much wider, detailed and reliable statistical database on external trade for purposes of analysis and decision making. As a result, two trends are pronounced in current reporting and accounting practices: first, the opening of "classified" or "restricted" databases, and, second, the application of existing statistical tools and methods to new areas of external trade or the development of new methods to obtain a better picture of external trade performance. The evaluation of external trade flows within the framework and application of input-output tables for the Ukrainian economy has been the most important recent development in this respect.

The disaggregated values of inflows and outflows of goods for the first time appeared in the 1987 issue of the input-output tables. Two major components were included: (a) goods going out to or entering from other republics of the Soviet Union (this flow is called interrepublic trade); (b) exports and imports of Ukrainian foreign trade to and from third countries, evaluated at domestic prices.

External trade data were provided by all enterprises on the territory of Ukraine and collected by regional statistical offices. They were checked against statistics collected by the state system of supplies and procurements (Gossnab) and foreign trade statistics. A special interrepublic 110 by 14 trade matrix was prepared corresponding to the number of branches of production and number of republics trading with Ukraine. The service sector, which is quite important—but which under Soviet macroeconomic theory is considered "nonmaterial" (for example, transportation and communication used by the population, banking, research and development)—was not included in the matrix. Like the rest of the input-output table entries in the interrepublic trade data were at end-user prices, which include trade commissions, sales tax, and subsidies. They reflect the existing price structure and movements of goods, leaving aside the issue of financial flows between the republics.

Another welcomed initiative of Ukrainian statistical authorities in 1989 was the publication of import/export breakdowns by administrative regions (oblasts) of the republic. These publications were greeted positively by scholars and the public at large. However, closer scrutiny reveals a fundamental deficiency in both statistical presentations. The underlying concepts make it difficult to rely heavily on these publications as a source or analytical tool. The inefficient pricing system in the domestic market, the remaining monopoly of the state in import/export pricing, administrative straitjacketing of producers and customers by means of state orders, the high degree of market monopolization—all distort any conclusions made on the basis of data provided.

There are also methodological issues complicating the interpretation of existing statistics. Until 1985 the total income from foreign trade, calculated by Goskomstat in Moscow, was apportioned to each republic rather arbitrarily, in proportion to the size of that republic's NMP. It is more logical to distribute such income in proportion to the share of each republic in the total exports of the USSR.

General Characteristics of External Trade

In this paper Ukraine's external trade includes both trade with other Soviet republics and with other countries of the world. This reflects some of the basic problems of the present economic system in the USSR. Such factors as the spatial division of labor, natural endowment, central planning, the state monopoly of external trade, and a distorted price structure are of major importance in any analysis of the external trade of Ukraine and other union republics. The interaction of these factors determines the structure of Ukrainian external trade and its share in the macroeconomic indicators of the republic.

The data on Ukrainian external trade for the three years for which they are available are shown below (in billion rubles) (Kvasniuk 1990, 39; "Ekonomicheskie vzaimosviazi" 1990, 36):

	Exports	Imports	Balance
1986	39.6	48.0	−8.4
1987	44.0	50.2	−6.2
1988	46.9	49.8	−2.9

The total turnover in current domestic prices, for example, in 1988 amounted to 96.7 billion rubles and accounted for about one-third of the Ukrainian gross social product (GSP). The data show that while exports were relatively stable, exports increased considerably, by 18 percent, during these three years. As a result, the negative balance was reduced to almost one-third in 1988 of what it was in 1986. The negative balance of Ukrainian external trade during these three years is surprising, because, according to some estimations (e.g., Plyshevskii 1989) the NMP produced exceeded NMP consumed in the republic, for example, in 1980 and 1985.

One of the reasons for Ukraine's overall negative balance is its negative balance of trade with other countries (see below). This deficit can be explained in part by the distortion of Soviet pricing, and the fact that Soviet current domestic prices are used for estimation of exports to and imports from foreign countries. Raw materials, the main component of Ukrainian exports abroad, are priced low in comparison with final products. On the other hand, imports, primarily of machinery and consumer goods, are priced relatively high. Moreover, domestic prices of imported goods include relatively high customs duties. In 1988, for example, these pricing practices led to a negative balance with other countries of the world, not only for Ukraine but also for all union republics, with the exception of Belarus and Azerbaijan. As a result, all republics combined had a negative balance in their external trade ("Ekonomicheskie vzaimosviazi" 1990, 37).

The composition of Ukrainian external trade is determined by the overall objectives for Soviet economic development. The development of major industrial centers specializing in particular products has been part of this strategy. For example, the production of metal processing equipment is concentrated in four republics, agricultural chemicals in seven republics, automobile tires in six republics. The majority of energy-intensive and ecologically harmful industries is located in the Russian Federation, Ukraine, and Kazakhstan. Considering individual commodities, while Ukraine exported about 16 percent of its Gross Social Product in 1988, this share was 41 percent for ferrous metallurgy, 45 percent for nonferrous metallurgy, and about 33 percent for chemicals and petrochemicals (*Narkhoz Ukrainy* 1990, 15).

Figure 17-1 shows the distribution of Ukrainian external trade by main economic sectors. As can be seen, industrial output accounted for 94 percent of exports, while agriculture, a traditionally important sector in Ukraine's economic structure contributed only 4 percent to the total. This is explained in part by the fact that the share of obligatory deliveries of agricultural products to the state which go outside Ukraine's borders are not included in the statistics of Ukrainian total exports.

Industrial goods exported from Ukraine predominantly consist of heavy industry products with consumer goods accounting for only 23.8 percent of the total exports (processed and semi-processed foods

13.7 percent, and consumer durables 10.1 percent) (Figure 17-2). Even the values of industrial consumer goods include a substantial share of raw materials. Without the raw material component the share of consumer goods is reduced to 15 to 17 percent of total exports. This composition implies that despite official claims of economic progress in Ukraine, its exports resemble those of countries with a relatively low level of economic development.

Consider now the structure of Ukraine's imports. Its diversified mineral base, favorable climate, and existing production capabilities allow it to cover more than four-fifths of local demand for raw materials, intermediate, and finished products. Ukraine's relatively high level of self-sufficiency, however, is tempered by the dependence of its economy on supplies of important raw materials and products from other republics and abroad. For example, 100 percent of natural rubber; 60 to 80 percent of nonferrous metals, cars and trucks, and chemical fibers; 40 to 50 percent of pulp and paper products, textiles, and cables come from other republics or abroad (Ivanchenko 1990). Ukraine's demand for energy is of special interest here. About two decades ago Ukraine was a net exporter of energy resources. However, as a result of a short-sighted policy of energy-intensive development, the republic has become a major energy importer. While in 1970 Ukraine covered 100 percent of its energy needs, in 1975 this declined to 98 percent, in 1980 to 75 percent, and in 1985 to 58 percent (*Problemy teorii* 1989, 116). Ukraine also imports various industrial products needed primarily by its dominant heavy industry. Finally, because of the underdevelopment of domestic consumer industries, a substantial share of its total imports, 18.7 percent, consists of consumer durables (Goskomstat SSSR 1990, 266–67, 287).

Interrepublic trade

A more detailed analysis of the structure and pricing of interrepublic and foreign trade, as presented below, will facilitate an understanding of the aggregate numbers in Figure 17-2.

As one might expect, economic relations with other Soviet republics predominate in Ukraine's external trade. They account for four-fifths of the total trade turnover. Figure 17-2 gives a breakdown of this trade by major industries. Incidentally, the breakdown by industries and not by products is a peculiarity of official statistics. The table shows that Ukraine runs a positive balance in trading in products of

ferrous metallurgy, engineering and metal processing, food processing, and agriculture. Ukraine is a net importer of oil, gas, petrochemical products, light industry products, wood and wood products, and
nonferrous metals. It had a positive balance of 3.6 billion rubles in
interrepublic trade in 1988.

The data in the above table are presented in official current prices
which are distorted by subsidies and turnover taxes, as well as other
factors. At best they represent an approximation of the situation which
would exist under market determined equilibrium pricing. Some para-
doxes arising from the official pricing can be illustrated by the example of the meat industry in Ukraine. In 1987 the contribution of the
meat industry to the republic's national income was valued at 700 million rubles. But since this industry received subsidies of 5.2 billion
rubles from the republic budget, it enters the national income estimate
with a negative value amounting to 4.5 billion rubles. In terms of
efficiency, industries incurring such losses should not be developed in
Ukraine and their products therefore should not be exported to other
republics. But considering the natural endowment and historical
experience of Ukraine this conclusion would be contrary to common
sense. Even if we assume that certain industries should remain in production and receive subsidies for whatever reason, the cost of their
subsidies should be proportionately distributed between the consumers
at home and in other republics so as not to fall entirely on the
Ukrainian budget. If this were done, Ukraine would gain 1.6 billion
rubles annually (Goskomstat SSSR 1990, 261).

Ukraine sold 410 thousand tons of meat and meat products to other
republics through direct trade in 1989. The all-union centralized fund
is another channel through which products are transferred from one
republic to another. Ukraine sold another 600 thousand tons of meat
and meat products to the fund in 1989 (*Narkhoz Ukrainy* 1989, 376).
How many of these supplies ended up in other republics and how
many were consumed in Ukraine by civilians and military stationed
on its territory is unknown. In view of the fact that the central government in Moscow remains one of the most important buyers of various
Ukrainian products, we fully support the proposal by Bandera
(Chapter 18, herein) to consider it a separate purchaser for the purpose
of economic accounting. Such a classification could become quite
important especially now, during the transition to a market economy.
The republic would then have the opportunity to trade according to its

best interests and to choose the most advantageous buyers of its products. Were such a situation to arise, the possible benefits to Ukraine can be demonstrated using again the example of the meat industry. The republic received 1.2 billion rubles through the sale of meat and meat products to the state fund at the official price of 2 rubles per kilogram. At the same time the average market price amounted to 5.5 rubles per kilogram. Had the meat been sold at this price, the republic's receipts would have been more than 2 billion rubles higher.

"Price zones" are another factor which affects the interrepublic balances of trade. This concept refers to regions with differentiated state purchasing prices (supposedly reflecting the differences in the cost of production) of similar agricultural products. Low procuring prices may cut profits on some products in some regions or republics. Other republics have an incentive to import the low-priced products from these regions or republics. The differential rent then benefits the buyers and not, as it should, the producers. Ukraine was a low-price zone with respect not only to meat and meat products, but also grain, sugar, vegetable oil, and some other products. It is not surprising that in 1989 and, especially, in 1990, when Ukraine attained some degree of freedom in economic decision making, it severed some of its economic links with other republics and all-union funds that had been previously imposed on it by central planners, and decreased its links in other cases.

The turnover tax and the ways it is collected is another factor which affects the external balances of the republics and their economic performance. This tax is a charge imposed by the central government on consumer goods and raw materials. In Ukraine, the total of this tax is equal to about 10 percent of NMP. The way the turnover tax is estimated and collected varies from industry to industry. Goskomstat estimates it at the place of production, while the Ministry of Finance at the place of sale. It complicates both the estimation of the real level of taxation and of financial transfers between industries and republics. Two important factors should be kept in mind while analyzing the effect of this tax: first, there is no tax imposed on producers of raw materials needed for the production of consumer goods; and, second, the consumer bears the brunt of the tax, because it is included in the price of final goods.

The turnover tax exerts an influence on interrepublic trade balances. In order to have a positive balance of trade, a republic would be interested in importing cheap agricultural products, e.g. unrefined sugar, cotton, wool—their prices do not include this tax—and export consumer goods, e.g. cars, alcoholic drinks, cigarettes, textiles. The prices of the latter contain the turnover tax. Republics can do very little to reduce the effect of the disadvantageous trade on their balances; their production specialization has been imposed on them by central planners. This is especially true in the case of Ukraine. Ukrainian exports consist primarily of domestically cheap and in many cases even subsidized products, e.g. meat and meat products, agricultural products, raw materials, and intermediary products of basic heavy industry branches. On the other hand, Ukraine imports products of light industry on which heavy turnover taxes are imposed.

A short overview of trade with the rest of the Soviet Union suggests that the possible restructuring and improvement of Ukraine's trade performance rests on two basic prerequisites. The first is the restoration of pricing and other economic mechanisms which allow decision making and trade development based on economic criteria. The second is a major restructuring of the economy itself. The predominance of heavy industry is to be replaced by consumer-oriented and high-tech industries supported by a strong and healthy agrobusiness. Both prerequisites or strategic goals are interconnected and both will strongly influence the pattern of foreign trade (trade with third countries).

Foreign Trade: A Hostage to Domestic Problems

Official statistics on Ukrainian foreign trade presented by Goskomstat show a highly unbalanced trade flow with 1988 exports equal to 6.9 billion rubles and imports almost twice as large as exports. Foreign trade is just one-fifth of the total external trade of the republic, however it is responsible for the overall negative trade balance.

The enigma of Ukraine's foreign-trade imbalance is very simple. Both exports and imports are calculated at domestic prices—producers' prices for exports and final consumption prices for imports. There are only two positive explanations for such an approach: first, it makes foreign trade data compatible with total external trade data; and, second, it allows an escape from the problem of a conversion rate for trade data expressed in currency other than rubles.

The foreign trade structure strongly resembles the intra-union trade structure for the republic and thus stresses the point of the basic structural problems underlying trade issues. It also resembles the trade pattern of the Soviet Union as a whole with raw materials and intermediate inputs dominating export. In Ukraine's exports these commodity groups account for 65 percent of the total. In 1988 Ukraine exported 16.8 million tons of coal and coke, 18.2 million tons of iron ore, 5.8 million tons of pig iron, steel, and metal scrap in addition to 3.6 million tons of rolled metal. The major exporting regions are Donets'k and the Lower Dnieper, where coal basins and most of the heavy industries are situated. L'viv region is an important exporter in the other parts of the country, accounting for 11.6 percent of total exports.

Ukrainian exports are mostly destined for Eastern European countries, where in the 1950s and 1960s major heavy industry projects were developed and were largely dependent on Ukrainian coal, coke, iron ore, and rolled metal. The majority of these commodities were and still are exported under long-term intergovernmental agreements signed by the Eastern European countries with Moscow. They are based on a clearing principle and the so-called "transferable ruble." In 1988 less than 9 percent of Ukrainian exports were sold for hard currency. A decision to move in 1991 to hard currency accounts with Eastern European countries is expected to boost the dollar share of Ukraine's exports. The data for the first quarter of 1991 confirm this expectation; the hard currency share of Ukrainian total exports increased to 60 percent.

In addition, the historical structure of foreign trade and its destinations is determined by the state monopoly of Ukrainian exports. Trade in raw materials and energy has always been subject to strict control and conducted through foreign trade organizations in Moscow. The latest available data for the first quarter of 1990 show that out of 1,200 Ukrainian exporters only 200 were trading directly and accounted for 5 percent of total exports. Recently, the central authorities are trying to substitute direct control over export flows by financial instruments like the compulsory sale of 40 percent of hard currency earnings to the USSR budget at a very low exchange rate.

The structure of foreign imports resembles the structure of imports from the rest of the union with the exception of oil and gas, nonferrous metals, and wood products. Major import groups are light industry goods (27.2 percent), products of engineering industry (26.2 percent), and processed foods (16.6 percent). Consumer goods that predominate in these groups are to be "blamed" for the negative trade balance. Under the Goskomstat procedure, imported consumer goods with relatively high retail prices in rubles tend to tilt Ukraine's foreign trade toward a negative balance (and for that matter the balances of most of the other republics).

Two principal factors undermine the analytical value of this type of estimation. The first is the fact that the local price system differs greatly from the world market system in its structure and the relationships between its major commodity groups. The second is the absence of any real bridge between the ruble and hard currency, which makes it impossible to link domestic costs and prices to those prevailing on the world market.

This is why any new attempt by Goskomstat to evaluate total external trade of the republics at world market prices (*Ob''em vvoza* 1990) simply cannot clarify the real picture. Again, the prices used in this exercise are not real contract prices but assumed average world market prices, which for many commodity groups is a questionable approach. Moreover, conclusions that are made in terms of comparing efficiency of trade within the Soviet Union in comparison to trade on the world market proceed from the completely unrealistic official exchange rate of the ruble. In this sense another negative balance of Ukraine's external trade, this time at the world market prices estimated by Goskomstat, is even less helpful than estimations in rubles.

Conclusions

Recently published statistical evidence, its drawbacks notwithstanding, gives more proof of the deep-rooted structural problems which plague the Ukrainian economy and are reflected in both Ukrainian interrepublic trade and foreign trade. In spite of the reforms initiated both at the union level and the republic level, major factors which deform trade relationships are still in force.

Inter-republic trade, which makes up almost 80 percent of the total turnover of goods across Ukrainian borders still does not entail direct financial transfers between the republics, as is characteristic of international economic relations. Such transfers are managed by and conducted via the union budget at the discretion of central authorities. In the present economic situation, economic authorities reacted to the balance settlement via the union budget by a number of hastily signed interrepublic agreements on trade and economic cooperation, and an epidemic of barter deals between republic enterprises.

Trade relations with the central government and its agencies involving defense spending and other government expenditures, which constitute an important part of the total transfer of goods, should be given a clearly defined contractual form based on rational prices. With or without the proposed union treaty such reform will only benefit economic and political relations between the republics and the center. A separate entry is also needed in each republic's trade balance to register these transactions.

Comparison of commodity structures, as well as the analysis of such issues as price system distortions, subsidies, and unequal transfers to the central monopoly clearly show that the inter- republic and foreign trade of Ukraine is more similar than dissimilar. Moreover, foreign trade—in terms of scope, influence, and existing planning, regulatory and organizational procedures—is subordinate to interrepublic trade as an element of the remaining system of central administrative controls. (A simple example is the provision for enterprises to export freely only that which is produced over and above the production quota or state order and is not destined for interrepublic trade flows.) In addition, the truly free foreign trade sector is well below 10 percent of total trade turnover for Ukraine. In relation to the gross national product (GNP) or NMP of Ukraine foreign trade is just a fragment of a percent.

It is only logical to conclude that if the Ukrainian economy seeks to turn fully to international markets, which is often proposed and much dreamed of, it still will be necessary to solve principal domestic issues including the major restructuring of trade with other republics. Otherwise, such a shift to international markets will hardly be possible.

New forms of international economic cooperation involving trade, such as joint ventures with foreign capital, can be more flexible and efficient since they largely exist outside the old administrative system. However their development is rather slow, especially in Ukraine, and their economic results are still insignificant. By mid-1990 about 60 joint ventures were operational on the territory of the republic.

The process of setting a new legal and organizational framework for Ukrainian foreign trade is in progress. New laws are being adopted, a Ukrainian Ministry of Foreign Economic Relations and a Ukrainian Customs Authority were recently formed. However, the newly born agencies will face the same deep-rooted structural problems faced under the old system.

We believe it essential to stress that the reorientation of Ukraine's foreign trade and its full-fledged development can be greatly facilitated and actually made possible by deep structural changes in the national economy according to a well-defined strategic program enjoying national support. However, major restructuring of both inter-republic and foreign trade is impossible without such fundamental changes of the economic system, which will trigger self-supporting mechanisms of real cost accounting, open pricing, and fair-market competition. A more reliable statistical coverage of external trade will develop both as a prerequisite and as a consequence of these processes.

Finally, looking into some intermediate future, Ukraine's foreign trade should be determined by the country's comparative advantages—natural endowment and geographical location.

References

"Ekonomicheskie vzaimosviazi respublik v narodnokhoziaistvennom komplekse." 1990. *Vestnik statistiki* 3:36–53.

Goskomstat SSSR. 1990. *Statisticheskii biulleten' vypuskov ekspress-informatsii v 1989 g.* Moscow.

Goskomstat USSR. 1990. *Narodnoe khoziaistvo Ukrainskoi SSR v 1989 g.* Kiev.

_____. 1991. *Narodnoe khoziaistvo Ukrainskoi SSR v 1990 g.* Kiev.

Ivanchenko, I. 1990. "Kto kogo kormit: neskol'ko tsifr, kharakter-izuiushchikh obmen USSR s drugimi respublikami." *Pravda Ukrainy* (March 17):4.

Kvasniuk, B. 1990. "Mizhrespublikans'kyi obmin i rynok." *Pid praporom leninizmu* 14:37–44.

"Ob'em vvoza i vyvoza produktsii po soiuznym respublikam za 1988 g. vo vnutrenykh i mirovykh tsenakh." 1990. *Vestnik statistiki* 4:49–64.

Plyshevskii, B. 1989. "Soiuznye respubliki: gotovnost' k khozrazchetu." *Ekonomicheskaia gazeta* 34:6.

Problemy teorii i praktiki upravleniia. 1989. No. 6.

Figure 17-1. Ukrainian External Trade (1988)
(in current domestic prices, million rubles)

Sector	Exports	Imports	Balance
Total	46,935	49,862	-2,927
Industry	44,538	48,122	-3,584
Agriculture	1,716	1,307	409
Other Sectors of Material Production	681	433	248

Source: "Ekonomicheskie vzaimosviazi" (1990, 40).

Figure 17–2. Structure of Trade with the Rest of the USSR (1988)

Branches	Exports		Imports		Balance
	(mil. rub.)	%	(mil. rub.)	%	(mil. rub.)
Total industry	37,930.0	94.7	35,964.4	98.7	1,965.4
Electric energy	159.7	0.4	157.7	0.4	2.0
Oil and gas	345.3	0.9	3,918.9	10.8	-3,573.6
Coal	256.2	0.6	295.2	0.8	-39.0
Ferrous metals	6,166.1	15.4	2,408.8	6.6	3,757.3
Nonferrous metals	913.7	2.2	1,896.5	5.2	-982.8
Chemicals and petrochemicals	3,294.9	8.2	4,189.4	11.5	-894.5
Machinery and metal processing	15,695.7	39.2	13,063.3	35.9	2,632.4
Forest, wood, pulp and paper	413.9	1.0	1,580.9	4.3	-1,167.0
Construction materials	727.5	1.8	342.6	0.9	384.9
Light industry	2,608.6	6.5	4,907.6	13.5	-2,299.0
Food processing	6,539.3	16.3	2,221.2	6.1	4,318.1
Other industries	809.1	2.0	980.1	2.7	-171.0
Agriculture	1,676.9	4.2	244.8	0.7	1,432.1
Other branches of material production	448.3	1.1	222.4	0.6	225.9
Overall Total	40,055.2	100.0	36,431.6	100.0	3,623.6

Source: "Ekonomicheskie vzaimosviazi" (1990, 40).

Figure 17–3. Structure of Ukraine's Foreign Trade (1988)
(current domestic prices)

Branches	Exports		Imports		Balance
		percent		percent	
	(mil. rubles)		(mil. rubles)		(mil. rubles)
Total industry	6,608.4	96.1	12,157.5	90.6	–5,549.1
including:					
Electric energy	525.0	7.6	0.0	0.0	525.0
Oil and gas	416.0	6.1	59.9	0.5	356.8
Coal	691.9	10.1	119.1	0.9	572.8
Ferrous metals	1,911.0	27.8	504.5	3.8	1,406.5
Nonferrous metals	45.7	0.7	165.3	1.2	–119.6
Chemicals and petrochemicals	629.8	9.1	1,167.9	8.7	–538.1
Machinery and metal processing	1,523.1	22.1	3,519.1	26.2	–1,996.0
Forest, wood, pulp and paper	40.9	0.6	436.3	3.3	–395.4
Construction materials	30.1	0.4	92.6	0.7	–62.5
Light industry	238.0	3.5	3,654.8	27.2	–3,416.8
Food processing	468.4	6.8	2,236.7	16.7	–1,768.3
Other industries	87.4	1.3	201.3	1.5	–113.5
Agriculture	39.0	0.6	1,062.4	7.9	–1,023.4
Other branches of material production	232.7	3.4	210.8	1.6	21.9
Overall Total	6,880.1	100.0	13,430.0	100.0	–6,550.6

Source: "Ekonomicheskie vzaimosviazi" (1990, 40).

CHAPTER EIGHTEEN

Income Transfers and Macroeconomic Accountability from the Standpoint of Ukraine

Volodimir N. Bandera

In conjunction with the ongoing transformation of the USSR, Ukraine and other republics have intensified their quest for economic rights. The national sovereignty proclaimed by Ukraine's parliament would be meaningless without the ability of the republic's government to control the process of production and distribution, to influence the content of international trade, and to determine fiscal relations with other republics or supra-national institutions. Therefore, it is not surprising that the principle of economic accounting, or *khozraschet*, was extended at the microeconomic level to embrace the accountability and self-financing of the republics at the macro level already in the early phases of perestroika. Moreover, Ukraine intensified its insistence that Moscow itself should become accountable to the members of the Union.

The measurement of interrepublic economic transactions in the Soviet system was unduly complicated. Writing in the spirit of glasnost, Koroteeva et al. (1989, 44) bluntly asserted: The question of economic relations of union republics is complex in two senses. First, at the present time there is no information about what republics give to the all-union fund and what they receive. Second, today there are no precise criteria regarding the justification of these flows. The situation could be clarified by detailed interrepublic balances of production and distribution in physical and value terms, as well as the resulting magnitudes of the republics' contributions to the all-union budget and subsidies from the budget. Fortunately, in 1990 M. Borysenko, the head of Derzhkomstat URSR, reported that his agency undertook fundamental reforms to provide statistics on income and trade, as well as other essential macroeconomic variables for the republic. In preparing this paper, the author had to rely on fragmentary historical evidence and substandard data for the latest available year, 1988. Actually, this was the last normal year for the USSR since the data for the subsequent two terminal years of the Soviet Union became hopelessly distorted by Moscow's deficit spending, accelerated printing of money and the resulting inflation.

Our objective to analyze the extent of regional imbalances and the corresponding interrepublic transfers of goods and services in the USSR is by no means easy. In the West, Bahry (1987), Bandera (1977), Gillula (1979), Holubnychy (1975), and Melnyk (1977) attempted to interpret the structure and significance of interregional transfers of capital and other resources. Western efforts to analyze interregional and international economic relations from the standpoint of particular republics such as Ukraine were hampered by the fact that Soviet publications typically reveal only fragmentary empirical evidence and conceal the essential primary data. As we are reminded by Treml (1988), the methodology of Soviet economic statistics as of 1988 still suffered from severe shortcomings inherent in a marketless economy with administered prices. According to Barymykov and Nevelev (1990, 6), interrepublic and international trade data originating in the republics were monopolized by Moscow.

This paper aims to interpret the income transfers involving Ukraine as a member of the Soviet Union. This issue was treated in Soviet publications rather superficially in terms of the more traditional analysis of budgetary relations between the republics and the center. Here, we try to focus on the transfers of output and explain the huge losses of Ukraine's national product over many years. It will be seen that the required measurement and evaluation of the republic's balance of trade is intricately dependent on the meaning of export and import prices. In that sense, the question of trade balances is part of a broader issue of the extent of a country's gain or loss from international specialization.[1] Our more specific task is to demonstrate that

---

[1] As I argued elsewhere (Bandera 1977, 247), we must distinguish the concepts of "the balance of trade" and "the terms of trade." Suppose trade is balanced, so that the value of exports equals the value of imports. Hence we can also write

Western-style balance-of-payments concepts, income-absorption analysis, and aggregate fiscal analysis of the republic can be very helpful in interpreting Ukraine's balance with the outside world.

Evidence of Protracted Income Losses

As a subordinate region within the centralized system of the USSR, Ukraine suffered protracted annual losses of substantial portions of its national product. The magnitude of these losses is summarized in Figure 18-1. This historical evidence shows that for well over half a century, at least 10 percent of Ukraine's national output has been given up annually.

A comprehensive analysis of the magnitude of income transfer out of Ukraine was provided in the report by the Ukrainian Academy of Sciences (Akademiia nauk 1963) for the years 1959 to 1961. The report revealed a huge net loss of 14.2 percent of the republic's net domestic product (NDP). The study was undertaken in conjunction with Khrushchev's short-lived decentralizing reform. Further compilation and publication of such revealing regional data was suspended, as was the experiment with the regional management of the economy (the so-called *sovnarkhoz* system). Since then, the regional inequities in the distribution of investment capital and in the burden of financing the imperial development policies could not be effectively challenged.

As shown by Bandera (1973), large income transfers out of Ukraine are confirmed in Soviet econometric studies by Emelianov and Kushnirsky (1974), Detneva (1967), and others. A sophisticated econometric project called OMMM (the Optimizing Intersectoral Interregional Model) pertaining to conditions in the 1970s, captured the extensive regional transfers of income in the Soviet economy and

---

$$P_x Q_x = P_m Q_m$$

where P_x and P_m are indexes of export and import prices, while Q_x and Q_m are indexes of export and import volumes, respectively. From the equation we can derive an index of the barter terms of trade

$$t = Q_m/Q_x = P_x/P_m$$

Now t indicates the amount of imports obtained per unit of exports, and t typically is measured as a ratio of import to export price indexes. Changes in t imply changes in the gains from trade. Clearly, manipulation of export and import prices by Gosplan and the Foreign Trade Monopoly affect the republic's gains from interregional and international specialization.

confirmed Ukraine to be a "net contributor." According to A. G. Granberg's report on that model (1973, 156): Regional balances of inflow and outflow of the gross output are comprehensive indicators of territorial economic interdependence. Counting external exports and imports, only the developed South (Ukraine plus Moldova) and the Ural regions make a substantive credit contribution to the country's economy. These two regions show a credit balance in their income accounts. If external exports and imports are not counted, also the West (Belarus plus the three Baltic states) would show a credit balance.

Specifically, the magnitude of contributed net exports (+) and received net imports (–) as percents of Gross Domestic Products in the seven macro-regions in the early 1970s was as follows: Ukraine with Moldova 7.5 percent, the Ural region 3.2 percent, the West 0.0 percent, the Center –4.2 percent, Western Siberia –0.5 percent, Eastern Siberia –9.1 percent, and the Far East –7.3 percent. As can be seen, the more-developed European regions were losing income to the benefit of the undeveloped Eastern regions of Asia, which are rich in natural resources.

Recent econometric models inevitably confirm that the net export balances were extracted from Ukraine systematically and perennially. Holubnychy (1975) correctly observed that the direction and persistence of such transfers of capital and human resources during the Soviet era reflects a geopolitical strategy aimed at developing the sparsely populated Asian regions, a strategy that had its origins in imperial Russia.

The magnitude of the net outflow of Ukraine's national product has historical comparisons. As elaborated by Bandera (1973, 149), the French indemnities to victorious Prussia were an estimated 5.6 percent of France's national income during the period of 1872 to 1875, and German reparations to the Allies amounted to 2.5 percent of Germany's national income from 1924 to 1932. More recently, East German reparations to the Soviet Union started at an incredibly high 28.6 percent of the GNP in 1950, dropped to 18.4 percent in 1953, 3 percent in 1957, and 0.6 percent in 1959. In view of these examples, the net extractions of output amounting to between 10 and 15 percent of the national product during the 1930s and similarly high sacrifices in recent decades were an exorbitant price to pay for Ukraine's captive membership in the Soviet Union.

The differences in the estimates of income transfers are not due only to the different historical periods being investigated, but also to the different methods used to assess the process and the extent of such transfers. Thus, the losses by Ukraine have been perceived as:

1. Net budgetary losses of the republic to the central government (Dobrogaiev 1927; Volobuiev 1928; Holubnychy 1971; Melnyk 1973, 1977; Bahry 1991).
2. Net losses of national product (Akademiia 1963; Emelianov and Kushnirsky 1974; Bandera 1973).
3. Net unrequited trade surpluses (Bandera 1973, 1977; Gillula 1979).
4. Net losses of capital (Wagener 1973).

We regard the net transfers of income as unjustified losses because they were imposed and extorted through the mechanism of a centralized planned command system. Moreover, these transfers were not on a loan basis with an appropriate rate of interest, rather, they were unrequited in the same manner as war reparation or tribute. Thus, the evidence of the extraction of national output from Ukraine indicates the extent of economic exploitation within the framework of the Soviet Union and the tsarist empire before it.

In addition to the inequity of unrequited income transfers, it has been argued persuasively that arbitrary transfers of income in the USSR involved a gross misallocation of capital resources. When capital is available to a developing region on a free basis and without regard to the cost of interest, the investment process is wasteful. There is ample evidence that the spatial allocation of investment in the Soviet Union has historically disregarded the marginal productivity of capital. Studies by Koropeckyj (1971) and Wagener (1973) demonstrate that marginal capital/output ratios in Ukraine have been lower than in other republics. Hence, the commandeered transfer of capital resources out of Ukraine, where the productivity of investment was relatively high, was economically unjustified under those conditions—not only does Ukraine suffer but also the total output of the union is not maximized. Holubnychy (1971) argued that while the favored developing regions of Russia were gaining at Ukraine's expense, the total output of the USSR was not optimized.

We shall not further pursue the problems of equity and efficiency engendered by the colonial policy of extracting capital and human resources out of a region such as Ukraine in an imperial-style system. In a climate of glasnost, these issues have been discussed in the Soviet Union. It is now widely recognized that accountability in the management of resources in the republics is an essential attribute of economic efficiency and political sovereignty.

From the standpoint of Ukraine, the aim should be to establish and promote equitable, mutually beneficial (non-exploiting) trade and financial relations with the former Soviet republics and the rest of the world. This implies that economically justified, interest-bearing capital movements (both credits and loans) have their place in an open economy. Hence, there is a need to formulate systematic statistical procedures that would track the balance of Ukraine's economic transactions with the rest of the world. The rest of this paper will consider methodological issues in measuring the balances of transactions in Ukraine as an open economy. It will be shown that the balance-of-payments account can be quite revealing, and its interpretation intertwines with national income and aggregate financial macroeconomic analysis of the republic.

The Balance of Payments of the Republic

It has been argued (Bandera, 1973; 1977) that the comprehensive annual balance-of-payments account can be the key to analyzing Ukraine's trade and financial transactions with the outside world. Unfortunately, balance-of-trade accounts first published during the 1920s have ceased to be compiled. More recently, Soviet economists have recognized the value of balance-of-payments analysis. Until recently, only occasional fractional data pertaining to trade in material goods have been published.[2] As a pleasant surprise, *Vestnik statistiki* (1990) contains data on exports and imports of material goods

---

[2] Using Soviet sources, Gilulla (1977, 1979) offers extensive data on Ukraine's intra-union and international trade flows in connection with his input-output analysis. Occasional statistics also can be found in Soviet monographs dealing with Ukraine's specialization or participation in the external trade of the USSR. But such data exclude services that are extremely important in intra-union trade, especially trade with the union government. Therefore, such data are of limited value in a comprehensive macroeconomic analysis.

(excluding services) for Ukraine with the Soviet Union and with out-side countries (the latter in internal rather than in international prices). Also, the yearbook *Ukrainskaia SSR v tsifrakh v 1989g.* (Goskomstat USSR 1990) included aspects of Ukraine's trade statistics for the first time. As will be shown, however, these and other Soviet sources are incomplete and contain serious price distortions.

A comprehensive balance-of-payments table must go beyond trade in "material goods" as found in Soviet sources. It is necessary to deal specifically with the peculiar interaction of payments between the republic and the rest of the union, and it is essential to take into account the peculiar fiscal interaction of Ukraine with the central government. Since it is necessary to identify the commercial and financial interaction between the Soviet government and the consti-tuent members of the union, the balance of payments of the Soviet republic can be patterned after a scheme devised for Puerto Rico by Isard (1960, 173–78).

As Figure 18-2 shows, this account encompasses all trade and financial transactions that occurred during one year. The transacting partners of Ukraine were: (1) countries outside the union receiving exports and supplying imports; (2) enterprises in the rest of the union that sell to, and buy from the republic; and (3) union government engaged in direct purchases in the republic, as shown in the current account, and involved in fiscal and banking transactions, as shown in the capital account.

The logic of this type of accounting requires that total in-payments (+, credits) must equal total out-payments (−, debits); whether the payments are actual or of a bookkeeping nature is irrelevant here. The overall equality of debits and credits is assured, since conceptually each transaction at the micro level involves a double entry. This accounting equality must remain when transactions are aggregated into convenient categories even though the pairing of debit and credit entries for specific transactions is obscured in the process of aggrega-tion. For example, an export of 100 million rubles' worth of wheat entered as a credit (or in-payment) must have somewhere in the state-ment an offsetting debit (or out-payment) entry of (1) 100 million rubles' worth of imports, or (2) 100 million rubles in cash receipts, or (3) 100 million rubles' worth of "unrequited" out-payments such as grants and tributes to foreigners, or (4) 100 million rubles loaned to foreigners, or (5) some combination of these. When bookkeeping inconsistencies result in a statistical discrepancy between total credits and debits, the required accounting equality between the two is assured by a correcting entry, "Errors and Omissions."

As we begin the analysis of the aggregate balance-of-payments account for 1988, a recent year for which data are available, four methodological issues must be kept in mind. These issues surfaced as we labored to construct Figure 18-2. First, contrary to expectation, the data on the republic's transactions with the rest of the Soviet Union are incomplete. To be sure, data in physical terms show Ukraine to be a net importer of lumber and consumer products (Gillula 1977, 218). But, although there is an abundance of statistics on the output and destination of producers' goods that fit into an input-output framework, corresponding data in value terms are unreliable and spotty. As explained in the notes to Figure 18-2, we used the more complete Western data on Soviet external trade to estimate Ukraine's exports and imports; to some extent this also compensates for the use of "internal prices" in *Vestnik*'s trade data for the republic.

Second, we deem it essential to estimate the current account transactions of the republic with the union government as a separate entity. This would be straightforward if the sale of goods and services to the Soviet government always involved exporting outside the republic's boundaries; such trade would be part of the entry "the rest of the union." However, sizeable defense expenditures and the provisioning of the military forces stationed in Ukraine did not involve exports across the republic's boundaries. The inclusion of the union government as a separate trading partner is needed in order to identify the real counterpart of the transfers of taxes, profits, and other payments to the Soviet Union, as shown in the financial account. To be sure, "normal trade" with union enterprises cannot be readily distinguished from "trade with the union government," especially since about half of the republic's annual budget is financed through the union budget.

The third methodological problem is the lack of data on trade in services, an anomaly that also typifies published trade statistics for the USSR as a whole. From the republic's standpoint it is necessary to account for the export value of such activities as the services of Ukrainian specialists in developing countries, sales to foreign tourists in the republic, support of foreign students (4,600 in 1967), and so on. According to Koroteeva et al. (1989, 44), new science and technology transfers between the republics occur free of charge, so that "...regions and republics that are most mature in terms of science and technology are losing colossal sums." Thus, the omission of service transactions in Soviet sources (and hence in Figure 18-2) undoubtedly reduces the credit side of the current account, diminishing the statistical estimate of Ukraine's unrequited net export balance.

Fourth, Soviet data underlying Figure 18-2 do not account for the arbitrary nature of prices. It is known that prices of primary producers' goods sometimes were set below the cost of production, while certain types of manufacturers often set their prices above their production cost. Since Ukraine generates substantial export surpluses in producers' goods and agricultural produce, the price system understated the opportunity cost of these exports. A further distortion was created by zonal price differentials for agricultural staples, producers' goods and centrally distributed inputs such as energy, while railroad rates favored long-distance shipments to less-populated regions beyond the Urals.

As if this were not enough, serious price distortions were created by union monopolies, organized vertically by sectors of production throughout the union; apparently, as much as 95 percent of Ukraine's industrial output was controlled by such monopolies. This industrial structure involved extensive intra-industry trade as well as intersectoral trade (both involving the republic's exports and imports) at internally set transfer prices or even on barter terms. Certainly, such arbitrary prices distort the aggregate values of exports and imports so that the meaning of trade balances becomes elusive. Thus a recent rash of publications (Baramykov 1990, 7) aimed to convince Soviet readers that Ukraine and most other republics were blessed with import surpluses as a result of their membership in the union. This illusion was created by selling external imports at inflated domestic prices, a practice that in fact exploited the buyers and generated huge profits for Moscow's Foreign Trade Monopoly. Indeed, imperial-style Soviet planning theories have maintained that price manipulation is a legitimate method to accomplish interregional transfers of resources.

The methodological difficulties that were just presented affected the construction of the balance of payments and have far-reaching implications for the economic analysis of interrepublic and international relations of Ukraine. It is not sufficient to assemble and interpret the trade balance on the basis of existing data as shown in the current account of Figure 18-2. In the spirit of true reform, one must also analyze the implications that arbitrary prices have on Ukraine's terms of trade. Aside from the balance of trade, these prices determine the extent of the gains from trade, that is the gains from international specialization. The issues of equity and efficiency in connection with lost trade surpluses and unfavorable terms of trade were impossible to overcome when Ukraine was a party to transactions within the framework of the command economy using administered prices, while the system was geared to exploit the republic as a colony.

Methodological problems notwithstanding, Ukraine's balance-of-payments account (constructed along the lines of Figure 18-2) could even now offer insight into the political economy of a republic within the USSR and the steps Ukraine must take to assert sovereignty over its open economy.

Thus, it is apparent that differences in the estimates of income transfers summarized in Figure 18-1 partly reflect the different definitions of the "net balance." In our case, if only the business-like trade that crosses Ukraine's borders is counted, then such "balance of trade" figures, consisting of lines 1 and 2 in Figure 18- 2, amount to a net export of 4.4 billion rubles, or a loss of 3 percent of the republic's gross social product (GSP). But, if non-defense purchases (line 3) and defense purchases (line 4) by the Soviet government in the republic are included, the net export balance of the entire current account is 22.2 billion rubles, or a loss of 14 percent of the republic's GSP.

The net balance of the republic may be interpreted not only from the real but also from the financial standpoint. In Figure 18-2, the capital and unilateral transfers account consists mainly of grant-like transfers into and from the union budget. In Western terminology these are unilateral transfers; that is, one-time non-repayable and non-interest bearing financial payments.[3] It was impossible to identify specific capital inflows and outflows, namely the loan-type interest-bearing transactions that add to Ukraine's external assets or liabilities. We may assume that "other union revenues" from Ukraine on line 6 include such capital transactions. In 1988, the Soviet budget required substantial deficit spending that was financed to some extent by utilizing the savings of Ukraine's population as well as by Ukraine's net

---

[3] These budgetary transfers between Ukraine and Moscow have been estimated by Melnyk (1977) and cited in Figure 18-1.

repayment of 12.7 billion rubles of short- and long-term credits to state banks (Goskomstat USSR 1989, 422–23).[4] Also, no attempt was made to estimate Ukraine's share of the USSR's external borrowing and lending, although such transactions, which intimately engaged Ukraine's economy, apparently increased the net international creditor status of the USSR in 1988.[5]

As can be seen, the overall balance of payments position of Ukraine in 1988 can be viewed from two standpoints: first, it can be considered the balance on current account amounting to a net credit of 22.2 billion rubles; second, it can be seen as the net financial debit of 22.2 billion rubles (allowing an error term to assure the accounting equivalence of the underlying double-entry bookkeeping). Like tribute, net export balance just discussed is unrequited, because rather than being purchased on credit, the balance was seized through an imposed budgetary process.

Another insight derived from the balance of payments exercise involves the contribution of the republic to the balance of payments of the USSR as a whole. This contribution was being circumvented, as Ivanov (1989) shows. Although *Vestnik statistiki* started to publish external trade statistics for the republics in 1990, the data were still incomplete and distorted the import values by using inflated domestic prices. Using our estimates, the international pattern of net trade flows

---

[4] Apparently, a significant portion of the large Soviet budget deficit since 1988 has been financed by an outright printing of money. The injection of such new money through government expenditures in Ukraine constitutes another method by which Moscow can acquire Ukraine's output. Moreover, the unwarranted expansion of money contributes to an actual and suppressed inflation for consumer goods, a malady over which the republic has no control.

[5] *PlanEcon* (May 25, 1990, 24–27), citing a minor Leningrad newspaper, *Chas Pik*, shows that that the USSR extended substantial hard-currency credits to Third World countries in the late 1980s, including $8.2 billion in 1988 alone. As of November 1, 1989, the outstanding indebtedness of the Third World to the USSR was $68 billion and of the socialist bloc 44 billion rubles. In 1989, Soviet liabilities to Western and CMEA banks rose from $36.8 billion to $44.4 billion, while Soviet deposits in these banks remained unchanged at $15.2 billion. Although Ukraine is starting to participate directly in international joint investment projects and is otherwise trying to attract foreign capital, aggregate data on these transactions is not available. However, since Ukraine's economy was substantially involved in overall international capital transactions of the USSR, an empirical interpretation of Ukraine's share is long overdue.

involving the republic, the outside countries, and the union can be represented as they are in Figure 18-3. For simplicity, transactions with the union government in Figure 18-2 are omitted. As can be seen, in addition to an export balance of 3.63 million rubles with other Soviet republics, Ukraine generated a trade surplus of 837 million rubles with outside countries.[6] Thus, national output drained from the republic through both internal and external trade mechanisms. The latter involved Moscow's Foreign Trade Monopoly, which assigned export tasks and import allotments and controlled the domestic prices of such external transactions. While perestroika made provisions for exporting businesses to claim some of the foreign currency that they earn, the elected parliaments (Supreme Councils) in Ukraine, the Russian Federation, and the Baltic states have claimed the right to manage foreign currencies earned through their respective exports. However, it still is unclear what the status will be of the imbalances that the republics might generate with foreign countries either directly or indirectly by participating in the combined transactions of the USSR. When the republics succeed in asserting their sovereignty over international transactions, they will be responsible for the imbalances incurred by such activity. This means that they will be able to incur foreign debts and to accumulate foreign assets.

---

[6] According to *Vestnik statistiki* (1990, 37), in 1988 Ukraine incurred a huge net import balance of 6.5 billion rubles in domestic prices as dictated by the Foreign Trade Monopoly (FTM). Thus a myth was propagated that Ukraine and most other republics—by being members of a happy union—enjoyed substantial import surpluses although, in fact, the intermediation of the FTM allowed it to extract more than 50 billion rubles in profits for the benefit of Moscow. Our method tries to mitigate the distortion created by the use of marked-up domestic prices for imports.

The implied pro-rated profit extracted from Ukraine was some 10 billion rubles. this recent revelation vindicates Melnyk's (1977) insistent inclusion of such trade profits in his estimates of the budgetary losses by Ukraine. Correction for such indirect transfers out of Ukraine would require a debit entry in the capital account, and a corresponding credit entry under "Transactions with union government" in Figure 18-2. We are thus reminded that the entry "Errors and omissions" in Figure 18-2 does not adequately represent the extent of distortions and concealment in the underlying aggregate data.

The harmful effects of the sytemic grip by the FTM are elaborated by Bandera (1977, 257–62; 1985, 110–17).

External Balance in Relation to Aggregate Income and Absorption

The income-absorption approach to the balance of payments as outlined by Dornbusch (1980) can help clarify the relation between output and its utilization within the confines of a republic functioning as an open economy. This method demonstrates the transfer of net balances out of (or possibly into) the republic as a process in which the trade activity intertwines with overall economic activity.

On one hand, not all of the production generated in the republic (as measured by its GSP) is used by the republic. On the other hand, not all goods and services absorbed or utilized by the republic originate on its territory. For a given year, the income and absorption may be interpreted accordingly. Define income, Y, as the value of the output or product generated in the republic, so that

$$Y = C + I + GR + GU + X \tag{18.1}$$

where C is the production of republic-destined consumption goods, I represents the republic-generated investment goods without the deduction for capital depreciation, GR is output paid for by the republic and local governments, GU represents net sales to the Soviet government exclusive of union enterprises, and X equals external and intra-union exports. Define absorption, A, in the republic as

$$A = C + I + GR + GU + M \tag{18.2}$$

where all variables, including imports M from other republics and outside countries, represent the sum of goods and services utilized in the republic.

The difference between income Y (Equation 18.1) and absorption A (Equation 18.2) is in fact the trade balance B in the following equation

$$B = Y - A = X - M \tag{18.3}$$

In order to apply Equation 18.3 to available statistical evidence, we must use estimated statistical aggregates that correspond to idealized theoretical variables. For our purposes, the value of the republic's output, Y, can be represented by the GSP, which was estimated at 157.2 billion rubles in 1988 according to Revenko's method (see Chapter 8, herein).

We do not have a comprehensive direct estimate of Ukraine's absorption, A, for 1988. According to Plyshevsky (1990, 54), the ratio of the indexes of per capita utilization to per capita production of national income in Ukraine was 87:90 in 1988. This implies that aggregate absorption was 152.0 billion rubles.[7]

In one interpretation, the proxies for X and M would count only trade that crosses the republic's borders, that is only lines 1 and 2 in Figure 18-2. Line 3, corresponding to the Soviet Union government's purchases of goods that are utilized mostly in Ukraine, would be excluded in that these purchases do not constitute exports in a strict sense. Under these narrow definitions, Ukraine's X equals 49.6 billion rubles and M equals 45.4 billion rubles.

Substituting the estimates just presented into Equation 18.3 and adding the required residual error term e, we can write

$$B = Y - A - e = X - M$$
$$4.4 = 157.2 - 152.0 - 0.8 = 49.8 - 45.4 \qquad (18.3a)$$

However, a second interpretation is possible. We can enlarge the definition of trade transactions to include the transactions with the Soviet government as estimated in the third line in Figure 18-2, making exports and imports embrace all transactions in section A, the current account. Now the balance on current account, BCA, can be seen in the following manner

$$B = (Y - A) + e = X - M$$
$$22.1 = (157.2 - 152.0) + 16.9 = 67.5 - 45.4 \qquad (18.3b)$$

The required discrepancy term becomes $e = 16.9$. Now Equation 18.3b implies that the estimates by Plyshevsky (1989; 1990) either understate the republic's income, Y, or overstate its absorption, A, probably the latter. It can be argued that although absorption involving Soviet government expenditures for defense and so on does take place within

---

[7] Here we deliberately use published Soviet estimates of the relation between income and absorption. Plyshevsky's (1989) analogous figures for 1985 and 1980 also indicate that Ukraine was losing about 3 percent of its national product. However, his data for all republics are disguised as per capita income and absorption without specifying the definitions of the underlying aggregates. Undoubtedly such data omit the services and embody other methodological weaknesses that were pointed out in conjunction with the balance of payments.

A more reliable estimate by Akademiia nauk (1963, 254) for 1959 to 1961 placed the net loss of the Net National Product of Ukraine at 14.2 percent. Granberg's (1973, 159) estimate applicable to the early 1970s was a 7.5 percent loss of the national product of Ukraine and Moldova combined.

Ukraine, such uses of the output are controlled by an outside entity
and hence do not constitute Ukraine's absorption.

The fundamental insight from our analysis is worth underscoring:
The unrequited trade surpluses involve equivalent losses of absorption
in the form of reduced consumption and/or investment in the republic.
Historical evidence summarized in Figure 18-1 as well as the analysis
of the most recent year for which data are available (1988) testify that
such unrequited losses by Ukraine have been burdensome indeed. We
can, therefore, appreciate why the issue of interrepublic income
transfers acquired such preeminence in the political economy of the
USSR, especially in the late 1980s.

Fiscal Balances and Net Transfers

Macroeconomic analysis of net income transfers can be further
enhanced by investigating how this process involved the aggregate
fiscal flows between the republic and the Soviet government. By
"fiscal flows" we mean the out-payments of various taxes to, and the
in-payments of budgetary allocation from the union. Here we would
also include banking credits and debits of Ukraine with union banks
and international institutions. An analysis of the budgetary balances
reveals the monetary counterpart of the net transfers of republic-
produced goods and services.

Consider the accounting definition of GDP of the republic as an
open economy:

$$Y = C + I + GR + GU + (X - M) \qquad (18.4)$$

where GR stands for expenditures by the republic's government and
GU for expenditures in the republic by union government. (For simplicity, transfer payments are disregarded here.)

An alternative statement of Equation 18.4 can be formulated by
subtracting from both sides taxes retained by the republic, TR, and
taxes transferred to the union budget TU, so that

$$Y - TR - TU = C + I + (GR - TR) + (GU - TU) + (X - M) \qquad (18.5)$$

Noting that $(Y - TR - TU - C)$ equals saving, S, we can state

$$S = I + (GR - TR) + (GU - TU) + (X - M) \qquad (18.6a)$$

Rearranging, we obtain

$$(X - M) = S - I + (TR - GR) + (TU - GU) \quad (18.6b)$$

Assume now that investment in the republic is financed partly through savings in the republic and by taxes retained in the republic, while the republic's budget is balanced. These assumptions were quite realistic in our case. This implies that $S + TR = I + GR$, or $S + TR - I - GR = O$. Thus, Equation 18.6 converts to a fundamental identity

$$(X - M) = (TU - GU) \quad (18.7)$$

This formulation of macroeconomic aggregates can further illuminate the meaning of the balance-of-payments data in Figure 18-2. Here again, two interpretations are possible. First, trade in Equation 18.7 can be defined as the goods leaving or entering the republic in the usual manner, as shown in lines 1 and 2 of Figure 18- 2. This would exclude sales to the Soviet government, that is, expenditures in Ukraine by the union government, as in line 3. On the budgetary side of the equation, net taxes acquired by the union, TU, are approximated by the "Capital and unilateral transfers" account in part B of Figure 18-2. Net union government expenditures in Ukraine, GU, correspond to line 3. thus we obtain

$$B = (X - M) = (TU - GU) + e$$
$$4.4 = 49.8 - 45.4 = 22.1 - 17.7 + 0 \quad (18.7a)$$

where the data below the variables are in billion rubles, from Figure 18-2. In other words, the net export balance, B, amounting to 4.4 billion rubles, is equivalent to the balance of the union budget as it pertains to Ukraine.

However, a second interpretation analogous to that in the previous section is possible. We can enlarge the definition of trade to include the transactions with the Soviet government, GU, on line 3 in Figure 18-2. Now exports and imports would embrace all transactions in the current account, analogous to Equation 18.3b. Consequently, the extent of the transfer may be viewed as follows

$$BCA = (X + GU) - M = TU$$
$$22.1 = 49.8 + 17.7 - 45.4 = 22.1 \quad (18.7b)$$

Now the left side corresponds to the entire current account, and
Ukraine's trade balance becomes 22.1 billion rubles. The right side
encompasses the "Capital and unilateral transfers" account. This
interpretation is similar to Melnyk's (1977) estimates of Moscow's
budgetary exploitation of Ukraine. But there is an advantage of juxta-
posing the trade balance and the financial balance. Now we can
observe how the financial means (taxes, profits, and so on) extracted
by Moscow are being converted into real value in the form of net
exports out of the republic plus union-controlled expenditures in the
republic (mainly for defense, police, and the union bureaucracy). As
can be seen, the transfer of income outside the republic's boundaries
in Equation 18.7a is substantially less than the loss of income to the
union in Equation 18.7b. In the first interpretation the loss amounts to
3 percent of Ukraine's GSP and in the second it is 14 percent of the
GSP.

Concluding Reflections

Historical evidence of burdensome income losses by Ukraine is
undeniable. Macroeconomic statistics needed for a thorough ongoing
analysis of this process are not readily available, however.

From our discussion we can appreciate that the discrepancies
between various estimates of net income losses by Ukraine (see Figure
18-1) are partly due to definitional and other methodological differences of various calculations. But certainly, the reality of protracted
and burdensome net losses by Ukraine cannot be doubted.

Recognizing that net income transfers (losses here) involve trade
imbalances (surpluses here), the republic cannot suffer indefinitely
such unrequited losses of capital. Ukraine must claim the sovereign
right to offer international credits and accumulate foreign assets and,
as the case may be, to incur external liabilities and become responsible for its foreign debts.

Applying Western analytical concepts to the Soviet system
highlights the fundamental problem of the reliability of data. Especially serious is the aberration of administered prices, which, in the
period under consideration, were further distorted by the intra-
enterprise transfer pricing practiced by union monopolies. As a result,
the economic values of traded goods were distorted and the allocation
of resources could not be guided efficiently. It is impossible to argue
logically about why and how the republic should specialize interna-

tionally when its apparent losses of trade surpluses and incomprehensible terms of trade render the gains from trade quite dubious. Certainly, it would be desirable to institute balance-of-payments accounts, making them consistent with income-absorption and budgetary data. Then it would be possible to trace the extent and content of income transfers as well as to provide a comprehensive picture of Ukraine's interaction with the rest of the world.

The recent outcry for macroeconomic accountability has far-reaching implications for Ukraine's participation in the bankrupt Soviet Union, which has been formally federated but, in fact, is managed as a centralized imperial-style system. As it claims national sovereignty and strives for independence, Ukraine will hardly remain subservient and continue to tolerate income losses ordained by the Soviet government.[8] As demonstrated, Moscow has wielded enormous fiscal powers in Ukraine so that the republic's losses of income have intrinsically involved union taxation and expenditures on its territory; consequently, center-ordained budgetary imbalances have resulted in losses of income and in losses of trade surpluses. The transfers that currently constitute a form of unrequited tribute must be eliminated, made voluntary, or contracted on a loan basis at negotiated rates of interest. Moreover, Ukraine must partake actively and directly in determining international prices: this could be attained by adopting market prices and dissolving the union monopolies, especially the Foreign Trade Monopoly. Ukraine should be able to negotiate the terms of trade with major trading partners, such as other republics, the Soviet government, the remaining union monopolies, and global multinational enterprises. After all, national sovereignty means being accountable and responsible for trade imbalances and terms of trade with the outside world.

In the Soviet case, the issue of interregional income transfers must be seen in the broad context of the imperial centralized system of the political economy. Here the budgetary, banking, and currency powers of the Soviet government have provided it with tremendous capability to control the republic's allocation of resources. The budgetary

---

[8] The applicability of the center-periphery paradigm to Ukraine's relations with Moscow is explored by Bandera (1977, 262–63; 1980; 1985; and 1988). Ukraine's evolving trade potential in the post-Soviet geopolitical system is discussed by Bandera (1991).

methods have been essential but they are not the only methods that the union government has used to extract net export surpluses as well as to utilize a huge portion of the republic's national product directly on Ukraine's territory. This process also has relied on the powers derived from Moscow's control of foreign and domestic banking, Moscow's ability to claim seigniorage profits from the issuance of money, the ability of the Foreign Trade Monopoly to generate huge profits from international transactions, and the ability of central authorities to allocate scarce foreign currency. The severe limitations on Ukraine's economic autonomy in the Soviet system have been oppressive. Ukraine must break these shackles on its road to sovereignty and independence.

References

Akademiia nauk URSR. 1963. *Natsional'nyi dokhod Ukrainskoï RSR.* Kiev.

Andreiev, V. 1989. "Ob ekonomischeskoi samostoiatelnosti respubliki." *Kommunist* 12:56–69.

Bahry, D. 1987. *Outside Moscow: Power, Politics, and Budgetary Policy in the Soviet Republics.* New York.

Bandera, V. N. 1973. "Interdependence between Interregional and International Payments: The Balance of Payments of Ukraine." In *The Soviet Economy in Regional Perspective.* Edited by V. N. Bandera and Z. L. Melnyk, 132–53. New York.

_____. 1977. "External and Intraunion Trade and Capital Transfers." In *The Ukraine Within the USSR: An Economic Balance Sheet.* Edited by I. S. Koropeckyj, 235–67. New York.

_____. 1980. "Structure of Economic Interaction Among the Neighboring Nations." In *Poland and Ukraine: Past and Present.* Edited by P. Potichny, 149–69. Toronto.

_____. 1985. "Międzynarodowe stosunki gospodarcze w cieniu dominacji Rosyjskiej." *Sučasnist (Zeszyt w języku Polskim)* 1-2.

_____. 1987. "The Political Economy of Chornobyl." *Soviet Ukrainian Affairs* (Summer).

_____. 1988. "International Economic Relations." In *Encyclopedia of Ukraine*, Vol. 2. Edited by V. Kubjovyc, 341–42. Toronto.

_____. 1991. "International Competitiveness of Ukraine." Temple University, Department of Economics *Working Papers* 55. Philadelphia.

Baramykov, Ie. and O. Nevelev. 1990. "Rozvytok mizhrespublikanskykh zviazkiv v umovakh rozshyrennia ekonomichnoï samostiinosti soiuznykh respublik." *Ekonomika Radianskoï Ukraïny* 5:3–12.

Borysenko, M. 1990. "Dokorinna perebudova statystyky v umovakh onovlennia suspil'stva." *Ekonomika Radianskoï Ukraïny* 6:3–12.

Detneva, E. V. 1967. "Nekotorye perspektivnye raschety: na osnove edinoi sistemy ekonomicheskikh schetov raiona." In *Statistika narodnogo bogatstva, narodnogo dohoda i natsional'nye scheta*, 253–77. Moscow.

Dobrogaev, V. 1927. "Problema finansovogo balansa Ukrainy." *Khoziaistvo Ukrainy* 3.

Dornbusch, R. 1980. *Open Economy Macroeconomics*. New York.

Emelianov, A. and F. I. Kushnirsky. 1974. *Modelirovanie pokazatelei razvitiia ekonomiki soiuznykh respublik*. Moscow.

Gillula, J. W. 1977. "Input-Output Analysis." In *Ukraine Within the USSR: An Economic Balance Sheet*. Edited by I. S. Koropeckyj, 193–234. New York.

_____. 1979. "Economic Interdependence of Soviet Republics." In *Soviet Economy in Time of Change*, 618–55. Washington.

Goskomstat SSSR. 1990. "Ekonomicheskie vzaimosviazi respublik v narodnokhoziaistvennom komplekse." *Vestnik statistiki* 3:36–38.

Goskomstat USSR. 1989. *Narodnoe khoziaistvo Ukrainskoi SSR v 1988 godu*. Kiev.

_____. 1990. *Ukrainskaia SSR v tsifrakh v 1989 godu*. Kiev.

Granberg, A. G. 1973. *Optimizatsiia territorial'nykh proportsii narodnogo khoziaistva*. Moscow.

Holubnychy, V. 1971. "The Soviet Economic System in Ukraine." In *Ukraine: A Concise Encyclopedia*, Vol. 2. Edited by V. Kubijovyc, 710–33. Toronto.

_____. 1975. "Teleology of the Macroregions in Soviet Union's Long- Range Plans, 1920–90." In *Development Regions in the Soviet Union, Eastern Europe, and Canada*. Edited by A. F. Burghardt, 82–150. New York.

Isard, W. 1960. *Methods of Regional Analysis*. New York.

Ivanov, I. 1989. "Problemy khoziaistvennogo rascheta vo vneshekonomicheskoi deiatelnosti." *Voprosy ekonomiki* 9:100–108.

Koropeckyj, I. S. 1971. *Location problems in Soviet Industry Before World War II: The Case of Ukraine*. Chapel Hill, North Carolina.

Koroteeva, V., L. Perepelkin, and O. Shkaratan. 1989. "From Bureaucratic Centralism to Economic Integration of Sovereign Republics." *Problems of Economics* 32 (no. 3): 36–56.

Melnyk, Z. L. 1973. "Regional Contribution to Capital Formation in the USSR: The Case of the Ukrainian Republic." In *The Soviet Economy in Regional Perspective*. Edited by V. N. Bandera and Z. L. Melnyk, 104–131. New York.

_____. 1977. "Capital Formation and Financial Relations." In *The Ukraine Within the USSR: An Economic Balance Sheet*. Edited by I. S. Koropeckyj, 268–99. New York.

Ministerstvo finansov SSSR. 1989. *Gosudarstvennyi biudzhet SSSR*. Moscow.

Ministerstvo vneshnikh ekonomicheskikh sviazei SSSR. 1989. *Vneshnie ekonomicheskie sviazi SSSR v 1988 g*. Moscow.

PlanEcon Report 20–21. 1990. Washington, D.C.

Plyshevsky, B. 1989. "Soiuznye respubliki: gotovnost' k khozraschetu." *Ekonomicheskaia gazeta* 34:2–3.

_____. 1990. "Narodnoe khoziaistvo v minuvshem godu. Territorial'nyi aspekt." *Planovoe khoziaistvo* 4.

Richytskyi, A. 1928. "Do problemy likvidatsiï perezhytkiv kolonializmu ta natsionalizmu." *Bil'shovyk Ukraïny* 2 and 3.

Treml, V. G. 1988. "Perestroika and Soviet Statistics." *Soviet Economy* 4 (1):65–94.

United Nations. 1990. *National Accounts Statistics: Main Aggregates and Detailed Tables, 1987*, Part II. New York.

Volobuiev, M. 1928. "Do problemy ukraïnskoï ekonomiki." *Bil'shovyk Ukraïny* 2 and 3.

Wagener, R. J. 1973. "Rules of Location and the Concept of Rationality: The Case of the USSR." In *The Soviet Economy in Regional Perspective*. Edited by V. N. Bandera and Z. L. Melnyk, 63–103. New York.

Figure 18–1. Historical Record of Income Losses by Ukraine

Researcher and Reference	Period Covered	Method	Net Loss of Funds as Percent of Budgetary Collections	Net Loss of Capital Funds as Percent of National Income
1. Volobuiev (1928)[a]	1925–27	Budgetary	20.0	n.a.
2. Melnyk (1965)	1928–32	Budgetary	23.2	9.0–12.0
3. Holubnychy (1971, p. 722)	1940	Budgetary	6.3	n.a.
4. Akademiia nauk (1963)	1959–61	Income & Budgetary	31.1	14.2
5. Melnyk (1973)	1959–61	Budgetary	31.1[b]	17.1[b]
6. Melnyk (1977)	1959–70	Budgetary	30.6[b]	19.9[b]
7. Bandera (1973, pp. 146–48)[c]	1960–68	Econometric	n.a.	5.8–39.2
8. Bandera (1973)	1960	Balance of payments	n.a.	6.2–16.9[d]
9. Bandera (1977)	1966	Balance of payments	n.a.	7.5–20.1[d]
10. Wagener (1973, p. 99)	1966	Capital transfer	n.a.	9.9
11. Emelianov and Kushnirsky (1974)	1959–69	Income	n.a.	15.2
12. Gillula (1979)	1961–72	Input-output	n.a.	11.0–14.0

Notes: a. During the famous debate of the 1920s, Volobuiev's estimate of the extent of "colonial exploitation" by Soviet Russia was based on budgetary estimates by Dobrogaiev (1928). Richytsky (1928) did not deny the existence of such exploitation but contended it was only 8 to 14 percent of Ukraine's total budgetary revenues during the period in question. b. Annual average for the period. c. The calculations were based on the formula in the econometric model by Emelianov and Kushnirsky (1970). These estimates are interesting in that they reflected Gosplan's anticipation of declining transfers of capital out of Ukraine. d. The first number excludes the expenditures by union government in Ukraine and hence represents "net transfer"; the second number includes these expenditures and hence represents "net loss." This distinction is elaborated in Figure 18–2.

Figure 18–2. Balance of Payments of Ukraine
(1988, million rubles)

		Credit entries (+) entailing in-payments	Debit entries (−) entailing out-payments
A.	CURRENT ACCOUNT[a] (exports +; imports −)		
	1. External trade[b]		
	With socialist countries	6,253	5,968
	With capitalist countries	3,533	2,981
	2. Trade with Soviet republics, Union government excluded[c]	40,060	36,430
	3. Transactions with union government		
	Defense expenditures in Ukraine[d]	13,200	
	Administration and other	4,500	
	Balance on current account	*22,167*	
B.	CAPITAL AND UNILATERAL TRANSFERS ACCOUNT		
	4. Transfers of taxes to union budget		
	Turnover tax[e]		6,103
	Taxes on population[f]		2,914
	5. Union share of enterprise profits[g]		17,985
	6. Other union revenues from Ukraine[f]		26,563
	7. Union budget allocations to Ukraine		
	To finance Ukrainian economy[h]	17,304	
	For social and cultural programs[i]	9,138	
	For Chernobyl cleanup[j]	5,000	
	Balance on capital and unilateral account		*22,123*
C.	ERRORS AND OMISSIONS (net)		*0,044*

Notes and Sources: a. Data on lines 1 and 2 exclude trade in services such as tourism.
b. External trade figures are derived from *Ministerstvo vneshnikh* (1989), which provides data for the union in "external prices," that is, in prices used in trade with various countries. The data were converted into rubles for purposes of aggregation at the official rates of exchange; thus total union exports were 67,115.4 million rubles, and imports 67,040.1 million rubles. However, this source does not identify trade data for the republics. Therefore, Ukraine's shares were calculated by applying the percentages from the data in *Vestnik statistiki* (Goskomstat 1990, 36), namely, 14.58 percent

for exports and 13.76 percent for imports. For 1988, *Vestnik* shows Ukraine's exports at 6.88 million rubles out of 47.18 million rubles union total, and 13.43 million rubles out of 97.62 million rubles, all in internal prices. This manipulation results in a huge import balance not only for Ukraine but also for all other republics. This dual pricing and bookkeeping allowed Moscow's Foreign Trade Monopoly to generate a huge profit of more than 50,000 million rubles in 1988 (37). c. *Vestnik* (March 1990, 36). Much of this intra-union trade takes place within union-controlled enterprises that are similar to multinational corporations in the West; their use of transfer pricing in intra-firm trade distorts the meaning of aggregated trade data. d. Ukraine's share was prorated according to population. We disregarded the figure for the union defense expenditure of 20,244 million rubles published in the official budget and instead used 73,400 million rubles in 1988, indicated by *Ekonomicheskaia gazeta* (No. 23, 1989, 3). Western estimates are still higher. e. 35.2 percent of total turnover tax collected in Ukraine. f. Prorated according to Ukraine's share of total USSR population. g. Ukraine's prorated share is 23.5 percent of the union total according to the method used by Melnyk (1977). h. Ukraine's share is based on Ukraine's proportion of 13.2 percent of the total USSR state investment. i. According to Bahry (1987), Ukraine's 17 percent share of the union total is somewhat lower than the republic's 18 percent share of USSR population. j. A discussion of the 1990 union budget indicates that it included 5,000 million rubles for the Chernobyl cleanup ("Finansovyi suverenitet respublik," *Ekonomika i zhizn*, no. 33, 1990). David Marples, a Western expert on Chernobyl, regards such a figure for 1988 as a reasonable guess. The cleanup is being managed by the Union Ministry of Nuclear Energy. It is assumed here that the funds allocated for the cleanup constitute a unilateral transfer of funds back to Ukraine.

Figure 18-3. Net Trade Flow (X – M) between Ukraine,
the Rest of the USSR, and Third Countries (1988)

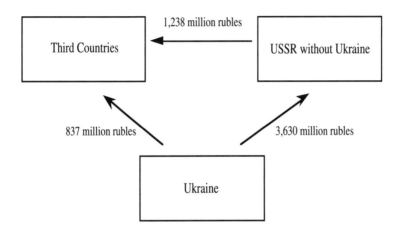

Source: *Ministerstvo vneshnikh* (1989) for aggregate USSR data and Figure 18-2 for Ukraine's data.

CHAPTER NINETEEN
Discussion

I. S. Koropeckyj

This session presented and analyzed selected problems of Ukraine's external economic relations, mainly using recently available statistical information. After offering institutional and political background information, the papers focused on issues such as the magnitude of economic relations, distribution among other union republics and foreign countries, the republic's commodity structure and balance of trade, the relationship between the republic and USSR budgets, the loss of part of Ukrainian national income and the relationship of this loss to some national income concepts, and the impact of external relations on overall conditions in Ukraine.

Ukrainian economic relations with the rest of the USSR and other countries of the world take place within the framework of the Soviet political and economic institutions. These institutions have existed since the late 1920s. Currently, they are undergoing changes, but what these changes will lead to is impossible to predict. Two factors seem to have been of decisive importance to Ukraine's external economic relations. First, the political decision making has been concentrated almost completely in the hands of the union government in Moscow. This has meant that the interests of the Ukrainian SSR have been subordinated to the interests of the entire Soviet Union. This relationship applies to all aspects of Ukraine's economy; with regard to Ukraine's external economic relations, Moscow's control has been practically absolute. Second, Ukraine's external economic relations, like those of any other republic, have been conducted according to state plans prepared by central planners without regard to either the economic interests of the republic or the welfare of the population.

Within the session Pakhomova and Mischenko analyzed Ukraine's external commodity trade, while V. N. Bandera conceptually incorporated both trade and financial flows, using them to estimate the balance of Ukraine-USSR economic relations.

Pakhomova and Mischenko show that Ukraine's external trade turnover, made up of transactions with other union republics and other countries of the world, accounted for one-third of the Ukrainian gross social product (GSP). Four-fifths of the total volume was transacted with other republics; one-fifth was transacted with other countries, mostly with the formerly socialist countries of Eastern Europe. Ukraine's commodity structure resembled that of a less-developed country: exports consisted primarily of industrial and raw materials; and imports mainly of machinery and nonfood consumer goods. Ukraine has earned some active balance of payments in inter-republic trade. Since its passive balance of payments with other countries was greater, Ukraine's overall balance was negative in the three years, 1986 to 1988, as indicated by recently published data. Although the data are deficient, the authors do not attempt to adjust their results. The authors do, however, draw attention to the fundamental problems of Ukrainian trade, which is determined not on the basis of economic criteria, but according to a plan formulated by central planners. The authors argue that Ukrainian external trade would fulfill its economic role if it were determined by natural endowments and the geographic location of the country—that is, guided by comparative advantages— and its operations were transacted in response to world market prices.

Bandera's primary objective is to investigate whether Ukraine has experienced a net loss or a net gain in national income in its relations with the central government and other union republics. Historically, it has been a net loss. Since Ukrainian resources were exported to regions with lower productivity than Ukraine, these transfers did not contribute to maximizing Soviet output as a whole. Unrequited transfers of the national income reflect the economic exploitation of Ukraine by the Soviet government in Moscow. On the basis of Ukraine's balance of payments for 1988, Bandera estimates the republic's unrequited loss to be about 20 percent of the national material product (NMP). This estimate depends on two crucial assumptions. First, in deriving Ukraine's active balance of trade with other countries, Bandera applies the official share of the republic in the Soviet Union's trade to the Western estimates of the Soviet

Union's trade. The same commodity mix of Ukraine's trade and the Soviet Union's trade and the same scarcity relations (and, implicitly, prices) in both are the implicit assumptions in this calculation. Second, the author assumes that all purchases by the union government from Ukraine are equivalent to its exports. Of course, some part of these purchases is consumed in Ukraine and, moreover, it may be argued that some share of the part spent outside Ukraine benefits the republic as well. Furthermore, a part of the Soviet government's products or services, bought outside Ukraine, is utilized in the republic. Bandera also relates the transactions, summarized in the Ukrainian balance of payments, to the macroeconomic concepts of income produced and absorbed and to various financial receipts and allocations of the Soviet budget. The results from these exercises are similar to those derived for the balance of payments. However, they also crucially depend on the two assumptions just presented.

The papers include a perceptive discussion of Ukrainian external economic relations. Among them, the continuous draining of Ukraine's national income by the central government has been of particular economic and political importance. Ukrainian resources served the following two purposes during recent times (Koropeckyj, 1990). First, Ukrainian trade with East-Central European countries, primarily the export of industrial materials, was intended to structurally bind these economies with and to make them dependent on the Soviet economy. Second, the purpose of the active balance of Ukraine's trade with the rest of the USSR was to support political and military activity abroad and at home, in which Ukraine usually has had no interest, and to finance the development of the Asiatic parts of the Russian Federation and the Central Asian republics.[1]

This transfer has been taking place without the approval of the Ukrainian people, has never been repaid, and has not earned any return. Thus, it has been Ukraine's tribute to the central government in Moscow. It is noteworthy that this occurred regardless of the economic system and political regime in Saint Petersburg or Moscow. It took place under the Tsarist autocracy, the mildly tolerant Soviet

---

[1] In his analysis of the republics' internal and foreign trade, McAuley (1991, 58) concludes that the Russian Federation gains welfare from the foreign trade and that the Central Asian republics benefit from their trade with the western republics (the Russian Federation, Ukraine, Belarus, Moldova).

regime of the 1920s, the regimes under Stalin and his successors, and, finally, in 1988 under Gorbachev's supposed democratization. The only logical conclusion that can be drawn from the historical record is this: only a politically independent Ukraine would be able to safeguard the most elementary principle of social justice, which is that income earned by a community of people should belong to that community.

Since the economic relations between Ukraine and the Russian Empire/USSR have been of obvious interest for so long, quantifying Ukraine's losses has a long tradition as well. Originally such estimates were undertaken on the basis of budgetary flows; in other words, whether Ukraine's contributions to the state budget were larger than its receipts from the state budget. Subsequently, researchers focused on estimations of the transfers of national income between the USSR and Ukraine. This can be accomplished by using two approaches. First, it is possible to estimate the country's (in our case, Ukraine's) balance of payments—consisting of transactions on the current account and transactions on the capital account—with the rest of the world during a certain period of time.[2] Second, the difference between national income produced and national income utilized can be calculated directly.[3] Various estimates for selected years until the 1980s have been summarized elsewhere (Bandera, Figure 18-1; Koropeckyj 1990, 47–48.)

The recent publication of trade data for the republics provided a convenient base for similar estimates. However, Western economists and, recently, Soviet officials and authors as well have been critical of the Soviet aggregate statistics, including the trade data, because of their deficiencies. Thus, the results obtained using these data are considered unreliable (Pogosov 1989; Mikhailov 1990; Rytov 1990). To provide a more realistic look at the balance of trade of the republics,

---

[2] The balance of payments consists of: (1) the balance of trade in goods and services and short-term financial relations and (2) private long-term investments and the change in the country's government assets in other countries.

[3] National income produced differs from national income utilized by the losses incurred after production, net surplus or deficit in the trade with other countries, and the redistribution of the national income among republics by the central government. See Bandera herein.

Goskomstat adjusted the official data for 1988 for some of these deficiencies (as discussed below; cf. *Vestnik statistiki* 1990a, 36, 38; and 1990b, 49). As a result of the adjustments, Ukraine's negative balance of trade increased from 2.92 to 4.80 billion rubles in domestic current rubles, or from 2.8 to 4.6 percent of the NMP (*Narkhoz Ukrainy* 1988, 4). Bandera also estimated Ukraine's balance of external relations (Figure 18-2) on the basis of aggregate data. However, he relied on a Western estimate of foreign trade for the entire Soviet Union and obtained a positive balance of Ukraine's inter-republic and international trade equal to 3.63 billion rubles, or 3.5 percent of its NMP, for the same year.

The following estimates attempt to show directly the difference between national income produced and national income utilized in Ukraine. Plyshevsky (1989) shows, on the per capita basis, that Ukraine produced 2.3 percent in 1980 and 3.4 percent in 1985 more in national income than it utilized. However, no explanation of the methodology is provided. According to McAuley (1991, 64, Table 6), who uses Soviet per capita data, this excess was equal to 5 percent in 1985. Belkindas and Sagers (1990) calculated the trend of this balance. They took the available data on NMP and estimated national income utilized with the help of data on consumption, investment, and changes in reserves. They conclude that the share of national income transfers from Ukraine in national income produced varied between 3.49 and 8.48 percent for the years between 1970 and 1988. All the authors warn the reader of the low quality of the Soviet statistics, which were used for their estimates.

As can be seen, there is consistency among all three sets of estimates just discussed (and among those for previous years, not cited here). The conclusion is that Ukraine has been losing a part of its national income to the Moscow government and to other parts of the USSR. The Goskomstat alone estimated that Ukraine incurred an overall deficit in its trade. The magnitude of this drain varies in the three estimates above, but in a narrow range. The differences are due to the choice of the period under investigation, the availability of the necessary information, and the methodology utilized by individual researchers. Because of Bandera's assumption that the national government purchases are not at all utilized in Ukraine, his estimate of the balance of payment deficit is raised to about 20 percent of the NMP.

Rather than offering still another estimate of this perennial problem in Ukraine under Moscow and Saint Petersburg's domination, it seems worthwhile instead to propose a conceptual framework for analyzing the problem. The framework that follows is intended to show the flows in real terms on the basis of transactions on the current account. In other words, if the value of all goods and services exported from Ukraine was larger than the value of all its imports, Ukraine lost national income in real terms.

While the publication of republic trade statistics for the 1986–1988 period is no doubt a positive event, these data are far from complete. The values of some of the omitted transactions, which follow, may be small in comparison with the trade data; but they should be included for the sake of conceptual completeness, nevertheless. Of course, the enumerated transactions could be imports to and exports from Ukraine, as well.[4] The following transactions have been omitted.

1. The export and import of services. Such nonmaterial production is excluded not only from the foreign trade statistics, but also from national income accounting in general in the USSR.
2. Agricultural raw materials. These are not included in Ukraine's exports abroad.
3. The transfer of commodities by union ministries among republics through their internal channels.
4. The transfer of the output of non-juridical persons (branches of enterprises, located in other republics) by main offices among republics.
5. Union government procurements in a republic when the procurements are utilized outside its boundaries.
6. Commodity exports by private individuals to other republics and other countries of the world.

Even if all six of the omissions were included, official trade data would still give a distorted picture of Ukrainian external economic relations for two additional reasons.

1. Under the price structure system in the USSR, domestic prices of goods and services are not equilibrium prices but are determined

---

[4] Despite searching in various sources and consulting some Soviet economists, no definite information on the magnitude of such transfers could be obtained.

by central planners. In general, Soviet prices of raw materials and food products are low and the prices of consumer goods other than foods and machinery are high relative to world prices. Thus, the structure of exports and imports is of major importance for the trade balance. Furthermore, agricultural zonal prices are supposed to be proportionally related to the costs of production. Implicit differential rent is then absorbed by the state and does not go to the producer.

2. Soviet financial arrangements also create problems. Two factors deserve mention in this respect. First, in some cases, such as meat and milk products, or coal, prices are set relatively low and producers receive subsidies from the republic budget to cover the costs of production. Since the data on Ukraine's external trade are given in current domestic prices (net of subsidies), the value of Ukrainian exports is biased down. Second, until 1990 a turnover tax has been collected either at the place of production—the method used in national income statistics, including external trade—or at the place of consumption, which is the method used by budgetary or financial statistics. Thus, a republic's exports containing a relatively high share of taxed commodities will positively bias and exports of non-taxed raw materials will negatively bias the balance of trade.

Hopefully, the trade data adjusted according to the framework just presented, assuming the availability of the necessary statistics, may serve as a reliable basis for the more precise quantification of the economic relations between Ukraine and the Russian Empire/USSR. They may be complementary to the direct calculations of its income produced and utilized. The results of both approaches will contribute to a better understanding of these relations in the past and can serve as a reliable basis for the development of future relations.

References

Belkindas, Misha and Matthew J. Sagers. 1990. "Economic Relations Among the Union Republics of the USSR, 1970–1988." Washington: Center for International Research, U. S. Bureau of Census, mimeo.

Koropeckyj, I. S. 1990. *Development in the Shadow: Studies in Ukrainian Economics.* Edmonton.

McAuley, Alastair. 1991. "Costs and Benefits of De-Integration in the USSR." *MOST-MOST* 2:51–65.

Mikhailov, L. 1990. "'Kto i kak zhivet.'" *Ekonomika i zhizn'* 10:7–8.

Plyshevsky, B. 1990. "Narodnoe khoziaistvo v minuvshem godu. Territorial'nyi aspekt." *Planovoe khoziaistvo* 4.

Pogosov, I. 1989. "Skol'ko stoit samostoiatel'nost'." *Argumenty i fakty* (16–22 December):6–7.

Rytov, Iurii. 1990. "Soiuznye respubliki, kto komu dolzhen" *Pravitel'stvennyi vestnik* 5 (January): 6–7.

Vestnik statistiki. 1990a. No. 3.

_____. 1990b. No. 4.

Index*

---

*Italicized page numbers refer to material in the tables.

Addresses of Contributors

Professor Alan Abouchar
Department of Economics
University of Toronto
150 St.George Street
Toronto, Ontario
Canada M5S 1A1

Professor Volodimir N.
    Bandera
Department of Economics
Temple University
Philadelphia, PA 19122

Professor Elizabeth M. Clayton
Department of Economics
University of Missouri
St. Louis, MO 63121

Professor Ralph S. Clem
Department of International
    Relations
Florida International University
Tamiami Campus
Miami, FL 33199

Professor Leslie Dienes
Department of Geography
University of Kansas
Lawrence, KS 66045

Mariian Dolishnii
c/o I. S. Koropeckyj

Professor David A. Dyker
School of European Studies
University of Sussex
Falmer, Brighton
England BN1 9QN

Professor Gertrude Schroeder
    Greenslade
Department of Economics
Rouss 114
University of Virginia
Charlottesville, VA 22901

Professor Holland Hunter
Department of Economics
Haverford College
Haverford, PA 19041

Professor I. S. Koropeckyj
Department of Economics
Temple University
Philadelphia, PA 19122

Professor F. I. Kushnirsky
Department of Economics
Temple University
Philadelphia, PA 19122

Ivan Lukinov
c/o I. S. Koropeckyj

Dr. Blaine McCants
209 Common Drive
Vienna, VA 22180

Serhii Mischenko
c/o I. S. Koropeckyj

Dr. Stephen Rapawy
Soviet Social Studies Branch
U.S. Department of Commerce
Scuderi Bldg. 710
4235 28th Avenue
Camp Springs, MD 02748

Tetiana Pakhomova
c/o I. S. Koropeckyj

Serhii Pyrozhkov
c/o I. S. Koropeckyj

Andrii Revenko
c/o I. S. Koropeckyj

Craig ZumBrunnen
Department of Geography
University of Washington
Seattle, WA 98195

Harvard Ukrainian Research Institute
Recent and Forthcoming Publications

Ukrainian Economic History. Edited by I. S. Koropeckyj. Harvard Ukrainian Research Institute, Sources and Documents Series. Clothbound, ISBN 0-916458-35-0. 1991.

The Hagiography of Kievan Rus'. Translated and with an introduction by Paul Hollingsworth. Harvard Library of Early Ukrainian Literature, English Translation Series, vol. 2. Clothbound, ISBN 0-916458-28-8, or paperback, ISBN 0-916458-52-0. October, 1992.

A Description of Ukraine. Guillaume Le Vasseur, Sieur de Beauplan. Translated, annotated, and with an introduction by Andrew B. Pernal and Dennis F. Essar. Harvard Series in Ukrainian Studies. Clothbound with separate map case and maps, ISBN 0-916458-44-X. November, 1992.

Republic vs. Autocracy: Poland-Lithuania and Russia, 1686–1697. Andrzej S. Kaminski. Harvard Series in Ukrainian Studies. Clothbound, ISBN 0-916458-45-8, or paperback, 916458-49-0. December, 1992.

To receive a free catalogue listing all Harvard Ukrainian Research Institute publications (including the journal *Harvard Ukrainian Studies*) please write to:

HURI Publications
1583 Massachusetts Avenue
Cambridge, MA 02138
USA